Presented to —
 Marshall & Sharlene Formby
From —
The Lukers —
 Christmas 1950

D1480695

THE WAY

BOOKS BY E. STANLEY JONES

THE WAY

THE CHRIST OF THE AMERICAN ROAD

ABUNDANT LIVING

IS THE KINGDOM OF GOD REALISM?

ALONG THE INDIAN ROAD

THE CHOICE BEFORE US

VICTORIOUS LIVING

CHRIST'S ALTERNATIVE TO COMMUNISM

CHRIST AND HUMAN SUFFERING

THE CHRIST OF THE MOUNT

THE CHRIST OF EVERY ROAD

CHRIST AT THE ROUND TABLE

THE CHRIST OF THE INDIAN ROAD

THE WAY

E. STANLEY JONES

ABINGDON-COKESBURY PRESS

NEW YORK   NASHVILLE

THE WAY

Copyright MCMXLVI
By STONE & PIERCE

K

PREFACE

THE WIDESPREAD BREAKDOWN IN INDIVIDUAL AND COLLECTIVE life is due to a loss of confidence. Men are not sure that what they are doing has cosmic backing and support. That sense of uncertainty sends a quiver of hesitancy into all they do. Something has snapped and left life dangling at loose ends.

The Christian scheme, which has been the cement that has held civilization together, has broken down in many minds; hence life is left without guidance, because it is without goal. When God goes, goal goes. Life turns dead on our hands.

When there are no long-range meanings to life which we are working out, then the present surrenders to itself, is not sustained by anything beyond itself. A Negro woman resigning her job said, "Life here is so daily." Life becomes "one ——— thing after another." It has no thread of meaning running through it. A student wrote concerning conditions at college, "Things are very contemporary here." What he was doing and thinking had no cosmic setting, no eternal values. He was a prisoner of the moment. He wanted to breathe something eternally meaningful and universal.

Schopenhauer, the philosopher and apostle of pessimism, sat slumped on a park bench, deep in thought. A policeman, mistaking him for a tramp, said to him, "Who are you? And what are you here for?" Schopenhauer slowly replied, "I wish I knew." He held no key in his hand to unlock the meaning of life, and the uncertainty made him a pessimist.

Amid all this gloom and uncertainty there is one bright spot—the Christian way. Here life lights up. It regains a sparkle, takes on meaning, goal. Here there seems to be promise of a way out. But the difficulty is that the Christian way has been presented as *a* way. It is an alternative alongside many others. It deals with the reclaiming and regenerating of the soul now, and heaven hereafter. It lacks total meanings for the total life—individual and collective. This does not grip us, for our faith must be everything or nothing. It must control the whole of life or none of it. It must not merely be *a* way—it must be *the* Way. And it must be the Way for everything and everybody, everywhere and in every circumstance.

Life must become a single piece—a whole. It must have total meaning. Unless it has total meaning, it becomes a total mess. But when it does gain total meaning, it lights up. A woman with radiant face said: "I've found life is a unit—a whole, all of a piece. And I have the Key." She had found what we must all find, or have a dead thing called life on our hands.

The breakdown in the individual is caused by the breakdown in his scheme of things. He cracks up under things because life has no cement. "The men in the armed forces don't break down," said a psychiatrist—"they fall to pieces. They were never put together, they were held up by environment, by home, by school and when these were taken away they fell to pieces." Life for them lacked a central cohesion, a lasting cement. People struck by sorrow, disappointment, and temptation go to pieces. They cannot stand up to life. They don't know how to take it.

Take the increase—the appalling increase—of nervous disorders. It is said that more than half the hospital beds of this country are occupied by patients suffering from mental and nervous diseases. The economic loss from these diseases runs over a billion dollars a year. And what about those who never get to a hospital, but drag themselves about their tasks inwardly defeated and at war with themselves? They are only half alive and making only a fifty per cent contribution to life. They are canceling themselves out with inner conflicts. A doctor came to our Ashram and said: "It's getting worse. Eighty-five per cent of the people who come to my office have nothing organically wrong with them. Their trouble is mental and spiritual. They are passing on the sicknesses of their minds and their souls to their bodies. I have come here to get something for myself to give to them." He found it!

In international matters we have lost "The Great Design"—some total pattern after which life in its completeness is to be shaped. Hence we go from one opportunism to another. We patch up peace, and it turns out to be no peace; it is a crazy quilt of expediences here and there. "Life is crazy," I thought I heard someone say. What he really said was, "Life is hazy." But life is crazy because it is hazy. We don't *see*, for we have lost, or haven't found, "the Master Light of all our seeing." When Rear Admiral Richard Byrd lost his bearings in the antarctic night, the awful realization came over him that he had missed the way: "I knew I was lost, and I felt sick inside." Men feel mentally, spiritually, and physically sick inside because they know they are *lost*. They are not sure of the Way. The old landmarks have been obliterated, and they don't know how to find their way about in a universe of this kind. They are puzzled and hurt and "sick inside." Even a bold exterior cannot hide the inner emptiness and loss of bearing. Like a blind man tapping with his cane on the sidewalk, so modern man is tapping from event to event by an everyday experimentalism trying to find his way Home. Somebody has said, "There is only one sickness, and that is homesickness." Whether modern man knows it or not, that is his chief sickness—he is Home-sick. He knows that he has one foot in time and another in eternity, and he doesn't feel at home in either one. He is afraid of both. He is afraid because he can't put these two together and make them come out as sense. His sums don't add up. Something is basically wrong.

What is it? Just one thing and only one thing—modern man isn't conscious of being on the Way. An airman doesn't mind clouds when he is "on the beam." But when he is "off the beam," he is rightly afraid of clouds—they may hold catastrophe. You can stand anything if you are sure you are on the Way. Can we be sure?

If so, it must not be a dogmatic assurance imposed upon life. That's out. That is a refuge, and we don't want a refuge—we want a release. The assurance must be a life assurance, appealing to the whole of life with self-verifying power. It must be as all-pervading, all-dependable, and self-verifying as gravity. It must be more than a weight of probabilities; it must be as self-verifying as love is to the heart. When we find our feet on the Way, we must know that, while we have not arrived at the Goal, nevertheless this is *it*—the Way.

This book is designed to put our feet upon the Way. It is not an argument, but an adventure. It is an experiment in living. If it doesn't work, don't take it. If it does work, then bet your very life upon it. If you do, you will not be working in the dark. As soon as you really get hold of it—or better, when it gets hold of you—you will know that this is the Way. Everything else will become irrelevant.

This book begins, not with those who have attained, but with those who *want* to attain. "All the prodigal son needed to bring home with him was a good appetite," someone has said. All you will need to begin with is to *want* to begin. For this book begins at the lowest rung of the ladder, where defeated men and women live. But it doesn't stop there; it goes through all the implications of the Way in the total life. It follows much the same pattern as *Victorious Living* and *Abundant Living*, but it attempts to go beyond them. It aims to give an advance course in human living. It will of necessity cover many things the other two books cover, but with different material and illustrations; and through it all, I trust, there will be a plus. For if there is just one book of the thirteen I have written into which I would like to pour a life message and in which I would like to sum up a life conclusion, it is this one. If I could say what I really want to say in this book, I would be willing to repeat, "Now, Lord, let thy servant depart in peace—I've said in life what I wanted to say." But I suppose that in the end I shall feel that I have not quite said it, for it is so utterly overwhelming and beyond one. And yet, while it is beyond one, it is available, at hand—and can be drawn upon for life now.

I try to tell *how*. That is the real thing men want to know. At the close of a service club luncheon address, a leading lawyer came up to me, grasped my hand as in a vise, and said, "Man, *how?*" Here I have tried to answer that word "how." Whenever we face a question, I will give a ladder of practical steps on *"how."*

The arrangement of the book makes possible a threefold use: (1) as a book of daily devotions, a page a day; (2) as a study book for classes and groups, for the subjects are arranged on a weekly basis; (3) as an ordinary book—it can be read straight through since it is a developing whole; the Way is treated throughout.

Some of the material of this book was given to four Ashrams in the summer of 1944 as a group study. I have discovered that this method is an almost perfect way to write a book. In the give and take —mostly take!—of group discussion you see the relevancies and irrelevancies, and you get a group reaction. Then to go off and write a book with the background of this group-experience—I repeat, it is an almost perfect way. I owe much to these groups.

But this book has been long in incubation. Twelve years ago when I went across disturbed Manchuria—there were sandbags up at the windows of the train with Japanese soldiers behind them—I said to my Chinese colleague, "If the bandits attack the train, please try to save my notebook, even if everything else is lost." It was a notebook with notes for a new book on the Way. On shipboard on my return to India I began to write on it. But in Singapore, while I was speaking through a Chinese interpreter on the subject of the use of suffering, the Inner Voice said, "This is the subject for your next book." Out of that quiet Inner Voice came *Christ and Human Suffering*. The bandits did not get the notes, but the Inner Voice scrapped them! And the Voice was right. I was not really prepared at that time to write on the Way. I glimpsed the message, but it hadn't taken full possession of me. Now it has.

E. STANLEY JONES

ACKNOWLEDGMENTS

ACKNOWLEDGMENT IS GRATEFULLY EXPRESSED TO THE AUTHORS and publishers who have granted permission for use of copyright quotations, as follows:

To Harper and Brothers for the scripture quotations—designated "Moffatt"—from *The Bible: A New Translation*, by James Moffatt.

To Harry Kemp for lines on page 49 from his poem "The Voice of Christmas."

To The Stratford Company for lines on page 119 from "Grace Before Work," in *First-Fruits*, by Margaret Bailey.

To the Bobbs-Merrill Company for selections on pages 162, 163, 166, 253 from *How Never to Be Tired*, by Marie Beynon Ray. (Copyright, 1938, 1944.)

To Harcourt, Brace and Company for lines on page 227 from "Prayer" by Louis Untermeyer.

To Little, Brown and Company for lines on page 297 from *The Poems of Emily Dickinson*, edited by Martha Dickinson Bianchi and Alfred Leete Hampson.

CONTENTS

SECTION II—*The Ways Within the Way*

THE WAY

THE INNER CONFUSION

An inner breakdown has taken place. Said an international thinker: "It is manifest that the breakdown in international comity is not solely due to economic and political causes." The breakdown is due to a breakdown in something back behind the economic and the political—a breakdown in the spiritual. Something has collapsed there, and the outer collapse is simply an outer expression of a more serious inner collapse. The outer arrangements of men are awry because the inner arrangements of men are awry. For the whole of the outer arrangements of life rests upon the inner. Men cannot get along with each other because they cannot get along with themselves, and they cannot get along with themselves because they cannot get along with God.

Perhaps you have the rather appalling sense that you are not on the Way. You are out of joint with the nature of Reality. You feel that the nature of things is not sustaining, backing, approving your way of life. You have a sense of uncertainty about the outcome of it all, for you are uncertain about the present. There is a sense of futility, of not getting anywhere, of being up against it. "We don't know what it's all about," said a returned airman from one of the battlefronts. He did not feel that they were working out any Great Design. You cannot advance in life with any buoyancy unless you are sure you are on the Way. "Why are we so faded?" asked a youth of his mother. People are "faded" because they haven't the red blood of an inner certainty coursing through them. The colors in which they have dyed life have "run." They were not fast colors. In the downpour of calamity and the stress of human living the colors of life have faded into a sickly gray.

If men are to get a sparkle, a buoyancy, a gaiety back into life, they can get it only as they are sure they are on the Way. Then they go singing down through life. Till then? Life simply won't sing. Something lies songless within. I once had a canary that wouldn't sing till after it had its bath. Our souls are like that: until we get a bath that cleanses away all fears, all uncertainties, all guilts—all sense of not being on the Way—the soul will not sing. Can we get that cleansing bath? From all doubts that there is a Way and that we are upon it?

O God, if Thou art, then there must be a way, yes, the Way. For that Way would be Thy Way. My ways don't lead me anywhere except to dead ends. I'm starting the quest for the Way. If Thou art, help me, help me to the Way. Amen.

AFFIRMATION FOR THE DAY: *"It is not given to man to imagine something higher than the reality of things."*

1

IS THERE SUCH A THING AS THE WAY?

This question confronts us as we begin our quest: Is there any such thing as the Way? Aren't we looking for something that isn't there? Philosophy has been facetiously defined as "a blind man searching in a dark room for a black cat that isn't there." Are we on the same kind of futile search when we search in a universe of this kind for the Way? Are we trying to impose on reality our way and making it out to be the Way? On the other hand, is it possible that the Way is written into the nature of reality?

In regard to all phases of life in the universe there is "the way" and "not-the-way." In chemistry H_2O produces water. You may fight with the formula and try to twist it into something else, but in the end you will surrender to it, accept it, obey it, or you will not produce water. Two parts of hydrogen and one of oxygen is the way, and everything else is not-the-way. There is the way to fly, and there is not-the-way. Aviators tell us that every moment they must obey those laws upon which flying depends—or else! There can be no moral holidays in the air. You obey or break. You gain mastery only by obedience. Aviation did not invent those laws or impose them; it discovered them.

This necessity of obedience to laws holds good in every single physical relationship, but what about it when we come to the business of human living—come over into more subtle relationships like the social, the moral and spiritual? Does chance reign there? Can you do as you please and get away with it? Or do you find there something which demands obedience if you are to live masterfully and well? And is that something which demands obedience not merely a set of conventions and customs built up by society, but is it something written into the nature of reality? When Kant the philosopher said, "Two things strike me with awe: the starry heavens above and the moral law within," did he mean that the laws of those two worlds are equally dependable and equally authoritative and equally inescapable? Is there a way and not-the-way written in both? If you obey the way, do you get results, and if you don't, do you get consequences?

O God, art Thou the author of both these worlds, or did they happen by chance? But how could that be? for then Chance would be God. I am feeling for Thee and Thy way. Help me as I grope in the dark. Amen.

AFFIRMATION FOR THE DAY: *I know the universe will respond in results or consequences. I am determined to get results.*

2

RESULTS OR CONSEQUENCES?

Yesterday we ended by saying that some people get results, others get consequences. We can see that at work around us. Some people know how to live; they seem to work with the grain of the universe; reality works with them—they get results in harmonious, happy, effective living. Others are not harmonious, not happy, not effective; they are up against it; the nature of reality is not with them; they are working against the grain of the universe—they get consequences.

Is there something here that always has the last word, no matter who has the intermediate word? A great many people don't believe that there is anything here that has the last word. A woman said to me, "It's all right to do these things [meaning sex license] provided you can get away with it." My reply: "That is a big 'provided,' for nobody gets away with it. The results register in you. You have to live with yourself, and the hell of being bad is a bad hell." I used to think that the passage, "Be sure your sin will find you out," meant, "Be sure your sin will be found out." It doesn't say so; rather it says, "Your sin will find you out"—will register in you, cause deterioration, decay; you will get consequences, in yourself.

An attempt to manipulate the universe and make it do what you want it to do ends in consequences. A young man wrote to the Duke University paper a letter to the older generation in which he said: "I'd like this older generation to get acquainted with this guy called 'Kick'—he is a wonderful guy—gives you thrills." I felt like replying: "Young man, may I suggest that you get acquainted with another guy called 'Kick-Back.' He is always a little behind the first guy and always has the last kick. You had better get acquainted with him, for everybody does, sooner or later." He overlooked the fact that when you strip off the first three letters of "thrills"—the beginning—you have "ills"—the end. It's not the beginning but the end result that counts.

Apparently we are free to choose, but we are not free to choose the results of our choosing. Those results seem to be in hands not our own. There is something here, something with which we must come to terms—or get hurt.

O Thou hidden God—hidden and yet there—I am seeking Thee. I want to come to terms with Thee. I know Thou wilt have the last word, so I would give Thee the first word. Speak and I obey. Amen.

AFFIRMATION FOR THE DAY: *There is a God, and I must come to terms with Him.*

CAN WE MANIPULATE LIFE?

We have seen that there is something written into the nature of reality—something with which we must be related in order to be released. Phyllis Bottome in *Survival* says: "We must not try to manipulate life; rather we must try to find out what life demands of us, and train ourselves to fulfill these demands. It is a long and humble business." "We must not try to manipulate life"; and yet how many are trying just that—trying to make life work their way. They and not life are the center; they demand of life instead of listening to what life demands of them. And the results are written in frustration and wreckage. If you won't be humble, you will be humbled.

The first step, then, is to be humble—to be teachable, to cease struggling and fighting and listen. Something is speaking, and speaking authoritatively. What is it?

Above we quoted, "We must try to find out what life demands of us." But "life" is vague, too impersonal. I want to relate myself to something that is both definite and personal, something that can answer me, something with which I can commune. Behind "life" is there "Life," and behind "Life" is there "God," and behind "God" is there "the Father"? Is "the Father" that infinite Spirit who creates us, loves us, and would redeem us, and whose character we have seen supremely and perfectly in Jesus? Is Jesus God become understandable? When we say "God" do we think "Jesus"? Is Jesus the human life of God? Is He God stooping to our understanding and to our need? With the consent of all my being I can answer all these questions in a glad affirmative. For in Jesus I see the uncovering of the nature of the Divine. And my heart almost skips a beat when the thought forms: I wouldn't, if I could, have God otherwise than what I see in Christ. If I were to sit down to try to think out the kind of God I would like to see in the universe, for the life of me, I couldn't think of anything higher than that He should be like Christ. The moment we arrive at this conception we feel we have arrived at an ultimate like two and two make four. Argument is at an end. We *see*.

O God, I am grateful that, as I reach up, Thou art reaching down. Thou art reaching down in terms lovable and understandable and, best of all, in terms redemptive. For I need to know that Thou dost care, dost redeem. Amen.

AFFIRMATION FOR THE DAY: *God is; God is like Christ. I am; I must be like Christ.*

4

CAN GOD BE PROVED?

Yesterday we came to the conclusion that God is, that in character He is like Christ, and that this is the highest and noblest—and to me the ultimate—conception of God. If I cannot think of God in these terms, I cannot think of Him in any terms. If He is not like Christ, I'm not interested. It is this—or nothing.

Can I prove this to you? No! But better, it can prove itself to you. As you follow through these pages day by day, you will come, I trust, not to a faith which you will hold, but to a faith which will hold you. It will be a faith that will hold not only your mind but also your emotion and your will. It will hold the total *you*. For this is not only an intellectual or an emotional or a volitional quest; it is a life quest. The whole person is involved—you and all your relationships.

The man who wants this proved to him is like a man who stands with his back to the sunset. I describe its breath-taking beauty. He says, "I don't believe it. Prove it to me." I reply, "I can't prove it to you. But turn around and look at it; it will prove itself to you." He replies, "I won't. Prove it to me." Is he fair? I hold a rose in my hand and describe the sweetness of its fragrance to him. He closes his nostrils and says, "I don't believe it. Prove it to me." "I can't," I reply, "but open your nostrils, and it will prove itself to you." He replies, "I won't. Prove it to me." Is he fair? He is unfair both to the sunset and to the rose—and to himself.

You are going to be fair to God, to life, and to yourself in this quest, aren't you? You are going to let down all your barriers of prejudice, of self-defense, of fear, and make this a life adventure, a life quest. You are going to find God, life, yourself. You are going to put your feet upon the Way. And the moment you do, something within you will whisper, "This is it. You've struck it—at last." And the whisper will be more certain than certainty, more real than reality. For it will not be a bare certainty or reality—it will be warm and tender and satisfying to the depths. It will satisfy the mind, appeal to the emotion, commit the will. It will have *you*.

My Father—for I begin to see Thee as just that—I will need Thee to take me by the hand as I start, for I shall be pulled in many a direction as I break with the old and begin the new. I start eager, but not sure. Help me. Amen.

AFFIRMATION FOR THE DAY: *I cannot prove God. I'm letting God prove Himself to me. My barriers are down.*

IS THE WAY WRITTEN IN US?

There is beginning to be formed in our minds that: (1) *There ought to be a God back of, in, and through the universe.* "If there isn't a God, we would have to invent one to keep people sane," said Rousseau, a skeptic. Life wouldn't add up, it would be "a tale told by an idiot, full of sound and fury, signifying nothing." There must be a God. (2) *This God, if he is to be a good God and trustable, must be like Jesus Christ.* The modern man is shut up to being religious after the pattern of Christ, or not at all. There is nothing else on the field. As a Hindu put it: "There is no one else seriously bidding for the heart of the world except Jesus Christ." God is Christlike or he does not appeal. (3) *If the very nature of God is Christlike, then we would expect that God has acted and still acts in a Christlike way, not only in the revelation in the Scriptures, but in creation as well.* In other words, when He made all things, He made them to work in a certain way, and that way would be according to Christ, for Christ is the revelation of God's nature. Is the Christian way, then, the Way? And is this Way not only written in the Scriptures, but written in the nature of reality as well?

If the Way is written only in the Scriptures, then a battle is precipitated around the authority of the Scriptures—their authorship, their authenticity, their worth. The foundation of authority is limited —limited to the Scriptures. It is not broadly based in the nature of reality. But suppose the Way is written in the nature of reality as well as in the Scriptures, then the Way is inescapable for everybody. For if you are not impressed with the authority of the Scriptures, then you will be impressed with the authority of life, of reality. That is inescapable.

If Jesus is a moralist imposing a moral code on humanity, then of course we can question that code and His authority. But suppose Jesus is the revealer of the nature of reality, then that makes Him different. He is not only revealing the nature of God—He is revealing the nature of life. Life then works in His way and only in His way. Then the Christian Way becomes not a side issue but the central issue of life—the one issue of life.

O God, I am starting something that grows on me. I have hold, precarious though it may be, of something that will fill my horizon, perhaps fill me. Help me, for I am weak and will need help—and grace. Amen.

AFFIRMATION FOR THE DAY: *The Way is; the Way is written in me. I cannot escape myself; therefore I cannot escape the Way.*

ARE WE PREDESTINED TO BE CHRISTIANS?

We continue to face the question whether the Christian way is *the* Way. If the Way is imposed upon life, then it is *a* way; but if it is a revelation of life, of life itself, then it is *the* Way. If it is written in the Scriptures only, then it is *a* way. If it is written in the nature of reality *and* the Scriptures, then it is *the* Way.

Elsewhere I have called attention to the fact that the Scriptures say that God created the world through Christ. He not only redeemed the world through Christ—He created it through Him. "Through him [Christ] all existence came into being, no existence came into being apart from him." (John 1:3, Moffatt.) "A Son whom he has appointed heir of the universe, as it was by him that he created the world." (Heb. 1:2, Moffatt.) "For it was by him that all things were created both in heaven and on earth, both the seen and the unseen . . . ; all things have been created by him and for him." (Col. 1:16, Moffatt.) Note: "All things have been created by him and for him." Do all things have the stamp of Christ upon them? Is His will wrought into their very structure? Will they work in His way and in no other way? Do the "by him" and "for him" mean that there is both a Christ touch and a Christ purpose in creation, that creation is made *for* Him—His will is its life and any other will is its death? If it doesn't work "for him," does it work its own ruin? Apparently a will from without doesn't decide the result of departure from His will; something inherent decides it. Something seems to be wrought into the texture of life—a way, a purpose, a plan. Is that way the Way—the Christian Way?

In Rom. 8:29 we read: "[Them] he . . . did predestinate to be conformed to the image of his Son." The doctrine of predestination—that some are predestined to heaven and some to hell—has been rightly thrown out of the window. But does it now come back again through the door of manifest fact? Is there a destiny written into the nature of reality, written into our blood, nerves, tissues, relationships —into everything? Are we predestined by the very nature of things to be Christian? And is that destiny not merely written in the Bible, but written in us, in the very make-up of our being?

O God, I begin to see that Thou hast fashioned me in my inmost and outmost being for Thy will, that there is something here which I did not create, but must accept—or get hurt. Teach me, for I follow. Amen.

AFFIRMATION FOR THE DAY: *There is a destiny written in me. That destiny is a Christian destiny. I am predestined to be a Christian.*

IS THE CHRISTIAN WAY THE WAY?

There is a hint that the universe is made in its inner structure to be Christian. Is the evidence overwhelming and inescapable?

In Acts 9:2 we read of those "belonging to the Way"; in Acts 19:9 of "decrying the Way"; and in Acts 19:23 that "a great commotion arose over the Way"; and in Acts 24:22 of "a rather accurate knowledge of the Way." (Moffatt.) What does "the Way" with a capital W mean? We usually interpret it as "the way of salvation." It is the way of salvation, for Christ is God's offensive of love invading us, redeeming us. He invades us in incarnation, in dying for us, in rising again, in coming into our hearts in the Spirit. It is the way to God, for it is the way from God. It *is* the way of salvation.

But this passage doesn't say it is "the way of salvation." It says it is "the Way"—"the Way" unqualified. Is the Christian way "the Way" unqualified? Is it the way to do everything—the way to think, to feel, to act, to be in every conceivable circumstance and in every relationship? Is it the way that is written into the nature of everybody and everything? And is it written into the nature of every relationship of everybody and everything? And does this hold good for God and man? Is the universe a universe and not a multiverse? Is the moral universe all of a piece? Do the laws that govern human conduct govern all conduct—divine and human? And are these laws not impositions upon reality but inherent in reality itself? Can God or man act in any way other than the Christian way and not act against reality? Is the Christian way imposed on life, or inherent? Is it the way we are made to work, as well as the way God wants us to work? Or is the Christian way the revelation of the Way written into the very structure of all being? If the creative touch of Christ is upon all creation, then does creation work His way or work its own ruin? And is the history of humanity nothing but a long confirmation of that statement? When Ching Chow, the newspaper sage, says, "This commonplace person believes the best preacher is time," can it mean that time is rendering a verdict, and that that the verdict is the Christian verdict?

O God, my Father, I am beginning to be confronted with something with which I must come to terms, something which is inexorable and yet tenderly redemptive. Help me as I begin to relate my life. Amen.

AFFIRMATION FOR THE DAY: *I belong to the Way—inherently. The Way belongs to me—inherently. Therefore we belong to each other —inherently.*

Matt. 7:24-27

Matt. 7:24-27 **Week 2—MONDAY**

ARE WE FINDING OUT HOW NOT TO LIVE?

We saw yesterday that there is a law of all being, that that law of being may turn out to be Christian, and that that law is an integral part of our make-up. It will not be clear at once, but it will unfold and become life's most important fact.

Is it true? Does all life sift down to just two things: the Way and not-the-way? And is this fact of the Way and not-the-way inherent in every situation and in everything? Does all life become a choice between the Way and not-the-way; and does that choice confront us in every thought, every act, every feeling—in fact, every time we do anything? Is the Christian way always the right way, and is the unchristian way always the wrong way? And does that refer to individuals and nations—the smallest and the largest? For individuals and nations, for God and man, in every conceivable circumstance in heaven and on earth, are there just two things: the Way and not-the-way? And is the Christian way always the Way, and is the unchristian way always not-the-way? With no exceptions anywhere?

If that is true, then it is tremendously true. Beside that one fact—if it is a fact—everything else dwindles into insignificance. A Hindu chairman said at the close of my address, "If what the speaker has said tonight isn't true, it doesn't matter; but if it is true, then nothing else matters." If the Christian way is a way among ways, you can take it or leave it and nothing much happens. It doesn't really matter. But if it is true—if it is *the* Way—then nothing else matters. This is the one thing in life with which we must come to terms, or ruin life itself.

Human beings are, in large measure, trying the experiment of how not to live. Rats, under scientific experiment, learn their way to the cheese amid a maze of ways by finding out that when they put their heads into the wrong way their noses get an electric shock. Only the right way is shockless. Human beings are in the process of finding out how not to live. We are sticking our noses into ways that are not-the-way, and we are getting hurt. Someday we will try the Way.

O God, in very fact I am finding out how not to live. I am running into ways that leave me frustrated and exhausted and hurt. Help me to find the Way. For in finding the Way I shall find Thee. And I would find Thee. Amen.

AFFIRMATION FOR THE DAY: *I have learned the bitter lesson how not to live. I am learning the better lesson how to live.*

9

WILL LIFE WORK ONLY IN GOD'S WAY?

Edison tried eleven hundred experiments, and they all turned out failures. Someone remarked, "Then you must have wasted your time." "Oh, no," Edison replied, "I found out eleven hundred ways how not to do things."

That is about where we are now. We are finding out how not to do things, how not to live. We are finding out that there are some ways that life will not approve, and some ways that life will approve. We must come to terms with the nature of reality. We cannot evade it, twist it to our ends, make it approve what cannot be approved. There is something "given"; we don't produce it, we don't build it up—it is there, built into the nature of things. Whoever has the first word, or the intermediate word, this moral order has the last word, and that last word is the final word. We choose, but the moral universe decides the results of our choosing, and those results are inexorable. We must come to terms with the moral universe or get hurt. We do not break the laws of God written into the nature of things. We break ourselves on them. Those laws are color-blind, class-blind, religion-blind. Break them, and you'll get broken. If you leap from a tenth-story window, you will not break the law of gravitation, you will only illustrate it.

These laws are God's preventive grace. They are barriers put up at the edge of precipices to keep us from going over. They are not put there to bind our freedom; they are put there to save us from using our freedom to destroy ourselves. They are the electric shocks upon the noses of the rats to keep them from going into ways that lead into confusion and away from the cheese. God is shocking us away from folly to food, away from confusion to the Way.

Humanity is finding out how to live by the hard way. God offers us the Way in Christ. We think we know better, take other ways of our own choosing, and are constantly getting shocks. These shocks are of various kinds—neuroses, inner conflicts, illnesses, guilts, inferiorities, fears. This modern age has put hell out of the door, but it has come back by the window. Dismissed from the universe, it has moved inside us in the form of inner neuroses and conflicts. Painfully we are finding out how not to live.

O God, I begin to see. I am not God—Thou art. And Thy will, not mine, must be my starting point. Help me to start with Thee and start with Thee this day. Amen.

AFFIRMATION FOR THE DAY: *God is shocking me to save me. His shocks are redemptive.*

THE WAY AND NOT-THE-WAY

We must spend some more days on the one thought, There is the Way and not-the-way, until this becomes a fixed conviction, almost as axiomatic as two and two make four. I say "almost," for it is not capable of such a simple demonstration as two and two make four, but it can become an insight that is corroborated more and more on a universal scale.

We first turn to the Scriptures to see what they say, and then we will turn to all life and get its word. Is it true that there is a Way which the universe will approve and other ways it won't?

When we find this passage, "The peace of an upright life" (Heb. 12:11, Moffatt), does it mean that an upright life brings peace, harmony, co-ordination, rhythm, and that an unupright life brings disturbance, disharmony, disintegration, discord? And does that happen now? Who decrees that? Does not the nature of reality decree it?

Again, we read, "See to it that no one misses the grace of God, that no root of bitterness grows up to be a trouble." (Heb. 12:15, Moffatt.) If you miss the grace of God, if you live life some way other than God's way, does "a root of bitterness" grow up to be "a trouble" to you? Does it spring up from the depths of you? Is life embittered at its sources? When you get out of joint with God, do you get out of joint with yourself? Do you become cynical and bitter—inevitably? When Bertrand Russell said that "life is a bottle of very nasty wine," did his judgment of life have any connection with his lack of faith in God? When God goes, does the meaning drop out of life? And does life actually become "a bottle of very nasty wine"? Do we then live in "a generally devaluated world"? Does life turn sour? There is only one answer: Yes! And the whole of life is one long comment on it!

I once saw in New Mexico, on a corrugated-iron-roofed mud hut, with a couple of other mud huts around it, and a mangy dog lying in front, this sign: "Radium Springs—Park Your Pains Here." Those surroundings—that sign! When you "park your pains" in some place other than God—in intoxicants, in money, in sex license, in yourself —do they stay parked, or do they come back to you multiplied? Is evil the great illusion?

O God, my Father, how often I've parked my pains of body and soul in places that have brought me nought but disillusionment and letdown. I bring them to Thee. For I know Thou art the answer. Amen.

AFFIRMATION FOR THE DAY: *Evil keeps the word of promise to my ear, and breaks it to my hope.*

WILL THE UNIVERSE BACK EVIL?

Yesterday we ended on the note that evil is not merely bad but futile. It is like Macbeth's witches, who "keep the word of promise to our ear, and break it to our hope." In I Pet. 1:18 (Moffatt) we read, "Ransomed from the futile traditions of your past." Is that word "futile" the word? Why did the "utilitarian age" turn into the "futilitarian age"? The Hindus and Mohammedans of India are bound by many "futile traditions." Are we also bound by "futile traditions"? That you can break the moral law and get away with it? That a self-centered life can be happy? That evil can bring something other than evil results? That you can hurt another without hurting yourself? That intoxicants, since they are a subterfuge, can bring something other than disruption to the personality? That the universe will back a lie? That evil isn't always evil and good isn't always good?

These "traditions" passed through society are both "futile" and fatal. That is not the imposed judgment of a moralist, but the inherent judgment of life.

This passage expresses it: "The world is passing away with its desire, while he who does the will of God remains forever." (I John 2:17, Moffatt.) Where "desire" instead of "the will of God" becomes dominant and determines life, does it "pass away"—does it tend to decay? For instance, who gets the most out of sex—the one who makes sex central, dominant, and controlling, or the one who puts sex under the guidance and control of the will of God? Make sex dominant and it will decay, will rot on your hands. Inevitably lust equals disgust. But sex dedicated to God becomes love, and love equals life. Who gets the most out of himself—the one who centers himself on himself and becomes a self-centered person, or the one who dedicates himself to the will of God and human welfare? A self-centered person "passes away," disintegrates. The God-centered person "abides forever." He goes on from strength to strength, goes on through difficulty and calamity. He has survival value; he stands up under life. He walks the earth inwardly stable, inwardly at peace. Doing the will of God, he abides forever; doing his own will, he inwardly breaks down, disintegrates.

O Thou gentle but firm Ruler, I begin to see that Thou art blocking me here and blocking me there, and through these blockings saving me, turning me to Thyself. So I come. Where else can I go? Amen.

AFFIRMATION FOR THE DAY: *To whom else can I go? Thou hast the words of eternal life.*

IS THE CHRISTIAN WAY IMPOSED OR INTRINSIC?

We saw yesterday that the universe will sustain certain ways of life and will not sustain others. It is said (I John 3:4, Moffatt), "Everyone who commits sin commits lawlessness"—commits chaos. Everyone who does right commits cosmos. Every thought, every attitude, every action produces either chaos or cosmos—it produces in some degree hell or harmony. Nothing from without decides which it will produce. The thing itself by its own nature will produce the result.

Intrinsically love is light and hate is darkness. Note: "He who loves his brother remains in the light—and in the light there is no pitfall; but he who hates his brother is in darkness, he walks in darkness and does not know where he is going, for the darkness has blinded his eyes." (I John 2:10-11, Moffatt.) Note these steps: (1) Anyone who hates his brother is "in darkness"—his general atmosphere. (2) Every advance is in darkness—"he walks in darkness." (3) It is not so bad to be in darkness if you know where you are going, but he doesn't—he "does not know where he is going." (4) The worst result is in himself: "The darkness has blinded his eyes." The punishment is a condition—blindness. Love brings cosmos; hate brings chaos.

There is another passage that teaches the same thing: "You may escape the corruption produced within the world by lust." (II Pet. 1:4, Moffatt.) Wrong desire—that is, lust—produces corruption, decay, death. Right desire produces health, well-being, life.

Punishments are inherent and from within. "Sin and its punishment are one and the same thing." In II Pet. 2:1 (Moffatt), we read, "Bringing rapid destruction on themselves." Note, not punishment from without, but destruction from within. The life forces clash and break down; there is "rapid destruction," a "galloping consumption" of the soul.

II Pet. 2:9 (Moffatt) says, "To keep the unrighteous under punishment till the day of doom." The unrighteous will not merely get punishment hereafter at "the day of doom"; they are "under punishment" now. The unrighteousness is the punishment, for it causes decay by its very nature—it is doom.

O my Father, I am trailed by Thy love. Thy love will not let me go. I know Thy purpose is to redeem me, save me, from myself and my follies. Help me this day to turn around into the arms of Thy love and be released. In Jesus' name. Amen.

AFFIRMATION FOR THE DAY: *God's law is my life. My sway is my suicide.*

IS EVIL STUPID AND DULL?

We look further at ways of life that are not-the-way. Jude 12 (Moffatt) reads, "They look after none but themselves—rainless clouds." Are those who look after none but themselves "rainless clouds"? Do they inevitably become noncontributive, useless to themselves and others? Down in Texas where they want rain badly someone pointed to a cloud in the sky in hope of rain, but an old Texan shook his head and said, "Nothing but empties." Are people who live for themselves "nothing but empties"?

Again, the same verse describes the self-centered as "trees in autumn without fruit." They come down to the autumn of their lives, the period of ripe fruitfulness when life should be laden with peace and calm and memories of life well spent, and instead what do they show themselves to be? Autumn trees without fruit. The saddest thing in life is to see a person come to the autumn time with nothing to show except a decadent self.

A verse below (16) says, "These people are murmurers, grumbling at their lot in life." The self-centered are always complaining of their lot in life. They haven't the key to life, so they try to find the cause of their failure in other persons or in circumstances around them. They blame others for everything, but do not realize that their self-centered attitudes are the cause of their grumpiness and dissatisfaction. Of all the unhappy people on earth the most unhappy are those who have nothing to do but sit on hotel porches and think about themselves, their aches and pains and troubles—most of them produced out of their own self-centered attitudes.

A passage says that "an unclean spirit . . . roams through dry places." (Matt. 12:43, Moffatt.) Is it a fact that when you are "unclean" with self-centeredness and other wrong ways of life, life "roams through dry places"? Does life turn insipid, dull, stupid? And do you have to do as one person said of himself, "I have to invent more and more ways to make life tolerable"? The inane stupidity and dullness of evil makes its devotees invent more and more extremes to get the same result. It is under "the law of decreasing returns."

O God, I am sure that Thy ways lead to fruitfulness—to life, to sparkle, to joy. And I am just as sure that the other ways lead to death, to dullness, to sadness. Help me to take Thy way, and help me to take it with my whole being. Amen.

AFFIRMATION FOR THE DAY: *When I am out of sorts with others, it is a symptom of being out of sorts with myself.*

14

SOME THINGS BITTER TO DIGEST

We must continue the emphasis upon the not-the-way. Rev. 18:14 (Moffatt) reads, "Vanished the ripe fruits of thy soul's desire!" Just as the soul is about to grasp the ripe fruit of its desire, it vanishes. That is the point about ways which are not God's ways: just as you think you are going to get the ripe fruit of your soul's desire, it vanishes. You never quite get to the realization; it's always around the corner. It is never just *there*. Someone has said that "all the fruit of sin is either green or rotten"—it is never just right! It never brings the soul its deepest satisfaction.

A passage used in another connection could be applied to this fact we are considering: "It did taste sweet, like honey, but when I had eaten, it was bitter to digest." (Rev. 10:10, Moffatt.) That is the point about evil. It does "taste sweet, like honey"—its beginnings are apparently sweet. But it is "bitter to digest"—it cannot be assimilated, cannot be related to the rest of life. For life is not made for it. Evil is alien—it is not food; therefore the system cannot digest it. The inner structure of our being is not made for hate, for resentments, for self-centeredness, for fears, for guilts; therefore the attempt to digest them, to make them a part of our being, ends in indigestion. And this indigestion is not only moral and spiritual; it is mental and physical as well. For in the inner structure of our life we are made for God-centeredness, for love, for faith, for reconciliation. Evil, then, is trying to live on that for which we are not made. Jesus said, "My meat is to do the will of him that sent me." Is God's will our meat, our food? Does it feed us, build us up, sustain us, and give us life? The answer is an unequivocal Yes! And does our own will, lived contrary to the will of God, poison us? It does. It lowers our sense of well-being, depletes us, starves us, poisons us.

Why? Because we are allergic to evil. I am physically allergic to shrimp. I have tried them four times, and it always ends in the same result. I am just as allergic to sin! I can't assimilate it. For I am not made for it. It disrupts me, soul and body. Gilbert Stuart, the painter, once looked at Talleyrand, the French statesman, and said, "If that man is not a scoundrel, then God writes an illegible hand."

I thank Thee, Father, that when Thou didst fashion me, Thou didst fashion me for Thyself—Thy ways are my ways. For I know when I do wrong it is wrong—wrong to everything connected with me, and others. Help me to do right. In Jesus' name. Amen.

AFFIRMATION FOR THE DAY: *God's will is my highest interest—always.*

THE PAY-OFF!

We are beginning to see, I trust, that "there is a way which seemeth right unto a man, but the end thereof are the ways of death." (*Prov.* 14:12.) Note that in the beginning the way "seemeth right unto a man"—the man lives without any God reference, lives by what seems right to his own unaided light. Result? "The end thereof are the ways of death"—not the beginning, but the end, the finished product, is "death." The person breaks down and decays. "The end thereof" is important. We have to put things under life to get the final judgment of life. "By their fruits ye shall know them"—not by the bud or the flower, but by the finished product. The fruits of evil are always evil. The fruits of good are always good. Evil is evil, and good is good, both in essence and in result.

Jesus speaks of a road that "leadeth unto life" and another that "leadeth to destruction." We used to think that He meant heaven and hell hereafter, but on closer examination we see that Jesus was talking about life here and now. Some roads lead to life, some to destruction—the life forces break down; they do not hold together; there is no inner cement. One road leads to "life"—life is the pay-off. All other roads lead to "destruction"—destruction is the pay-off. Jesus said, "A good tree cannot bear bad fruit," and, "A rotten tree cannot bear sound fruit." (*Matt.* 7:18, Moffatt.) The outcome of a good life cannot, by the very nature of things, be bad. The outcome of a bad life, by the very nature of things, cannot be good.

Ezek. 23:17 (Moffatt) says, "Till she grew sated and broke with them in disgust." Is that the history of evil—you grow "sated" and, by the very nature of things, you are compelled to break with it "in disgust"? You may not break with evil, but if you go on, you commit evil with the joy of it gone. Then it becomes treadmill.

In the first psalm we read "The way of the ungodly shall perish." Is it a fact that the way of the ungodly perishes now? Do his plans and schemes for happiness perish, turn to ashes in his hands? Does not *Rom.* 7:5 (Moffatt) express it when it speaks of ways "fruitful to Death"? When the whole thing is over, do you have "Death" on your hands—Death to everything worth while?

Something, my Father, is being burned into my consciousness—Thy judgments of life. I am not able to escape them. Nor would I, for to escape them would be to escape from salvation. I would accept them. Amen.

AFFIRMATION FOR THE DAY: *When I break with God, I break with life.*

SIN HAS NO FUTURE

When Amos says, "I make your steps collapse" (2:13, Moffatt), does he not put his finger on the fact that, the more evil advances, the more its "steps collapse"? The universe will not sustain it.

Again we read, "Because you have sold yourself to no purpose in doing what is evil in the sight of the Eternal." (I Kings 21:20, Moffatt.) Note the phrase "to no purpose." Does the doing of what God cannot approve always end in futility? Is it all "to no purpose"?

Luke 8:29 (Moffatt) says, "Driven by the daemon into the desert." Is that where evil always drives you—into a desert? It promises a garden, but ends inevitably in a desert. "I don't want you to think I'm happy," said a leery-eyed devotee of sin to me. He needn't have assured me he wasn't happy; it was sticking out all over him.

"Your doom appears; your sin has blossomed, your pride has budded." (Ezek. 7:10, Moffatt.) Note how sin blossomed and pride budded—and the fruit? Doom! By its very nature sin brought forth doom. No "day of doom" is needed to pronounce sentence. The very nature of evil dooms itself. In II Thess. 2:3 (Moffatt) we read, "The Lawless One, the doomed One." Do those things hang together? When you are lawless, break the laws of God written into the nature of things, are you doomed? No matter how that "Lawless One" may be implemented by money, by prestige, by military power, inevitably he is a "doomed One." Perhaps not today, not tomorrow, but inevitably evil is doomed. It carries the seeds of its own disruption in itself.

In Rev. 17:11 (Moffatt) we read, "The Beast which was and is not." Note: The Beast was and is not; evil has a past, but it has no future; it "was," but it will not be. No matter if "the Beast" is spelled with a capital *B;* it will shrivel; it is under the law of decay. Give evil enough rope and it will hang itself. If it is not constantly being bolstered up by the surrounding good, it will go to pieces. All evil is a parasite upon the good. You have to throw enough good around evil to keep it going. When it is pure "Beast," it is pure blight. It has no future. It is not-the-way.

Gracious Father, I have looked upon evil till my eyes are tired—tired of looking at death. Now lift my eyes and let me look upon good—upon Thee—and then I shall look upon Life. I want to live; help me to see and obey Thee. Amen.

AFFIRMATION FOR THE DAY: *Evil is the Great Illusion; God is the Great Illumination.*

THE GOD OF GRACE AND THE GOD OF NATURE—TWO GODS?

We have seen that the Way and not-the-way is written in the Bible. But there are many for whom the authority of the Bible has decayed. It doesn't grip or guide them. Like Solomon Richter they think that the Christian faith as contained in the Bible is "a set of scruples imposed on the framework of humanity to keep it from functioning naturally and normally." They therefore turn to the revelation of life through science and experience for their guide.

This is a serious situation if the revelation of life through science and experience turns out to be different from the revelation of life which we find in Christ. This would be serious for science and experience, for what we find in Christ is the highest we have seen on our planet, and for science and experience to be against *that* would mean that they are arraigned against the highest. On the other hand, for the Christian faith to be arraigned against science and experience would mean that the Christian faith is trying to live against life.

But suppose the Way that is written in the revelation of Christ and the way that is written in life around us turn out to be the same way, different revelations of the Way; then we can go on with abounding confidence, for then the Way is the way of everything, for everybody, everywhere.

There cannot be two Gods—the God of grace and the God of nature. There must be one God, perhaps revealing Himself imperfectly through nature and experience, for the medium is imperfect, and revealing Himself perfectly through Christ, for the medium is perfect. But they must be revelations of the one Way.

Is the Way written into the structure of reality? Is there a Kingdom "built from the foundation of the world"—a Kingdom built into the very foundations of life and therefore inescapable? I can escape the injunctions of the Bible if they are imposed from without upon life, but I cannot escape them if they are a revelation of life itself, a lifting up of laws written into the nature of things. For if I run away from them as written in the Bible, I meet them confronting me everywhere out of life. I'm "hooked"!

O God, my Father, Thou hast hedged me about, hedged me about so I cannot run away from Thy love. Nor would I run away, for if I run away from Thee, I run away from life. I come to Thee, for in Thee is life. In Jesus' name. Amen.

AFFIRMATION FOR THE DAY: *The God of grace and the God of nature are one God dealing with me in two ways for the same end.*

THE TWO APPROACHES TO LIFE

We are considering the Way as it is found in life and experience outside the Bible. Is there slowly emerging out of life and experience a body of truth which is revealing the Way? Is this body of truth a series of signposts that point to the Truth? In tracing these intimations we are not avidly gathering up the crumbs from the table of science and feeding upon them—poor relatives of a rich host. Rather we are seeing that science is working up through the facts to the Fact, through truths to the Truth. We pick up these crumbs because, when we taste them, they taste like the Bread of Life.

The Christian faith works down to life from the revelation in Christ. Science works up from the revelation of life—to what? Are these two approaches going to meet? They must, if life is one. I was tapping my way down a very steep mountain path in pitch dark. A misstep on either side would bring disaster. It was a slow and tedious process. When I was about halfway down, suddenly the lights came on. There was the pathway clear; I could abandon my tedious method of tapping my way and walk with confidence along a lighted way. My tapping in the dark was the way of science and experience; my assured walking in the light of a revelation of the pathway was the Christian way. They were not contradictory; they were different approaches to the one Way.

For instance, Charles A. Beard says that as a historian he has learned four lessons from history: (1) When it gets dark enough, the stars come out. (2) The bee fertilizes the flower it steals from. (3) Whom the gods would destroy they first make mad with power. (4) The mills of God grind slowly, but they grind exceeding small. Did he not discover through historical research that there is a moral law written into things and that this moral universe always has the last word—that if you fit into it, you live, but if you don't, you perish? That moral universe is not man's creation but man's discovery. History uncovered to Beard intimations of the Way. Beard could add to Kant's saying that "two things strike me with awe: the starry heavens above and the moral law within." He could add that he found a moral law not only within the individual but within the relationships of individuals, within history.

O God, Thou art speaking to me in the still small voice within and also in the stormy events of human history. Help me to listen to Thee whenever Thou dost speak. And help me to obey. In Jesus' name. Amen.

AFFIRMATION FOR THE DAY: *History is His story.*

THERE IS AN EVERLASTING RIGHT

There is direct evidence of the workings of a moral universe in the relationships of men. Henry M. Wriston, president of Brown University, says: "The history of tyranny is long. . . . Its transient character, the manner in which it has always nurtured the seeds of its own destruction make it desirable to follow its record wherever and whenever it has appeared in human history." Note "its transient character, the manner in which it has nurtured the seeds of its own destruction." What planted the seeds of its own destruction? There is one answer: the nature of reality. Tyranny is not-the-way.

This Way written into the nature of things is well expressed in Harry Emerson Fosdick's words: "There is an everlasting right to which our nations, our business, our racial relationships, our schools, our churches, and our personal lives must be adjusted, if salvation is to visit us." That "everlasting right" is not built up by custom and does not conform to it. It is there before customs are built up and will watch the inevitable decay of customs that do not conform to the "everlasting right."

Carlos Martins, the Brazilian ambassador to the United States, brings this "everlasting right" to bear upon the problems of the present: "The great powers, if they consider only themselves, can produce only universal wars. They can produce peace only if they co-operate with a world-wide system of liberty. In no other way can they win the necessary confidence, consent, and support of the rest of the world." Why is it that "great powers, if they consider only themselves, can produce only universal wars"? Who decides that result? The answer is that the nature of reality decides it. The Way is unalterably opposed to life that considers only itself, whether that life is that of an individual or that of a combination of great powers. They must think in terms of all—must "co-operate with a world-wide system of liberty"—or they cannot "win the necessary confidence, consent, and support of the rest of the world." If individuals or nations or combinations of nations think they can live against the Great Design and try it, the end will be disillusionment.

O Thou redeeming God, I come to Thee to help me to live this day according to the Great Design. Thy will is my peace. Thy plans are my very person. When I find Thee, I find myself. Help me this day to discover and do Thy will, In Jesus' name. Amen.

AFFIRMATION FOR THE DAY: *When I think only of myself, I produce a war—within myself.*

IS THE RIGHT THING THE HEALTHY THING?

In a Japanese relocation center I once quoted four people. First, a surgeon who said to me: "I've discovered the Kingdom of God at the end of my scalpel—it's in the tissues. The right thing morally is always the healthy thing physically." Second, a leading economist: "The right thing morally is always the healthy thing economically." Third, a leading sociologist: "The right thing morally is always the healthy thing sociologically." Fourth, an educator: "The right thing morally is always the healthy thing educationally." The head of the center commented: "If the right thing is always the healthy thing, why isn't the healthy thing also the right thing? Doesn't it work both ways?" I could agree wholeheartedly. Whether you work from standards of morality down to the tissues and their health, or whether you work from the tissues and their health up to standards of morality, you will come out at the same place. For morality is one, whether written in tissues or written in Testaments.

All life is of a piece. There are no dualisms, no compartmentalisms. Life is one, and the laws that govern all life have one source—God. The laws that govern our physical life are not other than the laws of God. They are the laws of God written into flesh and blood and nerve and tissue. Nor are the economic, social, educational, and political laws that govern relationships other than the laws of God.

Gladstone once said, "Nothing that is morally wrong can be politically right." The laws that govern right and wrong are of universal application, and politics are no exception. Hooker uttered this truth in a penetrating phrase: "Law, whose source is the bosom of God and whose voice is the harmony of the world." He saw that law, wherever found, when true law, had one source—the bosom of God. And he also saw that the purpose of that law is the harmony of the world. When you obey it, you obey the very laws of your being, so the result is harmony. The converse of that is true: when you break these laws, you break yourself. The result is disharmony and disruption.

O Gracious Father, author of me and of the laws that underlie me, help me to do Thy will, for only thus can I do my will. Help me, then, not to do Thy will grudgingly or of compulsion, but gladly and joyously as one who finds the Way. In Jesus' name. Amen.

AFFIRMATION FOR THE DAY: *God's will is harmony; my will against God's is discord.*

WRITTEN IN OUR RELATIONSHIPS?

We continue our search for the Way amid the ways of men. A state university president was talking to a businessman who did not attend church: "You don't give the vote of your life to them; do you want all the churches to burn down?" To which the businessman replied, "No, by Jerry, it would ruin my business." This business-man, uncommitted to religion, saw that unless there is a basis of morality in the community, then business is impossible. For the whole structure of life rests on that imponderable thing called character. If the character breaks, the confidence breaks. If the confidence breaks, the community breaks. If the community breaks, the country breaks. Nothing is more false than to say, "Business is business," for business that regards only itself and does not have regard to the moral universe sooner or later breaks itself upon that moral universe.

The vice-president of a bank at the age of seventy-five was about to get a divorce and remarry. The president of the bank was badly upset and said, "This is bad for the business of the bank." It would lower confidence in the moral integrity of a leading official, and that was bad for business.

A vice-president of one of the leading banks in the United States said, "The outstanding necessity of banking is unselfishness." He was right. You must think in terms of others' good or else life will not react to you in benefit. "He who serves most, profits most," may not be the highest motive for morality, but Rotarians who use this phrase see that there is a law of service written into life.

The head of a very practical institution, the Imperial Bank of India, said to me: "We have discovered that it doesn't pay us to break a creditor, for if he goes down, the financial situation goes down with him. So we find it better to nurse him along and help him to his feet. If we save him, we save a situation as well, and that is good for the bank." My reply: "So the Imperial Bank is also among the prophets—preaching redemption of the hurt and the weak! But that's the Christian position!" How did they come to that conclusion? Trial and error.

O God, I find the Way written in the common ways of life. Thou hast left Thy footprints everywhere. We follow them with bated breath, for we know if we find them, we find Life. Help us. Amen.

AFFIRMATION FOR THE DAY: *God's footprints are in my tissues, in my nerves, in me.*

"NOTHING THAT IS RIGHT IS FUTILE"

We continue our search for the Way amid the ways of men. Ignazio Silone, the Italian novelist, has told what has happened to some of his friends who have been ground down by wars, revolutions, and fascism. "One poor devil came to me the other day," he reports, "his eyes shining as if he had made an important discovery. *'One should always act toward others,'* he said with sober emphasis, *'as one would like to have them act toward oneself.'* I hadn't the heart," says Silone, "to tell him that his discovery was not exactly new, but expressed an ancient wisdom, for I saw he had seized upon it by dint of sufferings and struggles." Suffering had taken this poor fellow by the hand and had led him to the Way.

A little girl, reared in a lovely American home, tells what she discovered: "I'm not always good, but when I'm not good, I'm miserable." The little girl has discovered that there is a world of eternal goodness. When she fitted into it, she was adjusted and happy. When she lived against it, she received the results in herself.

A Des Moines editor captioned an editorial: "Nothing that is right is futile." He saw that the right is backed by the universe and hence cannot be futile. In the end it will come out on top. On the other hand, anything that is wrong cannot be anything but futile.

A high-school student came up to me at the close of my address and said: "You mentioned the young man who said he would take the beautiful without any reference to the good, but aren't the good and the beautiful the same?" This youth saw with rare insight that the bad could never be beautiful. On the other hand, the good is always beautiful, for it is according to the eternal loveliness.

When Benjamin Franklin said, "A lie is not useful," he said a very profound thing, for the universe is not built for the success of a lie. A lie breaks itself upon the nature of reality; therefore no lie can ultimately succeed. "Lies have short legs," says a German proverb, but that has been changed now by the Germans into, "Lies have one short leg," for Goebbels, the propaganda minister, had one short leg! Lies had defeated themselves.

O my gracious Father, I am finding Thy Way amid our ways. Daily, hourly, it is being disclosed before my astonished eyes. Help me to walk in Thy Way as I see it. For I know that when I take other ways they defeat themselves. Thy Way verifies itself. I thank Thee. Amen.

AFFIRMATION FOR THE DAY: *God is the Eternal Beautiful. Sin is the Eternal Ugliness.*

ALL CONVERGE ON THE WAY

An expert on family relations said: "You must give up yourself, you must serve others, or you cannot get along with others." This is interesting. This expert by the method of observation and trial and error found that you cannot get along with people unless you cease to be self-centered, unless you serve others. But that is Christian!

Listen to an economist, Arthur A. Hood, as he unfolds a discovery: "Mass production—the abundant life in material terms—is here. But we cannot have it or keep it until we learn mass distribution under the principles of the Golden Rule. Distribution involves the application of spiritual meaning to production." Hood discovered that mass production which emphasizes "Thou shalt love thyself" cannot succeed unless you have mass distribution which emphasizes "Thou shalt love thy neighbor as thyself."

No wonder an engineer said, "The great engineering word is awareness of people." Engineering word! We thought "awareness of people" was the Christian word! Are they one? Yes! Because not only "the sabbath was made for man, and not man for the sabbath," but engineering was made for man and not man for engineering. The effect on human personality is the criterion of its worth-whileness.

Bernard Shaw could scarcely be accused of Christian bias, but he sums up a life conclusion in these words: "After reviewing the world of human events for sixty years I am prepared to say that I see no way out of the world's misery except the way that Christ would take were he to undertake the work of a modern statesman." Shaw saw life getting tangled up as men try ways other than the Way.

Then here is Pitirim A. Sorokin, professor of sociology at Harvard, who says that the idea of selfish materialism underlying Western civilization is bankrupt and unable to sustain our civilization any further, and that the upset in civilization is over the search for a new idea around which life can revolve. The new idea? He points to the Sermon on the Mount—a co-operative order.

Here, then, a family-relations expert, an economist, an engineer, a socialist writer, and a sociologist all converge on one thing—the Way!

O Thou Father and God, we bow in humble wonder that Thou has shown Thy Way to us through many diverse ways. In the end they converge upon Thy Way—the Way we see in Christ. Help us to follow. Amen.

AFFIRMATION FOR THE DAY: *The Sermon on the Mount of yesterday is the Sermon for the Mart today.*

IS THE CHRISTIAN WAY THE NATURAL WAY?

We saw yesterday that we try ways other than God's ways, and get hurt. "He who sows for his flesh will reap destruction from the flesh." (Gal. 6:8, Moffatt.) Destruction? When? Hereafter? No, now! We see ways ending in decay, in death—death to joy, to peace, to personality, to contribution.

The Christian way is the natural way—the way we are made to live. Everything else is unnatural. Sin is not natural. It is the accustomed, but not the natural. Were it the natural we would bloom under it. Do we? On the contrary, sin blights. It is sand in the machinery of life—it is not-the-way. We have been taught very often that sin is natural. If so, then goodness is the unnatural and the good are the queer, a little off center. If that is true, then the Christian way has an impossible handicap; it is trying to live against nature. How can you live against nature and get away with it? No, goodness is the natural, and evil is the unnatural. If evil were the natural, how could you with justice he punished for living according to nature? That would be most unfair. But you are punished whenever you take sin into your life. The fact is that sin and its punishment are one and the same thing. By its very nature sin is disruptive —that disruption is the punishment. You don't have to punish a cancer for being a cancer—a cancer is its own punishment. You don't have to punish the eye for having sand in it—sand in it is punishment. "The word 'evil' is the word 'live' spelled backwards." It is life attempting to live against itself. And that can't be done. Evil is not only bad; it is stupid. It is an attempt to live against the nature of reality and get away with it. It is an attempt at the impossible. The result is inevitable—breakdown and frustration.

If sin were the natural, then why shouldn't it contribute to life, produce happiness, symmetry, harmony, effectiveness? It doesn't. But goodness does contribute to life, does produce happiness, symmetry, harmony, effectiveness. Then which is the natural? Which one fits into nature? The facts answer. Carlyle says, "Sin is, has been, and ever shall be the parent of misery." Why? There is only one answer— it is not-the-way.

O God, I see I am being shut up to Thee and Thy Way. I am being hedged in from every side—everything pressing me to Thy feet. So I come. I am finding that I cannot live any other way. So I come. Amen.

AFFIRMATION FOR THE DAY: *My way is frustration. Thy Way is fruitfulness.*

SIN IS THE UNNATURAL

We insisted yesterday that sin is unnatural and goodness is natural. But there are objections. One is the teaching of certain passages: "The natural man receiveth not the things of the Spirit of God." (I Cor. 2:14.) But Moffatt's translation puts it: "The unspiritual man rejects these truths of the Spirit of God." The contrast is not between the natural and the unnatural, but between the spiritual and the unspiritual. The Scriptures teach that God has made man in His own image, that there is a natural kinship between man and God, and that the laws of man's being are the laws of God written into flesh.

If this is true, then all departure from those laws written into man's nature is unnatural—a departure from nature. The most usual name for "iniquity" in the New Testament is *hamartia*—literally, "missing the mark." There is a mark, a standard, written within us, and all departure from that is sin, "missing the mark." Sin is the accustomed, but it is not the natural. If sin were the natural, it would feed us. On the contrary, the result of sin is to bleed us.

But there are those who do not accept the biblical account of man being created in God's image. They believe man has an animal heritage and therefore man is fighting with natural animal tendencies within him. Sin is therefore natural. The reply is that, even if we believe that man physically has an animal heritage, nevertheless there is a profound difference between man and animal. All men worship in some form. Animals do not. There seems to be in man a kinship with God that makes him yearn for God with unwordable yearnings. Even if man physically has an animal heritage, nevertheless, somewhere along the line of ascent God seems to have breathed into man the breath of spiritual life so that man became a living soul. That spiritual and moral nature makes a profound difference in man. It profoundly differentiates him from the animal. The difference between man and animal is not physical, but mental and spiritual. When man finds God, he finds the fulfillment of his mental and spiritual nature.

But, strangely enough, the same thing happens to our bodies. Our bodies are fulfilled when they do the will of God.

My Father, I see that Thou hast wrought, even into the texture of my physical life, Thy will and purpose. How can I escape Thee? Thou art intimate in these laws and purposes. Help me to align my life. Amen.

AFFIRMATION FOR THE DAY: *Nature works with me when I work with God, against me when I am against God.*

HOW DOES EVIL ARISE?

Note this passage: "Cleanse ourselves from everything that contaminates either flesh or spirit." (II Cor. 7:1, Moffatt.) If sin were natural, why should it contaminate? It should consummate. The fact that it contaminates shows that it is extraneous, does not belong to human nature, is alien.

If this is true, how does evil arise? If it is not inherent within us by nature, then how does it come into being? The clue can be found in these words: "Sin resulted in death for me by making use of this good thing." (Rom. 7:13, Moffatt.) Evil always uses a good thing— it is the perversion of the good. James gives us the clearest picture of this: "Let no one who is tried by temptation say, 'My temptation comes from God'; God is incapable of being tempted by evil and he tempts no one. Everyone is tempted as he is beguiled and allured by his own desire; then Desire conceives and breeds Sin, while Sin matures and gives birth to Death." (Jas. 1:13-15, Moffatt.) Here, then, are the steps: Simple, natural, normal "desire" is "beguiled," "allured," turned from its natural way into unnatural ways, breaks the laws written in its own being. Then it becomes "Desire" with a capital "D," and becomes dominant. Instead of "desire" submitting to and obeying the will of God, it becomes God—it is spelled "Desire." It rules us, dictates to us. That breeds "Sin." "Desire" has turned into "Sin," also spelled with a capital; it is God. Then "Sin matures and gives birth to Death." Here, then, are the steps: (1) "desire" becomes "Desire"; (2) "Desire" becomes "Sin"; (3) "Sin" becomes "Death."

Simple "desire" is God-given and natural and right. But "desire" can slip out from under the control of God and become "Desire." It controls us. It is master—we obey. The result of that is "Sin" and consequent "Death," not physical death only, but "Death" in general —"Death" to the whole person. But if Sin is natural, why should it breed "Death"? If to live according to one's nature breeds "Death," then we are queerly constructed. Besides, if sin is natural, why should we be punished for living according to our nature? Where is the justice?

O God, how could that which destroys me be native to me? I know in the inmost depths of my being that when I sin this is not the Way. I violate every law of my being, and I know it. Help me. Amen.

AFFIRMATION FOR THE DAY: *Outside of God there is nothing but death.*

IS EVIL ALWAYS DISRUPTIVE?

We saw yesterday that evil was a turning of the natural into the unnatural—it was a living against life. Self-love, the natural, can become selfishness, the unnatural. Self-respect, the natural, may be allured into pride, the unnatural. Love, the natural, can be beguiled into lust, the unnatural. Sex desire, the natural, can be allured away from its God-intended creative function, can become an end in itself and thus become Death to every portion of the being.

These simple, natural functions, dedicated to God and controlled by Him, bring Life—Life to the whole person. But if they become God, become ends in themselves, then there is one result, "Death"—death to development, to happiness, to the whole person.

Peter speaks of "the passions of the flesh that wage war upon the soul." (I Pet. 2:11, Moffatt.) But if they are natural and right, why should they war against the soul? The Christian use of sex does not war against the soul; it sets up the soul. Only the unnatural use of sex wars against the soul. The natural use, that is, the Christian use, contributes to the soul's well-being. Evil is good prostituted.

A passage says, "The face of the Lord is set against wrongdoers." (I Pet. 3:12, Moffatt.) We feel that to be true. But is the face of the universe also set against evil? When you do evil, do you feel naturalized, at home, related to the sum total of reality, the universe with you? On the contrary, you feel out of sorts, orphaned, estranged, furtive, underground, at cross-purposes with yourself and with life in general. Why? Because that is not the Way! Not only "the face of the Lord" but the face of the universe, the face of life, is set against evil. Note, is "set." It doesn't change like the fashions of the day; it is "set," for the universe has laws written in its very nature and hence unchangeable.

"For wherever jealousy and rivalry exist, there disorder reigns and every evil." (Jas. 3:16, Moffatt.) If jealousy and rivalry were natural, why should they bring "disorder" and "every evil"? Why not order and every good? For the simple reason that jealousy and rivalry break the law of love, and that means "disorder" and "every evil." The nature of reality decrees that. It is not-the-way.

O God, my Father, open my eyes that I may see, may see Thee at work all about me working through Thy laws. And deeper, help me to see Thy personal approach to me in Thy Son. And help me to follow. Amen.

AFFIRMATION FOR THE DAY: *The face of the Lord and the face of the universe are both set against evil.*

IS THE CHRISTIAN WAY PRO-LIFE?

We continue to consider this week the important question: Is the Christian way the *natural* way to live? When we live the Christian way, are we living the way we are made to live, made in the inner structure of our beings? Is life made for the Christian way as tracks and engines are made for each other? As blood and arteries have an affinity? As seed and soil are made for each other? Or is the Christian way at war with nature and therefore an unnatural way to live? Is its morality an imposed and alien morality—a morality for which we are badly made? Is the Christian an unnatural person living against nature, therefore off center and a little queer?

This is one of the most important questions concerning the Christian way. If it is unnatural and antinatural, then it would seem to be hopelessly handicapped, for you cannot hope to try to live against nature and get away with it. It is an unequal battle. In the end the sum total of reality will close in on you and break your puny efforts to live against it.

There is much to be said on the side that the Christian way is unnatural. Two arguments are cited: certain passages of Scripture, and the obvious bents of human nature. In addition to the Corinthian passage noted, a verse usually given to sustain this view is: "We . . . were by nature the children of wrath." (Eph. 2:3.) But Moffatt changes the sense of this passage thus: "We obeyed the passions of our flesh, . . . we were objects of God's anger by nature, like the rest of men." Translated thus it means that we are objects of God's anger by nature since we live this way. In other words, God is naturally against us when we sin. And rightly so. Another passage: "Jesus did not commit himself unto them, . . . for he knew what was in man." (John 2:24-25.) "He knew what was in man," namely, sin. But that verse is neutral. Sin may be in man—it is—and yet sin may be unnatural, not native to us. Sin is in man, deeply, tragically. It has gone down to the roots of his being and has depraved it. But the fact that it depraves us shows it is not natural. If it were natural, why should it deprave us?

O God, I am sure that sin is not native to me, for when I commit it, then I am disrupted, out of gear. I know that this is not-the-way. Help me, then, to take that for which I am made—Thy Way. For when I find Thy Way, I find my way. Amen.

AFFIRMATION FOR THE DAY: *In God I am in tune. Out of God I am out of tune, a discord.*

IS SIN ANTI-LIFE?

We saw yesterday that certain passages of Scripture which show man depraved by sin do not necessarily teach that sin is natural and goodness is unnatural. The fact that sin depraves human nature implies that sin is unnatural, for if it were natural, why should it deprave human nature? It should enlarge it, strengthen it, fulfill it. It does the opposite. Sin does deprave. Therefore sin is that for which we are not made. It is anti-life. It is an attempt to live against life and get away with it.

In Col. 1:21 (Moffatt) we read, "Your hearts hostile to him in evil doing"—not naturally hostile, but become hostile through wrong choices and attitudes and habits. Again, "To be consecrated and unblemished in his sight." (Eph. 1:4, Moffatt.) Evil, then, is a blemish, something that blemishes the truly natural. But if evil is natural, why should it blemish? Heb. 12:1 (Moffatt) speaks of sin as "clinging folds," but why "clinging folds" if natural? Another passage speaks of one who "suffered weakness from an evil spirit." (Luke 13:11, Moffatt.) Does an evil spirit always weaken us, and does a good spirit always strengthen us? If so, one is anti-life and the other pro-life; one is unnatural and the other natural. Heb. 13:9 (Moffatt) speaks of "one's heart strengthened by grace." Does grace always strengthen us, and does sin always weaken us? The answer is an unequivocal Yes!

A young man in a camp said, "We have come to the place where we can sin with assurance." If so, then it is a false assurance, for life speaks otherwise. All approaches to life are converging on one thing: some things disrupt life, throw confusion into it; some things build life, put harmony into it. And when we look at the things that disrupt, they are strangely like the things we have called by the old-fashioned term "sin." In other words, everything that is unchristian is unnatural, is against nature, and everything that is Christian is natural, is for nature.

In the words of an acute observer, "We become natural as Jesus comes into our lives." We do—thoroughly so!

O my Father God, I am beginning to see that when I am in Thee and in Thy purposes, I am in the way intended by life for me. When I accept Thee, I accept Life. I gladly do so, for I want to live and live fully. Amen.

AFFIRMATION FOR THE DAY: *Today I shall not fight with life. I shall yield to life and let it possess me.*

"THE ONLY SICKNESS IS HOMESICKNESS"

We must pursue the consideration of the question whether the Christian way is the natural way, and the unchristian way the unnatural.

We must grant that evil is the accustomed, the habitual, but we do not grant that it is the natural. It is true that men have been naturalized in the unnatural, but this naturalization is not the truly natural. Sin and evil are intrusions, aberrations—things for which we are not made. They are foreign bodies in the personality of man, and set up festering places exactly as a foreign body does in the physical.

We can become naturalized in the unnatural. Elsewhere I have written of a friend who became so used to riding a bicycle with the handlebars crooked that when someone straightened them he fell off. He was so used to crookedness that he thought straightness was crookedness! A woman, used to the dust-laden atmosphere of New York, went upstate to the country and said, "Why, the air was so pure it made me sick." She was naturalized in the unnatural.

When the prodigal son was in the far country, he "joined himself to a citizen of that country"; but he himself never became a citizen— he was never naturalized. He knew that it was not his homeland. He was out of joint, orphaned, estranged, starved, and homesick. Only when he was in his father's arms, a member of his father's household, did he feel he was where he belonged. There he was naturalized; that was his homeland.

"The only sickness is homesickness." It is. A strange nostalgia is upon humanity, and homesickness for God is responsible for most of our other sicknesses—mental, spiritual, physical, corporate. A prominent Christian leader threw over his Christian faith and followed his lusts. He tried to rationalize it all, tried even to make a new religion out of sexism, "a broader religion." As I sat beside him, old and haggard, lying in a hospital bed, he said pathetically, "I'm an ancient prodigal that never returned." He simply couldn't naturalize himself in evil. In the end homesickness got him.

O God, I know, I know I cannot run away from Thee, for I cannot run away from myself. For I am fashioned for Thee, and Thou art the life of my life, the joy of my joy, the being of my being. Nor do I want to run away; I want to run into Thy arms. For there I am at home. Amen.

AFFIRMATION FOR THE DAY: *God is my Home. When I am in Him, I am at Home. When I am out of Him, I am away from Home— I am Home-sick.*

NATURALLY PAGAN?

There are three attitudes one can take toward the soul. Tertullian, one of the church fathers, says, "The soul is naturally Christian." Reinhold Niebuhr says, "The soul is naturally pagan." Walter Horton says, "The soul is naturally half-pagan and half-Christian." I vote with Tertullian. The soul is unnaturally pagan. When it is pagan, it is off center, missing the way to live. When it becomes Christian, it has a sense of home-coming, of being reinstated, of being reconciled. The soul instinctively knows that this is the Way.

A radiant old man of eighty-two said to me: "I knew that this was the Way, for the moment I put my feet upon it I was no longer fighting with myself." That proved that the way of Christ and the way of the soul were one. When the soul found Christ, it found itself—it was no longer fighting with itself.

If the soul were naturally pagan, it would be very ill at ease in coming into the Kingdom. On the contrary, coming into the Kingdom means nothing less than coming into its own.

Besides, if the soul were naturally pagan, why should it be punished for its pagan ways? It would be unjust to punish it for living according to its own nature. But we feel that evil is evil and to be punished for it is just; therefore we witness to our feeling that evil is unnatural. In *The Screwtape Letters* a senior devil, writing advice to a junior devil, says: "We work under a cruel handicap. Nothing is naturally on our side. Everything has to be twisted before it is of any use to us."

There are three great driving urges in human nature: self, sex, and herd. The self urge is self-regarding; the herd urge is the social, the other-regarding; the sex urge is partly self-regarding and partly other-regarding. So there are just two urges: the self-regarding and the other-regarding; the egotistic and the altruistic. Then the other-regarding urge is just as natural as the self-regarding. As Professor Garnett says: "The desire for the good of others is just as natural to man as to desire his own good and just as incapable of further explanation." It is "incapable of further explanation" because it is a part of human nature.

O my Christ, I know when I meet Thee I meet that for which I am fashioned, that which fulfills me at the very moment it humbles me to the dust. I know I meet myself, my real self, in Thee. So I come knowing that I come to my destined way—Thy Way. I thank Thee. Amen.

AFFIRMATION FOR THE DAY: *I am natural only when I am in God.*

MY WILL AND GOD'S WILL—ALIEN?

There are a great many who still think with Ephraim, of whom God complained: "Were I to write for him my laws, he would but think them foreigner's saws." (Hos. 8:12, Moffatt.) Ephraim felt that God's laws were foreign sayings, or saws—something imposed from the outside. God says that His laws are native to us.

"There is something in the autumn that is native to my blood," wrote the poet Bliss Carman. There is something in Christ that is native to my blood. He is the author of my blood. He is at home there. It flows better, is warmer and purer when He is in it. He is native to my nerves. When He controls them, they are calm and creative and contributive. He is native to every organ of my body. When He controls them, they function well, perfectly, in fact, for they are made for His control. When they get under the control of resentments, of fear, of selfishness, they function badly.

Jesus said, "I have told you this, that my joy may be within you and your joy complete." (John 15:11, Moffatt.) Note: when His joy is within us, then our joy is complete, for His joy and our joy are the same. He is not imposing a foreign joy, trying to make me happy in something I can't be happy in. He is giving a joy which, when I take it, is my very own. My own joy is complete. Every joy, other than His, leaves me dissatisfied, incomplete. It doesn't hit the spot.

T. S. Eliot says: "We may say that religion implies a life in conformity with nature . . . and that not toward nature implies a wrong attitude toward God, and the consequence is inevitable doom." The Christian way is the way that conforms to nature, real nature. Anything else is doomed.

We must have hold of this until it becomes a basic axiom: My will and God's will are not alien. When I find His will, I find my very own. The idea that God's will always lies along the line of the disagreeable is false. The will of God is always our highest interest. It could not be otherwise and God be God. I am fulfilled when I make Him my center. I am frustrated when I make myself the center. I am destined to be a Christian.

O God, what a destiny I have—I am destined to be conformed to the image of Thy Son. Every portion of my being cries out in glad anticipation of the fulfillment of that destiny. I surrender myself to the loving purposes that would make me into His glorious image. Amen.

AFFIRMATION FOR THE DAY: *When my will and God's will coincide, I live. When they clash, I do not live.*

MADE FOR EACH OTHER?

We saw yesterday that my will and God's will are not alien. They fit as light and the eye fit, as truth and the conscience are affinities. Jesus said that man lives "on every word that issues from the mouth of God." (Matt. 4:4, Moffatt.) As the stomach and food are made for each other, so we are fashioned in our inner natures for the will of God as expressed in His words. So we "live" on them. We perish on any contradictory word. And it says "every"—there is no exception. Man perishes when he lives by every word that proceeds out of the mouth of hate, of greed, of fear.

Jesus said, "My food is to do the will of him who sent me." (John 4:34, Moffatt.) The will of God was "food"—it fed Him. Any other will contrary to God's will is poison. My poison is to do my own will when my own will clashes with God's. It leaves me frustrated, sick.

Whichever way you approach life, from the Christian revelation down to life, or from science up through the facts, you come out at the same place. The philosophers Moore and Otto "base their ethics on no theistic metaphysic, yet they have defined for us exactly what the enlightened religious consciousness declares—the duty to seek the good, not of ourselves alone, but also of our fellowmen." In other words, "Thou shalt love thy neighbor as thyself" is written in us as well as in the Bible. It is native to us.

To be good is good for you—your soul, mind, body, and relationships. To be bad is bad for you—your soul, mind, body, and relationships. You must love others in order to be able to love yourself. If you don't love others, you cannot get on with others or yourself. Apparently God has us hooked—if you don't love others as you love yourself, you can't get on with others, nor can you get on with yourself.

One of the first things you must learn in public speaking is not to think of your voice but to think of the people and the getting of the message to them. If you think of your voice, you will become self-conscious; and if you do, you go to pieces. To think of others is "native" to us—it is the way written in the constitution of us.

O God, when Thou didst fashion me, Thou didst fashion me for Thy will and purposes. In them I live—live radiantly, rhythmically, abundantly. In myself I perish. So I exchange my foolish ways for Thy will, and then I find my own wise ways hidden in me. I thank Thee. Amen.

AFFIRMATION FOR THE DAY: *Today I shall love my neighbor because I love myself. If I do not love my neighbor, myself will be too ugly to love.*

FINDING GOD—AND OURSELVES

Again we must look at the naturalness of the supernatural and the supernaturalness of the natural.

Jesus said, "If anyone does not remain in me, he is thrown aside." (John 15:6, Moffatt.) That is an amazing statement: "If you do not remain in me, then life throws you aside." Life says, "Sorry, I cannot use you. You don't fit." Right now before our very eyes that inevitable throwing aside is going on; those who live in hate, selfishness, fear, are inevitably thrown aside as unusable. Is that arbitrary? Oh no; the person who holds these things within him becomes unfit. The rest of that verse says, "He withers." Cut off from the source of his true life, he withers, becomes unfit for use. On the other hand, when you remain in Him, you are full of life and life giving.

Again, Jesus says, "He who does not gather with me scatters." (Matt. 12:30, Moffatt.) Life is scattered, goes to pieces, breaks down if it is not held together by Christ. On the contrary, he who gathers with Christ gathers up the forces of his own soul into a living unity. He is put together into harmony. "Do not be senseless, but understand what is the Lord's will." (Eph. 5:17, Moffatt.) If you know God's will, you have sense; if you don't, you are senseless.

There is a story of a child who couldn't get the jigsaw puzzle of the map of the world together and was well nigh in despair until she looked on the other side of the pieces and found they made a picture of Christ. When she put Him together, then the world on the other side came out all right. Get Christ right in your life, and then all of life will come out with it. For Christ and life are one.

This passage may well sum up our week's study of the naturalness of the Christian way: "All things have been created by him and for him." (Col. 1:16, Moffatt.) Note: We are not only made "by" Him; we are also made "for" Him. That is, life works in His way and in no other way. Look at everything in your life, every organ, every relationship, and you can see, if you have eyes to see, this written in everything: "Made for Him." When it finds Him, it finds its own fulfillment. His will is my peace.

O gracious God, Thou art overwhelming me with Thy generous grace. I thought I would have to climb up to heaven to bring it down, and lo, Thou hast brought it near—it is my very being if I will but accept it. I do accept it. I accept it now. And I thank Thee—from the depths. Amen.

AFFIRMATION FOR THE DAY: *Christ and life are one, and I cannot live against Christ without living against life.*

CAN WE BE TOO CHRISTIAN?

We must spend another week on the consideration of the natural-ness of the Christian way. A prominent member of the church showed in these words that he thought the Christian way is alien to life, that you might have too much of it: "You can have too much of religion. You must live a balanced life and make religion one of the interests of life." Of course you can have too much of religion that is off center, not centered in Christ; but if the Christian way is the Way, then it is not one of the interests of life—it is Life controlling all life.

Yesterday we quoted the passage, "All things have been created by him and for him"—we are made for Him and His ways. The rest of the passage is significant: "And all coheres in him." (Col. 1:17, Moffatt.) In Him all things cohere, or hang together. Out of Him all things are incoherent and go to pieces. When the pressures of life press hard or calamities strike, Christians know how to stand up under it better. Jesus said that if you build upon His way, then when the rain descends and the storm beats and the flood arises, your house will stand, for it is built upon a rock. Life will approve it, sustain it. It will cohere, hang together. But if you build upon something else, then when the rain descends, the storm beats, and the flood arises, your house will crash. Life will not sustain it; it will not cohere. In saying this He was saying what all life corroborates: The judgments of Christ and the judgments of life are the same. If you won't listen to the judgments of Christ, you will have to listen to the judgments of life. As I write this, at the beginning of a series of lectures in Lon-don, Ontario, a full-page advertisement of this series in the local paper this morning, put in by business and professional men, has this sentence in the center of the page, "If you will not live with God, you cannot live with yourself." These men found that the very pressures of modern life corroborate this fact. Revolt against God, and you revolt against yourself. Life is an incoherent mess until it finds the Way. Its sums won't add up; all its ways are ways to disillusionment. You have to find the key, or all your life you will stand fumbling with the lock of life, and it won't open.

O Christ, Thou art my key. When I find Thee, I find an open door, a way to live, a way to harmony, a way to everything I want in my inmost depths. I know life when I know Thee. I know death when I do not have Thee. Help me, then, to choose Thee. Amen.

AFFIRMATION FOR THE DAY: *Today my life will be a mess or a mes-sage. I choose.*

THE GOD OF LIFE AND THE GOD OF RELIGION

An outstanding Negro professor said in my hearing: "The biggest question with me is the question of making no distinction between the God of life and the God of religion." Are they one? The Christian's answer is an unequivocal Yes. The revelation of life that you see in Jesus Christ and the revelation of life slowly unfolding in history are the same. They speak the same story, render the same verdict regarding life.

The professor added these significant words: "If we nourish within our hearts fear and hate and self-centeredness, we shall spend our days stumbling in the dark." Why? For the simple reason that life is not made for fear, for hate, for self-centeredness. Take those ways, and you stumble in the dark. However, if you nourish within your heart faith and love and other-centeredness, you will spend your days joyously walking in the light. For the one way is for nature, and the other is against it.

A bishop spoke of the Christian way as costly—"It will cost you something to be a Christian." A management engineer said: "After hearing the bishop and hearing the message on the naturalness of the Christian way, my inner reaction was: 'How costly it will be not to be a Christian!'" To be a Christian you may have to give up some things, but not to be a Christian you have to give up everything— everything worth while. In giving up things for Christ I gave up nothing but what subtracted from me, and when I got Him, I got everything that added to me.

This passage in I John 5:3 (Moffatt) sums up this thought perfectly: "His commands are not irksome." Why? For He commands nothing that is not demanded by the necessities of life. If He did not command them, life would. His commands are not irksome, for when you obey them, you turn out happy, harmonious, and adjusted. And when you do not obey His commands, you turn out unhappy, inharmonious, and maladjusted. You may take it or leave it, but that is what life says.

O Christ, I know I had better listen to life. I get hurt when I don't. But why should I have to listen to life when I have Thee to listen to? For Thou art Life. In Thee I find everything I want and many things I never dreamed I needed or wanted. I thank Thee. Amen.

AFFIRMATION FOR THE DAY: *When God commands, life commends.*

MORE FUN TO BE A CHRISTIAN?

Yesterday we ended by repeating that "His commands are not irksome." I do not mean to say that it will not cause you pain and mental suffering to break old ways of life, to surrender your will to His ways. It will. To reverse one's habits causes upset. But it is an upset that sets up! The initial pain is the "pain divine"; it is the pain that leads to the profoundest joy that life knows—the joy of adjustment, of harmony, of Life.

Jesus puts it this way: "My yoke is kindly." (Matt. 11:30, Moffatt.) Why is His yoke kindly? Because He asks little of us? On the contrary, He asks our very all. He demands something that no one dare ask another—our all. And yet when we respond and give the all, we do find the yoke kindly. Why? Because it is of our "kind"; it fits us; we are made for it. His yoke is my yearning—my inmost yearning. His discipline is my desire—my inmost desire. His Life is my life.

He says, again, "My burden [is] light." It is not that He puts no burdens on us; He puts tremendous burdens on us. For if you follow Him, you will find the world and its burdens laid on your heart, these in addition to your own. But those who gladly accept His burden find it is light—the heart sings under it. His burden is a burden only as wings are a burden to a bird, fins are a burden to a fish, and love is a burden to the heart.

Some young people in Boise, Idaho, were discussing why they were Christians, and one boy spoke up and said, "I'm a Christian because it is a heap more fun to be a Christian than it is going to the devil." A heap more fun! Why? Well, one satisfies a life and the other satisfies an impulse, an impulse that throws confusion and disgust into the rest of life. A part determines the whole instead of the whole's determining the part. One ends in a mess; the other ends in fun.

The Christian way is literally goodness turned to gaiety. The Christian sings, and sings from the depths. He doesn't sing to make himself happy; he sings because he is profoundly happy. For his happiness is not dependent on happenings; it is founded on life.

O Christ, my every thought dances and sings when it thinks of Thee. For Thou hast set Joy within my heart. I knew some joys before I found Thee. But in Thee I know Joy, and in that Joy all lesser joys are contained and come to fulfillment. Am I grateful? Read my unspoken gratitude! Amen.

AFFIRMATION FOR THE DAY: *The Christian way is life set to music; the unchristian way is life set to misery.*

THE LIGHT TURNED TO DARKNESS

We continue our study of the Way as the natural way. Jesus calls Himself "the master of the House." (Luke 13:25, Moffatt.) He is literally just that—"the master of the House." When He masters it, the house of Mansoul is orderly and harmonious and livable. But when something else becomes master of the house, then you can't live in the house of Mansoul. Isaiah speaks of those who take hold of a clansman, crying, "Your house has a robe of office; come, be our chieftain, then, master this chaos!" (Isa. 3:6, Moffatt.) They had revolted from God, and the result was chaos, and they turned to almost anyone to try to "master this chaos." No one can "master this chaos" in the house of Mansoul except the Master—the real "master of the House."

Jesus says, "If your Eye is generous" (Matt. 6:22, Moffatt)—if your eye, your way of looking at life, is generous, is Christian—then your whole body is full of light. The generous eye generates—"gives birth"—gives birth to happiness, light, life. You are fulfilled, and you are creative. But "if your Eye is selfish," then everything you touch becomes darkness—money, sex, all relationships. The very self disintegrates and becomes darkness. This is not-the-way. When the very light turns to darkness, what a darkness it is! When your very goods become bads, how bad it is! The whole of your body becomes darkened. You cannot take a wrong attitude in one part of your being without that darkness' spreading to the whole of your body, affecting your whole personality. When all your foods become poisons, all your success is failure, all your light is darkness, all your sums come out wrong—what a tangled-up thing life becomes! That is not-the-way, and it is antinatural. Life won't respond to it. Chesterton says, "If the natural will not submit to the supernatural, it becomes the unnatural."

On the other hand, Jesus says, "I know that his orders mean eternal life." (John 12:50, Moffatt.) For His orders mean order—within, without, everywhere! Refusal of His orders means disorder—within, without, everywhere! For God orders only what life must have—if life lives.

O Thou living Christ, Thou art living, and Thou art life giving. I would know Thee, for I would know life. And now I'm beginning to know life as I am beginning to know Thee. Life steals into every portion of my being with healing and with health. I am alive—alive to my depths. Amen.

AFFIRMATION FOR THE DAY: *I submit my natural to the Supernatural that it may become more natural.*

LIFE-DENYING AND LIFE-AFFIRMING

The two types of religion, the unnatural and the natural, are embodied in John the Baptist and in Jesus.

John tried to show God in the unnatural, lived without a home in the desert, "neither ate nor drank," lived upon wild locusts and honey, beat upon the soul of a nation from without—an imposed morality. "You must not do this; you must do that"—a whipping up of the will. He imposed rites upon men.

Jesus revealed God from within the process of life. He ate and drank and lived in homes; He used parables taken from life and nature; He lifted up the laws underlying life—showed God in the regularities, the natural. Not that He stopped with the natural. He showed God in the extranatural—the supernatural. But it was all supernaturally natural. He revealed Life within life. There is a kinship between the natural and the supernatural. Life was of one piece.

Jesus said that "he that is least in the kingdom of God is greater" than John, for John was approaching life from the outside, and Jesus said, "The kingdom of God is within you"—in your nerves, your tissues, your blood, your very make-up. John presented religion as antinatural asceticism; Jesus presented it as a supernatural naturalism. John's religion was anti-life, and Jesus' was pro-life. The faith that John presented was world-denying and life-denying. Jesus was world-affirming and life-affirming. One was a No! The other was a Yes! John preached a baptism of repentance, a turning from. Jesus offered a baptism of the Spirit, a turning to—positive, receptive. John's movement died. Jesus' movement lives on. For you cannot live against life. The answer to life is not a reduction of life but an inner fullness of life that can master outer life.

The end product of the impact of Jesus on the lives of the disciples was this: "The Spirit enabled them to express themselves." (Acts 2:4, Moffatt.) The end was self-expression through Spirit—possession. They were most themselves when most God's. They were free from inhibitions, fears, guilts. Now they could be natural, supernaturally natural.

O Christ, I see Thee so poised, so natural, so altogether alive and spontaneous. I would be that way too. So I surrender my unnatural sin, my tied-up unnatural self, into Thy hands to be loosed and alive and gay and natural. I would be free—free to be myself in Thee. Amen.

AFFIRMATION FOR THE DAY: *In Thyself I am myself; outside of Thee I am beside myself.*

REACHING OUR FULL LIFE

There are three words that put into small compass what we have been saying these two weeks about the naturalness of the Christian way: "realized in him." (I John 2:8, Moffatt.) This phrase "realized in Him" can be written after every truth found anywhere in any philosophy; in Him the idea has become the *fact*. But there is something more than ideas realized in Him. We are realized in Him; we come to our own, become ourselves, are truly natural. It is a simple, literal fact that the more I belong to Him, the more I belong to myself. The more I am bound to Him, the freer I am.

Your code of morals can then be summed up in a sentence: "Love Christ, and do as you like." For then you will do what is right and what is good for you. And more, you will do what you really like.

Jesus said to the woman at the well: "Whosoever drinketh of this water shall thirst again: but whosoever drinketh of the water that I shall give him shall never thirst." (John 4:13-14.) "Shall never thirst"—why? Because of the ever-present source of satisfaction at the heart of life when Christ is there. Your thirsts are satisfied—in Him. For He is the natural satisfaction of natural desires.

In I John 4:9 (Moffatt) there is this penetrating sentence: "By him we might live." By Him we live—live fully, abundantly to our very finger tips. Out of Him we perish in every portion of our being. This passage sums up the matter: "It is in him that you reach your full life." (Col. 2:10, Moffatt.) Just as Jesus came not to destroy the law and the prophets but to fulfill them, so He comes not to destroy the laws and the prophecies written in us but to fulfill them. Everything surrendered to Him comes to its fulfillment—comes to its full life. Everything out of Him is runted and stunted.

In John 17:3 (Moffatt) we read, "This is life eternal, that they know thee, the only real God, and him whom thou hast sent." To know God as revealed in Christ, in the sense of participating in, is life eternal. It is also life natural.

O gracious Christ, I begin to see in Thee my life, my all. Thou art the life of my nerves, my flesh, my blood, my brain cells—my inmost being. In Thee I tingle with life; I overflow with it; I am submerged in it. And am I grateful? You will have to read the gratitude I cannot speak. Thank you. Amen.

AFFIRMATION FOR THE DAY: *As the flower in reaching toward the sun reaches its own full life, so in reaching toward Christ I reach my own fullest life.*

41

THE CHRISTIAN WAY IS SENSE

We come to the end of the week of our study of the naturalness of the Christian way. The real Christian is the most universalized person on earth, for he is the most natural. A great many people think they have to be less Christian to be more universal. That is a mistake. The more Christian you are, the more universal you are. You are at home in everything, everywhere except in one thing—evil. For in evil, life turns unnatural, lives against itself.

A doctor flung himself in a chair in front of me and eagerly asked, "Is religion natural?" His acceptance or rejection of it depended upon the answer. I could answer, "If you mean by religion Christ—for He is my definition of religion—then the answer is an unqualified Yes." Moreover it can be added: Everything that doesn't fit into His spirit is unnatural.

Charles Edward Pugh sums up the Christian way in these words: "It is horse sense. It is sanity. And anyone who acts differently is a damned fool, and I am not swearing when I say it." Everyone who has experienced Christ knows that he was reverent when he said it. For outside of Him we do damn ourselves to futility, to an impossible way of life. And we know that we are fools to try it.

I know exactly what happens when I do the Christian thing: I am universalized, at home in the universe; the sum total of reality is behind me; I walk the earth a conqueror; I am afraid of nothing; everything within me says, "This is the natural way to live."

On the other hand, when I go against the Christian way, I know exactly what happens: I am out of gear; something has slipped a cog; I feel orphaned, estranged, not at home with myself or people or God; my life sags and loses its music; everything within me says: "This is the unnatural way to live."

Some high school girls interviewed me for their paper and asked, "Is there anything you want that you haven't got?" I could reply, "I don't know of a thing that I want that I haven't got. All I want is more of what I have got." I had found the Way—the natural way.

O Thou living Christ, when my feet come to Thy Way, I am filled with a sense of surety, a sense of being at home, a sense of being rhythmical and harmonious and natural. All my complexities have been reduced to simplicities, all my clashes to concord. I thank Thee. Amen.

AFFIRMATION FOR THE DAY: *The Way is sense; all else is nonsense.*

IS THE WAY IMPERSONAL?

We have been glimpsing the Way amid the ways of life and experience around us. The Way is not merely written in the Book; it is written in us and in our relationships. I predict that this will become the most thrilling, exciting, rewarding adventure of human beings in the days to come. Science, philosophy, education, economics, business, politics, sociology—all branches of human approach to life—are going to converge upon one thing: the discovery of the Way. The discovery of gold amid the dust of the earth is going to be tame alongside the discovery of the Way hidden at the basis of life. Someday scientists are going to put it all down on the table, and they are going to say, "This is not the way to live," and, "This is the way to live." As we look at it, our eyes will bulge with astonishment, and we shall exclaim, "But, brother men, the way you say *is not* the way to live is the unchristian way, and the way you say *is* the way is the Christian way." They will reply, "We cannot say about that, for that is not our province; but this is not the way to live, and this is the way to live."

The Christian way is the ground plan of the universe. The earliest written document, written 3000 or 3500 B.C., says: "Life is given to the peaceful and death is given to the guilty, the peaceful being 'he who does what is loved,' and the guilty, 'he who does what is hated.'" This is the earliest written judgment on life. The writer saw that one way leads to a dead end, death; the other leads to an open way, life. From that day to this we are finding the same thing. The Christian way is not only sanctity; it is sanity. Take any way you will and pursue it and you will come out to one of two things: if it is not-the-way, you will come to a dead end; if it is the way, you will come to the Way. All the right ways lead to the Way.

While this is mentally reassuring and satisfying, yet it leaves one emotionally dissatisfied. For the Way seems impersonal. It is something on which to tread toward a goal. You can be grateful for a way, but you cannot love a way—it is impersonal. Is the Way personal? For I, who am deeply personal, cannot be satisfied this side of the Personal.

O my Father, I am grateful for the Way. But my heart is hungry for response, for love in return. I am grateful for principles, but I crave the Person. I want a heart to answer my heart. Must I obey principles, or can I love a Person? Show me. Amen.

AFFIRMATION FOR THE DAY: *Personality is our highest category of being. God may be more than personal; He cannot be less.*

RELIGION NEEDS A COSMIC GUARANTEE

We saw yesterday the craving that the Way be personal, something to love, to fellowship with. I can accept the multiplication table as true, but I cannot say my prayers to it. A weeping child cannot be satisfied if you offer him the principle of motherhood. He wants a mother. I am not a walking robot asking only for a path. I am a person asking for a Person. Is the Way a principle or a Person?

It is both! Jesus put them together in this statement, "I am the way." Here the Word became flesh, the Path became a Person. A white man was lost in an African jungle. He asked a native if he could show him the way through the jungle. As they trudged along, he became doubtful and asked, "Is this the way?" The native replied, "There is no way. I am the way." The shrewdness of the native got the lost man through a wayless jungle—the native was the way.

Christ is the Way. He said, "Follow me"—not merely follow a set of principles, a way of life, but surrender to me, get into living fellowship with me, find out my ways, and they will turn out to be the Way. For I am the Way.

Fortunately for us, we find that when we follow Him, the Way, we find that He is not a way through a trackless jungle. He is the Way in the midst of a universe which has the Way written in its very constitution. So He is not an imposition on life as the native with his intelligence was an imposition upon a pathless jungle. He is the Way written everywhere come to personification. He is the ways of life come to Life—all the paths become a Person. He sums up the meanings of life, for He is life. When you touch Christ, you feel you have not touched the margin of life; you have touched Life itself.

This is important, for religion needs a cosmic guarantee. If Jesus were an imposition on life, we would be afraid the universe would not sustain His way. The nature of reality might be against it. In that case the Way would be only an excrescence, an aberration, an imposition—it would be unnatural. But suppose the Way is supernaturally natural—is the exposure of Reality—then?

Yes, O Christ, then? If that should be true, I could give myself to Thee with all the consent of all my being. And something within me tells me it is true. For if Thou art not true, what can be true? If Thou art false, then life is false. But Thou art true. I know it. I come with all my heart. Amen.

AFFIRMATION FOR THE DAY: *I am following something which has a cosmic guarantee!*

LISTENING TO HIS MASTER'S VOICE

We saw yesterday that the Way is a Person. When you love Him, you fulfill all the principles embodied in Him. We are not then struggling to live up to a code; that is a force-pump type of faith. Our code is a Character. We love that Character, and we then fulfill the code embodied in Him. Our faith, then, is not a force pump; it is artesian. It is spontaneous and gay and released.

In India the newspapers came out with the headlines that the name of Mohammed written in the clouds was seen, so it was claimed, by many persons. This portent showed, said the Moslems, that the faith of Mohammed was to conquer the earth. But the name that will conquer the earth is not the name written into passing clouds, but the name that is written in the nature of reality, the name that brings into manifestation the very nature of being—that name will conquer the world.

Consider the familiar picture of the dog listening in the horn of the phonograph to "his master's voice" graven on a record. Is that not the picture of humanity listening to its Master's Voice as it is graven in the nature of things? If we would listen, we should hear His Voice from everywhere, from everything, except one thing—sin.

On an ancient papyrus is an inscription of a supposed saying of Jesus: "Cleave the wood and thou shalt find me, raise the stone and I am there." We can go further now and say: "Cleave the tissue and you will find His will written there; dissect every relationship of life and you will find it is made to work in His way and only in His way. Raise the stones, the hard bare facts of life, and you will find Him there beneath the facts of life." Just as the Rosetta stone furnished the clue to the hieroglyphics and made it possible to decipher all that ancient lore, so Jesus is the Rosetta stone that gives us the clue to the language of creation, to that hidden purpose running through all things. "He is God breaking through" into intelligibility, into redemption. He is God's open secret. A critic once said: "Wherever we seek to go in criticism, in coming back we always meet Coleridge." Wherever we go in life, we meet Christ.

O Jesus, I look through life, and I see Life, I see everything. The unfolding drama of creation comes into meaning in Thee. I see where I must head in, what I must become like. That is my glad goal. Amen.

AFFIRMATION FOR THE DAY: *I am not following the fixed letter of a law, but the unfolding of a living Mind. My good today may not be good enough tomorrow.*

GOD'S BEST PHOTOGRAPH

Yesterday we said that Jesus is the meaning of the universe come to concrete expression. A teacher was talking to some slum children and asked what they thought of Jesus. A little Italian boy answered, "Jesus is the best photograph that God ever had took." He is! The writer of Hebrews says that He is "the express image of his person," an exact likeness of God, "a speaking image," as we say, of the Father.

We have high-powered wires with such high-power voltage that it is unusable unless it goes through a transformer and is thus made available with safety in lowly cottages and for lowly uses. Jesus is the transformer of God. Here God enters our lowly doors and becomes intimate and tender and approachable.

In one place Jesus said to murmuring Pharisees, "To let you see that the Son of man has power on earth to forgive sins." (Mark 2:10, Moffatt.) That phrase "to let you see" is the key to the whole meaning of Jesus. In Him we do not hear things merely; we "see" them. In Him I "see" love, and love becomes Love. In Him I "see" goodness, and it becomes Goodness. In Him I do not hear of God; I "see" God. And what a God!

Someone overheard a Negro on the street saying to another, "Jesus is the only Somebody you can't match." His insight saw that here was the ultimate meaning of life. And now listen to what Alfred Adler, a psychologist and a Jew, said in answer to the question of a Los Angeles pastor, "What do you think of Jesus Christ?" The reply: "Whenever I hear his name, I stop for reverence to the greatest character of human history." But why is He great, and continuously great, unexhausted amid the passing of the centuries? Because in Him we see the meaning of God, of man, of life, of the whole cosmic process. He is great because freighted with great meanings, ultimate meanings.

Heb. 1:2 says, "Whom he hath appointed heir of all things." Why? Is that an arbitrary decree of God? Or will Jesus be heir of all things because all things that fit into Him will survive and all that does not will perish? So all that is, is His! "All things have been created by him and for him."

O Thou eternal Christ, understandable even to me, I thank Thee for putting the latchstring so low I can reach it. I can reach the Highest, for Thou art the Highest become lowly, reachable. And so I come, for in Thee I "see"—see everything I need. I thank Thee. Amen.

AFFIRMATION FOR THE DAY: *Today I shall let men "see" the definition of a Christian—in me.*

THE INDICATIVE BECOME THE IMPERATIVE

But in praising Jesus as you have been doing, aren't you over-praising Him? This same question was raised by the high priests and scribes when the children shouted, "Hosanna to the Son of David!" "Do you hear what they are saying?" "Yes," said Jesus, "and have you never read, 'Thou hast brought praise to perfection from the mouth of babes and sucklings'?" (Matt. 21:15-16, Moffatt.) Note: "Thou hast brought praise to perfection." Praise was brought to perfection when it praised Jesus. Why? Because here is one that cannot be overpraised. Whatever you say about Him is understatement, for the Word is bigger than our words, and the coming years and centuries will unfold new meanings in Him. A new meaning from a child: "Jesus was the one who gave God a good reputation."

Jesus said, "And blessed is he who is repelled by nothing in me." (Matt. 11:6, Moffatt.) I should have thought that He would have said, "And blessed am I if you can find nothing to repel you in me." But He didn't! He meant, "Blessed are *you* if you are repelled by nothing in *me*. For if you are repelled by anything in me, you are wrong; you are blessed if you approve me, for life will approve you."

When He finished the Sermon on the Mount, which some suppose to be idealism, "the people were astonished at his doctrine: for he taught them as one having authority." (Matt. 7:28-29.) What was the "authority"? An outer imposed authority? No, it was the authority of the facts. He was lifting up the meaning of life, lifting up the meaning of the laws underlying life. He was uncovering Reality. A good many people make the tragic mistake of considering Jesus a moralist, imposing a moral code upon humanity for which humanity is badly made. But Jesus was not a moralist in that sense at all. He was a revealer of the nature of Reality. He revealed first of all the nature of God, and the nature of God became the ground of God's conduct and ours. He then lifted up the laws written in the universe and the laws written in our tissues, our blood, our nerves, written in us. Instead of being an imposed idealism it was an exposed realism—it was Reality itself speaking. No wonder it was authoritative! Here was the indicative become the imperative!

O Christ, when I look upon Thee, I look upon Life. For I see in Thee my dream fulfilled, my longing become Fact. I see in Thee everything I have ever thought about goodness—and more! I thank Thee. Amen.

AFFIRMATION FOR THE DAY: *All of Christ's ways become the Way— for everybody, everywhere.*

"YOU JUST TOLD US THINGS"

We are considering the secret of this Man's authority. The best compliment I have ever heard given to a minister came from a Roman Catholic businessman who said at the close of a luncheon address, "You didn't preach at us; you just told us things." He saw the difference between a morality imposed by fiat from without and the lifting up of the laws underlying life, laws which are self-verifying.

"They were all so amazed that they discussed it together, saying, 'Whatever is this? It's new teaching with authority behind it!'" (Mark 1:27, Moffatt.) What authority was behind it? (1) The authority of God; when He spoke, God spoke. (2) The authority of Truth; Truth spoke when He spoke. (3) The authority of the Deed; the Deed spoke when He spoke. (4) The authority of Love; Love spoke and acted when He spoke and acted. (5) The authority of the sum total of Reality; Reality spoke and acted in Him.

We have often read passages like this as an arbitrary gift of God to Christ, "All has been handed over to me by my Father." (Matt. 11:27, Moffatt.) Why was "all" handed over to Him? All comes to Him because it came from Him. His will and way is written in "all," and hence "all" cannot exist or be fulfilled apart from Him. And note, it doesn't say "all spiritual things." It says "all" unqualified, and that means "all"—material, spiritual, secular, sacred, individual, social, national, international, heaven, earth—all. The Way is the Way—unqualified!

Again, it says, "Full authority has been given to me in heaven and on earth." (Matt. 28:18, Moffatt.) Many are willing to allow Him full authority in heaven, but "on earth"? Has He full authority here too? Yes, for everything both in heaven and on earth has a Christian destiny wrought into it. The earth belongs to those who belong to Christ, for no one else can run it—except into the ditch. There isn't a situation on earth, for the individual, for society, where the Christian thing is not the right thing. For earth is not only "crammed with heaven"—it is crammed with heaven's laws and ways as the very nature of its being.

O Christ, Thy will is in my lifeblood. It is woven into the texture of my being. I cannot run away from Thee, for I cannot run away from myself. Nor do I want to. Help me live in Thee this day. Amen.

AFFIRMATION FOR THE DAY: *The Way is the way for me to think, to act, to feel, to be in every conceivable circumstance. It shall be my Way today.*

CHRIST WRITTEN IN THE TEXTURE OF THINGS

Alfred Whitehead, the philosopher, says: "I hazard the prophecy that that religion will conquer which can render clear to popular understanding some eternal greatness incarnate in the passage of temporal fact." Note that it must be *"eternal* greatness." We cannot give ourselves to something that is time-bound, and therefore to be time-destroyed. It must be eternal. And then that "eternal greatness" must be "incarnate in the passage of temporal fact." It must meet us where we are, walk our dusty ways with us, redeem us, not by proxy but by proximity—the Word must become flesh. What other faith can fulfill the demand except that of Jesus?

But there is a further consideration. This Word which becomes flesh not only must be a revelation of God; it must have a kinship to the flesh, must be the interpretation not only of God but of life. In I John 1:2 (Moffatt) we read, "The Logos of Life." This Logos, or Word, was not only the Word of God; it was the Word of Life. In Him we see the meaning of life. He reveals God, and He reveals life. I see in Him all the half-hidden meanings of life, written in me and in the nature of things around me, come into full meaning.

These lines by Harry Kemp tell of this fact of Christ inherent everywhere:

"I cannot put the presence by, of him, the Crucified,
Who moves men's spirits with his love as doth the moon the tide;
. . . .
Again I see upon the cross that great Soul-battle fought,
Into the texture of the world the tale of which is wrought
Until it hath become the woof of human deed and thought."

Christ is in the texts of Scripture, but also in "the texture of the world." He is the revelation of God and life. Rev. 3:14 (Moffatt) sums it up thus: "These are the words of the Amen, . . . the origin of God's creation." His will is wrought into creation, and He is the "Amen," the affirmation of that creation. Creation comes to its own in Him. Out of Him it is not creation but chaos.

O Jesus, I see Thee as the summing up of the meaning of creation, and I see Thee as the author of my new creation. I need to be remade—remade into the image of Thyself. I present myself for re-creation. Amen.

AFFIRMATION FOR THE DAY:
"I see His blood upon the rose
And in the stars the glory of His eyes."
I shall see Him everywhere as I go forth today.

ONE GREATER THAN THE TEMPLE IS HERE

We have been studying the naturalness of the Christian way. If we get hold of that, it will transform our attitudes toward the Christian way. We will no longer tend to be afraid of it. It will be easier to surrender to it, for in doing so we find ourselves and our own way. A woman arose in a meeting and said: "The Christian way is the natural way. But we haven't been taught that. That's news—let's go out and give it." We must. But one word of reminder before we do. While the Christian way is the natural way, the Christian way is not a mere naturalism—it is supernaturally natural. It is within the natural, but it is above it.

A passage which shows the relationship of Jesus to everything is this: "One greater than the temple is here." (Matt. 12:6, A.S.V.) The temple was the center of the religious life, the very life of the Jewish nation. People came to it from all over that ancient world because it was the center of their faith and hope. Jesus stood in the midst of that ancient grandeur and quietly said: "One greater than the temple is here." It seemed preposterous. And yet the ages have corroborated Him. The temple is gone; all that is left is a Wailing Wall. He lives on, the most potent power in human affairs.

A man looked at some pictures in a famous gallery and said, "I don't think much of these pictures." The reply of the attendant: "Excuse me, sir, the *pictures* are not on trial." The people who viewed them were! Jesus is not on trial now. We judge ourselves by our judgment of Him.

Said a German, "At the end of the last war stood one personality —Jesus." At the end of this one stands one personality—Jesus.

One greater than the temple was there—is here. Jesus is bigger than all our systems. They are related to Him, not He to them. He is the absolute; they are the relative. They must all stand before the judgment bar of His person. If they fit into Him, reflect His mind and spirit, they are valid. If not, they are not valid. The acid test of anything Christian is: Is it Christ-ian? Is it centered in Him, and does it work out from Him?

O Christ, Thou art my center, and Thou art my circumference. I begin with Thee, and I end with Thee. For if I don't begin with Thee, I end in disillusionment and disgust. Help me this day to begin every thought, every secret longing, and every act and project with Thee. Amen.

AFFIRMATION FOR THE DAY: *"Our little systems have their day." Christ has towered and will tower over the wrecks of time.*

GOD BECOME INTIMATE

We are thinking upon the words, "One greater than the temple is here." Had we kept that emphasis, the history of Christianity would have been different. Very often Christianity has become ec-centric, off the center, away from Christ. For Christianity *is* Christ.

The editor of a farm journal with millions of readers wrote me: "The South is suffering from the lack of a Christ-centered religion. It is wasting its time and energy on irrelevancies. Write me an article on 'A Christ-centered Religion.'" Not only the South but the whole of Christendom is suffering from the same lack.

We must get our values straight, and the central value of the Christian faith is Christ. If the reply is made that God is our central value and starting point, the answer must be that apart from Christ we know little about God. If we try to start from God, we do not start from God, but from our ideas about God. But our ideas about God are not God. We must start from God's idea about Himself, and God's idea about Himself is Christ. Jesus is God breaking through to us. He is the great simplification—God speaking to us in the only language we can understand, a human language; showing us His life in the only way we could grasp it, a human life; uncovering His character in the place where your character and mine are wrought out, a human character. Jesus is the human life of God. He is the God become intimate. Jesus is God the vague become God the vital. He is manifest God.

Someone has said: "The important things are two: What is your center? And what is your circumference?" They depend on each other, for you soon get to the end of your circumference if you have the wrong center. Your faith exhausts itself against the problems of life. Christ must be the center. From Him we work out to God, and life, and human problems. He is the Master Light of all our seeing. He is our Starting Point. And where is our ending point? Our circumference? There is no ending point, and there is no circumference —it is all infinite, boundless. But if you begin at any other place it is not infinite, it is not boundless—it is earthbound.

O Christ, when I get hold of Thee, I know that I get hold of infinity. Thou art the language of eternity speaking to me in the speech of time. I hear, I heed, and I am at rest, for in Thee the final word speaks, speaks to my need, speaks to my inmost being, speaks to me. I thank Thee. Amen.

AFFIRMATION FOR THE DAY: *If I begin with a problem, I'll probably end with a problem, and in the process I'll become a problem.*

ONE GREATER THAN THE BIBLE

One greater than the Bible is here. We love the Bible, honor it, assimilate it, for it leads us to His feet. But the Bible is not the revelation of God. It is the inspired record of the revelation. The revelation was seen in the face of Jesus Christ. Jesus said: "You search the scriptures, imagining you possess eternal life in their pages—and they do testify to me—but you refuse to come to me for life." (John 5:39, Moffatt.) "Imagining you possess eternal life in their pages." Eternal life is not in the pages; it is in Christ, who is uncovered through the pages. The Word was not made printer's ink. The Word was made flesh, not a page but a Person.

One greater than the Bible is here. A prominent theologian said, "The Bible is the supreme method of intercourse between man and God." Is it? I thought Christ is the supreme method of intercourse between God and man. "There is . . . one mediator between God and men, the man Christ Jesus." (I Tim. 2:5.) It is true that we know little about Christ except through the New Testament. But it is also true that "Jesus was above His reporters." We believe that those reporters through the heightening of their insights—in other words, through inspiration—have caught the essential meaning of Christ. To all intents and purposes we have the essential Christ through them. Nevertheless, we always have the feeling they were trying to tell the untellable and express the inexpressible. Paul calls Christ the "unspeakable gift"—he couldn't quite speak Him. A minister asked me if we shouldn't preach Paul's epistles? I replied, "I do not preach Paul's epistles. I preach Christ, who was revealed through Paul's epistles and through other channels. But He is bigger than all the channels." The Word is greater than Paul's words.

Moreover, Christ was here before the New Testament. He created it; it did not create Him. It was His impact upon life that produced this literature. The Person is greater than the product. We love and honor the product, but only as it leads us to His feet and to an allegiance to Him. One greater than the Bible is here.

O Christ, I know that Thou art greater than all our descriptions of Thee. When we have said all, then we stand in dumb adoration before the wonder of Thee—the Inexpressible. But I see enough of Thee to love Thee and to give my heart to Thee fully. I do so, and I do so now. I thank Thee. Amen.

AFFIRMATION FOR THE DAY: *If I begin with Christ, I'll probably come to a crisis and go on to a conclusion.*

OUR CODE IS A CHARACTER

Yesterday we stated that "One greater than the Bible is here." He made Himself supreme even in Scripture. The Old Testament is the period of preparation for Christ. It is not Christianity; it is both pre-Christian and sub-Christian. Revelation was progressive, moving on till it found its completion and perfection in Christ. All Scripture must be brought before the bar of His person to be judged. He made Himself final even in Scripture. He said, "Ye have heard that it was said by them of old time, . . . but I say unto you." He changed the standards and made His own word final. I accept everything in the Old Testament that fits into His mind and spirit, and what does not I gently lay aside as belonging to the imperfect stage of revelation and accept Him—the perfect stage.

Moreover, One greater than the Ten Commandments is here. We honor and love those commandments, but Christ transcended them: "A new commandment I give unto you, That ye love one another; as I have loved you." (John 13:34.) Many quote it and stop at "That ye love one another," but that would not have been "new"—the Old Testament and other Scriptures enjoined that. The new thing was "as I have loved you." His conduct produced a new code. This is fully stated in these words: "Treat one another with the same spirit as you experience in Christ Jesus." (Phil. 2:5, Moffatt.) Here morality reached its high-water mark. Our code is a Character. It is not a set of commandments—that is legalism. It is a Character—that is life. I believe in the Ten Commandments, and very, very much besides— I believe in Him. The Ten Commandments are an injunction. Jesus is an injunction, plus an inspiration.

Besides, to obey commandments is to obey an imposed morality— "Thou shalt," and "Thou shalt not." But to follow a Person and to do the thing He does is an inspired morality. It comes from within, and its source is love. One is a legal morality; the other is a love morality. One is artificial; the other is artesian. One binds you; the other frees you. One makes you tense and gloomy; the other makes you relaxed and spontaneous and gay. One greater than the commandments is here. Our code is not a commandment but a Character.

O Christ, I know that Thou art my code and my commandment. I love Thee. I shall be free—free to live and do the Highest. For Thou art the Highest. Amen.

AFFIRMATION FOR THE DAY: *Love Christ supremely; hold all else in relationship to that supreme love; then all else is yours.*

ONE GREATER THAN THE CREEDS

We saw yesterday that Christ is greater than the commandments. To love Him is to fulfill the commandments—plus. To fulfill the commandments produces the Pharisee. To love and obey Christ is to produce the Christian. The Christian feels that he has never attained; the more he obeys in Christ, the more he sees there is to obey. It is not a fixed but an unfolding morality. We follow a living Mind, and hence we are under the law of eternal growth.

That leads us to say: One greater than the creeds is here. The creeds attempt to fix in statement what we see in Christ. We are grateful for those attempts—grateful, but not satisfied. For we cannot fully catch and confine the Word in the web of our words. The Word is greater than our words. Hence our creeds must be eternally open on the side of revision—revision toward larger, fuller meanings. A fixed creed becomes a false creed. For Christ is forever beyond us, calling us to new meanings and new surrenders and new adventures.

This does not mean that there is nothing fixed. There is. In the incarnation, the life and teaching, the death and resurrection of Jesus something has been fixed. We have a Norm. We do not hold to a meaningless theosophy that takes in everything—and in the process becomes nothing. We are not adrift. Something is fixed in the historical Jesus. Yet the fixed is also the unfolding. "I have yet many things to say unto you, but ye cannot bear them now. Howbeit when he, the Spirit of truth, is come, he will guide you into all truth. . . . He shall glorify me: for he shall receive of mine, and shall shew it unto you." (John 16:12-14.) Here Jesus provided for an unfolding revelation of Himself. That saves the Christian faith from being a road with a dead end as Mohammedanism has become. Moslems were caught by the letter; we were released by the Life. They are static if they follow the Koran; we are dynamic if we follow the Christ. Mohammedanism finds a desert or makes one; Christ finds a desert and makes it blossom like the rose. One decays; the other develops. This puts life under an eternal growth. We shall approach the Divine forever, and in that approach find our eternal happiness.

O Thou Living Christ, how, oh how, can I ever be grateful enough that I see in Thee something fresh every morning and something new every night. Thou art a constant surprise to me. I hold my breath as new meanings unfold and my soul is atingle with expectancy. I thank Thee. Amen.

AFFIRMATION FOR THE DAY: *"A Christian never is; he is always becoming."*

ONE GREATER THAN RITES OR CEREMONIES

One greater than rites and ceremonies is here. We do not disparage rites and ceremonies. They can and often do express our loyalty and love for Christ. They are the outer expression of an inner love. But to make any rite, any ceremony, essential to salvation is to make an idol of it. No rite, no ceremony, of any kind is essential to salvation. If it were, then we would be saved by a rite or ceremony. We are saved by Christ—not by a rite or ceremony. In front of Christ a rite or ceremony may be an idol and a stumbling block. Behind Christ, as an expression of our love to Him, it may be a beautiful sacrament.

A radiant Baptist friend of mine was asked about baptism, and he replied, "It's all right, but you mustn't hang around the river too long." Some do. And soon the river becomes dry of meaning, becomes an end in itself, and we stand beside dry river beds while Christ has passed on. But baptism in its place as an expression of faith in Christ is beautiful and helpful. As such I love it and love to administer it.

"Neither circumcision availeth any thing, nor uncircumcision, but a new creature." (Gal. 6:15.) Neither baptism availeth anything, nor unbaptism, but a new creature. The new creature is the criterion.

The Holy Communion is a beautiful sacrament—behind Christ. But if it gets around in front of Christ, becomes the exclusive possession of exclusive groups, then it is the good turned bad. "If therefore the light that is in thee be darkness, how great is that darkness!" (Matt. 6:13.) If the Communion leads to communion with Christ and with all others who belong to Christ, then it is the Holy Communion. But if it leads to exclusiveness and special claims about validities, then it is an unholy communion. One greater than the Communion is here.

Then One greater than faith is here. We sometimes say we are saved by faith. That would make faith the means of our salvation. We are not saved by faith, but by faith in Christ. The end is Christ and not the faith. I do not have faith in my faith; I have faith in Christ. If you try to have faith in faith, you are tense and trying; if you have faith in Christ, you are relaxed and receptive.

O Christ, I thank Thee that I can have faith in Thee when my faith in everything else fails. For Thou and Thou alone art worthy of faith. I rest in Thee and receive from Thee everything I need for this day. I am so grateful I cannot express my gratitude in words. Amen.

AFFIRMATION FOR THE DAY: *Rites and ceremonies come between me and Christ and become an idol, unless they point beyond themselves—to Christ.*

ONE GREATER THAN THE CHURCH

One greater than the cross is here. We sometimes say we are saved by the cross. Rather, we are saved by the Christ who died for us upon the cross. The cross can become a matter of contention instead of conversion if detached from Christ. On the cross He took into His own heart all we have done and been and made it His own. If therefore I identify myself by surrender to and faith in Christ, identify myself, not with my past life and its sins, but with Christ, who thus died for me on the cross, I am saved. But I am saved by Him, not by the cross. One greater than the cross is here.

One greater than the Resurrection is here. We do not have faith in His resurrection; we have faith in the resurrected Christ. He says, "I am myself resurrection and life." (John 11:25, Moffatt.) He is Himself the Resurrection. We do not have faith in an event, a resurrection, but in one who went through the event, and is bigger than the event. One greater than the Resurrection is here.

One greater than the Church is here. The Church is a fellowship of believers, a fellowship around Christ, not around themselves. He, and not they, is the center. When they become the center, the light has turned to darkness. And how great is that darkness!

John said to Jesus: "Master, we saw a man casting out demons in your name, but we stopped him because he is not a follower of ours." Jesus said to him, "Do not stop him; he who is not against you is for you." (Luke 9:49-50, Moffatt.) John tried to make "in your name" and "a follower of ours" synonymous. We still do that. We make our group the issue. Jesus showed the difference: "He who is not against you is for you. For 'you' are not the issue, but as for me, I am the issue. He who is not with me is against me. Here you must take sides: if you are not for me, you are against me." A greater than the Church is here. The Church behind Christ is the greatest serving institution on earth; in front of Christ it is an idol. If it becomes an end in itself, it loses itself. If it loses itself in Christ and His Kingdom, it finds itself again.

O living Christ, Thou art greater than all the things that serve Thee. And yet Thou dost serve all things. Thou art greater than all, for Thou art the servant of all. Thou hast given Thyself, and I can do nought else but give myself, first of all to Thee, and then to *all*. Amen.

AFFIRMATION FOR THE DAY: *Belonging to a group does not save me. Belonging to Christ does.*

DESTINED TO POSSESS ALL THINGS?

We have seen that "One greater than the temple is here"—also One greater than the Bible, the commandments, the creeds, rites and ceremonies, faith, the cross, the Resurrection, the Church. Jesus not only towers "o'er the wrecks of time"; He also towers o'er the good things of time. He is the Best to which all lesser good points. He is the Absolute from which all relativisms get their worth and meaning.

If the objection is made that you cannot call the limited Jesus an absolute—look at the limitations of His birth and surroundings and the fact of His own humanity—the answer must be that there are relativisms in Jesus, but rising out of those relativisms is an Absolute. When He speaks, finality speaks. When He says, "Full authority has been given to me in heaven and on earth" (Matt. 28:18, Moffatt), we feel that this is not a pompous claim, but the statement of an inherent fact. Everything not only "in heaven" but "on earth" is made in its inner structure by Him and for Him, and works only when it works in His way. If it tries to work in some other way, it works its own ruin. Again, "That all things in heaven and earth alike should be gathered up in Christ." (Eph. 1:10, Moffatt.) "All things" in heaven and on earth have a Christian destiny in them—they will be gathered up in Christ. Out of Him they go to pieces, disintegrate. He is the Way unqualified—for heaven and for earth. The moral universe is one.

Further, when He says, "No one knows the Son except the Father" (Matt. 11:27, Moffatt), we know that the Way is an infinite Way. Only God knows it in its entirety. The Way will have no end. It will be eternally explored, and it will be an eternal surprise. We have hold of something that cannot be exhausted.

Again, when it says, "Whom he hath appointed heir of all things" (Heb. 1:2), we know this is not an arbitrary predestination; He is destined to possess all things, for all things that do not obey His will and work in His way will perish. Those things that survive will be His, inherently so. By the very nature of things He will possess all things. For all things know their Master's voice.

O Thou living Christ, by whose hands all things were made, and into whose hands all things will return, I gladly render up to Thee what is Thine own. I am Thine, for I know that apart from Thee I wither and perish. In Thee I live and live abundantly and fully and freely. Thou art my fulfillment and my fullness. Amen.

AFFIRMATION FOR THE DAY: *Christ is destined to possess all things. I am in Christ; therefore in Him I possess all things.*

IS THE KINGDOM OUR GOOD?

We have been studying the fact that loyalty to Christ is to be sought first, last, and always, for when supreme loyalty is fastened on Him, then there is complete life fulfillment. But, strangely, Jesus did not begin with Himself as the center of loyalty. He said, "Seek ye first the kingdom of God . . . ; and all these things shall be added unto you." He made the Kingdom the center of loyalty.

Philosophers have said that we must have a *Weltanschauung*, world view, a cosmic framework in which we live and work and think. That cosmic framework must give validity and meaning to all we do. That world frame of reference gives a sense of moral security.

The breakdown of that world frame of reference in the minds of people is the cause of the sense of loneliness and homesickness in modern man. He is going on to a hand-to-mouth existence day by day, and what he does and thinks does not seem to be related to the Whole. This has made life empty and jittery because it is insecure.

The Chinese have a saying, "In a broken nest there are no whole eggs." The nest, the world in which we live and think and create, has been broken up; our central life unity is gone. As a consequence of the broken nest there are no whole eggs; the individual's unity and security have broken down. This can be seen on a small scale when the home is broken. Nearly all the boys in the reformatory at Plainfield, Indiana, are from broken homes. Nearly all the problem children in high schools also come from broken homes. Why? The framework in which they have lived has broken down and has left them inwardly homeless and confused. As a consequence morals break down. Man needs a new Home—a cosmic Home.

That cosmic Home is the Kingdom of God. Jesus said, "Seek God's Realm [Kingdom] and his goodness, and all that will be yours over and above." (Matt. 6:33, Moffatt.) He makes the Kingdom and goodness synonymous. His rule is our good—our physical, intellectual, emotional, spiritual, economic, social, political, and international good. God's rule is good for us, is our highest interest. Any other rule is bad for us. Self-rule equals self-ruin. God-rule equals good rule. The Kingdom is our cosmic Homeland—our total Security.

O Christ, I am so grateful that I do have a Homeland, a land in which I live and move and have my being. I feel the sense of belonging and that at the heart of things is utter security. I am grateful. Amen.

AFFIRMATION FOR THE DAY: *The Kingdom is my Homeland; therefore I am at home in all lands.*

THE KINGDOM OF GOD IS OUR FATHERLAND

Yesterday we saw that man needs a sense of a cosmic framework, a cosmic Home, cosmic approval. That cosmic Home, we said, was the Kingdom of God. Begin there, and everything will come out all right. Begin some other place, and everything will come out all wrong. On a sales bulletin board were these words: "Get the idea, and all else follows." But the idea must be the Idea; all else follows.

Someone has said: "The most basic problem in community organization and leadership is formulation of the central idea to be achieved." Get the center right, and the circumference takes care of itself.

Around the frescoes in the Nebraska Capitol are these words: "He who would duly enquire about the best form of the State ought first to determine which is the most eligible life." Jesus defined "the most eligible life" as the life that seeks the Kingdom first, last, and always. When you do, then everything you need will be added. And if you don't, then everything will be subtracted. As Henry Drummond said: "If you seek first the Kingdom of God you will have that problem, but if you don't seek first the Kingdom of God then you will have nothing but problems."

For instance, Jesus says, "So do not seek food and drink and be worried." (Luke 12:29, Moffatt.) Note the sequence: If you seek something less than the Kingdom, for example, food and drink, you will be worried—you will have the sense of missing the mark, of being insecure, of out-of-gearness. Why? For the reason that the mind is worried, feeling a sense of nonfulfillment and frustration until it seeks first its natural Home, the Kingdom of God. When it finds the Kingdom, worry and insecurity drop away. This is It!

Prominently displayed in a seminary were these words: "Harmony of sound is music; harmony of line is sculpture or architecture; harmony of color is art; harmony of truth is poetry; harmony of life and goodness is fellowship with God and man." And we may add: Harmony of the total life is the Kingdom of God.

Heb. 11:14 (Moffatt) speaks of those that "are in search of a fatherland." The Fatherland is the Kingdom. We are alien to all else, and all else is alien to us.

O God, I know that when I find Thy Kingdom I find myself and all I want to be. For here I can breathe freely and feel a sense of at-home-ness. Here I can become a child again, unafraid and spontaneous. Amen.

AFFIRMATION FOR THE DAY: *The Kingdom is harmony. I am in the Kingdom; therefore harmony is in me.*

AN UNSHAKABLE KINGDOM

Yesterday we ended by emphasizing the necessity of living in harmony with the Kingdom. Rev. 1:9 (Moffatt) speaks of "your companion in the distress and realm and patient endurance which Jesus brings." If the word "realm" is spelled "Realm" (Kingdom), as it obviously should be, to make sense, then on each side of the "Kingdom" is "distress" and "patient endurance." If the Kingdom is at the center, then you have an unshakable center even though it is flanked by "distress" and "patient endurance."

No wonder the writer of Hebrews says, "Let us be grateful for receiving a kingdom that cannot be shaken." (Heb. 12:28, R.S.V.) I am grateful with every fiber of my being that we have an unshakable Kingdom. For the kingdoms of this world and the rotten civilizations they have built up are going down in blood and ruin. They are shakable. Paul speaks of "the dethroned Powers who rule this world." (I Cor. 2:6, Moffatt.) These Powers still rule, though they are dethroned. Life has passed judgment on them, but they still rule on under the law of decay.

Jesus spoke of "the so-called rulers of the Gentiles." (Mark 10:42, Moffatt.) Think of saying that: "the so-called rulers"—of the mighty Roman Empire! But the years and the centuries have spoken against the hours, and the so-called rulers and their empires have perished. And note that He contrasted a group of disciples with the so-called rulers: "The so-called rulers of the Gentiles lord it over them; . . . not so with you." He implies, "You are rulers, but you are different, they are so-called, you are real rulers." It is literally true. Those disciples rule our thoughts and conduct; the principles and teachings they passed on have molded, and still mold, a civilization.

Now our confidence is being shaken in our own kingdoms even at the moment of our victory in war. Listen to these words of Drew Pearson: "Maybe we will wake up to the futility of old-fashioned diplomacy and the hopelessness of big armies and put our faith in friendship. In other words, everything else having failed, we might finally come around to practicing the Sermon on the Mount." Then —and then only—will we come to an unshakable Kingdom.

O Christ, I know in my heart of hearts that Thy reign is It. It has the feel of the real and the eternal upon it. It will never grow stale or wear out. It is eternally fresh and eternally creative and new. I thank Thee. Amen.

AFFIRMATION FOR THE DAY: *I belong to an unshakable Kingdom; therefore passing events cannot shake me.*

THE KINGDOM OF GOD IS TOTALITARIAN

We have seen that the Kingdom is the world view of the Christian. It can be summed up in these words: "May Thy Kingdom come and may Thy will be done on earth as it is done in heaven." Three things here: (1) The Kingdom is. It is a Kingdom that is in operation, and its operation produces heaven. Where it is not in operation, that is hell. (2) The Kingdom that is, nevertheless, comes on earth as earth is willing to accept it and submit to it. (3) The Kingdom comes in a total way. The coming of the Kingdom means the doing of the will of God on earth as it is done in heaven. How is the will of God done in heaven? In the individual will? Yes. In the collective will? Yes. In the total social arrangements in heaven? Yes. Then may the Kingdom come in this total way on earth as it is in a total way in heaven.

The Kingdom of God is a completely totalitarian order demanding a total obedience in the total life. It was presented to the individual will; it was presented to the collective will: "The kingdom of God shall be taken from you, and given to a nation bringing forth the fruits thereof." (Matt. 21:43.) "But," cries my reader, "we are getting rid of one totalitarianism, and you are introducing us to another, even more thoroughgoing and absolute." True. But there is this profound difference: When you obey the Kingdom of God, you find perfect freedom. When you obey other totalitarianisms, you find perfect bondage, for they are not the way you are made to live. When you obey the Kingdom of God, you find perfect self-fulfillment.

As the stomach and poison are not made for each other, and when brought together produce disruption and death, so life and other-than-Kingdom ways are not made for each other and produce disruption and death. As the stomach and food are made for each other and when brought together bring health and life, so life and the Kingdom are made for each other and when brought together produce health and life and fulfillment.

The Kingdom of God is release, is salvation. "Now it has come, the salvation and power, the reign of our God and the authority of his Christ!" (Rev. 12:10, Moffatt.) The "reign" of God brought "salvation"—release—and "power"—fulfillment.

O God, Thy Reign is my realization. My rule is my ruin; Thy Rule is my release. I submit to Thy Rule, for to me it is life, and life abundant. I thank Thee. Amen.

AFFIRMATION FOR THE DAY: *The Kingdom demands my all and offers its all. The demand and the offer are not equal.*

"THE OPEN SECRET"

We emphasized yesterday that obedience to the Kingdom is the fulfillment of life. Why? The reason is that the Author of the Kingdom and the Author of us is one and the same, and we and the Kingdom are made for each other. "Come into your inheritance in the realm prepared for you from the foundation of the world." (Matt. 25:34, Moffatt.) When the world and we were founded, the Kingdom was built into its very nature, into its very foundations. The laws of the Kingdom are the very laws of our being. They are not a set of laws imposed from without; they are written in us as the nature of our being.

A man said in one of our Ashrams: "I have always followed the line of least resistance. I have always found it harder to do wrong than to do right." As the flowers have a sun bent within them, so we have a Kingdom bent within us. We are made for it.

If we and the Kingdom are not made for each other, then religion is hopelessly handicapped. It becomes an unnatural imposition. A laborer put the matter thus: "You can pass all the laws you want, but what is in the seed will come out in the plant." But if the Kingdom is "within you," as Jesus said, then the very nature of our being demands that we accept it, freely choose it, or end in self-frustration.

If it is all as simple as that, then why do we not see it more easily and live by it? Jesus speaks of things "hidden since the foundation of the world" (Matt. 13:35, Moffatt.) These things are hidden in the nature of Reality. Jesus disclosed them in parables. We are discovering them as laws, as facts. Jesus again speaks of "the open secrets of the Realm of heaven." (Matt. 13:11, Moffatt.) It is all "secret," but it is an "open secret"—anyone can discover them who will. This runs true to everything else hidden in nature. Electricity was a "secret," but an "open secret," and those who paid the price of discovery discovered it. The wireless was a "secret," but an "open secret," open to the humble, obedient, inquiring mind. So the Kingdom is "secret," but it is an "open secret," ready to be revealed to the humble, the obedient, the responsive person.

O God, Thou art so intimately near, in my very being. I have reached up to heaven to bring Thee down, and lo, Thy Kingdom is within me. Help me humbly to obey it, that it may be revealed to me as life of my life and being of my being. Amen.

AFFIRMATION FOR THE DAY: *I shall know as much of the "all" of the offer as I am willing to obey the "all" of the demand.*

THE KINGDOM INVADES AND PERVADES

We close our week's inquiry by recapitulating what we have been saying. If we walk against the lights, we're going to get hurt—inevitably. These "lights" are seen supremely and finally in Christ—He is "the light of the world." But these "lights" are also in us—the very laws of our being.

I find ten laws written into our beings, and as we study them, they turn out to be the very laws of the Kingdom of God. They are these: (1) The universe is a universe of moral consequence. (2) The morally and spiritually fit survive. (3) The Christian way is written in the structure of the universe. (4) Humility and obedience are the secret of knowledge and power. (5) An organism expends as much as it receives and no more; therefore receptivity is the first law of life. (6) The second law of life is that you must lose your life to find it again. (7) Greatness comes through service. (8) Love is the fundamental law of human relationships. (9) Life is an eternal growth. (10) All life is lifted by self-sacrifice, by a cross. Wipe, then, the gospel of Jesus from the pages of the New Testament and you will find intimations of it in yourself.

Ours is a cut-flower civilization. We are living without roots. Our morality has no roots in the cosmic order, but only in changing customs, and hence they fade. Our happiness has no cosmic backing, and hence it too easily withers and dies.

The Kingdom of God both invades you and pervades you. It invades you from without and pervades you from within. It descends and it ascends. We are made for it; therefore its coming is like a home-coming, a naturalizing, a finding of one's self.

"Why aren't Christian students as enthusiastic over Christianity as Nazi and Fascist and Communist students over their systems?" was asked of a Christian student a few years ago. He thoughtfully replied: "These systems are looked on as realism, while Christianity is looked on as idealism; you can't get enthusiastic over idealism." True! But if the Kingdom is the only realism, since it is written in the nature of Reality, then we can be enthusiastic to the depths.

O satisfying Christ, I give Thee my all with the consent of all my being, for I know that Thou hast the keys to everything. Thou art unlocking God, myself, and life. I see in Thee just what I want. Beyond Thee I cannot go, for anything. Amen.

AFFIRMATION FOR THE DAY: *The Kingdom of God is above me; the Kingdom of God is around me; the Kingdom of God is within me.*

THE ORDER AND THE PERSON

We must pause to gather up our definition of the Way. Just what is the Way? Is it the Person—Christ? Or is it the Order—the Kingdom of God? In one place He makes loyalty to Himself the supreme loyalty: "If anyone comes to me and does not hate [love less] his father and mother and wife and children and brothers and sisters, aye and his own life, he cannot be a disciple of mine." (Luke 14:26, Moffatt.) Here He made loyalty to Himself supreme and absolute. But in another place He said: "Seek ye first the kingdom of God" (Matt. 6:33.) In one place the Person—Christ—was first. In the other place the Order—the Kingdom—was first. Which *is* first?

We must now state what to my mind is one of the most important, and one of the most overlooked, facts in the New Testament. Jesus began with the Kingdom of God. He went out "preaching the gospel of the kingdom." (Matt. 4:23.) But before He was through He began to preach the gospel of Himself: "I am the way, the truth, and the life." (John 14:6.) "Come unto me, . . . and I will give you rest." (Matt. 11:28.) He made "for the kingdom of God's sake" (Luke 18:29) and "for my sake" synonymous. He made Himself and the Kingdom synonymous. The Person and the Order were one.

The Way, then, is impersonal—an Order. It is personal—a Person. If it were impersonal only, it would be unsatisfactory. I can be loyal to an Order, but I cannot love it; I can love only a Person. But if it were a Person only, then religion would be reduced to personal relationships with a Person—good, but not good enough. Religion would lack total and corporate meanings. But when it is both the Order and the Person combined into a living whole, then it satisfies the need for the intimate—the Personal—and it also satisfies the need for the ultimate—the Order. It makes religion by its very nature at once individual and social. For in having relationships with the Person we have relationships with the new Order embodied in the Person, and that Order is completely totalitarian.

The Way, then, can be defined as Christ, the Person, embodying the Kingdom, the Order. The Way thus becomes the Way for all life—individual, collective—for God and man and things.

O Christ, at last I have come out to Thy feet. I know in my heart of hearts that Thou art the Way. My inmost being witnesses to it, and in doing so sings. I am satisfied. Amen.

AFFIRMATION FOR THE DAY: *The Way is the way for God, for all men, and for me.*

THE FIVE STAGES

We ended yesterday with a definition of the Way: The Way is Christ, the Person, embodying the Kingdom of God, the Order. The Way is the Person-Order. But the end is not a definition, but a decision. Christ is not to be reviewed but to be received and followed. The end is not to see but to seek. It demands that we cease other unworkable ways of life and give ourselves to the Way.

The stages through which we pass in getting from our ways to the Way are: (1) Contact. (2) Conflict. (3) Conversion. (4) Cultivation. (5) Contribution.

The first is *contact*. The contact comes from the side of the Divine. He takes the initiative. "We love him, because he first loved us." (I John 4:19.) He has come to us through a Divine Invasion: an Incarnation, an atoning Death, a Resurrection, and a coming into our hearts by the Spirit. To get contact with us was not easy, for our sins stood in the way of fellowship. So He had to come to us wearing our sins in His own heart in atoning love. The cross is the price God pays to get to us in spite of our sins. But He made the contact. Result?

Conflict! There is an instinctive reaction against any seeming intruder. The instinct of self-preservation rises up to oppose any invasion of our personal selves. So we erect barriers. There is conflict. Jesus always brings initial trouble, for we know that He will demand change. And we don't want to change, even though it is a change from chaos to cosmos, from our present hell to a heaven of release. We hold to the securities of the old, even though they may be in shreds. We fear "lest having Him I must have naught beside."

When Jesus appeared, it was said that "the news of this troubled king Herod and all Jerusalem as well." (Matt. 2:3, Moffatt.) Jesus brought trouble in the beginning! He always does. But it is the same trouble that comes to us when on a journey we are told that we are on the wrong road. There is initial trouble in having to retrace our steps, but it saves us from an infinite amount of complicated trouble later on if we don't retrace them. Jesus upsets us to set us right.

O Christ, Thou troubler of human hearts, O Christ, Thou healer of troubled human hearts, I come to Thee. Trouble me, trouble me till I face the last sore spot; then heal me. For I would be whole. In Thy name. Amen.

AFFIRMATION FOR THE DAY: *"All things betray thee, who betrayest Me."*

WHAT IS CONVERSION?

We saw yesterday that the first two steps were contact and conflict. The impact of Christ produces initial upset; there is convulsion before expulsion. Things always get worse before they get better. The gospel is disturbance before deliverance. The contact and the consequent conflict do not end there. The end is *conversion*.

What do we mean by "conversion"? Conversion is that change, gradual or sudden, by which we pass from the kingdom of self to the Kingdom of God by the grace and power of Christ. Note that the center of the old life is the self. A self-centered person is in the old life no matter how religious he may be. An upright Pharisee talked earnestly with Jesus at midnight, and Jesus said, "You must all be born from above" (John 3:7, Moffatt). The "all" may mean "all persons," but it also may mean "all of the person." You may be righteous and moral, and yet the center may be all wrong. You may be doing good things from a bad motive—a motive of self. In Jesus' view the Pharisee needed conversion as much as the publican and the harlot, and needed it especially. For the Pharisee sins in his disposition—pride, prejudice, censoriousness, self-righteousness. These are respectable sins—Brahmin sins. They are not easy to be repented of. They are "elder brother" sins. The younger brother sinned in his flesh—lust and appetite. These sins are not respectable—they are outcaste sins. It is easier to repent of these sins of the flesh; hence, as Jesus said, the publican and the harlot get into the Kingdom of God before the Pharisee. Both need to be converted, to change the center from self to God. Elizabeth Fry, before she was converted, saw that she was a Pharisee: "I feel like a contemptible fine lady, all outside and no inside." The converted Pharisee became a marvelous Christian.

A pastor left one of our Ashrams and called his family circle together and said to them: "Let us have a family in which we decide things together. You elect someone to preside over our meetings." He thought, of course, that they would elect him. Instead they elected the eldest daughter. It shocked the pastor. He went to his knees and surrendered his hurt self to God and arose a new man.

O God, I see that if I am centered in myself I cannot be centered in Thee. And I want to be centered in Thee. For when I am centered in myself I am off center, out of adjustment, unhappy. In Thee I know adjustment and joy. So I come with all my heart. Thou hast me. Forever. Amen.

AFFIRMATION FOR THE DAY: *I am converted, for God is my center—not I.*

THE NEW HEREDITY

Yesterday we saw that both the "down and out" and the "up and out" need conversion. Some say that you cannot change human nature. A minister said to me: "My father had a temper, and I have a temper too. Heredity determines it, and that is all there is to it." I replied: "But you have a heavenly Father and therefore the possibility of a new heredity. Surrender to Him and you will have a new heredity with the temper left out." Human nature is the most changeable thing on earth. They tell me that peaches were once used by Persians to poison the arrow tips. If so, then peach nature has been changed from poison to luscious food. The wild fowls of the Himalayas are the progenitors of all the chickens of the world. Then chicken nature is convertible— convertible from the little brown fowls into Rhode Island Reds, Wyandottes, Brahmas, into endless varieties. But human nature can be converted more radically. The worst can become the best.

Take two contrasts: When a young man, I preached in a Kentucky town on court day in the public square. A drunk stood near the box on which I stood and kept commenting to the crowd about my preaching. "That young fellow makes me feel like crying." He had a long stick around which he leaned. At the close of the address I asked those who wanted to be converted to come to the mission. Among others, he came. I asked him if he wanted to be converted, and he replied, "I'm drunk." "I know you are drunk," I replied, "but God can change you." "If you say so, it must be so," he replied, and we bowed in prayer. As I was praying, he opened his eyes with a surprised look in them and said, "Why He has saved me! And I am drunk too!" He arose and handed me his whisky bottle, saying, "I don't want that." I threw it out of the window. He handed me his stick, upon which he leaned for support, and said, "I don't need that either." And he walked out of there perfectly straight. God had not only saved him; He had sobered him as well.

A highly cultured woman, a student of philosophy, underwent a spiritual change and described it thus: "I feel like a newborn babe." Both were profoundly remade.

O God, I see the untold possibilities for change when I come to Thee. For in Thee I can have a new heredity; a new Blood can flow within my blood; a new Life can take the place of my old life. I arise with new expectancy and joy. Amen.

AFFIRMATION FOR THE DAY: *I am a part of a new Heredity, a new Lineage. I can do nothing this day beneath the dignity of my Birth.*

WANTED—A NEW PHILOSOPHY OF LIFE

Yesterday we saw contrasting types of conversion. We must pursue this until our faith grows that any man can be changed.

A man with a hard and dirty face went to an altar of prayer and prayed in desperation, "O God, if you can save a sinner like me, why in hell don't you do it quicker?" Then his face melted into tenderness, and upon it came the smile of heaven, and the happy man said, "Boys, He's done it." And He had!

The head of a large manufacturing plant was fighting with himself and at loggerheads with his workmen. He was nervous and upset. He went to an outstanding doctor, who gave him a thorough checkup and, finding nothing physically wrong, said, "What you need is a new philosophy of life. Go home and get one." And he handed him a bill for three thousand dollars. He knew that if he charged anything less the man wouldn't be impressed. The businessman went home furious, called up his pastor, and made the air black and blue with these words: "What do you think that blankety-blank doctor said? 'You need a new philosophy of life.' And what do you think he charged me? Three thousand dollars for that!" The pastor quietly said, "He's right, that's what you need." The businessman quieted down and abruptly asked, "What shall I do?" The pastor recommended certain books, among them *Abundant Living*. The man is now completely changed. He no longer fights with himself or with his men. He has found God and therefore is in right relation to himself and others. He thinks the three-thousand-dollar fee was cheap! He is putting his new philosophy of life into the industrial situation in America.

Someone arose in one of our meetings and said, "I've had a wonderful healing, a healing of attitude." Conversion from wrong attitudes is just as necessary as conversion from wrong acts—perhaps more so. A missionary to China said to us, "I've been a missionary for eleven years, and I've been a part of the disease rather than the cure." Another said, "I can be perfectly ethical and know nothing of being a Christian." A businessman put it this way, "I gave my best for these young people, and my best was not good enough." They all needed conversion.

O God, my Father, I am coming to Thy feet. I need to be healed at the heart, healed from every sore of resentment, fear, and pride. My being is open; heal me to the depths. In Jesus' name. Amen.

AFFIRMATION FOR THE DAY: *I am healed in actuality, in attitude, and in act. I belong to the healed.*

RELIGION AN IRRITANT

We have been insisting that conversion is necessary equally for those whose sins of the flesh and for those whose sins of the disposition disclose that the center of life is unchanged. A minister said in one of our meetings, "I see clearly, and I see the cross, and I don't like it." The cross confronted his essential self-centeredness, and he reacted in opposition to it. It challenged the basis on which he was living. He was religious, but not Christian, for Christ did not control the center.

A great many have introduced just enough Christianity into their lives to set up a conflict. There isn't enough Christianity to produce control, but just enough to produce conflict. Christianity then becomes an irritant. It upsets instead of sets up. A businessman sat down in a hotel room with me, and the first thing he said was, "I'm trying to live the Christian life, and I'm having a hell of a time at it." Why was the Christian life issuing in a hell of a time instead of in a heaven of a time? He disclosed the reason: "Twenty times a day the self will be ready to do anything as a compromise, provided it be allowed to stay at the center, on the throne." The Way was operative in the minor issues of life, but the way of self was operative in the major issue—the issue as to who makes the decisions. The self made them—in the interests of the self. Result? A hell of a time! The center needed conversion. Christ needed to take over—at the center.

We often appeal to outsiders with the text, "Behold, I stand at the door, and knock." But that was not spoken to outsiders, but to insiders —the Church. Christ was trying to get inside—the Church! "So, because you are lukewarm, neither hot nor cold, I am about to spit you out of my mouth. You declare, 'I am rich, I am well off, I lack nothing!'" (Rev. 3:16-17, Moffatt.)—Nothing but Christ! Self was at the center, and Christ was at the door, knocking. The center of life needed to be redeemed.

It was said of Joseph of Arimathaea that he was "a disciple of Jesus but a secret disciple—for fear of the Jews." (John 19:38, Moffatt.) Fear held the center. Result? He found a dead Christ instead of a living one. Fear, not Christ, was operative. He needed conversion.

O Christ, I do not want a dead Christ, for there is no such thing. Thou art alive! I want Thee to live in me. I give Thee the center, that Life may be in every part. I do it now. Amen.

AFFIRMATION FOR THE DAY: *"I give thee an undivided heart; oh never may I stray from thy control."* (Ps. 119:10, Moffatt.)

"A BIG SMILE INSIDE"

Whatever our sins or our goodness, if anything other than Christ is the center and spring of our lives, we need conversion. I know of an Anglican archbishop who was converted at seventy-two. For him, he said, "life began at seventy-two!" It did! Contrast that highly moral religious leader who needed conversion with this: "I was drunk when I got hold of your *Christ of the Indian Road*. It converted me."

Contrast again the coming of the drunk with this coming of a child: "I heard a knock at the door, and I saw it was Jesus, and I asked Him to come in. He did. I heard another knock, and I said, 'Jesus, you go to the door.' He did, and Satan was there. When he saw Jesus he said, 'Oh, I've made a mistake. I'm at the wrong place.' " The conversion of the archbishop, the drunk, and the child were all authentic, but different—different and yet the same: Christ was at the center of life. When that happens, there is conversion.

The psalmist says, "Awake, my soul! awake, my lute and lyre!" (Ps. 57:8, Moffatt.) When the soul was awake, then the lute and lyre were awake. When the soul centrally and fundamentally sings, then the instruments of the soul sing with it. But you can't make life sing at the edges until you make it sing at the center.

A person radically changed said to us, "The dogs that have dogged my footsteps for years are all dead and buried. I'm free!" Another one put it this way, "I have a song in my heart and wings to my feet." You can never have wings to your feet unless you have a song in your heart.

Still another said, "I have a big smile inside." When Christ is at the center of life, then life has "a big smile inside." When something else is at the center, there is a big frown inside. A college girl put it this way, "I felt as though I had swallowed sunshine." A lot of people look as though they have swallowed gloom.

Some people were looking at a sunrise, and a little girl, a lovely Christian, exclaimed, "That's just how I feel inside." Christ is a sunrise. The old life is a sunset. One is heaven, and the other is hell. You'll have to take your choice: the heaven Way, the hell way?

O Christ, I am tired of wearing hell within my bosom. I turn all this inner hell over to Thee. Thou hast it. Bury it—bury it at the foot of the cross. I henceforth belong to heaven, not to hell. I'm free! Amen.

AFFIRMATION FOR THE DAY: *"O thou Eternal, thou wilt light my lamp, my God, thou wilt make my darkness shine."* (Ps. 18:28, Moffatt.)

"THE TEN STEPS TO VICTORY"

We come now to the steps we must take to put our feet upon the Way. Perhaps you have been impatiently asking, How? We could not answer the How until we had looked at the What and the Why.

But let me remind you that you have come to a crisis. You are going to be called on to choose. You will have to say Yes or No. And heaven or hell—here and now—will be in that Yes or No. Hitherto we have been seeking information. Now we are seeking transformation. That involves throwing the will on the side of transformation. That can be done only in an atmosphere of inner prayer. Inwardly commit yourself to follow simply and humbly the steps to the Way.

Just now a man left my room, and one of the things he said about his tied-up spiritual life was: "No use to try to kid yourself about this matter of surrender. You do or you don't. I haven't been willing, so I'm tied up." Your question marks will never be straightened out into exclamation points of certainty and realization unless you pass from the question to the quest. For there comes a moment in life when to get further light you must decide something—the light you have will turn to darkness unless it ends in decision. Light turns to life through decision. In a moral universe the only way to get more light is to act on what you have.

We will call the ladder "The Ten C's." (1) *Consider your ways*. See if they correspond with the Way. Take an honest, straightforward look at your life. (2) *Change your directions*. Where you are wrong, decide to change. (3) *Connect with Christ*. You will need His grace and power. (4) *Consent to surrender*. He is Lord, not you. (5) *Cease from struggling*. Don't try to do this yourself; let Him do it. (6) *Concentrate on acceptance*. He is making an offer to you; accept it. (7) *Cleanse your past*. Make restitution where it is necessary and possible. (8) *Christianize your relationships*. Take the spirit of the Way into your total life. (9) *Cultivate the Quiet Time*—preferably in the morning. (10) *Create outlets and activities*. The Way is outgoing.

These are the ten steps to release and victory. As you look at them, are you ready to begin?

O Christ, I am ready to begin. I'm eager to begin—anything that will get my feet upon the Way. So I begin, all eager and atingle within to start the adventure. Take my hand as I do. Amen.

AFFIRMATION FOR THE DAY: *"Teach me what is thy way, thou Eternal, how to live loyal to thee."* (Ps. 86:11, Moffatt.)

CONSIDER YOUR WAYS

We come now to the steps that are going to lead you from the complicated entanglements of not-the-way to the simplicities of the Way.

1. *Consider your ways.* See if they correspond with the Way. You will probably find, like the rest of us as we considered our ways, that they do not. But it will not be easy to take a straight look at yourself. Three possible attitudes may keep you from it:

a) You will be tempted to defend yourself. Emotional attachments gather around the old ways. Had they not done so, you would not have been able to have remained in them so long. These emotional attachments gather reasons around themselves to justify themselves, as a magnet gathers iron filings. We think with our emotions in very large measure. We rationalize our wrongs, give excuses for the inexcusable, try to bolster up impossible positions by propping them up with props gathered from anywhere. A minister living in secret sexual sin said, "But I preach better than ever." He probably did—worked harder on his sermons to justify himself in the unjustifiable. In the end his defenses crashed, as they must, either by consent or by their breaking down of their own accord because not backed by reality. A couple living in sex sin had a fixed hour for a quiet time each day in which they lived in communion with each other and supposedly with God. The quiet time was used to hallow the unhallowed. They broke from this. Freed from this impossible position, the woman said, "I'm free—and happy." Only the truth can make you free.

b) You will be tempted to justify yourself by the actions of others —"Everybody does it." You are not going to dodge into that road with a dead end; you are out for reality. The conduct of others cannot be your criterion. Christ is. You are going to be a person and not a thing.

c) You will be tempted to fasten upon marginal sins, confess them, but leave the central ones alone. You will probably try to keep the self intact, central, and controlling, while you confess to sins of anger and impatience. You may be selfish in your business relationships and confess personal sins.

These three attitudes may keep you from a frank, honest-to-goodness appraisal. The first step to release is complete honesty.

O Christ, Thou of the honest eyes and the honest attitude, help me to have honest eyes and honest attitudes, for I would be free. Amen.

AFFIRMATION FOR THE DAY: *"I will obey thee eagerly as thou dost open up my life."* (Ps. 119:32, Moffatt.)

CHANGE YOUR DIRECTIONS

I trust we have taken that first step to freedom: "Consider your ways"—honestly. We come now to the next step:

2. *Change your directions.* There is no use going on in a wrong attitude, for going farther in a wrong direction simply means that you have farther to come back to get to reality. Every step you take away from the Way wastes three steps—the one in going away, the one in coming back, and the one you might have been taking on the Way. "What's the use in doing evil," says Rufus Moseley, "for you have to eat humble pie every time in order to get straightened out." What's the use of justifying yourself when you have to humble yourself to get away from the justification?

You will probably be tempted to make the "change" indecisive by one of three things: (*a*) You may be prepared to change in some things but not in all things. Ananias and Sapphira gave up everything to be Christian except one thing: they "kept back part of the price." That one part kept back was their undoing. It was said of Herod: "For Herod feared John, . . . and when he heard him, he did many things." He did everything except one thing—give up the unlawful relationship with the woman. That one thing he held back was his undoing. You don't have to have all the known diseases to die; one will kill you. (*b*) You may be prepared to change everything, but only partially. You may be prepared to turn around in everything but to turn around partially. You may cut down a habit instead of cutting it out. You may end up indecisively, leaving yourself neither here nor there. That will get you nowhere. All compromise will end in confusion. (*c*) You may be hindered from a clear-cut change by putting off the time of it. Augustine's prayer, before he was converted, was, "O God, make me pure, but not now." He wanted to be pure, but wasn't willing to bring it into the "now"—which meant that he really didn't want it. For you do not want a thing unless you want it *now*.

We have now come to the second step: "Change your directions—and change them, not in *some things*, and not *in all things partially*, and not *in some future time*; change everything fully, and do it now.

O Christ, I do not want to shirk, to dodge, to slur over, or to put things off. Help me, and help me now, to change completely my directions. For I cannot keep going—away from Thee. Amen.

AFFIRMATION FOR THE DAY: *"Give me a willing spirit as my strength."*
(Ps. 51:12, Moffatt.)

CONNECT WITH CHRIST

We come now to the third step:

3. *Connect with Christ.* You need His grace and power, and you need to have life centered in Him. You might give up sins and still fail to be a Christian. For the giving up of sins is not an end in itself; it is in order to get in saving touch with Christ. The Way is not negative. You are not a Christian because you don't do this, that, and the other. You are a Christian when life is centered in Christ and not in yourself. You are emptying your hands to grasp a whole Christ.

Here you may miss your step by one of these things:

a) You may change but change toward the wrong ones. Judas changed; he "repented himself," went to the high priests, threw down the money, and said, "I have sinned in that I have betrayed the innocent blood." They sneeringly answered, "What is that to us?" Sin doesn't care. Judas repented toward the wrong direction. Had he gone to Jesus, thrown down the money, and said, "I have sinned," we would have seen the most remarkable reconciliation and restoration in history. Some turn toward their sins and mourn in useless regret. No release comes from that. "Nor all your Tears wash out a Word of it."

b) You may connect with an institution and fail to get through to Christ. The Church is wonderful as a place of worship and spiritual cultivation, provided you go beyond it to Christ. If your relationship to it makes you stop in self-satisfaction this side of a personal, saving relationship with Him, it is a stumbling block. It leaves you at a half-way house this side of the Way.

c) You may stop at principles and miss the Person. You may say, "I'll live by Christian principles," and yet not get into a warm, living fellowship with Him. Your spiritual life will be a tense striving to live principles instead of a trustful fellowship with a Person, issuing in relaxed spontaneity. Mahatma Gandhi took the principles of Christianity, but missed the Person—Christ. Hence he sees "through a glass, darkly."

Go beyond your sins, beyond the institution, beyond the principles, to the Person. Then religion will be to you a long falling in love.

O Christ, I see that I must not stop this side of Thee, for if I do, I stop this side of Life. Help me, then, to take the steps that lead to Thee. I come; with all my being I come. In Thy name. Amen.

AFFIRMATION FOR THE DAY: *"Make me alive to follow thee, and turn mine eyes from cravings vain."* (Ps. 119:37, Moffatt.)

CONSENT TO SURRENDER

We come now to the next step in our quest:

4. *Consent to surrender.* Christ is Lord, not you. This is the crucial step. If you slur this over, then nothing will come out right. And the step is simple. Everyone goes into the shrine of the heart and bends the knee to something; something has the place of supreme allegiance. Some bow the knee to what others will say. They look around before they act. They don't act; they only react. Their god is public opinion. "Everybody does it," decides it for them. Others bend the knee to themselves. Self-interest is supreme. Their first reaction is: How will that affect me? Their god is self. We could name others: money, sex, ambition, fear—any one of these may be the center of allegiance. Everybody bends the knee to something. If so, I choose—I choose Christ. I am not God; He is! I whisper the inner consent, the consent of abdication. He commands; I obey. From this moment I do not belong to myself. I let go the one thing I own—myself. I am free from self-domination; I choose Christ-domination. I let go at the center.

Perhaps you are afraid to surrender to God. A young woman, very much a woman of this world, wanted to find God; and when I suggested surrender as the first step, she replied, "Why, if I did that, I would be at God's mercy." She thought God was looking for a chance to make her miserable. She did not understand that God's will and her highest interest were one. God's will is love in action—perfect love in action. As Rufus Moseley, a modern saint, puts it, "Jesus said to me, 'I am perfect everything, and I give you perfect everything.'" But we don't believe that. We are afraid that the will of God lies along the line of the disagreeable.

A rich woman said, "I was afraid to surrender to God, for I was afraid He would drive my last cow out of the pasture." But when she surrendered, she found God's will was not only perfect love but perfect reasonableness. The cows were all there, only she and God were partners in raising them, and partners in their disposal. Life was a partnership, with God as senior Partner. She was released and free and effective. She was relieved that she was no longer God.

O God, I lay down the burden of trying to be God. For I am not God. Thou art. So I yield to Thee the throne. I abdicate, now and forever. And am I relieved and released? I am. I'm grateful that I am now no longer centered in myself—I'm centered in Thee. Amen.

AFFIRMATION FOR THE DAY: *I surrender nothing, except what was a trouble to me—unsurrendered.*

CEASE FROM STRUGGLING

We now come to the next step:

5. *Cease from struggling.* Don't try to do this yourself; let Him do it. After having consented to surrender, you will be tempted to struggle and try instead of relax and trust and receive. "When I gave all trying over, simply trusting I was blest." There is a profound truth in that simple statement. For as long as you are trying, you are on the basis of yourself; but the moment you begin to trust, you are on the basis of Christ; He becomes the center, not you.

"But as many as received him, to them gave he power to become the sons of God, even to them that believe on his name: which were born, not of blood [you do not receive this new life through being born of Christian parents], nor of the will of the flesh [you do not receive it by whipping up your will, by trying], nor of the will of man [no man can bestow it on you through rite or ceremony or institution], but of God." (John 1:12-13.) It is quite clear. This new birth which leads to a new life is a gift accepted by faith, by those who *"believe on his name."* But that belief is not mere intellectual assent; it is believing with your life, self-committal to Another. It means letting down the barriers of your inmost being and letting Him come in and take over, take over as Sole Owner.

The two laws of life are receptivity and response. But first *receptivity.* Many reverse this and try to respond, respond, to try, to do. No, first receive—receive by a quiet appropriating faith. Then you will respond, naturally and out of the resources which receptivity brings. But if you try to respond before you receive, you will be responding out of emptiness. Your religious life will be strain, hence drain.

A theological student was tense and trying, striving hard to be good. His jaw was set, his nerves tense; he would be good at any cost. When I showed him the possibility of accepting the Gift, he seemed incredulous. But he relaxed and received, and rejoiced! He kept saying over and over, "Why it's too good to be true! All my life I've been fighting; now I'm receiving!" He was free, released, and happy—overflowingly so. Faith is pure receptivity.

O Christ, I come. In my hands no price I bring. I come claiming no worthiness. I have no right to anything, except grace. I have no right to that, except that Thou dost offer it to me. I take—humbly, joyously take. Now. Amen.

AFFIRMATION FOR THE DAY: *I accept what is my own—in Thee.*

CONCENTRATE ON ACCEPTANCE

We come to the next step:

6. *Concentrate on acceptance.* He is making the offer to you; accept it. These last two steps are parts of one step—negative, cease from struggling; positive, concentrate on acceptance.

A woman who became an author of several remarkable books, but who up to the age of sixty had produced nothing, walked out of her spiritual emptiness into spiritual fullness through the story of the man with the withered hand. Jesus asked the man to do the impossible— He asked him to lift an arm that he couldn't lift, a withered arm. But the man threw his wavering faith on the side of receptivity; he connected with the power of Christ by offering his willingness. He offered willingness; Christ supplied power. This woman did the same. By accepting faith she raised her withered life to Christ.

A remarkable Indian woman, head of a prominent school, passed from emptiness and defeat to fullness and victory by taking simply and gladly a book which a friend offered. She then saw that, just as she had taken the proffered book, she could and would take the proffered gift of God. That moment she was released.

A man who has become a world leader was defeated and discouraged and about to give up his work in India. He was sick in soul and in body. Then the verse spoke to him: "Whosoever drinketh of this water shall thirst again: but whosoever drinketh of the water I shall give him shall never thirst, but the water that I shall give him shall be in him a well of water springing up into everlasting life." (John 4:13-14.) He saw that this well of water within was a gift, began to drink by faith, and from that moment was completely changed. "I haven't had a discouraged or blue hour for thirty years," he humbly and joyously testifies.

A dean of girls, inwardly tied up with fears and inhibitions and frustrations, sat reading these words: "If the Son . . . shall make you free, ye shall be free indeed." (John 8:36.) She quietly let their significance sink in—freedom was a gift which she could take. She did! "I felt like shouting it to the world," she triumphantly said.

Faith is pure receptivity, alert receptivity, aggressive receptivity.

O Christ, I come to Thee believing that Thou art completely trustable. I cannot trust myself. I am not trusting my faith, but my faith is trusting Thee. I rest my case, and myself, with Thee. Amen.

AFFIRMATION FOR THE DAY: *The Son makes free; He makes me free; He makes me free now.*

CLEANSE YOUR PAST

We must continue the steps to the Way:

7. *Cleanse your past.* Make restitution where it is necessary or possible. I say make it where "necessary or possible" because sometimes it is not possible. There are things beyond your recall. Do not spend time in useless worrying over a past you cannot change. He forgives; let that suffice. He wipes it from His "book of remembrance." So must you. God forgives you; you must forgive yourself. Bury it all at the foot of the cross, and put "No Resurrection" over it. The past is buried. Its effects may carry over into the present, but it itself is buried. Even those continuing effects He can help you counteract and cancel, by starting new redemptive influences. He restores the years which the caterpillar and the locusts have eaten.

Some things it is not necessary to bring up. If more harm than good comes from bringing things up, let them rest, especially if they involve others. Do not develop a back-looking conscience, morbidly mourning over the past instead of bravely facing the present and the future in His name.

But some things may have to be straightened out before you can go on. A stately New England woman rocked an audience with laughter, and at the same time shook their consciences, by this story: She and her neighbor hated each other like poison. The point of contention was the neighbor's ducks, which used to get into her garden and spoil it. One day she found her opportunity. She put all the ducks into a cement-weighted bag and dumped them into the river. Later she became spiritually changed, and one day in the quiet hour those ducks came up. She would have to confess. Her response was: "Now Lord, this is carrying things too far. I'd be ruined if I confessed *that.*" One day when the neighbor was on the lawn, she started tremblingly toward her. She managed to blurt out the truth, told the whole story. The neighbor's jaw dropped. "My heavens, I always wondered what happened to those ducks." The woman volunteered to pay for the ducks, but the neighbor said she was just as responsible. The whole matter was buried. They are wonderful friends now, and the subject of ducks is never mentioned. Restitution often comes before restoration.

O Christ, give me courage and power to do the right thing though the heavens fall. I know they won't fall, for Thou requirest only the possible, and the healing thing. Help me. Amen.

AFFIRMATION FOR THE DAY: *"Cleanse your hands, you sinners, and purify your hearts, you double-minded."* (Jas. 4:8, Moffatt.)

WASHING WOUNDS

Since this matter of cleansing the past as far as possible is so necessary, we continue it today. You may be afraid of making an apology, of righting a wrong—afraid of what people will think about you. But only small people are afraid to apologize. "I'd die before I would apologize," said a telephone exchange operator. To which the superintendent of the hospital replied, "Oh, I do that a dozen times a day. It's the easiest thing I do." Result of these two attitudes? The telephone girl stayed a telephone girl, the other woman climbed to the top. The telephone girl got caught in herself; the superintendent was released from herself every time she made an apology.

The president of a state university once told me that he had received a diploma with an accompanying letter saying: "I cheated in the final examination. This thing has burned me for seventeen years. I can't keep it any longer. I feel relieved already. A great burden has been lifted." One member of the board of regents wanted to take the name off and hang the letter in the university as a warning to others. "No," said the president, "that would leave suspicion on other students. I'll bury it in my safe. No one shall ever know." He invited the man to come to see him whenever he came to town. The incident has never been mentioned.

Some university girls slipped out at night through a window and were caught. They lied about it. They afterward told the dean that they had lied. He suggested that they go to the dean of women and confess the whole thing. They did. The dean brought it before the university council, and then she moved that the girls be forgiven and the matter dropped. This was passed unanimously.

Gypsy Smith preaches on the Philippian jailer washing the wounds of Paul, wounds which he had inflicted the night before, as a sign of his penitence and change. If we wash the wounds of the past with our tears and our sincere apologies, they will be sterilized and will quickly heal. Cleanse your past from everything that might fester.

O Christ, Thou hast forgiven that past, and where Thy forgiveness is, there can be no infection. But show me if there is left anything for me to do in righting that past ere we go on together. For I want no open wounds, anywhere. Amen.

AFFIRMATION FOR THE DAY: *"Search me, O God, and know my heart, test me and try my thoughts; see if I am taking a wrong course, and do thou lead me on the lines of life eternal."* (Ps. 139:23-24, Moffatt.)

CHRISTIANIZE YOUR RELATIONSHIPS

We come now to the next step:

8. *Christianize your relationships.* Take the spirit of the Way into your total life. You have now one more set of relationships to bring into line with the Way—your present relationships.

To be a Christian is to be in Christian relations. Of course that must be qualified: Do it as far as it depends on you, for other wills are concerned, and you may not be able to establish Christian relations with them. "As much as lieth in you, live peaceably with all men." (Rom. 12:18.) "As much as lieth in you" is important. But we are to do the Christian thing even though the other person doesn't respond.

a) The home. Where there are points of friction, talk over things objectively. Try to see the matter from the standpoint of the other person. Project yourself in imagination into the very self of the other person and see things from his or her position. That will take sympathetic imagination. Don't confess the other person's sins; confess your own. That will beget confession in the other person. Even if it doesn't, you have done something to yourself; your peace has returned unto you. I have just received a letter containing this sentence: "I think he feels that in admitting that he is wrong he shows weakness." A strong person doesn't hesitate to confess wrong; a weak person does, lest his weakness be exposed. But the refusal makes him weaker.

Then go beyond talking over points of friction, come together each day in a corporate spiritual quest—a prayer time together. In that prayer time you will be melted into a common purpose and a common mind. In God you will become one.

b) Your daily occupation. That daily occupation can be the extension of your spiritual life, your spiritual life become incarnate in material things. The head of a great foundry told me that the defects of character in the individual workman sooner or later become revealed in the castings. If the character goes wrong, the casting goes wrong. The opposite of that can be true. Your Christian character can be registered in the work you are doing. God and we make men and things in our own image.

O Christ, I am beginning to extend Thy life and purposes into my contacts which are the extensions of me. Help me to create no longer in my image but in Thy image. That will not be impossible if Thou art in me —wholly. Come in, then—wholly. Amen.

AFFIRMATION FOR THE DAY: *I cannot keep my contact with Christ unless I Christianize my contacts with others.*

CONCERNING CLASS AND RACE RELATIONS

We continue the Christianizing of our relationships:

c) Your class and race relationships. Perhaps class feeling and race feeling have been determining your conduct, not Christ. Two young people, a boy and a girl, came in to interview me about race relations. You could look at their faces and see which one was on the Way. The boy's face was bright and assured; the girl's face was clouded and confused. The boy was working from Christ out to race relationships; the girl was working from the attitudes and opinions of society around her. One ended in tangles, the other in triumph.

d) Your international relations. Perhaps you are becoming embittered and corroded by the acids of prevailing hatreds. Surrender your international attitudes to Him, and let Him cleanse them. There you will be immune to prevailing hatreds.

e) Your relationships with the person next to you. Become a witness to the new life. Nothing is yours that is not shared. On the jacket of the little book *God Calling*, by "Two Listeners," are these words: "When supply seems to have failed, you must know that it has not done so. But you must look around to see what you can give away. Give away something." The simplest and most effective thing you can give away is just the thing you have received. Share it.

f) Your relationships with money. Bishop Edwin Holt Hughes preached a sermon on "God Is Owner"—we are debtors; we own nothing. A wealthy man invited him home to lunch, and they drove to a hilltop overlooking hundreds of beautiful acres. The man waved his hand toward the horizon and said, "Bishop, if this doesn't belong to me, to whom does it belong?" The bishop quietly replied, "Ask me that question a hundred years from now." There was no answer. A girl said to me, "My mother taught me that we can take nothing out of this world except our characters." Nothing except our characters, and what we deposit in other characters through personal activity, influence, and dedicated money invested in others.

g) Your relationships with the Church. If you are not in the Church, get in. If you are marginally in, get into the center.

O Christ, I see that no relationship can remain outside Thy sway. Here, take them all. I reserve nothing. For everything is made for Thy ownership —for the Way. I thank Thee that my hands and my heart cling to nothing —nothing but Thee. And, having Thee, I have all. Amen.

AFFIRMATION FOR THE DAY: *I hold nothing—nothing except in relationship to the Kingdom of God.*

"CULTIVATE THE QUIET TIME"

We now come to the last two steps in putting our feet firmly upon the Way:

9. *Cultivate the Quiet Time*—preferably in the morning. We have talked about Christianizing your relationships; we come now to the central relationship—your relationship with God. When that relationship is intact, then every other relationship is toned up. If that relationship gets loose, then every other relationship goes loose with it. For the Christian, there is one responsibility and only one responsibility—to keep in union with God. When that union with God is intact, everything flows from it. I know of no one thing that cultivates union with God more surely and constantly than the regular practice of the Quiet Time. If I have a Quiet Time, I have a quiet heart; but if the Quiet Time goes, the quiet heart goes with it. I can take it or leave it, but that is one of life's inexorables.

Close your eyes, drop into the silence of the heart, and then listen to God as He tells you how much time you can spend in the Quiet Time. Take the figure that fixes itself in your mind with a sense of approval, and start it. Pray by the clock. If it starts being mechanical, it will soon become medicinal—it will heal you at the heart.

10. *Create outlets and activities*. The Way is an outgoing way. The first law of life is intake, and the second law of life is outflow. If you try to continue the intake without a corresponding outflow, it will all end in an impasse. The inflow will cease.

The outlets and activities do not need to be great and significant. They may be small and insignificant. But the fact that they represent an outgoing attitude and a sharing purpose makes them significant. For the law of sharing, which is the law of love, which in turn is the law of life, is in operation.

We now sum up the steps: Consider your ways, change your directions, connect with Christ, consent to surrender, cease from struggling, concentrate on acceptance, cleanse your past, Christianize your relationships, cultivate the Quiet Time, and create outlets and activities. Your feet are now on the Way!

O Christ, how can I thank Thee enough that I am taking these ten steps to freedom. For I feel in my bones that this Way is the way to freedom. For my bonds are breaking, my heart is being released. I know that I am in the process of redemption. I am on the Way. Amen.

AFFIRMATION FOR THE DAY: *The alternate beats of my heart this day shall be "cultivate" and "contribute."*

"THE STEPS TO THE DIVINE RELATIONSHIP"

We are reluctant to go on in our pilgrimage with anyone left be-hind; so we turn back in these last two days of these weeks of quest to gather up the not-yet-arrived souls. Perhaps as we have talked about the Way it has seemed to lack the warmth of a personal fellowship.

So I must give you a shorter and simpler ladder around the idea of getting into saving touch with a Person. How do we set up a warm human friendship? What are the stages through which we pass?

These stages are five: (1) *The stage of drawing near*—the inde-cisive, uncertain stage where we alternately want to and do not want to give ourselves to the other person. It is the stage of exploration. (2) *The stage of decision.* The mind ceases to alternate; it is made up. (3) *The actual surrender of the self to the other person.* There is nothing weighed out or measured, nothing that the eye can see, but inwardly you say, "That person has my heart—has me." (4) *The taking of the gift of the self of the other*—the stage of appropriation, of acceptance. There is a merging of the selves; inward union takes place. (5) *The stage of growth*—a blending of will with will, mind with mind, being with being, down through the years.

These are the stages through which we pass in setting up a beauti-ful human relationship. We go through the same stages in setting up a saving relationship with Christ.

(1) *The stage of drawing near*—the tentative, explorative, uncer-tain stage. You have been in that stage with all its wistful, hungry longings, a stage when you alternately rebel against God and long for Him. You wish you could dismiss the divine Lover, and yet you can-not. You are torn between worlds.

Then you come to the second stage: (2) *You make up your mind.* The decision is made. Your will is thrown on the side of Christ. Of one woman who was indecisive about the Christian way someone remarked, "She is always hovering; she never alights." Now you have ceased hovering. You have alighted. For better or for worse, for life or for death, you have decided.

O Christ, I am grateful that at last, at long last, my indecisive will has come to rest, and has come to rest in Thee. How can I be grateful enough that it has not come to rest elsewhere, for then that rest would turn to restlessness. In Thee I know I can be forever at rest. Amen.

AFFIRMATION FOR THE DAY: *"Thou hast saved my life from death, mine eyes from tears, my feet from stumbling."* (Ps. 116:8, Moffatt.)

FURTHER STEPS

We come to the third rung in our ladder: (3) *Surrender to Christ.* That sounds simple—after it is done! But before, it seems vague and unreal. You are now so near that all you will have to do is to say, "Yes," and the relationship is set up. Christ has already said His Yes. All His barriers are down.

A student sat on a log bridge over a mountain stream and made her life decision. As she sat there, she took twigs of wood and one by one threw them into the stream and watched them float away. She named those twigs: "There goes my pride." "There goes my fear." "And there goes my self." That self was the last thing she threw in, and the decisive thing. When she threw in that last twig, she rose radiant. "I have been laughing ever since, ever since I got my self off my hands." You too will be glad and relieved to get your self off your hands and into safer hands—the hands of Christ.

That surrender is important, for there can be no love between persons unless there is mutual self-surrender. If either one withholds the self, then love simply will not spring up. It cannot spring up, for love by its very nature is mutual self-surrender. In the inmost depths of your being whisper to Him: "You have me and all I have—forever."

You now come to the next step: (4) *Acceptance of the self of the other person—Christ.* Your very surrender of yourself will give you an inner boldness and confidence that you, having surrendered yourself, have a right to take the very Self of Christ into yourself.

Someone has said, "We don't make friends; we recognize them." You don't make Christ a Friend, a Saviour; you recognize Him as such. He has always been and is your Saviour and Friend; now you are recognizing Him as such. That is receptive faith.

The last step is: (5) *A continuous, mutual adjustment of being to being, of purpose to purpose.* This is the stage of a continuous growth, and this will go on forever.

But one thing is settled, and settled forever: You belong to Christ; Christ belongs to you. You are forever each other's. The eternal pact has been made.

O Christ, how can I ever be grateful enough that I have come to this hour, this hour of the permanent choice. I am relieved that my self is off my hands and on Thy hands. For in Thy hands I am safe and adjusted and usable. I am now where I have always longed to be—at Home. Amen.

AFFIRMATION FOR THE DAY: *"This is a day we owe to the Eternal; let us be glad and rejoice in it."* (Ps. 118:24, Moffatt.)

ROADS WITH DEAD ENDS

We have seen in our quest that there is the Way and not-the-way, and we have marked out the steps in finding the Way. Having our feet upon the Way—firmly, I trust—we may now look at some roads with dead ends. For many people starting upon the Way get sidetracked into roads that lead nowhere. We shall look at sixteen roads that lead to the Never-Never Land. The signs that we shall put up over these roads that lead to dead ends are commandments: "Thou shalt not enter." That sounds dogmatic and authoritarian, but in reality these commandments are simply the distilled experience of the race. We shall look at some ways humanity, by the method of trial and error, is finding out how *not* to live.

The first road with a dead end is *Fear*. When fear is spelled with a small *f* it may be contributive. For fear may have useful biological ends. Fear makes the frightened deer alert and fleet; it makes the surgeon skillful, for he sees the dangers that beset him if he does the wrong thing; it makes the soul alert lest it hurt itself through wrong choices. Fear harnessed to constructive ends may be constructive. When we use fear and control it, then it is good. When fear uses us and controls us, then it is bad. When fear becomes Fear, then it becomes master and runs us into roads with dead ends. Then Fear becomes fearsome.

Fear has three things against it: (1) It is disease producing. (2) It is paralyzing to effort. (3) It is useless.

If these three things are true, then to conquer fear is one of the first conquests of life. Without that conquest we limp through life. I asked a doctor, "Is fear Enemy No. 1?" "Enemy No. 1? It's Enemy No. 1½," he replied. If it is Enemy No. 1, then we must face it first of all and get it out of the way before we can walk upon the Way with heads up and our hearts released and unafraid. The first word of the gospel was the voice of the angel, "Fear not." The first word of Jesus after His resurrection was, "Have no fear!" (Matt. 28:10, Moffatt.) Between that first word and the last word the constant endeavor of Jesus was to get men released from fear. We must learn His secret.

O Christ, how fearlessly Thou didst move down through life, and yet Thy courage was not a screwed-up courage; it was calm and assured and unstrained. Give me that courage. I too would face life calm, assured. Amen.

AFFIRMATION FOR THE DAY: *"Be strong, take heart, and do it; . . . the Eternal your God . . . is with you."* (I Chron. 28:20, Moffatt.)

MANY DISEASES ROOTED IN FEARS

We said yesterday that fear first of all is disease producing. Apparently we are made in our physical and mental makeup for faith and confidence and calm. Faith builds us up; fear tears us down. When Jesus was always saying to people, "Fear not," He was not imposing an exhortation upon life; He was exposing a necessity inherent in life.

A teacher of psychology said to me, "I know that I wouldn't have an ache or a pain in my body if I didn't worry about my son. But I do worry about my son, so I am filled with aches and pains." As a psychologist she knew that worry and aches and pains were bound up together. She worried and wearied, and knew the cause.

But sometimes the cause is not known. A college girl went to the doctor to find out the cause of her vomiting every morning. Bound by physical traditions, he could suggest nothing but the possibility of pregnancy. The real cause was a certain teacher who seemed to take a delight in humiliating students. The fear of that humiliation made her lose her breakfast every morning before that class. The doctor, belonging to the era when everything was rooted in the physical, did not inquire into the mental and spiritual upset at the base of the trouble.

A doctor, after an operation, couldn't get well. He was about to become chronic. A pastor said to him: "Doctor, you're worrying. You are afraid to die. You haven't done anything with your life, so you're afraid to face the future." The doctor said, "Perhaps you are right. Pray for me." The pastor did, and then and there the doctor surrendered his life to God. The next day the pastor, visiting him, saw the change. "You're trying it, aren't you?" The man got well and joined the church. Later he said: "If that man had not talked to me to get me to surrender to God, I would never have become well." We know how fear and worry cause disease and how they hinder convalescence. Wounds do not heal, or heal slowly, if fear is at the center of life. Faith is healing and fear is hindering.

Release from fear is a physical necessity as well as a moral and spiritual necessity. It is a life necessity.

O Christ, I see that Thou hast fashioned me for faith and confidence. Forgive me that I have allowed fear to invade me. For I know that faith is of Thee and fear is not of Thee. I therefore lay my fears at Thy feet. I surrender them. In Thy name. Amen.

AFFIRMATION FOR THE DAY: *Fear ties me up. Faith releases me. Therefore I choose faith.*

86

MANY DISEASES ARE FUNCTIONAL

We must pursue our consideration of the effects of fear upon the body. A woman was the chairman of one of my meetings, but failed to appear. It turned out that the fear of presiding had made her physically ill. She went to bed instead of to the platform.

A letter in this morning's mail begins this way: "For some years I have had trouble with fears. It began when I was in company of some of my friends and they began to speak of heart disease. As I tried to imagine what it would be like, my own heart began to beat very rapidly, and of course I thought there was something wrong. . . . I have heart skip which is due to nervousness, but the doctor tells me that many people have it, that it is merely functional and not organic. Nevertheless, since then I have been 'heart conscious.' . . . I have had nervous sick spells, and my stomach seems to be tied up in a knot."

Another letter in the same mail from a woman who finds herself unable to walk and puts her finger on her trouble in these words: "The real cause was fear—fear of not walking again, fear of losing my husband's love, as he says he dislikes such people. Fear, fear, fear!"

Another fine woman said to me, "I get arthritis and pains in my shoulder, and I know it comes when I begin to worry and am upset." She saw clearly the connection.

We must make it clear that we do not believe that all arthritis is functional and a result of wrong attitudes. There are structural diseases, and they are real; and there are contagious diseases, and they too are real. But the consensus of medical opinion is that from 40 per cent to 60 per cent of diseases are rooted in wrong attitudes of mind and spirit. The American Medical Association puts it about half rooted in the physical and half in the mental and spiritual. Apparently the ratio is growing. One doctor said that 85 per cent of the patients that come to him don't need medicine—they need to change their mental and spiritual attitudes. These people are passing on the sicknesses of their minds and souls to their bodies. They will get well only if they change their attitudes. States of mind can determine states of body.

O Christ, I see that when Thou dost tell me not to fear Thou art not imposing a precept; Thou are exposing my deepest need. I would be loosed from all my fears. Help me to lay them at Thy feet. Amen.

AFFIRMATION FOR THE DAY: *God has no fear. I am in God. Therefore I have no fear.*

WORRY IS SAND IN THE MACHINERY

As we are conquering the physical side of disease, we are being more and more defeated on the mental and spiritual side of disease. We know *about* life, but we don't know how to live it. One doctor said to another: "If I could find a purely physical case of disease, I would begin to think I'm a doctor again."

A woman told me that her husband suffered from gastric ulcers. "Does he worry?" I asked. "Worry?" she replied. "He doesn't do anything else but! And then I got to worrying over his ulcers, and I had a nervous breakdown. And then he worried over my nervous breakdown and got worse." There is a vicious circle—very vicious. It cannot be broken except by getting rid of the fear. A woodsman, apparently strong, was suffering from a stomach ulcer. When I asked him if he worried, he replied, "I guess that's my trouble." The worry produced an overacidity, which in turn produced the ulcer.

A woman writes: "Every time I get upset and start to worry my stomach hurts and I cannot eat for three or four days." Another said: "I was worried sick." The wife of a pastor got high blood pressure because of a trouble that came to her husband. It made her tense and anxious and sent up her blood pressure.

Of a fellow prisoner a C.O. wrote: "He hasn't eaten anything for the last four days, evidently from worry. His bowels have moved only twice in twenty-two days." Worry and fear may produce a diarrhea or constipation. Fear and worry upset the natural functioning of the digestive tract—about the first place they strike. "The digestive tract mirrors with fidelity every emotional state," says a doctor.

Fear also upsets the mental processes. Wrote a woman: "I am so filled with fear that I cannot think. I'm losing my power of mind, for I react only emotionally and not rationally." This woman could not think straight, for fear distorted and twisted everything.

Someone sent my book *Abundant Living* to a woman bedridden with arthritis. She saw that her arthritis was rooted in a fear of death. She surrendered that fear of death, and her arthritis left her. Today she is doing her own housework.

O Christ, Thou hast come to remove all fears; remove mine. For I know I cannot be at my best, Thy best, unless I am delivered, completely delivered, from fear. I would be whole. Amen.

AFFIRMATION FOR THE DAY: *"He has no fear of evil tidings; he trusts the Eternal with a steady heart."* (Ps. 112:7, Moffatt.)

NO ORGAN IMMUNE

We continue our study of the effect of fear and worry on the body. A nurse gives this case: A girl, married to an older man, came to a hospital complaining of pain in both sides. She was unable to tolerate any food, and whenever she attempted to eat she had severe attacks of vomiting. It was discovered that she was unhappy with her life at home and did not wish to return. Her physical condition was rooted in a fear of home conditions.

John Evans says in the *Calvary Evangel*, October, 1943: "In peptic ulcers, so common among white men between twenty and fifty, which someone has called the 'Wound Stripe of Civilization,' we know that worry plays an important role." He further says: "Mucous colitis, simple colitis, is nearly always a nervous phenomenon. For many years the treatment has been that of simple, easily digested diet and nerve sedatives. A study of these patients in one of the large general hospitals showed that 92 per cent of them were harrowed by worry and emotional strain."

A man became ill on his way to work every day for two months. When questioned, he explained that his easygoing boss had been replaced just two months before by an efficiency expert. A change in his job cured him.

John Evans gives the striking case of a radio executive who had distressing stomach and intestinal symptoms for about six months. It was rooted in this incident: While waiting for a verdict on his case, he copied out four long words from the doctor's records while the doctor was out of the room. He failed to ask the meaning of the words, but felt they meant an incurable condition. He carried that crumpled paper around with him. He was sick and miserable. When another doctor examined him and explained the meaning of the words, he went away relieved and had no further symptoms.

An optometrist says that fear can distort vision. "When one is frightened and there is a tension in the muscle of the eye, the fright will make it worse, and then he is the more frightened."

O God, my Father, I see that to be well I must have confidence and faith. I would be well—every whit whole. Then help me to confidence and faith. I have little, but I offer what I have to Thee. Multiply it—beginning now. In Jesus' name. Amen.

AFFIRMATION FOR THE DAY: *Fear is paralysis. Faith is power. Therefore I let in faith.*

FEAR PARALYZES

We have seen first that fear is disease producing. In the second place, it is paralyzing to effort. No one can be at his best unless he is free from all fears. Jesus speaks of the seed that was "choked with worries." And note that He puts the choking things in this order: "choked with worries, . . . money, . . . pleasures." (Luke 8:14, Moffatt.) We would have reversed that order and would have said that the pleasures of sex and appetite—lust and drunkenness—and the love of money are the chief sources of arrested development. Jesus said worry is. And life bears Him out. More people are mentally, spiritually, and physically arrested by fear and worry than by any other single thing. Of Peter it was said "He was afraid, and began to sink." (Matt. 14:30, Moffatt.) Fear makes you sink.

When Jesus cured the paralytic, He saw that the paralysis was rooted in fear, which in turn was rooted in sin. So his first word was, "Courage, my son!" and His second was, "Your sins are forgiven." (Matt. 9:2, Moffatt.) When He lifted the guilt, that lifted the fear, and that in turn lifted the paralysis.

Jesus said to His prostrate disciples: "Rise, have no fear." (Matt. 17:7, Moffatt.) Fear always gets you down; faith always lifts you up. The man who buried his talent brought back the unused talent and said, "I was afraid, and I went and hid thy talent in the earth." (Matt. 25:25.) His lifework was a hole in the ground! Fear did it.

Again, it was said of the disciples: "The disciples had gathered within closed doors for fear of the Jews." (John 20:19, Moffatt.) Fear puts you behind closed doors—an introvert, an ingrown person.

Joseph of Arimathaea was "a secret disciple—for fear of the Jews." (John 19:38, Moffatt.) Fear always drives you underground. Fear brought to Joseph a dead Christ. It will do the same for us. If we live by fear, Christ will be dead within us.

Jesus said to the woman with the hemorrhage, "Courage, my daughter." (Matt. 9:22, Moffatt.) Fear had made her tense, and that had made her bleed, and the more she bled the more she was afraid. Jesus turned her from fear to faith, and she was well.

O Thou living Christ, our souls and minds and bodies have been bled white with fear. Say the word of "courage" to me and help me to respond to Thy faith. I have little; give me Thine. Amen.

AFFIRMATION FOR THE DAY: *Fear puts me behind closed doors. Faith throws open the doors and makes me free and unafraid.*

FEAR AND COLD FEET

We saw yesterday that fear and worry cut down the personality and its effectiveness—sometimes as much as half. That leads us to the last observation: Fear is useless. A woman who was a nervous wreck from fear and worry, when urged to surrender it all to God, replied: "Why, if I didn't worry, things would go to pieces." She actually felt that by her worrying she was holding things together.

One pastor said: "I am a worry wart. I've worried myself sick about what might happen to my wife and daughter coming to this Ashram." He saw the futility of worry and surrendered it to God; the lines of his face relaxed, and he was transformed—radiant.

A Y.M.C.A. worker among boys said: "I was tense, holding up the world. Atlas and I together were holding it up. I was defending the Christian faith, arguing, struggling, trying to set everybody right. Every night I went to bed with my socks on, my circulation was so bad. Then I surrendered my whole tense self to God. I said I would follow truth wherever it led. Truth would have to defend itself; my business was to follow it. My tensions are all gone. My circulation is normal. I don't wear socks at night. People say I'm not the same person. I'm not. Now God uses me." He does, greatly. The man is no longer trying to do things for God; He is allowing God to do things in and through him. He used to be a tied-up bundle of nerves. Now he is a relaxed channel of God's grace.

A woman came to our Ashram provided against every possible sickness. She had brought eight dollars' worth of medicines: sleeping powders, aspirin, a doctor's prescription for asthma, and so on. She had stopped up every possible hole—beforehand! Then she surrendered all this tense anxiety to God, and when she was about to leave, she said: "Now I'll have to cart all this stuff back again. I haven't needed a bit of it." Had she not let go her tensions, turning them over to God, then she would have needed all these medicines. For if we will not take God's way, we have to provide stopgaps. Worry and fear are useless—and worse.

O calm Christ, come into my heart and take out all useless fear and worry and let Thy calm and adequacy reign. For where Thou art, there is peace and power and poise. Where Thou art not, there is worry and disintegration. Come in, calm Christ; I consent. Amen.

AFFIRMATION FOR THE DAY: *Christ was always calm. I am in Christ. Therefore I am in the Eternal Calm.*

ONLY TWO FEARS ARE INHERENT

We come now to the steps to deliverance from fear. Breathe a prayer as you put your feet upon the road to complete freedom. Let the prayer be this: "O God, help me not to be afraid to face my fears. Give me strength not to evade or to cover, but to face things honestly."

1. *Remember there are no inherent fears, except two; the rest are acquired.* The two inherent fears, born with us, are fear of falling and fear of loud noises. Some psychologists examined five hundred people and found that they had about seven thousand fears. All but two of those were acquired. Five hundred people loading themselves down with 6,998 unnatural and useless fears! There is a caste in India in which the women add on each birthday four rings of heavy brass, one on each ankle and each arm. By the time they are of middle age they walk with difficulty under this senseless burden. But this is no more senseless than weighting one's self down with inward fears: fear of failure, of the future, of growing old, of sickness, of being dependent, of the opinions of people, of death, and so on.

Most of these fears are home-grown fears. They come out of wrong home teaching and example—making children afraid of the dark, of bugaboos, of this, that, and the other thing. Parents who try to control their children by fears and threats often succeed too well—the children grow up controlled by the fears themselves. On the other hand, where the home is released from fear, the children have no fear. Two parents belonging to our Ashram began singing, "I will not be afraid," and one night they heard their little three-year-old singing in her bed in the dark, "I will not be afraid." There was a home-grown faith.

A woman says in a letter: "All my life I have been subject to fear and tension. As a child I was afraid of everything any child ever dreamed of fearing, and I added others of my own invention. My nightly prayer was, 'I thank Thee for not letting anything happen to me today!' As I grew older, my fears became less material and more intangible. As a Christian I considered these fears and tensions my cross to bear, my thorn in the flesh, and thought it my duty to keep them under control." You need not keep them under control; you can get rid of them. They don't belong to you; they are unnatural.

O Christ, no fears lurked within Thy bosom to cripple and hinder. Thou didst have the unafraid heart. Give that to me. For I want no enemies within. Cleanse the depths. Amen.

AFFIRMATION FOR THE DAY: *All my fears are home-grown fears. I cease to rear them—from today.*

STEPS TO VICTORY OVER FEARS

We come to the next steps in the conquest of fear:

2. *Talk over your fears and anxieties with someone.* Carefully choose the person and go over the whole matter. I say "the whole matter," for sometimes we bring up a marginal fear and leave the central fear untouched. We are afraid of that fear. It may be a fear around which a reticence, a hesitation to mention, has gathered. For instance, the fear of being left without a life mate, the fear of losing the love of the mate we now have. Both of those fears are self-defeating; they help to accomplish the thing they fear. Sterilize those and other fears by bringing them up and frankly talking them through. But having talked them out with one person, do not retail them. To talk about them too much is to aggravate them. They become a complex. Having relaxed and allowed every fear to come to the surface, if nothing more comes to the mind, then take it for granted that your fears are all exposed. Don't fear that you haven't brought up all fears.

3. *Decide on a plan of action.* These fears have invaded you; they are not a part of you; they are extraneous, not natural, not permanent. You allow them to come in, and you, and you alone, can decide that they shall go out. Vash Young, radio broadcaster, tells in "My Conquest of Scarecrows" (*Reader's Digest,* July, 1932) how he took a look at himself and said: "Your factory is a menace to yourself and a nuisance to others. Look at your products—fear, worry, impatience, anger, doubt." He made a list of the qualities that seemed ever-enduring: love, courage, cheerfulness, activity, compassion, friendliness, generosity, tolerance, justice—nine magic words—incidentally, all of them Christian! He determined to replace his old, dead, festering words with these new, living, health-giving words. Soon he was no longer, as formerly, losing his breakfast in the gutter when he thought of going to see a client. One of his secrets of victory: "I have tried it as a rule to devote less than half of my time to my own affairs."

The point of this step is that you are now on the offensive. You are no longer being invaded; you are outgoing, positive. You are beginning to be no longer afraid of fear, for you see it for what it is—a scarecrow.

O Christ, I begin to see that my fears are my uninvited guests—guests that have taken over control. And now, by Thy grace and power, I am again in control. I have my feet on the Way. I am grateful. Amen.

AFFIRMATION FOR THE DAY: *I shall think no fearful thought, speak no fearful word, give way to no fearful act. I belong to faith.*

LOOK IN THREE DIRECTIONS

Now take the next step:

4. *In deciding on your plan of action look in three directions:*

a) Look at your surroundings. Some psychologists are convinced that the root of all personal problems is in the environment. "By the crowd thou hast been made, and by the crowd thou shalt be saved," is the saying of one of them. This is an exaggeration, of course, but it holds a truth. There are three influences that determine character: innate heredity, social heredity, and a person's own choices. Within the framework of the innate and social heredities there is room enough for one to choose and determine his own character.

But the surroundings do influence one and influence one greatly. A Negro student whose brother was missing in action broke out with swellings on her lips and eyes. She thought it was a food allergy. But it was an allergy to worry and fear.

A woman was secretary to two brothers who were at tension point. Every night she would have to take tablets for her indigestion. When the brothers were reconciled and the tensions eased, the secretary's digestion returned to normal.

b) Look at your past. There may be something in your past, some childhood emotional shock, some fear that has been pushed into the subconscious and the lid closed upon it. There it festers underneath. Sit relaxed with your head back, your eyes closed, and let your mind wander over your past to see if it fastens itself upon some incident. Gently bring it up, look at it, pull its sting. It can hurt you no longer. If it is some guilt buried there, bring it to the redemptive love of God. He forgives, washes it out. You are free.

c) Look at your present ideas and attitudes. Your fears may be rooted in a wrong set of ideas and attitudes now operating in you. A fine woman came to a crisis in her life when she needed God, but her idea of God had been fixed by a preacher when she was a child so that she thought of a God throwing people into hell. When she turned to God with her fear, she could get no help, for her idea of God created fear in her. A wrong idea of God blocked the release.

O Christ, cleanse away from me all wrong ideas about the Father, and life, and the future. Thou art cleansing away my wrong ideas and attitudes by the wholesome sanity of Thy love. Thou art sterilizing all my fears. I am being released. I thank Thee. Amen.

AFFIRMATION FOR THE DAY: *My soul, set no sail to fear. Lift thy full sail to faith, and sail the seas with God.*

LOOK FOR WRONG IDEAS

A wrong notion of God can produce fear. A Jewish high-school girl said that, though her home life was happy, she was filled with a dread of routine, the routine of going to school and being grooved. She could not sleep on Sunday night, for Monday began the cramping. This fear was rooted in the idea she had of God: He was an impersonal Fate who fates us. That wrong idea of God made life all awry, a pitilessly grooved thing. She was afraid of it. Her idea of God needed to be changed to a Father who wills nothing but the best.

Your maladies may be rooted in a wrong idea about yourself. David Seabury says 98 per cent of our troubles are imaginary. A famous Chicago psychiatrist says that of people who imagine they are going insane only one in a hundred actually is. A girl, a fine musician and beautiful, left college because of worry and excessive fatigue. Her inability to relax caused a breakdown. She thought she had intestinal trouble. She surrendered her fears to Christ, and her relaxation was so complete that she accepted a proposal of marriage. She is now living a happy, useful life as a minister's wife.

In looking at your ideas and attitudes you may find that you are magnifying your fears, looking at them through a magnifying glass.

> "Worry is an old man with bended head,
>   Carrying a load of feathers
>   Which he thinks are lead."

And when he thought they were lead, then they felt like lead. Paul speaks about "the renewing of your mind"—sloughing off all fears.

5. *After having looked at your fears, don't think too much about them—think faith.* Fear feeds on itself. The more you think about it, the more you have. "As he thinketh in his heart, so is he." (Prov. 23:7.) Your habitual thinking becomes you. Ideas are actions in the making. Whatever you hold in your mind will pass into your acts, automatically. For ideas are not passive; they are active. Show me a man who thinks negative, fearful thoughts and I'll show you a failure. Show me a man who thinks positive thoughts, thoughts of faith, and I'll show you a success. One is paralysis; the other is power.

O Christ, Thou didst affirm life in the face of life's direst calamities. Thou didst talk faith in the face of failure. Help me to affirm Thy affirmations and to believe Thy beliefs. Amen.

AFFIRMATION FOR THE DAY: *Today I shall think faith, act faith, be faith—and spread faith.*

DON'T FIGHT YOUR FEARS; SURRENDER THEM

We continue our steps in the conquest of fear:

6. *Don't fight your fears; surrender them to God.* If you fight your fears, your mind will be upon those fears, and it cannot be repeated too often that "whatever gets your attention gets you." If your fears get your attention, even though it be a fighting attention, they will get you. A struggle will ensue between the imagination and the will, and in any such struggle the imagination always wins. You must not fight your fears, but surrender them into the hands of God.

7. *When worry comes to the door, don't give it the best seat and entertain it.* Gently close the door and say: "I have surrendered you into the hands of God. You have no place or part with me any more. I'm free from you." A Jewish high-school girl was afraid of a certain teacher. This made her work so unsatisfactory in her other classes that the authorities were about to give consent for her to change schools. She heard my message, went home to her mother, and said: "Mother, the message was for me. I've surrendered my fear to God. I'm no longer afraid of that class, and I don't want to be moved." God had her fear; she wasn't struggling with it, or entertaining it; it was gone.

8. *Learn the art of prayer, for fears dissolve in an atmosphere of prayer.* A missionary in Japan lived in inward fear of earthquakes in that land of earthquakes. She became sick at the stomach and had heart palpitation at the thought of going to Tokyo. It had never occurred to her to turn her fears over to God. She surrendered them into His hands and lo, they were gone. She said she actually looked forward to going through earthquake experiences just to prove her freedom to herself, though she needed no proof. She went through several and did not even know they had happened.

A Negro singer was asked to sing at a university church to a white congregation on the Day of Prayer. She was filled with fear. She read *Abundant Living* and surrendered her fear to God in prayer. "I felt like singing my head off after I got rid of my fears through surrender of them." One woman, trembling with fear, found release through repeating the Lord's Prayer.

O Christ, these fears of mine I've held within my heart, and now I'm turning them over to Thee. I cannot master them, but Thou canst. From this time on they are in Thy hands and off mine. Amen.

AFFIRMATION FOR THE DAY: *In an atmosphere of prayer my fears are not solved so much as dissolved.*

KEEP YOUR SENSE OF HUMOR

We continue our steps to freedom from fear:

9. *Look at the facts precisely and see them in the total setting.* The thing or things you fear may have come out of focus—they occupy the center when they should be on the margin. God is now at the center of your life; therefore fear is on the margin. Your fears are now being dissolved in the great fact of God. This marginal thing has no right to determine your life. God determines it.

10. *Remember that nothing that happens to you can ever be as bad as the fear itself.* The words of Montaigne are relevant, "Who feareth to suffer, suffereth already because he feareth." And the words of Francis of Sales to a fearful friend, "Fear is a greater pain than pain itself." It is absolutely true that nothing that can happen to you will be as bad as the fear itself. In the words of Emerson, "Never set a sail to fear"—it will drive you on the rocks. But you can use the winds of adversity and calamity to drive you to your goal.

11. *Keep your sense of humor.* When you get too tense and begin to take yourself and your troubles too seriously, walk to the looking glass and burst out laughing. I often do it; it lets down tensions. As you stand before the looking glass, repeat these words: "O fool, to carry thyself upon thine own shoulders! O beggar, to come to beg at thine own door!" And then burst our laughing—at yourself.

12. *Think faith, speak faith, and act faith.* I overheard the following conversation in a train: "A man is what he eats. America is the greatest nation because we eat better than others." But you can upset the digestion of what you eat by wrong emotions, fears, worries. So it's what you think that determines the effect of what you eat. Therefore think faith, speak faith, and act faith.

13. *Fear is self-centered; faith is God-centered.* Fear turns you toward yourself; faith turns you toward God. One is ingrowing, the other is outgrowing. One is illth, the other is health. Fear nervously tries to hold your world together; faith surrenders your world to God, and you and He work it out together.

O Christ, I see, I see I've tried to be my own savior by my fussing and fuming and worry. Thou art my Saviour. I turn over to Thee, forever, myself, my worries, my all. Thou hast me, and I'm released. I'm grateful. Amen.

AFFIRMATION FOR THE DAY: *Think of self and trouble grows. Think of God and trouble goes.*

GOD AND YOU MEET LIFE TOGETHER

We continue the steps for overcoming fear:

14. *Do something for someone every day.* A businessman, nervous and upset, was ordered by his doctor to go to Grand Central Terminal, New York, and look for someone who needed help. He felt like a fool in obeying, but found a woman seated on her suitcase weeping. Someone had failed to meet her. He found out where she wanted to go, got a taxi, went with her, bought her some flowers on the way, and delivered her to her daughter's home. He went to the telephone, called his doctor, and said, "Doc, it works. I feel better already." He was well—when he thought of someone else!

15. *Identify yourself, not with your fears, but with Christ.* By surrender of fears to Him you are no longer identified with them. You are identified with Him. "In the world ye shall have tribulation: but be of good cheer; I have overcome the world." (John 16:33.) He has overcome your world of fear. You have become identified with Him, and therefore you are identified with His victory.

Here is a man who did just that: He was getting thinner and more nervous all the time. He was told that he would die if he stayed in his job, but he couldn't get out. He heard me talk on wrong attitudes producing illness. He surrendered his fears to Christ, and today he is happy and released and is getting fat—in the same job! Christ had overcome his world, and when he accepted that fact, he was released. Jesus said, "It is I, have no fear." (Matt. 14:27, Moffatt.) Where Jesus is, there is no fear; where He is not, there is fear. Here is a life equation: — Christ = + fear; + Christ = — fear.

16. *Surrendered to God, you and He can work out life together.* You are not alone; you are not facing life alone. You are facing the future with God. As a wise man put it: "I do not know what the future holds, but I know who holds the future." Someone asked a Negro, a radiant soul, how he managed to keep that way. He replied: "I know that God won't let anything come my way that He and I together can't handle." You and God are now working co-operatively. You supply the willingness, and He supplies the power.

O God, I thank Thee that at last I have come to the place of release, for I have come to Thee—Thou art my solution. "Without Thee, not one step over the threshold; with Thee, anywhere!" I am not afraid of anything, for Thou hast conquered all things. Amen.

AFFIRMATION FOR THE DAY: *"It is no weak Christ you have to do with, but a Christ of power."* (II Cor. 13:3, Moffatt.)

WHERE CHRIST IS, FEAR IS NOT

Howard Thurman says: "The religion of Jesus saves us from fear, hate, and deception—all strongholds of the weak."

A simple faith in Christ does deliver from fear. A young minister writes: "After I had written the last letter, I decided to make one more effort to combat my fears. My nervousness was almost unbearable. There have been times in my life when I have suffered bodily pain, but I never knew that one could feel so sick without pain in the body. I overcame it somewhat by struggling against it. But on New Year's Eve, after a terrible night of suffering, I realized the futility of it all. Toward morning I prayed: 'Here I am before Thee, Lord; take me from this earth or heal me, for I can't go on this way any longer. Do with me as you like.' As soon as I finished, a Voice seemed to say, 'Perfect submission.' It went through my whole being. As soon as I realized its meaning, my entire body and soul relaxed completely, and I lay there as one coming out of a terrible dream. It seemed like heaven itself when I realized that I didn't have to struggle with myself any longer. . . . He can't fail; therefore I can't fail. My health is returning rapidly. There is very little nervousness, and my appetite is almost normal. Now I feel like 'a new man in Christ Jesus.' I have tried to discipline myself without surrender. This way is much easier: surrender first, then discipline."

Surrender identified this minister with Christ, and where Christ is, fear is not. One of the saintliest persons I have ever known was a woman in Kentucky who, when I went to India, made a compact with me: she would pray, and I would work, and in the end we would divide the results! When she died, her husband said: "All my life I've been afraid of death, but seeing her going through death so triumphantly has cleansed away all fear of death from me." Jesus has done just that. As you go into the future, remember:

> "The light of God surrounds you,
> The love of God enfolds you,
> The presence of God watches over you,
> The power of God protects you,
> Wherever you are, God is."

O God, as long as I am in Thee I am immune to all fear and anxiety. I am able to throw off fears as a healthy body throws off disease germs. In Thee I am alive and life-giving. In Thee I am on the offensive. Amen.

AFFIRMATION FOR THE DAY: *"All my fears are dissolved in the great Quiet of God."*

FROM THE CELLAR TO THE SKY PARLOR

We can be released from fear and anxiety. "Anxiety," as someone has said, "is the measure of the distance between man and God." When God comes, anxiety goes; when anxiety comes, God goes. A minister surrendered his anxieties and fears to God and then said: "I came back to my work, not with tight lips and clenched fists in determination to do better, but with the feeling of renewed strength." He had settled down in God.

The following extracts of a letter from a Ph.D., a dean of girls, show a real victory over a life-long, deep-rooted fear: "I built up a wall between me and the outside world. This attitude was resented by others and created a dislike in them. Added to this, I had an undue sense of duty or justice and demanded too much of myself and others. There was nothing lovable in my whole make-up. . . . I became ill from it all. . . . I began to read *Abundant Living,* and for the first time I glimpsed a life of freedom; I no longer needed to control fear, I could dispense with it. So I moved out of the dark, dank basement of my life, where rats of fear and nervous tension made life unbearable, and moved up into the sky parlor, where I threw open the windows of my soul and let God's sunshine penetrate every recess of my being. . . . I could elaborate at length on the evident results—a joyous happiness I had never known, a loving, not critical, attitude toward others, loss of abnormal appetite, no further need of sleeping pills. Many people remark that I am like a different person. Causes of irritation have disappeared. The walls between me and the world have melted away. Restraint and diffidence are gone. I have lost undesirable inhibitions. I am walking in the Light!"

What God has done for this brilliant woman, He can do for you. Surrender your fears and trust Him.

A nurse had a lifelong fear of dropping a teacup at a tea party. The more she fought it the worse it became. She surrendered it to God and was released.

O Christ, so beset by tragedy and everything that produces fear, and yet so completely free from fear, come into my life and release every tension, every anxiety, and make me unafraid. I co-operate to the full—together we can meet anything, everything. Amen.

AFFIRMATION FOR THE DAY: *"So let each loyal heart in trouble pray to thee: the floods may roar, but they will never reach him."* (Ps. 32:6, Moffatt.)

ANOTHER ROAD WITH A DEAD END—RESENTMENTS

Another way with a dead end—the way of *resentments and hate.* On a large scale we are taught to hate. An American general speaking before an audience said, "At the close of this war we must hate, hate, hate." And vigorous applause greeted the statement. Suppose we do just that, what will happen? We will go to pieces, for life is not made for hate. Here is an example of what happens when you live by hate: An American correspondent was told by an assistant to Goebbels: "My work is very bad for me. The copy we send out is so depressing that the bureau personnel is always on edge; nervous breakdowns are common, and there have been cases of insanity. Hideous creatures gnaw at our souls continuously, and these,. I am sure, are our own fantastic creations." The mind, not made for hate, broke under it. Hate is not-the-way.

It is true that there is a legitimate anger which can serve life's purposes. Paul says, "Be ye angry, and sin not." (Eph. 4:26.) If so, then you must be angry only at sin. It is said that Jesus "looked round about on them with anger, being grieved for the hardness of their hearts." (Mark 3:5.) Here anger was grief, a sense of being hurt at the attitudes the religious leaders were taking toward an unfortunate man. If your anger is grief at what is happening to others, it is right and Christian. If it is personal pique at what is happening to you, it is wrong and unchristian.

Charles Baudelaire says: "Hatred is a precious liquor, a poison dearer than all the Borgias, because it is made of our blood, our health, our sleep, and two thirds of our love." Hatred consumes the consumer. Elsie Robinson puts it truly thus: "But even if our rage seems fully justified, and our plans succeed beyond our blackest hope, we will never get even. For life doesn't work that way. Instead of finding peace, renewed self-respect, and healing for our hurt, each attempt at revenge leaves us frustrated, cheated. Instead of punishing our enemies, we've simply played our own debasing game and sold ourselves down the river." Hate is not-the-way.

O Christ, we see that Thy way of love is our own way, the way for which we are made in the very structure of our beings. For love builds us and hate blasts us. Help us, then, to love, even the unlovely, and in so doing we shall become lovely ourselves. Amen.

AFFIRMATION FOR THE DAY: *"Let all you do be done in love."* (I Cor. 16:14, Moffatt.)

THE PHYSICAL EFFECTS OF RESENTMENTS

We must see the effects of anger and resentments upon us, physically, mentally, spiritually, socially. Take the physical effects of anger and resentments. The body is made for good will, not for ill will. Experiments have shown that when anger sets in, the process of digestion stops. In a group of mucous colitis cases 85 per cent of the patients confessed they had resentments—against employers, parents, life in general.

A woman said to me: "You're right. I lived with my son-in-law for five years under great tension. At the end of five years he had a stomach ulcer and I had arthritis. We separated, and we both got well!" The resentments threw a functional disturbance into the system. If it had stayed there long enough, it would have passed into structural disease.

When the word "mother-in-law" was repeated to a hypnotized patient, his stomach would secrete acid. He was not getting along well at home. Said one who knew, "Anger will produce varicose veins straight off." A leading optometrist, knowing that anger disturbs the vision, made it a habit whenever he became angry to drive to the side of the road and stop until his anger cooled down. He knew that there is truth in the saying, "I was so angry I couldn't see." A man said to me with a sigh, "My sister-in-law is upsetting the digestion of the whole family." Wherever there is an atmosphere of ill will, there you will find upset digestions. A young man was so angry with a garage man who took his tire, slashed it with a knife, and said, "This tire is no good," that he could have killed him. He nourished this resentment until he went into schizophrenia, split personality. The anger disrupted and divided his whole person, left him a wreck.

The headlines of a newspaper read: "Chronic grouch shoots, kills two partners, two women, and self." The sad narrative ends with the words, "He nursed a chronic grouch." A grouch within the soul throws everything out of balance; every organ is affected, especially the brain.

A banker would get up and leave the denominational conference every time a Negro spoke. Later this banker committed suicide. He wouldn't live with others, so he couldn't live with himself.

O Christ, I see that if I do not live in love, I do not live—my life forces break down and go to pieces. Take from my heart all resentments, all ill will against everybody and everything, and help me to love. Amen.

AFFIRMATION FOR THE DAY: *Today I shall hate hate, and I shall love love.*

SENTENCED BY GOD

We must continue to look at the effects of hate and resentments. Jesus said, "Whoever is angry with his brother without cause will be sentenced by God." (Matt. 5:22, Moffatt.) Note, not by the Sanhedrin or the Gehenna fire, as the contrast shows, but by God in the silent processes of judgment: inner decay, frustration, conflict, neurosis. These are the modern sentences by God. If you give out hate, you will become hateful. If you are resentful, you will be resented. If you do not like people, you will not be liked by people. That is the sentence of God. And it is going on silently around us.

Howard Thurman says: "If we nourish within our hearts hate and fear and self-centeredness, we shall spend our days stumbling in the dark." Why? Well, hate and fear and self-centeredness are not-the-way. Life won't work that way. As someone has said, "Revengefulness is a powerful poison. It will destroy you if you try to repress it, and it will destroy you if you express it in action." Either as repression or as expression it is poison.

Said a friend: "Resentments have divided our family. I have two brothers and two sisters. I am the only one who is friendly with all the others. Some of these resentments are twenty-five years old. Their lives lack a theme song. Love is the only way to keep a family together." Love not only holds a family together; it holds the person together; it holds everything together. It is the Way.

A nurse wanted a night shift so she could attend the university in the day. The request was refused. The nurse entered the hospital a few days later as a patient, severe pain in her side, inability to eat, a temperature of 102 degrees. Nothing organically wrong could be found. After a few days' rest the night shift was granted her; she became well and did the night shift and the university work with no ill effects. The resentments had made her ill.

A man said to me: "Six men did me injuries. I refused to retaliate. All six men, I'm sorry to say, were buried in suicides' graves." But if it doesn't eventuate in outer suicide, it certainly ends in suicide of the spirit. Everything good is slain by hate and revenge.

O Christ, I know that I cannot wrong another without wronging myself. I know that this fire of hate consumes me, consumes everything noble and fine within me. Quench it within me. Let no smoldering embers remain. I consent for the last spark within me to be put out. Amen.

AFFIRMATION FOR THE DAY: *Today I have a theme song: "I love everybody in God."*

LIVING WITH A STONE IN THE HEART

We must continue to see the effects of hate and revenge. A teacher said, "Whenever I went to see my sister, I was unwell. The reason was that I did not like my brother-in-law." The dislike was dis-life. It threw disturbance into life.

A woman·was resentful of the attitudes of her brother, who was a doctor. She asked him to take her blood pressure. It was much above normal. She went back home and surrendered her resentments to God, and her blood pressure returned to normal. Had she kept the resentments, her heart might have been affected permanently.

A returned missionary said to me: "I was given up to die. The doctors said I could not live. I was holding resentments down in the depths of me. I surrendered them to God. I got well. Today the doctor says laughingly, 'You are so healthy you are ready for hard labor.' "

Sometimes these resentments are buried deep in the subconscious and there work disruption. A banker wanted his wife never to have her name in the society column, for he wanted to be known as a conservative banker. She resented this role of being in the shadows. She became an invalid. Her husband spent a fortune on her. When the husband died, she left the invalid's chair. She was no longer resentful at her role in life. Both had paid heavily for wrong attitudes—the one in money, the other in health, both in unhappiness.

A woman of seventy gave herself to Christ and was released from a life-long inner burden. "I've lived with a stone in my heart all my life," she said. "Ever since the day my mother said to me, 'I hate you,' because I stood in the way of her going to another man, I've had this stone of resentment within me. I'm grateful that at last it is gone."

When I was in Mexico, I was told of a man who became so angry with his son that he turned green and died. The Mexicans believe that the bile had killed him. Whatever the scientific conclusions may be, we know that something within us dies when we allow hate and resentments to lodge within us. Good will is food; hate is poison. Good will is a forced option: if you take it you live; if you don't you die.

O Christ, Thy ways are so inescapable. I cannot escape from them, for when I do, I escape from life, I am saved from salvation. Help me, then, to come to terms with Thee and to take Thy way—the way of love. Amen.

AFFIRMATION FOR THE DAY:
> How can hate have a part in me?
> For I belong to a Man who died on a tree—
> For those who hated Him.

THE DICE ARE LOADED AGAINST ENMITIES

Einsworth Reisner says: "The dice are loaded against enmities. The natural affinity of human nature is good will. Never bet on enmities, but always bet on love, for the dice are loaded against enmities in human relations." Anyone who is trying to play the game of life against love is a dead-sure loser.

Why is it that in human history peace treaties have lasted only on an average of two and one half years? For one simple reason: They were founded on revenge. So the universe upset them. They broke down fighting against reality. You can have peace or revenge, but you cannot have both. They are incompatibles. And all human history is a comment upon that.

A woman said to me: "I've found out the cause of my headaches: I get angry with my roommate. I confessed it to her, and my headaches left." The world is a vast headache because it is a vast hate. We will never get rid of our world headache until we get rid of our hate.

A banker was chronically ill. He held resentments against the directors of the bank. He got out of the bank, gave up his resentments, and found to his amazement that he was walking along the street whistling. "Why, I'm well," he said joyfully to himself. He was, for his resentments, with the consequent conflicts, were gone.

A pastor's wife, whenever she became upset with people, would break out in a rash. We are now breaking out in a rash on a world scale—the rash of war and conflict. We break the law of love and we break out into wars and outer conflicts. Our trouble is that we won't live by love, so we do live with sickness, individual and collective.

Some boys played a prank on a man with a long beard. While he was sleeping they buried a piece of Limburger cheese in his beard. When he awoke, he sniffed and said, "This room smells bad." He went out into the open and said, "The whole world smells bad." The source of the evil smell was in himself. The world smells bad to us because we have hatred within. Go out with love within and the world will be lovely. It will respond in love, for you are living with the grain of the universe—you are living by love.

O Christ, Thou revelation of the heart of the universe, Thou hast revealed love as the secret. We have lost that secret; hence we spend our days griping and groping. We will not see Thy way, and we cannot see ours. Help us to see Thy way that we may find ours. Amen.

AFFIRMATION FOR THE DAY: *Love shall be in my bosom, and then I shall find love everywhere.*

THE STEPS OUT OF RESENTMENTS

We now come to the steps we are to take to get rid of resentments. Breathe a prayer. You are not just reading a page; you are ridding yourself of a plague.

1. *Remember that resentments have no part nor lot with a Christian.* You cannot hold both Christ and resentments. One or the other must go. Do you want to go through life without Christ, chewing on resentments, a bitter, crabby, poisonous person? That's what you are headed for if you allow resentments to fester within you.

It may be that your resentments are justified: someone has mistreated you; you have been disappointed in a life plan or ambition; you have met with a bitter calamity; there are those who rub you into soreness; you have to live in an uncongenial environment—all of these things may be very real and apparently justify your resentments. But whether justified or unjustified, resentments are disastrous to the inner life—they are poison. The probabilities are that the resentments are not justified, that they are rooted in a touchy, self-centered self, a self that is full of self-pity. Those who harbor self-pity haven't the key, for life will back good will and only good will. Decide that resentments are going to have no part nor lot within you.

2. *Remember that no one has ever treated you worse than you have treated God, and yet He forgives and forgets.* God isn't asking you to do something He himself is not doing. Here is one of the most wonderful passages in literature, "Treat one another with the same spirit as you experience in Christ Jesus." (Phil. 2:5, Moffatt.) He forgives you, graciously and without reservation. You must do the same. If not? Then Jesus tells what happened to the man in the parable who was forgiven a debt of "three million pounds" and then went out and refused to forgive a fellow servant who owed him "twenty pounds"— he was handed "over to the torturers, till he should pay him all the debt. My heavenly Father will do the same to you, unless you each forgive your brother from the heart." (Matt. 18:21-35, Moffatt.) The "torturers"? They are within you—resentments mean inner conflict, division, unhappiness, torture.

O Christ, I know how Thou hast treated me: forgiveness, gracious and undeserved. Help me to treat others with the same spirit. Only as Thy spirit takes the place of my old spirit can I do it. Amen.

AFFIRMATION FOR THE DAY: *Today I shall treat everybody as Christ treats me.*

THE THREE LEVELS OF LIFE

3. *Remember the three levels of life and decide which one you are going to live on.* (*a*) The level of life where you return evil for good—the demonic level. (*b*) The level where you return evil for evil—the human, legal level. (*c*) The level where you return good for evil—the Christian level, the divine level.

"You become born of the qualities you give out." If you give evil for good, then you become evil, you become the thing you give out. If you give evil for evil, you become a tit-for-tat person, legalistic, unlovely, and unloved. If you give out good for evil, then you are born of the good, you become good.

But suppose the person is undeserving? That doesn't matter. As someone says, "If you give out love to an undeserving person, it will be a bright spot to him on his way to hell." It will be a bright spot to you too, for there you have risen to the divine level of life. John Beilgalhausen is a converted Jew, a very learned man. The Nazis deliberately starved to death his mother and his father. For some time he fought against resentment and hate. Then he did something better and more decisive: he surrendered it all to God. His resentment and hate were taken away. And when he says these words, they fall upon the soul with an almost divine authority: "A Christian has no enemies." No enemies? No, for he has no enmity. This is a simple way to get rid of enemies: have no enmity and your enemies are all gone, at least as far as you are concerned.

When someone remonstrated with Lincoln that he had forgiven an enemy, he replied: "Our business is to get rid of our enemies, isn't it? Well, I got rid of this one by turning him into a friend through forgiveness." The only possible way to get rid of an enemy is to turn him into a friend, and the only possible way to turn him into a friend is to forgive him. For two hates never made a love affair.

A man gave a golf ball the name of his enemy and struck it. But he struck it into the rough, for if you hate you cannot see straight nor drive straight. You cannot hurt another without hurting yourself. "He who spits against the wind spits in his own face."

O Christ, I see I cannot be an echo of the treatment people give to me. I must echo Thee and treat people as Thou dost treat them. But I cannot do this except by Thy grace. May Thy love melt down all my resentments and heal all my hurts. I accept that love now. Amen.

AFFIRMATION FOR THE DAY: *I shall overcome evil with good, darkness with light, hate with love.*

DON'T LET THE ACTIONS OF OTHERS DETERMINE YOURS

4. *Don't let the actions and attitudes of others determine your conduct and attitudes.* Be Christ-directed instead of circumstance-directed. If you allow the conduct and attitude of other people to determine your conduct and attitude, you will be changing with every person you meet. You will be on the legal level of life—tit-for-tat. You will be below the Christian level, the law of karma, instead of the law of Christ. Remember Jesus said that if you give up attitudes of grace—of forgiving enemies, of agreeing with your "adversary quickly, whiles thou art in the way with him"—and take legal attitudes, then you surrender yourself to legal processes, and you will have to pay "the uttermost farthing." There is no stopping this side of exhaustion.

Today I read an account of an important meeting in which it was stated that I had offered a resolution but "it was defeated." I found myself inwardly glorying in that "defeat," for while I am often wrong, this time I know I was right. I can wait for the years to speak against the hours. One does not need to get excited or exasperated when he knows that reality is behind him. "He that believeth shall not make haste"—shall not make haste to avenge, to pay back, to retaliate. He can be contented with temporary defeat, provided he is linked with long-range victory. "It makes me content, for Christ's sake, with weakness, insults, trouble, persecution, and calamity." (II Cor. 12:10, Moffatt.) "Content," not with the weakness, insults, and the rest in themselves, but "for Christ's sake." That phrase "for Christ's sake" transforms you from becoming "everybody's door mat into everybody's temple of refuge." You have an inner core of dignity, of assurance, of glorying, for you know that in the end the right will emerge. You can trust the processes of God where you cannot trust the persons of men.

Remember the word of George Fox: "To outlive all wrath and contention and to weary out all exaltation and cruelty or whatever is of a nature opposite to itself." "To outlive" and "to weary out"—that is it! When you surrender to love, you "outlive" and "weary out" everything. For love lives and gives, and gives and lives. Hate dies.

O Christ, Thou wilt outlive and weary out all that is contrary to Thy love. For love is eternal; hate is of a passing hour. I surrender myself to love, to love even where I do not like. For Thou canst make me love the unlovely, and perhaps in the process they too shall become lovely. Amen.

AFFIRMATION FOR THE DAY: *I will not descend to the level of the person who has wronged me by trying to pay him back.*

LIKING PEOPLE AND LOVING PEOPLE

5. *Remember to "shake off the dust."* Jesus told His followers that when people would not receive them they were to "shake off the dust." This is usually interpreted as meaning that we are to give the people a final warning in the dust-shaking process. Would it not be nearer to His spirit to say that it means that we are not to let the attitudes of people cling to us—their very dust must not become a part of us? Very often we leave a situation, get partial victory over it, but some dust of resentment, of inward hurt, of lingering mental debate still clings to us and spoils the complete victory. "I will forgive him, but"—and because of that "but" the dust clings. "I will forgive, but I won't forget"—the dust is still there. "I will forgive, but I won't have anything to do with him"—the dust is evident. The dust must go completely. There must be full and free forgiveness with no strings attached. You must forgive others as God forgives you.

6. *This does not mean that you have to like people and what they do.* Christians are people who love people whom they do not like. Impossible? Oh no, for they love them for what they might be when they cannot love them for what they are. They see in every person another person, the person he might become. That very love and faith helps to create that person.

7. *Go beyond praying for people who do you wrong—bless them in His name.* A woman told how she got rid of her resentments: Every time she thought of the person who had done her wrong, she then and there said inwardly, "I bless you—in His name." This goes beyond praying for enemies, for when you pray you ask God to bless them; here you bless them. That makes the act yours and makes it firsthand. You are not touching people through God. God is touching people through you.

If you cannot attain to this, then take an intermediate step. Meet the object of your dislike with a prayer. Every time the name of the person you dislike is mentioned, breathe a prayer for that person. You beat down rising resentments by a barrage of prayer. Make this a life habit, so that it does not become an issue each time.

O Thou Christ of the unalterable good will, help me to have that same unalterable good will, no matter what others may do. Help me to have the fixed purpose to love, to answer all opposition with patience, all insult with instant prayer, all nagging with patient good humor. Amen.

AFFIRMATION FOR THE DAY: *"Goodness shall have justice done to it—the future is with men of upright mind."* (Ps. 94:15, Moffatt.)

SMILING A SMILE OUT OF THE BABY

8. *Remember that the sum total of reality is behind you when you love—you are behind you when you hate.* Love is positive; hate is negative. Love heals; hate wounds. Love lasts; hate stings itself to death.

I watched some pigeons feeding. One pigeon was very pugnacious and was constantly fighting the rest. But I noted it was a losing game, for when he was fighting he wasn't feeding. The rest stepped out of his way and kept on feeding while he wasted time and temper and nourishment in fighting others. Do not fight—feed!

Lao-tse, the Chinese sage, said: "You are to conquer as does a stream when it reaches a rock; it goes around it, and when strong enough overflows it." In a home, or in any life situation, when you meet opposition, flow around it. Quietly set up your own inner satisfactions when you cannot get them from your surroundings. Live within when you can't live without. Then one day you'll be strong enough to overflow the obstacle, to inundate it with love. You will then do as one saint said: "If you had anything against me, I'd hug it out of you." And those who know him know that this is no exaggeration; he would do just that—or the moral equivalent of that! I cannot refrain from another quotation from this radiant soul: "The only thing the devil can't get into is the love of Christ, for if he did get into it, he wouldn't be the devil." The devil can get into our virtues and by a twist can turn them into vices. He can make righteous indignation into unchristian resentment. He can turn self-respect into pride, can make humility into mush, can corrupt everything except one thing—the love of Christ. Here is one thing he cannot get into and remain the same. Here, then, you take your stand. You will give out love and only love, no matter what the other person gives out to you. A friend tells how he "smiled a smile out of the baby." That's it! We must smile a smile out of the unsmiling, love a love out of the unlovely, create a new birth in the spiritually unborn. We must answer death, not with death, but with life. Then we ourselves live!

O Christ, I come to Thee to help me to be no longer tangled in what other people do. Help me to be emancipated by starting from Thee and by doing what Thou wouldst have me do, for then I am free—free to return good for evil, love for hate. I thank Thee that I am now beginning from Thee and Thy Way. Amen.

AFFIRMATION FOR THE DAY: *"In God I trust without a fear: what can man do to me?"* (Ps. 56:11, Moffatt.)

DON'T FIGHT RESENTMENTS; SURRENDER THEM

Resentments can slip in under the cover of something else. I have just read where Paul had what he calls moments and attitudes "not inspired by the Lord." (II Cor. 11:17, Moffatt.) He allowed the attitudes of his detractors to determine his conduct: "If anyone has no love for the Lord, God's curse be on him!" (I Cor. 16:21, Moffatt.) "Whoever preaches a gospel that contradicts the gospel I preach to you, God's curse be on him!" (Gal. 1:8, Moffatt.) And then he adds: "Now is that 'appealing to the interests of men' . . . ? Trying to 'satisfy men'?" Someone had said, "He's soft," and Paul lashed out in these curses upon people to prove he was no "softy." He allowed other people to determine his conduct. Here he was "not inspired," and not inspiring. We seldom quote those words.

Perhaps you feel disappointed with life and what it has brought to you. Self-pity sets in. Perhaps you have been denied, for one reason or another, a life partner. It is no use to fight against that fact. Surrender it to God and let Him help you make something out of it. Here are the triumphant words of one who did just that: "I am one of the old maids you have helped to see the way to take life and *love* it!"

That leads to another step:

9. *Don't fight your resentments—surrender them.* When you fight them, they grow. When you surrender them, they go. A doctor says: "There was a time when I held a strong resentment against an individual for nearly a year. But almost the moment my letter of apology dropped into the mailbox the resentment vanished. It has never returned." But some of us are willing to do everything except surrender the resentment. Walter B. Pitkin tells of nettles along the walk on the grounds of a California old ladies' home that scratched so many legs and brought on so many cases of nettle rash that the gardener finally dug up the plants. Whereupon a committee visited the superintendent and demanded that the nettles be restored. "They gave us something to talk about," said the spokeswoman; "now we just sit around for hours saying nothing." Back went the nettles. Some people would miss the possibility of a grouch. They are so negative that they fear they would be lost in turning positive.

O Christ, Thou in whom no resentments lodged, help me to be the kind of person in whom no resentments can lodge. Inoculate me with Thy love so I will not be susceptible to resentments. Amen.

AFFIRMATION FOR THE DAY: *I belong to the Way of Love. I cannot step down to any lower way.*

GOD FORGIVES YOU; YOU FORGIVE OTHERS

We come now to the last steps in getting rid of resentments:

10. *In surrendering the resentments to God you may have to expose them to man.* Dr. Loring Swain, who has been very successful in helping arthritics to health and release, says: "Together, the patient and I try to expose his resentments, fears, conflicts, or actual hatreds. . . . For example, without any physical reason we could find, a woman in the hospital began vomiting every morning after breakfast. It was discovered she was full of self-pity and resentment against others in her ward who had visitors and she had none. She was blind to her jealousy which was back of the emotional upset causing her illness. Repentance freed her and apology restored friendly relations with her neighbors. These two acts cured her resentments and her vomiting."

So surrender your resentments to God and expose them to someone, possibly the one against whom you hold them. The exposing does what oxygen does when impure blood is exposed to it—it purifies it.

11. *Then be so inwardly outgoing and happy that resentments can have no part nor lot in you.* As Luther said, "My soul is too glad and too great to be the enemy of any man." Someone else has put it, "He is below himself who is not above injuries." The temptation will be to descend from the Christian level of returning good for evil to the lower level of returning evil for evil. Here you leave Christ and return to the pagan level of Cyrus, of whom it was said: "No one ever did more good to his friends and more harm to his enemies."

When Tokichi Ishii, awaiting his death sentence in a Japanese prison, stumbled accidentally upon the passage in the New Testament, "Father, forgive them; for they know not what they do," he said that in a flash he saw the whole meaning of Christianity. That verse, he said, "pierced my heart like a five-inch nail," and he was forever changed.

Since God forgives you, you can forgive others. But if you shut off others from your forgiveness, then you shut off yourself from God's forgiveness. The wonder of God's forgiveness to us should send us out joyously to forgive others.

O Christ, can I ever get over the wonder of Thy forgiveness to me—to me? Help me to pass this on in just as gracious a way as Thou didst pass it on to me. Thou didst forgive me not grudgingly but graciously. Amen.

AFFIRMATION FOR THE DAY: *I am so rich in forgiveness that I can afford to dispense it prodigally to others.*

ANOTHER ROAD WITH A DEAD END—NEGATIVISM

Negativism, or retreatism, is a road with a dead end—it gets you nowhere. There are three possible attitudes regarding reality: (1) escape it, (2) rebel against it, (3) co-operate with it. Many do not want to co-operate with Reality; much less do they want to rebel against it; so they try to escape from it. Escapism becomes a life attitude. This, of course, may be almost entirely unconscious. For the self would not try to escape from reality unless the self could save its self-respect by convincing itself that the attitude is justified. This self-justification takes many forms, sometimes the development of an illness. Such a person says, "I could do this if I were only well, but I am not well, so I am justified in not trying."

A very conscientious man, given a job which was too big for him, developed asthma every time he got into a jam and couldn't handle the situation. This was unconscious, of course, for he had to provide himself with a reason for not being able to handle the situation. Asthma was the reason. It was mentally induced. It has been estimated that five sixths of the cases of heart trouble among servicemen in 1917-18 were wrongly diagnosed as heart disease. "Patients by the thousands were discharged and pensioned on that basis, and, in fact, became chronic heart disease cases," says Francis Sill Wickware. These persons, under the stress of battle, would want to get away from it, but it is awful to be a coward. They would reason: "I'm not a coward, but my heart is acting up, so my desire to get away is justified." To keep up the self-justification the heart condition has to be maintained—and is, unconsciously. So the person settles down to chronic invalidism. The heart trouble is not structural but functional.

I know of a woman who has an underlying self-pity because of her troubles in life. She has a continuous series of accidents, far more than the laws of chance would justify. Unconsciously she produces these accidents to justify her self-pity. She has powers which could be greatly used if she could get rid of her self-pity. Another woman, self-centered, has stomach upsets and pains constantly. Her husband had a stroke, and she complains that sympathy is given to him when he has no such pains as she has. She is living by negativism.

O Christ, Thou didst come to save us from all running away, all evasion of responsibility, all subterfuges. Save me from all unreality. Help me to be real—in everything. For I cannot evade; I must master. Amen.

AFFIRMATION FOR THE DAY: *"Be strong, take heart, and do it. . . . The Eternal . . . is with you."* (I Chron. 28:20, Moffatt.)

THE RETREAT INTO THE ANONYMOUS

We continue to look at this road with a dead end, retreatism. A Swedish girl was jilted. She went to bed and was a chronic invalid for six years. She retreated into invalidism from the hard, cruel world. A friend helped her to surrender her negativism and her fear of life to God. She was released, became positive. Now she is a deaconess, a radiant, outgoing, helpful person.

Many are canceling out their lives and effectiveness by more subtle and less obvious negativism. For instance, many people retreat into prevailing attitudes and customs to avoid the responsibility of acting up to their highest light. "Everybody does it," is the soporific excuse. Society demands conformity. If you fall beneath its standards, it will punish you; if you rise above its standards, it will persecute you. It demands a gray average conformity. So many succumb and become echoes instead of voices, things instead of persons. The retreat into the anonymous is going on all around: "I'm not going to put my neck out." So convictions are stifled, personality is stunted, spiritual life dies. "Come to the cocktail lounge for smooth sophistication," says a sign. Note the word "smooth." You fit in, no issues are raised, you conform, you are flattened out, you stand for nothing, you fall for everything, including folly. This creeping paralysis is killing the soul of America. When a service club was about to pass a resolution embodying soul-destroying hate and race prejudice under the appeal of a superpatriot, a leading citizen arose, stemmed the tide, and was greeted with prolonged applause. The resolution was defeated. Why did that group applaud the courage and sense of this man? Because they saw in him what they would like to be, but didn't dare be, for they were under the sway of our most prevalent philosophy of life, the philosophy of not putting your neck out, the philosophy of negativism. This is creating a morally dull, colorless civilization.

Women, as well as men, are often afflicted with this creeping moral paralysis. They look around, not up, before they act. They don't act; they only react. They are fast becoming a ditto mark. They lock-step down through the innocuous years. "It's smart"—to be innocuous, to fit in, to retreat into vacuity, to be a cipher.

O Christ, of the steadfast will, of the unbroken purpose, of the heart that dared die rather than conform to wrong, help me to be positive, outgoing, unafraid. Help me to catch Thy quiet courage. Amen.

AFFIRMATION FOR THE DAY: *"The turtle never gets anywhere till he puts out his neck."*

THE STEPS OUT OF NEGATIVISM

We now come to the steps to get rid of all negativism and retreatism.

1. *Will to be positive*. This is important, for you have been willing to be negative, perhaps unconsciously. The first question of Jesus to the man by the pool was, "Do you want your health restored?" (John 5:6, Moffatt.) That question was important, for the man had been living by ill health, by arousing pity, by negativism. If he was not willing to reverse his attitudes, nothing could be done. A psychologist said to a nervously upset man, "Do you want to get out of this prison?" He didn't, since that would make him confess to himself that he was getting a weird satisfaction out of his misery, that his retreatism was a life strategy.

The first thing to decide is: Do I will to be well? To be positive? To go out and meet life and master it? When you decide this affirmatively, then all the resources of God are behind that decision. In the inner quietness of your heart throw your will on the side of freedom.

2. *Remember that you are made in the inner structure of your being for creative activity*. You are fulfilling yourself when you are creative and positive. You are frustrating yourself when you are non-creative and negative. Now that you have decided to become a plus instead of a minus, the sum total of reality is behind you instead of against you. All the resources of God are at your disposal.

3. *Remember that your happiness does not come through what happens to you, but through what you make happen to others*. Plan to go out of your way to do something for others, and plan it today, plan it now. And don't let it end with a plan; let it end with a performance. Begin, on however small a scale. You will gather strength as you go.

You have been saying to yourself, "I would be happy if only this would happen to me." It has failed. It is not-the-way. Now you are saying, "I will make others happy, and I will begin now." Happiness doesn't come to you; you join happiness on the way to doing something for others. Like the waves thrown up by the ship as it plows to its goal, happiness will be a by-product of your creative activity.

O Christ, I see, I see. Help me to follow this gleam. I am afraid of failure, afraid of my own fears. But I know that with Thee anything is possible, everything is possible. So I do will to be positive, creative, and I believe Thy will is now behind my will. I thank Thee. Amen.

AFFIRMATION FOR THE DAY: *"Thou wilt not drop the work thou hast begun."* (Ps. 138:8, Moffatt.)

115

I CAN DO ALL THINGS THROUGH CHRIST

We continue our steps to the affirmative life:

4. *Surrender your negativism and retreatism into the hands of God.*
You are not the center of it any more; you have transferred that center
to God. You and He are going to work it out together.

5. *Say to yourself: "This does not depend on my ability, but on
my response to God's ability."* Or, as it has been put, "This is not my
responsibility, but my response to God's ability." You are now not
alone; you are strong in strength not your own.

6. *Accept the gift of positive, outgoing energy.* "The breath of life
from God entered them; they stood on their feet." (Rev. 11:11, Moffatt.) The breath of life from God is now entering you; you are going
to be an upstanding person—unafraid of life and its demands.

7. *Refuse to think negative thoughts.* If you think negative, you
will be negative; if you think positive, you will be positive. "As he
thinketh in his heart, so is he." (Prov. 23:7.) Squash a negative
thought as you would squash a louse, and for the same reason. A louse
is a parasite living on life; a negative thought is also a parasite living
on life, on the positive. Negative thinking is lousy thinking.

8. *Refuse to speak negative words; cleanse them from your vocabulary.* A certain management engineer takes hold of sick businesses
and puts them on their feet, and also takes hold of sick personalities
and puts them on their feet too. He says that he cannot get a man
started unless he says Yes twenty times. He has been saying No to
himself in various forms and under various guises for so long that he
has become a No. You are born of the thing you habitually give
out. Now you are going to be born of the Yes. Go over your vocabulary and one by one root out all negative, weak, and doubtful words.
Put in their stead words that breathe positive attitudes of faith.

9. *Keep repeating to yourself: "I can do all things through Christ
which strengtheneth me."* (Phil. 4:13.) Say it the last thing before
you drop off to sleep, for the subconscious mind is susceptible then.
Say it the first thing as you open your eyes in the morning, and keep
saying it during the day. You will turn from being a nay-saying to
being a yea-saying person—a plus instead of a minus.

O Christ, Thou art life's supreme affirmation. I look at Thee and anything becomes possible. I am merging my life with Thy creative life. In
Thee I too am creative—we are creative together. Amen.

AFFIRMATION FOR THE DAY: *"Give me a willing spirit as my strength."*
(Ps. 51:12, Moffatt.)

ANOTHER ROAD WITH A DEAD END—
INFERIORITY COMPLEXES

Another road with a dead end similar to the one we have been considering: *the road of inferiority complexes.*

Seneca pictures a child in the womb saying, "I don't want to be born. I'm afraid to go out into that strange world. I am comfortable and secure here; I don't want to be born." That fear of ongoing life would stunt the child forever. We must yield to the processes of ongoing life with confidence and joy. And we must do it with no sense of inferiority. We must feel our importance to the sum total of things. We must feel that destiny, however limited, is centered in us.

The Way is the way of importance—to everybody. Whenever Christ touches life, that life takes on significance, the nobodies become the somebodies. "Why don't you accept your inferiority?" someone asked a Negro. "How can I?" he replied. "I'm a child of God."

In spite of this a great many people develop inferiority complexes. A woman with more than average powers became dependent on her family for support. To justify to herself and others this leaning on the family she developed various ailments. She told herself, and was told by others, that she couldn't do this, that, or the other thing—she was too weak. She was weak, but it was a mentally induced weakness to justify her dependence. She got herself a pair of crutches, and these crutches further weakened her.

Inferiority attitudes are shown in putting up such high standards for yourself and others that, not being able to reach them, you do nothing. Because you cannot do everything, you do nothing. Because you cannot change the world, you refuse to try to change the situation at hand. The reaction is from perfectionism to pessimism. This lets down easy the person with an inferiority complex. We have no right to be thinking of world-changing plans unless we are doing all we can to change the situation around us. The healthy-mindedness of Jesus was seen in the fact that, while he proclaimed an absolute Order, the Kingdom, he was willing to sit down with an individual and lead that individual to change.

O Christ, Thou art adequacy and power. So I come to Thee to get adequacy and power to live by. I throw open every pore of my being to let Thee come in to change me from inefficiency to efficiency. Amen.

AFFIRMATION FOR THE DAY: *"Happy the man who reverences the Eternal, who finds rich joy in his commands!"* (Ps. 112:1, Moffatt.)

STEPS OUT OF INFERIORITY FEELINGS

We now consider steps, a ladder, to climb out of inferiority feelings:

1. *There is no superiority and inferiority in the Christian scheme of things.* Paul repudiated this whole conception of superiority and inferiority: "If the foot were to say, 'Because I am not the hand, I do not belong to the body,' that does not make it no part of the body" —here was an inferiority complex; and here a superiority complex— "The eye cannot say to the hand, 'I have no need of you.'" (I Cor. 12:15, 21, Moffatt.) To feel and act superior or inferior is wrong. Feel and act what you are—in God.

2. *To cover an inferiority feeling, don't act superior.* Loud, aggressive talking and self-assertion is often based on a fear that people will find out an inferiority. The aggressiveness is the obverse side of inferiority feelings. It shows an inner strain, a lack of confidence and poise.

3. *Don't struggle against your feelings of inferiority.* That might drive them into the subconscious, where they would work against you. Bring them up and look at them calmly. See where you are below par and where you are above par.

4. *Accept correction and improvement from yourself and others.* Da Vinci put such artistry into two cups in his picture of the Last Supper that friends remarked about them. Da Vinci wiped them out. "I don't want you to see the cups primarily, but the faces." His willingness to accept correction made him a master.

Jack Minor, the naturalist, could not read or write until he was a grown man. His Sunday-school boys sat around him—their teacher— and taught him to read. "Wasn't that lovely of them?" he said in later years when he came to fame. When he was lecturing at the University of Toronto, a man sent up a note afterward: "Don't use that expression—it is this way." Again Minor remarked: "Wasn't that lovely of him to do that? I'll never make that mistake again." His simple, humble Christian spirit saved him from both inferiority and superiority and made him a great man. "When one is on the defensive, he has lost his grip on life." Don't defend yourself; accept correction from yourself and others.

O Christ, I am accepting myself, but I am accepting myself in Thee. In Thee I am no longer inferior—I take on Thy adequacy and Thy power. In Thee I meet life with a cheer and a song. In Thee I am strong. Amen.

AFFIRMATION FOR THE DAY: *"In Him who strengthens me, I am able for anything."* (Phil. 4:13, Moffatt.)

FURTHER STEPS OUT OF INFERIORITY FEELINGS

5. *Accept your limitations and dedicate them.* A professor long refused to accept his deafness and was always nervously strained. He finally surrendered his deafness to God, got a hearing aid, became happy, and is now head of an association for the hard of hearing.

6. *You can make your inferiorities serve.* The Negro woman who pioneered in taking the kinks out of kinky hair had unruly hair herself. Her sisters had lovely hair, and the family teased her about her hair. She determined to do something for people who had unruly hair, experimented on a kitchen stove, evolved the process, and made a million. More, she made self-respecting young people. She said to an audience: "I am not merely taking kinks out of hair; I am taking kinks out of character." She made her inferiority serve.

7. *Do everything, even the insignificant things, in a significant way.* The insignificant things take on significance when you do them significantly. The spirit in which a thing is done makes it significant. I watched a waiter in a railroad diner wait on a table so rhythmically and harmoniously that he made it an art. Later in that diner again I recognized the graceful flourish of the elbow, knew it was the waiter who did little things in a great way. The professor who bowed to his class was bowing to greatness—to potential greatness.

8. *Do everything for the love of God.* The secret of Brother Lawrence's greatness was that he did everything—the scrubbing of floors, the washing of pans—for the love of God.

9. *When you do the insignificant in a significant way, you are working out a larger plan of God.* Here is a telling passage: "The due activity of each part enables the Body to grow and build itself up in love." (Eph. 4:16, Moffatt.) When you perform the "due activity" of your part, you are making possible a larger whole.

Pray in the words of Margaret Bailey:

"God, give me sympathy and sense
And help me keep my courage high.
God, give me calm and confidence—
And, please—a twinkle in my eye."

O Christ, I am a part of eternal significance, eternal plans working themselves out through me. I can contribute spirit when I cannot contribute bigness—and maybe the spirit is the bigness. Amen.

AFFIRMATION FOR THE DAY: *"Thy promise puts life into me."* (Ps. 119:50, Moffatt.)

ANOTHER ROAD WITH A DEAD END—SELF-CENTEREDNESS

We come now to another road with a dead end—*self-centeredness*. It is a way that is not-the-way. Paul, describing a self-centered life and its results, ends by asking this question: "Well, what did you gain then by it all? Nothing but what you are now ashamed of!" (Rom. 6:21, Moffatt.) The end was zero. That is the inevitable end of a self-centered life—nothing. No matter what the outer shell of life may contain in the way of prosperity or fame, the soul is dead; it died of being off center.

Our civilization teaches self-interest as the primary driving motive— "Every man for himself and the devil take the hindmost." But when you do that, the devil not only takes the hindmost but takes us all, and especially the one who takes that attitude. And takes him first of all. For the self-centered are the self-disrupted. They are making themselves God, and they are not God, so the universe won't back their way of life.

Jesus penetratingly said, "Whoever wants to save his life will lose it." (Luke 9:24, Moffatt.) He doesn't actually save it; he *wants* to save it. But it goes to pieces; he *loses* it. Why? The sum total of reality decrees it. Life will not back it.

First, it is unnatural. The idea that life is made up of one driving urge, the self-regarding urge, is a false view of human nature. There is not one urge in human nature, but three great urges: self, sex, and the herd or gregarious urge. The self urge is obviously self-regarding; the herd urge is other-regarding; the sex urge is partly self-regarding and partly other-regarding. There are just two dominant urges in human nature: the self-regarding and the other-regarding—the egoistic and the altruistic. Suppose you organize life around the self-regarding urge; then that leaves the other-regarding urge unfulfilled and frustrated. Therefore the self-centered person is at war with himself, waging a personal civil war. The self-centered are the unhappy, the frustrated. I have never seen a happy self-centered person. They do as they like, and then they don't like what they do. They express themselves, and the self they express sours. That is not-the-way.

O Christ, Thou hast come to deliver us from the dominance of ourselves. Thou hast come to free us to be natural. Save me from myself and from the futilities of a self-centered life. I know this—experience tells me so—but give me power. Amen.

AFFIRMATION FOR THE DAY: *"To please and serve thee is my joy, thy law lies deep within my heart."* (Ps. 40:8, Moffatt.)

A SELF YOU CANNOT LIVE WITH

Self-centeredness produces a self you cannot live with. If you won't live according to God's way, you can't live with yourself.

I once saw a cartoon of a very sick-looking world with a doctor holding its pulse. He shakes his head and says: "You are in a bad way—you are allergic to yourself." If you make self-centeredness your driving urge, it will drive you into conflict with yourself, will drive you into complexes; you will be allergic to yourself.

An intelligent young woman said to me in alarm: "I've tried to charm people, using any means to win them. Now they've found me out. I've lost all my friends. Even my little boy has found me out. I'm losing him. What shall I do?" She wanted some magic medicine by which she could be saved from the results of her self-centered life. There was only one thing she could do to save herself from the fruit of her life, and that was to cut the root—herself.

Another woman said: "I've been self-centered all my life, and I've been able to get away with it. Now it has caught up with me, and I'm empty—incapable before a real task." Yes, you can get away with it for a while, but sooner or later that which is whispered in the ear is proclaimed from the housetops. A self-centered life turns out empty; everybody sees it.

A prominent man with an oversized ego, whose great powers were canceled out by his egoism, asked me to speak in public on his behalf so that the community would recognize and use him. I couldn't. For the thing that was canceling out his usefulness was himself.

> "There was a young lady of Guelph,
> Who was wholly wrapped up in herself;
> It would have been kinder,
> To try to unwind her,
> But they left her in knots on the shelf."

Life will leave you "on the shelf," will refuse to use you, if you are wrapped up in yourself. If you think of others, then others will think of you. But if you think of yourself, then others won't, except to despise you or leave you alone.

O Christ, when life is centered in Thee, it is fruitful; when it is centered in me, it is frustrated. So I shift the center, by surrender, from myself to Thee. And I do it now. Amen.

AFFIRMATION FOR THE DAY: *"He that findeth his life shall lose it: and he that loseth his life . . . shall find it."*

SELF-RENUNCIATION IN ORDER TO FIND
SELF-REALIZATION

Self-centeredness produces disease. Much of this disease is functional in the beginning, but it often passes into structural.

All life is made on the principle that it must think in terms beyond itself if it is to be healthy. This is true of the basis of life, the cell. We are told that all cells, when they begin their existence, are capable of being the whole. But they renounce being the whole and surrender themselves to be a differentiated portion of the whole, in order to serve the whole. In that renunciation they are realized. They lose their lives to find them again. But if they should refuse that renunciation to serve the whole and try to be the whole, try to make the rest serve them, what is the result? A cancer. A cancer is a group of unsurrendered cells trying to be the whole, making the rest serve them. It is a group of cells turned self-centered and selfish. The cancer eats its way to its own death and to the death of the organism upon which it feeds. It has broken the law of being, and death results.

Every organ looks to something beyond itself, to the service of the whole, and thus finds itself. If you think about your voice while speaking, your voice will work badly, will probably go back on you. Those who know say that you must project your voice about two feet beyond your eyes. May I, who have had no voice trouble through years of speaking, suggest that it must go further than two feet? You must think of getting a message to an audience and forget all about the voice. Then the voice is realized.

Just now, as I write on a train, a man sighed and said, "I'll be glad when I get back home." His wife replied, "You make yourself tired by worrying about yourself." His self was the center of his world, and it was a tired self, tired of itself.

"You know, I'm very sensitive," said a patient to Dr. William Sadler, the psychiatrist. "Yes," he replied, "you are very selfish." "But I didn't say 'selfish,'" said the woman. "I did," replied the doctor. She went away angry, but came back in ten days, chastened, and confessed it was true. That was the basis of her illness.

O Christ, Thou hast fashioned me in my inner depths for the health of Thy self-giving. I am sick when I break that law. Help me now to become well by thinking of Thee and others. Then life shall blossom and bloom where now it withers and dies. Amen.

AFFIRMATION FOR THE DAY: *Self-realization comes through self-renunciation.*

CREATING ILLNESSES

We must continue our study of how self-centered living creates illness in mind and body.

A brilliant woman, released from alcoholism, said: "Before, I was always striving to be happy and was therefore unhappy most of the time. Now I am not dwelling on anything. Then, if I was not happy, I would dwell on that, resenting it and saying, 'Poor me!' Now I am not unhappy about being unhappy." She was well.

A mother dominates her daughter. The daughter had a good year away from home teaching. The mother, to get her back home, developed an illness. The daughter came back home with nothing to do but to serve a mother who was ill because of self-centeredness, and she herself became frustrated and ill—a vicious circle. The center and spring of that household mess was the mother's self-centered illness.

Another case: A mother develops asthma to get her children back home to attend to her. They stand around her bed and fuss over her, and that is what she wants. She is willing to make herself sick to have her way and gain attention.

Whenever there is a family gathering, an aunt always comes, but always comes ill. The family fusses around her and gives her sympathy, and that is what she wants. When mealtime comes, she always eats, and eats heartily—in bed where they can attend to her.

All of these people were trying to take a strategy of life which is not-the-way. The Man who was the most healthy person that ever lived on our planet, a Man who radiated health—only to touch Him was to be well—lived beyond Himself for others, always. He was never ill, for He lived the Way. Our not-the-way ways produce disruption and disease.

Luther says: "No tree bears fruit for its own use. Everything in God's will gives itself. Only Satan and men under his influence seek their own." Note: "Everything in God's will gives itself," and thus fulfills not only the will of God but the law of its own being. The outgoing, the unselfish, are rhythmical and harmonious; the incoming, the selfish, are discordant and inharmonious. They are ill.

O Christ, I see I am made for Thy way of outgoing love. I have asked to be loved and in that asking have received nothing but ashes. Help me to be loving, outgoing, thinking of Thee and others, and then life shall catch its freshness and its flavor. I know this. Help me to do it. Amen.

AFFIRMATION FOR THE DAY: *I am off center when I am self-centered. I am on center when I am Christ-centered.*

THE THREE STAGES OF LIFE

The stages of life through which we pass to maturity: dependence, childhood; independence, adolescence; interdependence, maturity.

The first stage, dependence, the childhood stage, is a necessary stage, in which the child is the recipient of the experience of the past and takes what is passed on. That is the stage of receptivity; and Jesus said that if you do not become as a little child, become receptive, you cannot enter the Kingdom of God. The first lesson of the child is receptively to obey.

Then comes that difficult second stage, difficult for the parent and the child, the stage of independence, adolescence. The child, now growing up, wants sufficient room around himself to develop, to be a person in his own right, to express his personality, to make his own mistakes, and to suffer his own consequences or reap his own rewards. Sometimes the parents want to retain a repressive hand of authority, and the child gets rebellious. Sometimes the child runs mentally amuck and wants to obey no one but himself. Someone has defined adolescence as "a period of temporary insanity." I quoted that at a meeting, and a mother came up and said: "That was the most hopeful thing you said. I thought it was permanent!" She had been dealing with an adolescent boy—and knew!

But after independence is gained, one finds that independence isn't what it is cracked up to be. You long to be interdependent—to relate yourself helpfully to other people, to establish right relationships. This is maturity. In maturity you lose your life to find it again.

Some people never become mature. They are always adolescent, always insisting on their rights, their places, their selves at the center of the picture. They may be sixteen or sixty, but they have never grown up. They are immature. A judge who dealt with family relations in his court said that the greatest cause of divorce is "emotional adolescence"—people who never grew up emotionally. They never knew the joy of surrendering to something beyond themselves, of saving life by losing it.

O Christ, Thou hast shown me how to live. Help me to live Thy way, so that I may truly live. I would abound and not drag leaden feet to dead tasks. I would know what it is to be purged of all self-centeredness and to be free to give myself to others—a heart leisured. Amen.

AFFIRMATION FOR THE DAY: *I grow up only as I go up—to Calvary. I die to live.*

STEPS OUT OF SELF-CENTEREDNESS

We now give a ladder leading from a self-centered life to a life released from oneself:

1. *Don't act as though you have no love for yourself.* You do. You are bound to. The Way teaches that you are to love yourself: "Love thy neighbor *as thyself.*" A healthy self-love is legitimate and right. If you try to act as though you have no love of yourself, then self-love will dress itself up in other guises and come back again. Love yourself—healthily.

2. *To love yourself healthily you must lose yourself.* "To be truly selfish, you must be unselfish." For the self is realized only as it is unselfish. The happiest people are the people who deliberately take on themselves trouble for other people. Their hearts sing.

On the "Titanic" an author had a manuscript upon which he had been working for many years. When he plunged into the sea, he held to one precious thing, his manuscript. He saw a child in the water—the manuscript or the child? He dropped the manuscript and swam to the child. It was dead. He found another child, alive, held it up, tried to get into a lifeboat, but the boat was too full. He grasped a nail on the side of the lifeboat. It pierced his hand, and there he hung by that nail. But he had saved the child. The manuscript was lost, but his soul was saved. And the story of what he did is more deathless than his manuscript could ever have been. He lost himself and found himself—forever. Had he not done it, he couldn't have lived with himself.

3. *The only way to be able to live with yourself is to love others.* As you love others you will have a self you can live with. Frank Laubach, lonely and a failure, went out to Sunset Hill and talked with himself: "You have been too much concerned with yourself. You have been thinking too much of yourself. You have been working for people, not with them." He lost himself by surrender and was transformed. If you love your neighbor as you love yourself, you can get along with your neighbor, and you can get along with yourself. "Interesting people are people who are interested. Bores are people who are bored."

O Christ, I thank Thee for Thy interest in everybody and everything. Break these bonds of self-centered interest that choke my soul and my mind and my body. Give me freedom to love—widely and deeply. Amen.

AFFIRMATION FOR THE DAY: *I can have a self that is lovable only as I love something more than myself—God.*

THE SIGNIFICANCE OF THE CAUSE

We continue our ladder out of a self-centered life:

4. *Deliberately surrender yourself to the highest—the Kingdom of God.* "Seek ye first the kingdom of God, . . . and all these things shall be added unto you." "All these things"—including yourself. When you deliberately surrender yourself to the Kingdom, then the self falls into the right place—subordinate. Then it can be loved.

5. *You now take on the importance of the cause with which you are identified.* You are identified with the Cause of causes—the Kingdom—so you are really important in its importance. The best introduction I have ever received was given by a Negro minister who introduced me to a mixed audience in these words: "I will introduce the speaker by quoting from one of his books: 'The significance of Mahatma Gandhi is not in the person, but in the cause with which he is identified—the cause of India's freedom.' The significance of the speaker is not in himself, but in the cause with which he is identified—the Kingdom of God!'" The perfect introduction. One could speak after that, for supreme values were supreme. When you are identified with the Kingdom, then when you speak the Kingdom speaks, when you act the Kingdom acts.

But if you are self-centered you are unimportant, for you are identified with nothing important, no matter how importantly you may act. "He looked importantly about him, and the world passed by without him." It always passes by the self-centered.

6. *Deliberately take on yourself obligations and interests that will make you forget yourself.* A businessman retired at sixty because his family thought that he would kill himself if he kept up the pace. Three weeks after he retired he had a nervous breakdown. A rest cure gave no relief. A doctor found that in his early days the man had been interested in juvenile delinquency. He himself had narrowly escaped going to a reformatory as a delinquent. He decided to give himself to delinquents, snapped out of his nervous condition, and has never had a relapse. He forgot himself and became important in the importance of his task.

O Thou living Christ, so tremendous in Thyself and so tremendous in Thy impact upon others, because so identified with the Kingdom, help me this day to be great only in the greatness of the Kingdom and to be significant only in the Kingdom's significance. In Thy name. Amen.

AFFIRMATION FOR THE DAY: *The Kingdom of God is Significance; all else is insignificance.*

ANOTHER ROAD WITH A DEAD END—CRITICISM

Another road with a dead end, a way which is not-the-way—*the way of criticism of others.*

It is an enticing way, for criticism seems to provide satisfaction in two directions: (1) toward the one criticized, in that it is done for his good, and (2) toward one's self in the self-satisfaction of being superior to the one criticized. It ends in hurt to both. It is not-the-way. It is the way of Pharisaism. It ends in self-righteousness instead of self-realization.

The Pharisees actually believed that it was their moral duty to try to correct people and make them good by criticism. When they held aloof from men, they did it for the sake of the wrongdoer. It was salvation by isolation. The sinner must be shown that sin estranges, and the Pharisee was the agent to embody and proclaim that estrangement. He was the embodiment of the Moral Order which pronounced judgment on men. There was a truth in that attitude, a truth which made the attitude float—for a while. And then it sank. A Chinese interpreter in Malaya interrupted me when I used the word "Pharisee" with this question, "What sea was that?" I might have answered, "The Dead Sea." For the attitude of Pharisaism produced nothing but "Dead Sea fruit." Jesus warned His disciples, "Beware of the leaven of the Pharisees"—beware of letting their spirit get into you and produce the Pharisee instead of the Christian. For they are quite distinct.

A good many Christians think that the Christian task is to give the Christian criticism of life. If so, we are on the edge of a vortex of Pharisaism. This makes the Christian faith a judgment seat from which life is criticized and judged. But the center of the Christian faith is not a judgment seat but a cross—a cross where men are not merely criticized but died for. The center is not a sideline criticism but an identification with man which makes his sin its own, and in the process cries, "Father, forgive them; for they know not what they do." Redemption is by suffering with and for and instead of, rather than by a sideline pointing out of sin by criticism. Men are not converted by criticism. They are converted by a cross.

O Christ, I thank Thee that Thou didst not approach me as the divine Pharisee, else I would have hardened and revolted. Thou didst come to me silently bearing my sins, and lo, I am melted and redeemed. Help me to take Thy attitudes toward others. In Thy name. Amen.

AFFIRMATION FOR THE DAY: *"So do not criticize at all."* (I Cor. 4:5, Moffatt.)

NOT THE JUDGE OF ALL THE EARTH

Yesterday we ended by saying that the center of the Christian faith is not a judgment throne but a cross. And yet that cross becomes the most awful judgment throne imaginable. Jesus said: "Now is this world to be judged. . . . But I, when I am lifted up from the earth [on a cross], will draw all men to myself." (John 12:31-32, Moffatt.) The judgment of the world took place from a cross. And yet it was a judgment that drew men to itself. In one act Christ judges men and draws men—criticizes and converts. Nothing but divine love and divine wisdom could have put those two things together.

I think I could stand up pretty well to a judgment seat out of sheer bravado, but I cannot stand up to a cross—it melts me, sends me to my knees in broken penitence; it judges me to my depths. Nothing is more terrible than the judgment of the cross.

The business of the Christian, then, is simple. He is not to go around judging people, pointing out flaws here and picking motes there, trying to save the world by judgment and criticism. It was a great relief to me to find that I was not the judge of all the earth. In my early days I was trying to decide who was going where. Then I saw that was not my business—it was God's. I was not good enough or wise enough to judge others. When that assumed responsibility was taken from my shoulders, I felt a great sense of relief and freedom. My task was simple: Live and preach redemption, and leave judgment to God.

A group of self-appointed judges of all the earth sat with me one day. They took seriously their responsibility. Their brows were knitted; their souls were tense; they were weighted down with their responsibiltiy—they were out to convert by criticism. If it hadn't been serious, it would have been laughable. Their religion was a burden instead of a blessing; they were jittery instead of joyous. They were being slowly made into perfect Pharisees and into very poor Christians. Their Christianity was being criticized out of them.

They waved aside the command of Jesus, "Judge not, that ye be not judged" (Matt. 7:1), and the echo by Paul, "So do not criticize at all" (I Cor. 4:5, Moffatt). We are not God Almighty.

O Christ, all Thy judgments are redemptive, for there is a cross at the heart of them. All my judgments of others are hardening, producing self-defense and resistance. Help me, then, to suffer for and with men, but leave judgment to Thee. May I give out love and only love. Amen.

AFFIRMATION FOR THE DAY: *"Judge not, that you may not be judged yourselves."* (Matt. 7:1, Moffatt.)

THE DISGRUNTLED

Every Sunday morning just before he preached, a prominent minister of a great church received from another prominent minister a telegram denouncing him. It was his Christian duty to straighten out the other man! The critic's wife, dying, said to him, "My dear, I think we have been on the wrong track." In the light of a dawning eternity she saw their pettiness, their sin. The husband, telling another minister what his wife had said, rolled on the floor in an agony of remorse. But it was too late. The minister who had been·criticized was beyond criticism—he had passed on, leaving behind a man who had wasted his powers and was left with a lump of remorse in his bosom.

A disgruntled preacher didn't like the attention being given to Moody as a local committee prepared for him. "Has Moody a monopoly of the Holy Spirit?" he asked. Someone quietly replied, "No, but the Holy Spirit has a monopoly of Moody." One attitude ended with criticisms, and the other with conversions. Another man criticized Moody's method of conducting a revival but did nothing himself. Moody's reply was quiet and simple, "I like my way of doing things better than your way of not doing things."

The only valid criticism is the criticism of a better deed. Our words of criticism must become flesh in a better deed; then the criticism is vital and redemptive, instead of verbal and resistive. Jesus said that the way of trying to correct people by picking motes is not-the-way. The Way is: "Take the plank out of your own eye first"—right your own life—"and then you will see properly how to take the splinter out of your brother's eye." (Matt. 7:5, Moffatt.)

The people who influence you are not the people who are always trying to correct you by criticism, but the people who believe in you, who love you and inspire you. A Negro minister heard a certain Christian speak and in telling about it afterward said: "After hearing him speak I came away feeling I wanted to throw away something. I reached in my pocket, found some cigars, threw them away, and I've never touched them since." Come in contact with Christ, and though He says not a word, you feel you want to throw away something.

O Christ, whenever I see Thee I see myself, and in the contrast I want to throw away something—my pride, my self, my fear, my pettiness. Without a word Thy love strips me, strips me of all ugliness. Amen.

AFFIRMATION FOR THE DAY: *"Who are you to criticize the servant of Another? It is for his Master to say whether he stands or falls."* (Rom. 14:4, Moffatt.)

STEPS OUT OF CRITICAL ATTITUDES

We come now to the steps for overcoming critical attitudes.

1. *Make up your mind that the way of criticism is not-the-way, is fruitless and futile.* It defeats its own purpose. Instead of begetting reform it begets resistance. The criticized becomes critical of the criticizer. Two criticisms never made a fellowship.

2. *When tempted to criticize, switch your mind to all the good things you can find in the person.* Repeat them to yourself and to others. Someone asked about a glass on a table. One person said, "It is half empty." The other said, "It is half full." One speaker was negative; the other was positive.

3. *Negative people never have any following; people will follow only the positive, appreciative person.* If you are critical, your friends will drop away. A porcupine is an uncomfortable bedfellow. The Pharisee withdrew from the people in criticism; the people withdrew from the Pharisee and left him high and dry—mostly dry.

4. *Never repeat a criticism of others which you may have heard.* Bury it in the love of God in your heart. Repeat that criticism only to the person concerned, and when you do, "do it in love." Let your heart be a graveyard for gossip.

5. *Meet every critical thought with a barrage of prayer.* If there is a basis for the criticism, prayer will lead you to help the person.

6. *Project yourself in love; put yourself in the other person's position and see why this criticism has arisen.* When you know all, perhaps you will forgive all. Someone said, "We don't understand each other; therefore we cannot stand each other." When you understand the other person, perhaps you can stand him.

7. *Even if you don't like the other person, you can love him.* A Christian is a person who loves the person he doesn't like.

8. *Keep in close touch with Christ; the closer the touch, the less the criticism.* I find I am loving to the degree that I am in touch with Christ, and critical to the degree that I am not in touch. Remember the words: "It is the faith He inspires which has made the man thus hale and whole." (Acts 3:16, Moffatt.) Christ inspires faith in people.

O Christ, Thou didst give out love and only love. Help me to give out love and only love. I know that love will quicken new life in dead hearts, and a desire for goodness in the bad. Help me to be a faith-inspiring person. For Thou dost have faith in me. Amen.

AFFIRMATION FOR THE DAY: *The measure of my spirit of criticism is the measure of my distance from Christ.*

ANOTHER ROAD WITH A DEAD END—OVERSENSITIVITY

We have considered the person who criticizes. Now we must think of the person criticized. His reaction to criticism is important—it may make or break him.

Oversensitivity is a road with a dead end—it is not-the-way. And yet the thing that is at the base of man's progress is sensitivity. In the onward march of life the oyster did an apparently wise thing: he put his skeleton on the outside—his shell is his skeleton—and his nervous system on the inside. He would protect himself from all suffering. He fastened himself upon a rock and stayed there. Life swept on past him. He never developed. On the other hand, we men did a dangerous thing—we put our skeleton on the inside and our nervous system on the outside. That means that we are capable of great sensitivity, hence great suffering, also great development.

Someone has defined life as "sensitivity." The lowest life is sensitive only to itself. The higher in the scale of life you come, the wider range and deeper depth of sensitivity you find. The highest range of life was where Jesus said, "I was an hungred"—every man's hunger was His hunger. He was infinitely sensitized, therefore had infinite life. For life is sensitiveness. Therefore it is the secret of our rise. It can also be the secret of our downfall. If we are sensitive, we rise; if we are oversensitive, we fall. Perhaps to say "oversensitive" is wrong, for you cannot be oversensitive—you can be wrongly sensitive, sensitive toward yourself. Sensitiveness directed outwardly toward others is the secret of developing life; sensitiveness directed toward yourself is the cause of disrupted life.

Someone gave a prominent man a jack-in-the-box for Christmas. When he opened the present, the toy jumped into his face. It offended his dignity. He became resentful, lost what religion he had. In some places the Kiwanians give the new member an "Eleventh Commandment": "Don't take yourself too seriously."

O Thou universally sensitized Christ, so open to all the winds that blew, and yet so utterly un-self-conscious and hence so healthy-minded, give me that sensitiveness that makes me self-forgetful and healthy-minded. For I would grow and grow and grow—in sensitivity. In Thy name. Amen.

AFFIRMATION FOR THE DAY: *An oversensitive ego makes me what native Africans call "a smalltime man."*

ASK TWO QUESTIONS ABOUT CRITICISM

As a public man I am subjected to a great deal of criticism. People think that because I have learned to smile I must be a very thick-skinned individual. On the contrary, my skin has been very thin. I remember staying in my stateroom on my way to India the first time, lest if I walked on deck someone should say something about me. Believe it or not, I was shy! Now I've had to thicken my skin until I sometimes wonder if it isn't a rhinoceros hide. I've had to do so to survive.

When criticism comes, I ask, Is it true? If it is true, I will change. I am only a Christian in the making, and I'll let this criticism make me. Therefore I owe much to my critics; they are "the unpaid watchmen of my soul." Bless them! But suppose it isn't true. Suppose the criticism is unfair and unjust. I have determined that I would not change my attitudes toward the criticizer. I would not let his actions determine mine. As far as I know, I have no enemies. I have no enemies because I have no enmity. It is an easy way to get rid of your enemies: have no enmity and your enemies have gone! Someone remarked, "I don't believe you know when you are insulted." In either case, whether the criticism is true or untrue, you win—provided you take the Way!

Dr. Dubois, the psychiatrist, says: "In all these patients, you will observe the difficulty of adapting themselves to life as it is given to us, of supporting its vicissitudes with patience and courage. It is in this insufficiency of the intelligence, particularly in the ethical domain, that one has to recognize the primary trouble. The patient may be gifted in other ways, be very intelligent, have many admirable qualities of mind and heart; he lacks that good sort of stoicism necessary to the struggle of life."

William James divides people into the tough-minded and the tender-minded. Perhaps it would be better to put it as someone has done: Be tough-minded toward yourself and tender-minded toward others. In other words, don't let your sensitivity become ingrown. Keep it directed outward toward others, and you will grow to the degree that your sensitivity grows. For life is sensitiveness.

O Christ, pull up the adhesions of self-centered sensitivity which have been thrown around my inner life, and make me free to love widely and deeply. Help me to be free from constant self-reference. Deepen my other-reference. Amen.

AFFIRMATION FOR THE DAY: *My critics are my correctors. I use them. They make me.*

STEPS OUT OF OVERSENSITIVITY

We now come to the steps we must take in overcoming sensitivity:

1. *Remember the end of the Christian redemption—it is to save you from yourself.* "He died for all in order to have the living live no longer for themselves." (II Cor. 5:15, Moffatt.) The center of our problem is ourselves. The center of Christ's redemption is to save us from ourselves. If we are not saved from ourselves, we are not saved.

2. *As a Christian you are committed to seek first the Kingdom— not yourself.* What happens to you is of secondary concern. What happens to the Kingdom is the primary concern. Paul, in prison, could say: "My affairs have really tended to advance the gospel. . . . Over that I rejoice; yes, and over that I will rejoice." (Phil. 1:12, 18, Moffatt.)

3. *Dedicate your sensitivity to God; it is your greatest Kingdom asset.* I know a person who is as sensitive as an aeolian harp on a mountaintop. Her sensitiveness drove her to distraction. She took to liquor, to smoking, to drugs—anything to deaden this distracted sensitivity. But to no avail. Then she surrendered her sensitive self to God. Now her sensitivity is not a distracted sensitivity but a directed sensitivity. She has the makings of a saint. Paul was such a person. Before his conversion his sensitivity became disrupted, distracted, and destructive. After his surrender to Christ he was still sensitive, but now constructively so. Dedicate your sensitivity to God.

4. *Become so interested in your life cause that you do not feel life hurts.* Fighting a forest fire for ten hours in the Himalayas, only afterward did I notice a smashed toe. I could not even remember when it happened. Be so wrapped up in your task that you do not notice the personal hurts. Livingstone did just that. When his wife died in Africa, he went out to assuage his grief by seeking to heal Africa's wounds.

5. *Don't allow a toe hold of self-pity to get hold of you.* Laugh it out of court at the very threshold. If a sensitive self knows that it is going to be laughed at every time it appears, then it will lie low and behave itself. It can't stand being laughed at. It thrives on being coddled.

O Christ, Thou didst take Thy sensitive soul and didst dedicate it to heal the wounds of others. Give me power to dedicate my sensibilities to Thee. Thou hast them—they are not mine. Use them. And let me smile at the hurts that come. Thou canst use them too. Amen.

AFFIRMATION FOR THE DAY: *A self-pitying self is a pitiful self.*

THE HOUSE DIVIDED

We come now in our study to another road with a dead end—*the house of Mansoul divided against itself*.

Both psychology and the Way are crystal clear upon this point: To be at your best there must be no inner division or conflict. "If a house be divided against itself, that house cannot stand"—not merely will not stand but *"cannot,"* for it is of the nature of reality that inward division brings inward disintegration.

Psychology tells us that at the basis of every nervous breakdown is a conflict. The idea that men break down through overwork is exploded. Overwork does not break us down; it is underbeing. The nerves and the body in general can stand almost anything provided there is inner harmony and absence of conflict.

This conflict must be surrendered. Dr. Harry M. Tribout, in *The Act of Surrender in Therapeutic Process*, says: "The person has lost his tense, aggressive, conscience-ridden self which feels isolated and at odds with the world, and has become a relaxed, natural, more realistic individual who can live in the world on a live-and-let-live basis. The act of surrender is an occasion wherein the individual no longer fights life, but accepts it." He then gives an instance of a released alcoholic: "Before, if there were the Ten Commandments, I had to be at the bottom of them. I was a queen without a kingdom. Gradually a change came in me. You might say Nancy did not live in this body any more. Everything seemed so good I wanted to tell everybody. It seems silly to feel so wonderful. Something has taken place in how I feel about other people." She had surrendered her conflicts.

There is one thing and only one thing that causes breakdown in people—a conflict. And there is one thing and only one thing that makes people with a conflict well—a surrender of that conflict. The conflict must be discovered, revealed, and related to the rest of life. A woman, speaking of her husband, said, "I have been as confused as he is now. My whole mind and body have been sick in the confusion." The confusion came out of a conflict of ideas and emotions, and that confusion spread sickness to the body.

O God, perhaps I've been off the track treating symptoms instead of the disease itself, the disease which is rooted in my mind and soul. Help me this day to be willing to face the facts and go to roots. For I would be every whit whole. I ask Thee to probe me to my depths. Amen.

AFFIRMATION FOR THE DAY: *A house divided against itself cannot stand—not will not, but cannot, stand.*

THE INNER CONFLICTS

We saw yesterday that inward division and conflict is at the root of all nervous breakdowns and is at the root of many functional diseases. Mental work leaves almost no trace of fatigue, though it is prolonged over many hours, provided the mental work is not accompanied by mental conflict. There is a slight metabolism in mental work, but so slight that it is almost impossible to measure it. And yet the metabolism caused by the lifting of the arm can be measured. Thinking does not tire one. It is the conflicts in the thinking that produce the strain and consequent weariness. Harmonious thinking is creative and recreative; it leaves you with a sense of well-being, of being built up.

Conflicts may be of various kinds. Christianity has introduced into your life a new standard of life, a new set of loyalties. But the Christian life thus introduced is allowed to function only partially. Certain areas are reserved for other standards and other loyalties. A conflict is set up. Instead of becoming harmony and rhythm, religion sets up conflict. A lot of people have just enough Christianity to make them miserable. They are not free to act according to the standards of the world, nor are they free, through lack of self-surrender, to do what the Christian way demands. They have just enough religion to create irritation and not enough to create iridescence. The businessman who began an interview, "I'm trying to live the Christian life, but I'm having a hell of a time at it," added these words: "I've read little history, but I understand that history is largely a description of battles. If that is true, then I've had enough inner battles to fill ten books." All of this was unnecessary, for if he had consented to let God control his whole life, he would have had a heaven of a time of it. For hell is conflict; heaven is harmony. Someone has described heaven as "the regions where there is only life, and therefore all that is not music is silence." Hell can be described as the regions where there is only conflict, and therefore all that is not discord is the silence of death. We must learn to be unanimous or live in hell.

O Christ, Thy single-minded devotion to the Father's will brought Thee poise and peace and power. I too would know that poise and peace and power. Then help me to Thy single-mindedness. I give Thee my conflicts—take them. I am unanimous from this hour. Amen.

AFFIRMATION FOR THE DAY: *No heart is big enough for two mutually exclusive loves.*

BACKSTAGE

We must continue our study of the effects of inner conflict. A girl came up to me at the close of an address and said, "You told of that girl who said she was a civil war. That's nothing. I'm a world war." And her unhappy face showed that it was not an exaggeration. She had known God once and then had deliberately sacrificed her spiritual birthright for a mess of physical porridge—sexual freedom. She grasped at the lurid colors of the sunset, and lo, all she had was the dark.

The man in the tombs afflicted with evil spirits called out to Jesus: "Do not torture me. . . . There is a host of us." (Mark 5:7, 9, Moffatt.) Note: "me" . . . "us." He was a person but a divided person, single yet multiple. If you allow conflicting devils to come within you, then you are headed for a dwelling in the tombs, a graveyard of possibilities and peace. You will cancel yourself out. The man who said, "I'm in harmony with chaos," was describing where he lived—the hell of conflict.

Often I go behind stages which are all cluttered up. Thus many of us live with outward stages all set, but behind this frontage we are all cluttered up with conflicts and fears and resentments and frustrations. We keep up a brave front, but behind the curtains!

Peter speaks of "illicit idolatry." (I Pet. 4:3, Moffatt.) It was behind-the-scenes idolatry—out on the stage of life apparently seeking altruistic ends, but behind the scenes practicing illicit idolatry, bowing the knee at the shrine of self. Paul speaks of those who "proclaim Christ for their own ends" (Phil. 1:17, Moffatt)—Christ is being proclaimed, but in the service of the self. The pulpit is used as a stage for self-display. Of one politician it was said: "He couldn't use the Lord's Prayer without weighing its political significance—for himself." There are many politically-minded people in religious positions using religion as the frontage to backstage political maneuvering for position, place, and power. They are not bad men—they are divided.

O Christ, whose inner motives and outer acts were crystal clear and all of a piece, and whose impact upon life changed the world, give me that singleness of motive and life that I too may change my little world—for Thee. For I am now leaving a blur; I want to leave a mark—for Thee. Amen.

AFFIRMATION FOR THE DAY: *I shall take care of my motives. Then my actions will take care of themselves.*

THE DOUBLE-MINDED MAN

We continue our consideration of the divided life. It is said that the mother of the sons of Zebedee "waited on" Jesus. (Matt. 27:56, Moffatt.) And yet in the midst of that waiting on Jesus she wanted something for her two sons—seats at Jesus' right and left hand in His Kingdom. That beautiful ministry to Jesus was spoiled by ulterior motives. She wanted to use the Kingdom for purposes of display for her sons. A woman had a nervous breakdown because she wanted her daughter to marry an officer whom she could display as her son-in-law. She convinced herself that it was for the daughter's happiness, but really it was only for her own display. The conflict broke her.

It was said of Amaziah: "He did what was right in the eyes of the Eternal, but not with an undivided mind." (II Chron. 25:2, Moffatt.) Paul put the danger in these words: "I am afraid of your thoughts getting seduced from single devotion to Christ." (II Cor. 11:3, Moffatt.) There is first the division in the thought, then the division in the act; then the division is registered in the person himself.

We are held together by a single-minded devotion; otherwise we begin to fall to pieces. It was said of the prodigal son that "he squandered his means in loose living." (Luke 15:13, Moffatt.) It was so "loose" that he fell to pieces; so his living could better be called, not "loose living," but "falling-to-pieces living." Life had no inner cement.

James sums up the whole matter in these words: "A double minded man is unstable in all his ways." (Jas. 1:8.) The inner division projects itself into "all his ways" and makes the man unstable and ineffective. A sign over an express office in Shanghai said: "Your baggage taken and delivered in all directions." We are delivering ourselves in too many directions. We haven't decided to be one person, with one motive, toward one goal.

Conversion means cohesion. A man saved from alcoholism put it this way: "I feel all of a piece now, not rushing around in all directions at once." Conversion means conservation too. It means you are no longer wasting energy and time in conflicts which cancel you out.

Thou single-purposed Christ, infuse within the chaos of my divisions the singleness of Thy purpose. Let me will the highest with my very all. May all these clamoring voices be stilled at the voice of Thy command. Let me give Thee a simple and sincere devotion—with all my heart. Amen.

AFFIRMATION FOR THE DAY: *"If therefore thine eye be single, thy whole body shall be full of light."* If thine eye be double, thy whole body shall be full of darkness.

STEPS OUT OF INNER DIVISION

We now come to a ladder for getting out of inner division:

1. *Remind yourself that inner division is not natural.* You are made in the inner structure of your being for unity. Inner division is an introduction from without. It is the product of divided loyalties. It is our making. So it can be our unmaking.

2. *God has originally willed, and does now will, unity for you. You must will it too.* Not merely wish it—will it. Throw your will, your whole will, on the side of inward unification.

3. *Make up your mind what you want—really want—and then give yourself to that one thing wholeheartedly with no reservations.*

4. *Be sure that the thing to which you give yourself is capable of sustaining you totally and of fulfilling you wholly—something infinite and eternal.* Anything less than that will let you down somewhere along the line.

5. *The will of God is the only thing capable of fulfilling your life demands. Decide to make the will of God your supreme loyalty.*

6. *Surrender your divided self into His hands.* From this moment He has you—not merely this thing, that thing—He has *you*. You are no longer on your own hands; you are on God's hands. He has control.

7. *Believe that here and now the Holy Spirit takes over control of the depths of your being.* The area of the work of the Holy Spirit is largely, if not entirely, in the subconscious mind. The subconscious mind has been the place where your inner divisions lie. Now the Holy Spirit cleanses and controls that subconscious mind. You are brought, by His power, into an inner living unity.

8. *This surrender is once and for all and yet continuous.* This is a life choice, and all the lesser choices of life fit into it—not it into them. Fix the habit of surrendering the little things as they come up.

9. *Now that your "eye" is "single," "your whole body" is "full of light." Your whole being is filled with the Light.* Rejoice in that Light; walk in it; and if you "walk in the light, as he is in the light," you will have "fellowship one with another," and "the blood of Jesus Christ" will cleanse you continuously "from all sin," all division. You are free.

O Christ, I know that in Thee I am free—free from all conflicts and divisions. I am now "in Thee"; so I am free, now and forever. Help me to keep my freedom intact. Help me to bring to Thee each day my ransomed powers to be used as Thou wilt, and when and where. Amen.

AFFIRMATION FOR THE DAY: *I am surrendered to God; therefore I surrender to nothing else.*

138

GOING WHERE WE ARE PUSHED

We must look at another road with a dead end, akin to the way of inner division which we have just been studying—*the road of indecision*.

Inner division produces indecision, and indecision produces weakness of character. I am writing this in a plane over the Andes, 12,000 feet above sea level. A voice behind me just spoke the oft-repeated word in Latin America: "manana"—tomorrow. That word has produced more blight in Latin America than any other word. Jesus said to the disciples: "You have a saying, have you not, 'Four months yet, then harvest'?" (John 4:35, Moffatt.) In other words, "There is plenty of time—four months yet, then harvest." Then He added: "The fields are white for harvesting!"—now. He was correcting the attitude of being unwilling to face things now, the attitude of indecision. We have a saying that "procrastination is the thief of time." It is worse than that—it is the thief of character. For character is decision.

Others become weak through allowing circumstances to decide matters for them. A Negro caretaker, having difficulty with the men who were running a men's church supper, was asked, "If you have so much trouble with us, what do you do when the women are here?" He replied, "That's easy. I just throw my mind in neutral and go where I am pushed." That allowed him to *get along,* but he didn't *get on*. His character became spineless. A teacher asked her pupils what would happen if we didn't have backbones, and a little boy replied, "We'd be worms."

Then there are those who, after they decide, are always undeciding. They go over their decisions and undecide them by continuously worrying over whether they have made the right decision. That indecision regarding one's decision is as weakening to character as no decision. Decisions must be decisive in order to develop character.

Someone has defined prayer: "To bring the whole of life into the light of God's presence for cleansing and decision—that is prayer." It is also power. For when you are bringing things up into the light of God's presence *for decision,* then you are a positive person. And positive persons influence men and situations. They are contagious. The vacillating are not. They cancel themselves out by doubt and dilemma.

O Thou Christ of the face "set" to go to Thy cross with no wavering, give me the decisive mind and attitude. For the times demand that I take sides, take my stand upon the truth. Give me the decisive will. Amen.

AFFIRMATION FOR THE DAY: *Today with calmness of heart and faith in God I will decide my decisions and will let them stay decided.*

STEPS OUT OF INDECISION

We come now to a ladder to get out of the habit of indecision:

1. *Remember that not to decide things is worse in character result than an occasional wrong decision.* An occasional wrong decision may do harm in that particular thing, but indecision weakens the whole character.

2. *Decide things, not on the basis of a prediction of results, but on the basis of principles.* If you are always trying to foresee the results of an action, you are always in a dilemma of doubt. But if you decide on the basis of principles, leaving the results to the moral universe to take care of, then you are always on sure ground.

3. *Remember that indecision is the result of self-reference or self-centeredness.* "How will this decision affect me?" rather than, "What is the right thing to be done, regardless of what happens to me?" When you do the right thing morally, the result cannot be bad.

4. *A quick decision is just as liable to be right as a prolonged, agonized weighing.* The agonized weighing and debating unfits you for clear insight and decision.

5. *When you get into the habit of quick decision, all your powers get the habit of being summoned for quick weighing and decision.* But if your powers know that you won't decide anything, they will become lazy and sit down on you when you need them in a crisis.

6. *Bring things up in the presence of God and decide them there.* His judgments will get into yours; you will decide things together.

7. *After you have decided things, let them remain decided.* There may be occasions when you may have to reverse your decisions. Let them be the exceptions rather than the rule. Useless regret over possibly wrong decisions is more harmful than the wrong decision honestly made. Do your best and leave the rest.

8. *God can and does overrule wrong decisions honestly made.* He can bring good out of wrong honestly done. He makes things work together for good. The things themselves may not be good, but He makes them work together for good. Decide, and then further decide to let your decisions remain decided.

O Christ, I thank Thee for Thy decisiveness. Through the dark hours of Gethsemane Thou didst emerge with these words: "Rise, let us be going." Give me that same final decisiveness that will rise and be going, to meet anything, even a cross. Amen.

AFFIRMATION FOR THE DAY: *Since I am a surrendered person, I will do my best and leave the rest.*

140

THE ROAD OF UNDISCIPLINED SEX

We now consider perhaps one of the broadest roads that lead to dead ends—*the road of undisciplined sex.* Note that we do not say that sex leads to a dead end, but *undisciplined* sex.

Sex in itself is neither moral nor immoral—it is amoral. Sex in itself is natural, as much a normal part of us as eating. It is what we do with it that determines whether it will be a blessing or a curse, whether it gives us heaven or hell. In no other area of life is it more true than in sex that some people get results, others get consequences.

Take, for instance, Solomon. If any man could have made sex work his way and do his bidding, it was he. He had everything: position, wisdom, youth, opportunity, and a philosophy about sex. He puts it startlingly clear in his opening verses: "The song of all songs, which is Solomon's. Oh for a kiss from your lips!" (Song of Sol. 1:1, Moffatt.) The song of all songs—the chief emphasis in life is what? "Oh for a kiss from your lips!"—life is sex. To this Freud would agree.

Other philosophies of life could be stated thus: "The song of all songs. Oh for recognition!"—life is self. "The song of all songs. Oh, for security within the group!"—life is the herd. But if life is identified with any one of these, it will run into a dead end. Each of these—self, sex, the herd—is right in its place; but if it gets out of its place, it ends in disillusionment. It did with Solomon.

He started out by saying that "the song of all songs," the chief emphasis, is sex: "Oh for a kiss from your lips!" and ended up in cynicism and pessimism. Listen to his verdict in later years: "Nothing I coveted did I refuse myself; I denied my heart no joy. . . . Then it was all vain and futile. Nothing in this world is worth while. . . . So I hated life; for all that goes on under the sun seemed evil to me, all of it vain and futile. . . . What does he gain by all his futile toil, spending his days in gloominess, privations, deep anxieties, distress, and fits of anger? . . . Utterly vain—such is the Speaker's verdict—everything is vain!" (Eccles. 2:10, 17; 5:17; 12:8, Moffatt.) Why did life turn dead on his hands? He was seeking the wrong thing first.

O Christ, here I enter an area in which I shall need Thy special guidance, for my emotions get tangled up, and to think straight is difficult, yea impossible if Thou dost not give me the guidance I must have, the guidance I crave. For here I must not make a misstep lest it lead to disaster everywhere. For here the issues of life center. Help me. Amen.

AFFIRMATION FOR THE DAY: *Since sex is the creative part of me, I shall see to it that it is creative, not chaotic.*

THE SLOUGH OF DESPOND

We saw yesterday that Solomon, the wisest and the most foolish man that ever lived, was not upon the Way in regard to sex, for his philosophy ended in cynicism and pessimism about life. Depend upon it: any philosophy of life that leads you into a slough of despond is off the track. Life is not approving it. Examine the roots when the fruits begin to taste bitter.

Lupe Velez, a film actress, had defied the moral laws and done as she pleased. She committed suicide and left a note: "I am getting to the place where the only thing I am afraid of is life itself." She was expecting a baby, something that should have brought only joy had sex been used as the Way ordains. To her it brought only fear and dismay. Why? It was not-the-way.

Why is it that an age which has laid such supreme emphasis on sex seems to enjoy it least? Those who are freest in sex get most tied up. Hollywood is a symbol of sex freedom, and it is also a symbol of sex dissatisfaction, with its procession of divorces and remarriages. They are specialists in sex and also specialists in sex dissatisfaction. They spend most time at it and get least out of it.

A well-fed man said to a radiant friend of mine who lives abstemiously, "I couldn't live the way you live; I enjoy my meals." My friend replied with his characteristic twinkle, "I enjoy myself more between meals than you do." It is the between acts that count. What happens to you between acts determines the nature of the act. "By their fruits ye shall know them"—the outcome is the criterion.

A prominent pastor deliberately walked out of his pulpit, deserted his family, and ran away with an intelligent and respectable school-teacher, disregarding the advice of friends and the protests of conscience. "I have a right to enjoy myself," he said. Years later, after the man had died in disillusionment and misery, the woman came back to her family with the simple but revealing comment, "I don't see why I should have done it." The between acts determine the nature of the act. To pay a lifelong regret for an hour's pleasure is a fool's bargain. It is an attempt to make life work other than the Way, and it simply will not work. And anyone who tries it is not only bad—he is a fool.

O Christ, I see that Thy laws are written into our relationships with each other, that we cannot be free from them at any time, anywhere, except in one way—by obeying them. Then, and then only, are we free. Amen.

AFFIRMATION FOR THE DAY: *Sex is going to bring me heaven or hell. I choose that it bring heaven.*

THE ROAD AWAY FROM GOD

When the emotions get entangled then the mind can't think straight. You have to be straight in order to think straight.

A man who had lived a morally straight life allowed self-pity to justify his taking up with another woman because his sex relations with his wife were unsatisfactory. "I did what nine out of ten men would have done under the circumstances," he replied to my urging to keep true to his marriage bonds. He justified himself by saying that other men would have done the same. But that justification didn't make his face light up, nor did it relieve the inner conflict. He was a civil war, and his face showed it.

The words of Weatherhead are to the point: "Yes, life will work only one way, and that is Christ's way. There is a precipice at the end of every other road. Broken, bruised, disillusioned, despairing, we know then that of ourselves and in ourselves there is no hope of finding anything but the hell of a great despair. 'Outside of God there is only death.' I wish I could persuade the reader of that before he finds it out for himself."

And yet we go far afield to find justification for wrong courses. A woman, writing to a married man, suggesting that he have another woman since his own married relationships were not happy, said that Jesus must have approved such extramarital relationships since he said to the woman taken in adultery, "Neither do I condemn thee." She stopped short of the last portion, "Go, and sin no more." She was prepared to blaspheme the holy to justify the unholy.

A doctor says to his patients: "Your brain is your chauffeur. If the brain gets drunk with a wrong idea, you'll land in the ditch." The wrong idea is that you can enjoy sex against the will of God.

"O man of God, there is death in the pot!" said the guild of prophets to Elisha as he was about to eat the poisonous herbs. Elisha threw some meal into the pot, and "there was nothing wrong with the pot." There is death in every pot—self, sex, herd—until the meal of the will of God is mixed into it. Then there is nothing wrong with it; it can be eaten safely.

O Christ, Thou didst cleanse everything, especially sex. So I bring to Thee my sex life—so clamorous, so ready to go astray. Where I have failed alone, with Thee I can succeed and can succeed gloriously. Amen.

AFFIRMATION FOR THE DAY: *"Put ye on the Lord Jesus Christ, and make no provision for the flesh, to fulfil the lusts thereof."* (Rom. 13:14.)

THE STEPS TO SEX VICTORY

We come now to the steps we must take in regard to sex:

1. *Remember that sex is God-given, and hence can be God-blessed and God-used.* God has put sex within you as an integral part of your being. It cannot be escaped, cannot be side-stepped or disregarded. It is *there*. It cannot be eliminated as Hindu ascetics vainly try. I have seen them try to get rid of it in strange ways, but the attempts to get rid of it call attention to it all the more and aggravate it.

2. *There is a Way written in sex; that Way is God's Way.* Don't fight against that Way; you'll lose the war. You will win all the skirmishes, even some battles, but you'll lose the war. In the end the Way will have the last word. A friend of mine, about to walk across the street against a red light, had a hand laid on his shoulder with this word, "My friend, if you want to live long, walk with the lights." Say to yourself, "My friend, if you want to live long and happily and usefully, walk with the Way."

3. *That Way is not the way of taboos and suppressions.* We are not advocating unnatural attitudes toward sex. Someone wrote to me, "I have read your book *Victorian Living.*" We are advocating "Victorious Living," not "Victorian Living"—they are not the same. Unnatural ways tie you up; the Way frees you. The most unnatural use of sex is to suppress it and drive it down into the subconscious mind and put the lid on it and sit on it. That is self-defeating, for sex, then frustrated, works as subconscious conflict. There is a disturbed uneasiness, and one scarcely knows why. It is frustrated, suppressed sex working at hidden levels. The lid must be lifted and sex brought up and faced.

4. *Remember the clarifying words of Paul:* "I know, I am certain in the Lord Jesus, that nothing is in itself unclean." (Rom. 14:14, Moffatt.) He was "certain in the Lord Jesus." You do not have to turn to pagan ethics to find natural attitudes toward sex. When you discover and obey the Way in regard to sex, then you discover the way of harmony, of peace, of rhythm, of creative power. Rom. 1:28 (Moffatt) speaks of "a reprobate instinct"—an instinct naturally right, but turned reprobate. That is the genesis of sin—the good twisted.

O Christ, I know that Thy stamp is upon my body, Thy laws are written in me. I would know them, would obey them and live by them. For they are life. Everything else is death. I would live. Help me, then, to be as natural as Thou wast—and as victorious and radiant. Amen.

AFFIRMATION FOR THE DAY: *I am afraid of nothing Thou hast made, except that I unmake them—and myself in the process.*

FURTHER STEPS TO VICTORY

We continue our steps to victory over sex. We saw yesterday that in the Lord Jesus "nothing is in itself unclean." Jesus did not hesitate to call husband and wife "one flesh," not merely "one spirit," as the over-spiritual would have done.

5. *The God who made sex provides the power to use sex aright.* It seems, as someone has said, that sex has been overloaded, that to get the species to propagate itself the sex impulses are greater than the inherent necessities. But this is because we have misused sex and have turned its energies into destructive channels and have aggravated the impulses. If the wrongly used impulses are strong, then the rightly used impulses can be strong in the direction of construction. They can be harnessed and made to pull life into creative channels.

6. *Shun like poison the advice of pagan psychiatrists and others who advise extramarital relationships as a cure for sex problems.* The advice to "find a man," or "a woman," as the case may be, has resulted only in further frustration. It introduces into the personality a mental and spiritual conflict worse than the sex problem itself. And it cures nothing. Honest psychiatrists are increasingly agreed on that. An eminent psychiatrist says: "From the point of view of cures, the advice to go out and express your instincts is foolish. In actual experience I have never known a true neurosis cured by sex libertinism."

7. *Like everything else, sex must be surrendered to God.* It must come under His guidance and His purposes. It must not be first—God must be first. If sex climbs into the saddle and tries to guide your life, you are in for a fall. God, and not sex, is God. You must deliberately decide that you turn over to God your sex life and therefore plan to use it only under His guidance. That surrender breaks its tyranny and its power. Since God controls it, you have no longer the responsibility of controlling it. If sex is not surrendered, it is on your hands, you have to control it; but if it is surrendered, the center is changed from you to God. And the tensions are let down. That means that you are no longer tense and fighting; you are surrendered, relaxed, trusting.

O Christ, of the pure heart and mind and act, I would know Thy secret. I think I see it: everything was aligned to the will of the Father. Help me to align everything to the will of the Father. Then the victory of the Father will work in me. Amen.

AFFIRMATION FOR THE DAY: *"God led them not through the way of the land of the Philistines, although that was near."* I shall take no near ways that are not God's Way.

DON'T FIGHT; SURRENDER

We come now to the next step:

8. *Don't fight your sex passions; that aggravates and intensifies them.* To fight them puts your attention upon them. And it is a well-known law of the mind that whatever gets your attention gets you. Therefore a great many people fall into sex temptation and sex act at the very moment of fighting it. The strategy is wrong. When you no longer fight sex but surrender it to God, then your attention is drawn away from sex to God. You are looking at Him—not at it.

9. *Since, in any battle between the imagination and the will, the imagination always wins, let God be the center of your imagination.* That is not as difficult as it may sound, for "where your treasure is, there will your heart be also." Your treasure is in God, not in sex; therefore your heart or imagination is there too. Peg that down. Sex is to be used only as He approves and directs.

10. *If you are to have a God-directed sex life, then watch the place of your thinking.* Whatever you hold within the mind tends to pass straight into act. Ideas are not passive; they are active. Keep them long enough within the mind and they will inevitably pass into act, no matter what the will may say. They will brush past the will into act. Ideas held within the mind are destiny. So if you allow sex imagination to stay within the mind, you must not then expect God to save you from the sex act. But you cannot walk up to the precipice by undisciplined sex thinking and then expect God to keep you from a fall. The place to kill a cobra is in the egg. The place to kill wrong sex act is in its very incipient presentation—at the threshold. "Shut your mind," says Paul, with wrong sex thoughts on the outside. "Never think how to gratify the cravings of the flesh." (Rom. 13:14, Moffatt.) "Never *think how*," for if you *think how* you will soon *plan how*. The answer is in the first portion of the verse: "Put on the character of the Lord Jesus Christ"—put Him in at the place of your incipient thinking, and He will be in at the place of the resultant act. "Temptation knocked at my door; I asked Christ to answer, and no one was there!"

O Christ, I know that Thou art my only hope and my only redemption—from evil thought. When the evil thought presents itself, be Thou my first refuge and my last. For in Thee I am strong and free. And in Thee I am pure. I would be pure—in thought. Help me, for I'll co-operate. Amen.

AFFIRMATION FOR THE DAY: *"Let the words of my mouth, and the meditation of my heart, be acceptable in thy sight."*

MAKE SEX SERVE

We come to our next step in sex victory:

11. *Take a course before or after marriage on how to make marriage happy and useful.* Among those who take such a course only one in seventy go to divorce courts. Every church should have such a course to teach its youth regarding courtship and marriage. To those who believe in love at first sight the advice will be: Take a second look. For you'll have to look a long, long time. These courses will help you to take a second look. They will help you to see which dispositions get along with each other. The sins of omission and commission are bad, but the worst sins are those of disposition.

12. *Make sex serve you and your life ends.* Sex in the saddle will ride your life into ruin and regret. But sex harnessed to great life ends can contribute to victorious living. Its powers can be sublimated into creative activity. They need not be suppressed; they can be expressed on other levels. The creative urge in sex can be made creative in mothering the weak, the orphaned, the dispossessed. It can become the father of movements, of hope, of art, of poetry, of creative activity in every department of life. It can give birth to newborn souls. In yourself it can be sublimated into quickness of decision, into a sparkling personality. Alexis Carrel says that the people who do the greatest work in the world are strongly sexed people who subordinate sex to the ends for which they live. The creativeness of sex pours through all their activities and makes them creative activities.

This possibility fits in with this verse: "Dedicating your members [context: sex members] to God for the service of righteousness." (Rom. 6:13, Moffatt.) When sex is dedicated to God, then it becomes an asset for the service of righteousness. Sex, then, should not be looked on as an enemy to be fought but as a friend who is an ally in the service of righteousness. The strongly sexed can be strongly used. Within the marriage relationship, procreation; outside the mariage relationship, productivity. In both cases, usefulness.

The homosexual can also be spiritually useful if his homosexuality is dedicated to God. For he still loves men, but uses that love to lead men to Christ instead of himself.

O Christ, Thou pure-hearted Christ, give me Thy purity, for I want Thy power. For they are linked. I would link them in my life. Help me, then, to have the strength of ten because my heart is pure. In Thy name. Amen.

AFFIRMATION FOR THE DAY: *My creative powers are in the hands of the creative God. We go forward together.*

THE ESCAPE METHOD

We have said that there are three possible attitudes toward reality: First, escape it. Second, rebel against it. Third, co-operate with it. The first two bring disaster; the third brings development. There is only one way to live—to co-operate with reality and get its resources behind you.

One of the commonest methods of trying to escape reality is through narcotics. In taking narcotics you build up an unreal world and live in it for the time being. If you are unhappy, you seem to be happy; if you are inhibited, you seem to be free; if you are inferior, you seem to be superior—at least for the duration of the effects of the narcotics. Someone asked a man in Manchester, England, why he drank liquor, and his reply was, "It's the shortest way out of Manchester." He had no courage, no nerve to face Manchester, so he sought to escape from it by way of a bottle. But the difficulty with the method was that in the morning Manchester was back again, and back again stronger than ever, since he had less resources to meet it. Each time he tried to escape it he was less capable of meeting it, for each attempt at escape weakened his personality by the very attempt. The whole process was under "the law of decreasing returns"—he had to put more into it each time to get out the same result. The result was inevitable—decay.

The attempt to make drinking "smart" is an attempt at rationalization. It dresses up an escape mentality in the dress of social smartness, an attempt to make a personal weakness into a social strength. The attempt is to provide compensation. Elvin M. Jellinek says: "Inferiority feelings may be present in some degree in all drinker-types." Note that he does not say the "drunkard-types," for the desire to escape from reality is present both in the drinker-types and the drunkard-types. It is just a matter of degree how far you have slid down the line of escapism. Dr. Carver says: "Alcohol, by producing euphoria, blunting the critical power and progressively relaxing inhibitions, permits a flight from reality." Drinking is the refuge of the weak; it is crutches for lame ducks.

O Thou strong Christ, who didst refuse while upon Thy cross the deadening drug, and who didst match Thy inner courage against outer circumstance, give me that same courage that I too may take no subterfuge, but face bravely everything with Thee. For I want no half answers that let me down. I want to live, and to live abundantly and courageously. Amen.

AFFIRMATION FOR THE DAY: *I am a Christian—I lean on no staff that will break and pierce my hand and my heart.*

INFERIORITIES AND ALCOHOL

We saw yesterday that the taking of narcotics is the refuge of the weak. It is a sign of frustration or of inferiority feelings. Dr. Stracher says: "Alcohol is utilized as an escape from the responsibilities and burdens of mature emotional life and its decisions. It provides wish-fulfillment." It makes a man think, for the moment, that he is strong and brave, even if he is the same frustrated person who took to alcohol to escape. The story is told of a mouse that found a cask of wine dripping in the cellar. He took one taste and began to feel his muscles, took two tastes and, standing on his hind legs, faced the world and said, "Now let the cat come on!" Mice-men, under the influence of alcohol, feel capable of meeting the cats of human existence.

Dr. Wall sums it up: "Alcohol offers an escape to the blissful state of infantile omnipotence." On a Sunday morning in a hotel lobby a rather bunged-up individual, battered from a night before, stepped up to me and without preliminary words said, "I'm a big shot too." His inferiority compelled him to assert himself as "a big shot too." It was a "blissful state of infantile omnipotence."

I overheard this remark: "One of those funny things happened—you know, one of those things that happens when a gang has four or five cocktails each." Then followed a disgusting recital of beastliness. Inhibitions gone, moral barriers swept aside, lust without restraint. It is a fact that alcohol deadens the brain cells that preside over the moral faculties and awakens those that preside over the lower instincts, so that the stage is set for "one of those funny things" that happens after a few cocktails. Funny? Fiorello La Guardia said: "Don't forget that 80 per cent of the cases of the magistrates courts are alcoholics." But what of those that don't get to courts? What about the reaction in "hangovers," in decreased efficiency, in wasted powers? "But I don't get drunk," is the reply. No, but if it takes ten drinks to get you drunk, then when you take one you are one-tenth drunk. You are on the way to the other nine tenths. And more, each drink weakens you and makes the other nine easier. You are a deteriorating personality.

O living Christ, give me power to rise out of this descending spiral of weakness leading to greater weakness. Give me grace that I be not shackled with any self-imposed habit. Help me to complete self-mastery. Amen.

AFFIRMATION FOR THE DAY: *"All things are lawful for me? . . . Yes, but I am not going to let anything master me."* (I Cor. 6:12, Moffatt.)

SOME WRONG NOTIONS ABOUT ALCOHOL

You must clear out of your thinking certain illusions about alcohol:

1. *It is not a stimulant; it is a depressant.* "In the early stages there seems to be a stimulation, and many people still think of alcohol as a stimulant. This is incorrect. The apparent stimulation is interpreted by those who have studied it carefully as due to the loss of some control, to the blunting of the feeling of self-consciousness, and to the decrease in self-criticism and concern as to the opinion of others. In other words, certain of the highest and most important activities of the brain have been depressed." This statement issued by the Department of Public Instruction of Michigan is corroborated by Dr. Robert Fleming of Harvard: "Wherever the alcohol comes in contact with the tissues, it exerts its characteristic and single effect, which is that of a depressant: alcohol depresses, retards or stops, the functions of any protoplasm upon which it acts directly." Note: "It exerts its characteristic and *single* effect, which is that of a depressant." Alcohol has one effect and only one effect—it depresses. The "lift" that one apparently gets out of it is the lifting of controls, of inhibitions, of restraints.

2. *Alcohol does not increase muscular strength.* Dr. Howard W. Haggard says: "The results of such investigation showed that alcohol does not restore or increase muscular strength. Industry then adopted rules against drinking in factories. . . . The labor organizations joined a ainst drinking."

⟍   *Alcohol does not increase warmth.* "When alcohol is used before o.   g exposure to cold, it may bring more blood to the surface, where   nerves for perceiving warmth lie, and make one feel warmer, but actu. y there is a greater loss of heat as a result." A man under alcohol feels warmer for the moment, but is actually colder.

4. *Alcohol does not make you more capable—for anything.* "In both Swedish and French armies tests with expert marksmen showed that their scores were always lower after small amounts of alcohol. Many such experiments show that alcohol, even in small doses, interferes with the accurate co-ordination of the muscles of the body."

O God, I do not want to live my life amid illusions, making a present fool's paradise into an ultimate hell. I want to be real, and I want to live really. Help me to break the chain of illusions which I have foolishly bound around myself. Help me. Amen.

AFFIRMATION FOR THE DAY: *I am a follower of the Way. I have resources within. I do not need to try to take them from the end of a bottle.*

TAKE IT OR LEAVE IT ALONE?

Alcohol lowers the whole tone of the personality while seeming to heighten it. This apparent heightening is the result of a loss of control. For instance, says the Michigan Department of Public Instruction: "When the effect of alcohol on reaction time, that is, the time which elapses between stimulation and response, has been measured, it has been found in every case that this time is lengthened. Such an action becomes very important in the case of the person driving an automobile. . . . Similarly, tests of learning and memory, committing poetry, learning to associate pairs of words, all reveal a decreased effectiveness after even small doses of alcohol. . . . After alcohol the individual is less competent physically, less critical of himself, less alert in his attention, less responsive to emergencies that may arise, and may be quite unaware of any decrease in his capacity."

5. *Drinking to relieve symptoms sets up a vicious circle.* Dr. Robert Fleming says: "It is a curious and essential fact that many symptoms which originally owed their existence to the chronic action of alcohol may be temporarily relieved or forgotten by taking more alcohol. A person drinks to assuage feelings of inferiority and remorse arising out of previous alcoholic excess, or to relieve indigestion or decreased appetite due to alcoholic gastritis, or a result of the social dislocation attendant upon loss of job or wife because of drinking—then the person has been caught in an addictive vicious circle."

6. *The idea that you can take it or leave it alone may become a snare.* Dr. Robert Fleming gives these two important generalizations: "First, moderate drinking is forever impossible for the alcoholic addict; the only therapeutic objective that has any chance of success is total abstinence; secondly, *anybody,* if he drinks enough over a long enough period of time, will become addicted; it takes some people longer than others to attain addiction, but no human being can be regarded as immune."

7. *Remember that every single addict has come out of the ranks of moderate drinkers.* Every moderate drinker is a potential addict. Every drink sets the skids for the next—the toboggan slide has begun.

O Thou Christ of the complete control and of the complete freedom, give me that same control, so that I may have that freedom. For subtle bondages are taking over the control of my life. I would be bound to nothing—nothing except Thee. Amen.

AFFIRMATION FOR THE DAY: *I am a servant of Christ; I will be the slave to nothing else.*

151

SOME POSITIVE STEPS OUT OF ALCOHOLISM

Now that we have cleared our minds of certain illusions about drink we may be ready to take the next positive steps.

We take the steps outlined by Dr. Peabody, who has probably exerted more influence than anyone else on the psychotherapy of alcohol addiction. His re-education program has nine steps, to which I have added comments: (1) A mental analysis and removal of doubts and fears created in the past. Go over your past with someone skilled and trusted and get up and out any buried doubts and fears which may be at the basis of your drinking. (2) Permanent removal of tension, which is only temporarily removed by alcohol, by formal relaxation and suggestion. Say to yourself: "This tension can be and is being removed by the power of Christ, to whom I am surrendering the tension." (3) Influencing the unconscious mind by suggestion "so that it co-operates with the conscious to bring about a consistent, intelligent course of action." Suggest to yourself as you drop off to sleep at night: "I shall be well, strong, and free. Deliverance is working." (4) Control of thoughts and actions. When the thought of taking a drink presents itself, bat your eyes rapidly and pray the prayer, "O Christ, save me." The batting of the eyes breaks up the thought, and in that moment you recover your equilibrium. (5) Hygiene. Keep your body clean by a daily bath as the symbol of a soul cleanness. Take exercise morning and evening. (6) Daily routine of a self-imposed schedule to keep occupied, to train will power and efficiency, and to give the feeling of doing something about the problem. Draw up a list of the steps you should take in your particular situation. (7) Warning against unexpected pitfalls. If you fall, fall on your knees. Don't give up. (8) Provision of some means of self-expression. Take on yourself a task for others which will show that you are not a worm but a worker, not a thing but a person. (9) Realization that the same force which drove to disintegration will, under conditions of sobriety, carry beyond the level of average attainment. You can be strong where you have been weakest.

O Christ, I am affirming release and victory, not in my poor strength, but in Thy strength and willingness. I can rely on Thee when I cannot rely on myself. I have faith in Thy faith in me. I will rise to Thy faith and live by it. Amen.

AFFIRMATION FOR THE DAY: *"When a man's life pleases the Eternal, he gives him a sure footing; he may fall, but he never falls down."* (Ps. 37:23, Moffatt.)

A TRIED METHOD OF RELEASE

Take the steps which Alcoholics Anonymous, after long and fruitful testing of the ways of release, has outlined: "(1) We admitted we were powerless over alcohol—that our lives had become unmanageable. (2) We came to believe that a Power greater than ourselves could restore us to sanity. (3) We made a decision to turn our wills and our lives over to the care of God *as we understood Him.* (4) We made a searching and fearless moral inventory of ourselves. (5) We admitted to God, to ourselves, and to another human being the exact nature of our wrongs. (6) We were entirely ready to have God remove all defects of character. (7) We humbly asked Him to remove our shortcomings. (8) We made a list of all persons we had harmed and became willing to make amends to them all. (9) We made direct amends to such people wherever possible, except where to do so would injure them or others. (10) We continued to take personal inventory and when we were wrong promptly admitted it. (11) We sought through prayer and meditation to improve our conscious contact with God *as we understood Him,* praying only for knowledge of His will for us and the power to carry out that will. (12) Having had a spiritual experience as a result of these steps, we tried to carry this message to alcoholics and to practice these principles.

Captain Conger was an alcoholic, beaten, had no grip on his job, but he has been saved from even the desire for alcohol for eight years. During a period of great struggle the Inner Voice said: "Look into that cupboard at those bottles." As he looked at them, his tensions were let down: "The alcohol in those bottles had no more effect upon me than if it had been ink or glue. I was released."

Dr. Charles Mayo says: "You can get along with a wooden leg, but you can't get along with a wooden head. It is the brain that counts, but in order that your brain may be kept clear you must keep your body fit and well. This cannot be done if one drinks liquor." Thomas A. Edison adds: "I am a total abstainer from alcoholic liquors. I have a better use for my head."

> "I do not think   For when I drink
> That I should drink,   I do not think."

O God, I'm committed, soul and body, for time and eternity—committed to freedom from every enslaving habit and desire. And now help me to reach out a helping hand to some struggler. Amen.

AFFIRMATION FOR THE DAY: *"I have soothed and stilled my soul . . . ; my soul is like a weanèd child."* (Ps. 131:2, Moffatt.)

A GROWING ADDICTION

We must spend this day on the growing addiction to the cigarette habit. That it is an addiction no one can doubt. Look at a long line of people, in wartime Hammond, Indiana, queued up at ten o'clock in the morning waiting to get a pack of cigarettes at three o'clock in the afternoon. Five hours of standing in line through the most important part of the day, including the lunch hour! Something has gripped them, enslaved them. They are not free people; they're victims.

On an airplane coming across the Caribbean, I watched a woman with parched, yellow skin, incessantly puffing on a cigarette. The doctor inspecting the passengers pulled her out of the line for further inspection. Medical science is increasingly pulling cigarette addicts out of line and warning them of deterioration. Dr. Raymond Pearl, the medical statistician, says: "Between the ages of thirty and forty-five, the mortality rate is double among the heavy smokers (that is, ten or more cigarettes a day) over the nonsmokers." You cut your life expectancy in half between those ages. Dr. Bertha Van Hoosen, says: "The prospective mother who smokes can expect overstimulation of the nervous system, unnecessary rise in blood pressure, lessened desire for food, disturbed and decreased action of the lungs, injury to the kidney substance, and this culminates in the interference in the growth and development of the child."

Two letters, one from a World War I veteran: "I never smoked until I went into training. . . . Now I have to smoke all the time, even during the night. It is making me nervous, and I cannot concentrate on what I am doing. I am only about fifty per cent efficient in business. I have tried in vain to stop smoking. Can you help me?" Another from a World War II veteran: "I have been ordered by the doctor to quit smoking, but to date have been unsuccessful. As it is ruining my health and nerves, I would like to quit for the sake of my wife and two children, as well as for the sake of my health."

To smoke because it's "smart" is a rationalization of a weakness. It is not smart to smoke; it is weak. The cigarette is a minus sign.

O Christ, who didst come to make men free, make me free. I surrender into Thy hands this habit. I cannot break it, but I am willing for Thee to break it. I rise up strong in Thy strength to throw off this foreign yoke. Amen.

AFFIRMATION FOR THE DAY: *"Revere the Eternal and draw back from sin: that will mean health for your body and fresh life to your frame."* (Prov. 3:7-8, Moffatt.)

A ROAD WITH A DEAD END—UNDEDICATED MONEY

We must pause to consider a road *that perhaps more than any other leads to self-atrophy—the road of undedicated money.*

Jesus mentioned two things that choked the growing wheat and made it unfruitful: "As for him who is sown 'among thorns,' that is the man who listens to the word, but the worry of the world and the delight of being rich choke the word; so it proves unfruitful." (Matt. 13:22, Moffatt.) Here "worry" and "the delight of being rich" are classed as the two outstanding enemies of growth.

Now note that Jesus didn't say that "riches" was Enemy No. 1, but "the delight of being rich," that is, riches as an end in itself. The "delight" was in the thing itself rather than in what it could do. It was undedicated wealth. Had the "delight" been in what could be done through the riches to help others, it would have saved it from decay. But the riches became an end in itself, hence became Mammon, became God. And Jesus said: "You cannot serve both God and Mammon." (Matt. 6:24, Moffatt.) You can serve God with mammon, but you cannot serve God and Mammon. Note that "Mammon" becomes "mammon" when it is a servant of the will of God, but when it is an end in itself, then it is "Mammon," a god—a false god that determines destiny, a destiny that becomes decay.

"Is not the life more than meat?" asks Jesus. No, says the biochemist; life is food—you are what you eat. Life = food, says the biochemist; life = emotion, says the sensualist; life = money, says the materialist; life = Christ, says the Christian. To the Christian, Christ is supreme. He controls the food, the emotions, the money. They are servants of a divine purpose, hence purified and redeemed. Without that purpose the purification turns into putrefaction. There is a Moslem quotation from Jesus: "Whoever craves wealth is like a man who drinks sea water; the more he drinks the more he increases his thirst, and he ceases not to drink until he perishes."

Jeremiah speaks of "idols" that "break down when the test arrives." (Jer. 10:15, Moffatt.) The idols that break down when the test arrives are these: egocentricity, power, fame, and money.

O Christ, who didst enrich the world without riches, help me to take my riches—small or great—and make them the instrument of Thy purposes. Thy purposes purify. I would have my wealth dedicated to the purpose of Thy Kingdom. In Jesus' name. Amen.

AFFIRMATION FOR THE DAY: *"A grasping nature is its own undoing."* (Prov. 15:27, Moffatt.)

A STRAIGHT, SAFE COURSE FOR OUR GOODS?

Two attitudes with two results: "Woe to the careless citizens, . . . dining off fresh lamb and fatted veal, crooning to the music of the lute, composing airs like David himself, lapping wine by the bowlful . . . —with never a single thought for the bleeding wounds of the nation." (Amos 6:1, 4-6, Moffatt.) Result? "So now . . . that dissolute crew shall disappear." (Vs. 7.) Men who care nothing for the bleeding wounds of a nation shall decay and "disappear."

But here is another picture: "Then I proclaimed a fast . . . , that we might humble ourselves before our God and obtain from him a straight, safe course for ourselves, our children, and our goods." (Ezra 8:21, Moffatt.) Result? He built the temple—a lasting memorial.

Are we asking for "a straight, safe course for our goods"? That is doubtful. Eighty-five per cent of the income of the United States is spent for living; 12 per cent is saved or put in various investments; 3 per cent goes to schools, hospitals, and churches—the culture, the curative, and the spiritual. Only 3 per cent into them! And the point is that if you didn't spend that 3 per cent, what about the 97 per cent? It wouldn't be worth anything; it would go to pieces.

"One gives away, and still he grows the richer: another keeps what he should give, and is the poorer. . . . Life thrives like a tree on generosity, but grasping greed is death to men." (Prov. 11:24, 30, Moffatt.) If we do not take God into partnership with our material life, then a curse will rest upon our riches. "But what he won he cannot keep, the harvest of his gain he cannot reap." (Job 15:29, Moffatt.) He cannot take it with him when he leaves this life. "There are no pockets in a shroud." Only that which is laid up in unbreakable banks, banks of character, will remain. Said an oilman to a missionary as both were evacuated from Malaya with the coming of the Japanese: "My life work has gone into oil wells, which I had to blow up; your life has gone into people, into their character and development. My life work has gone; yours will remain. I've failed; you've succeeded." The only permanent investment is an investment in people.

O Christ of the productive way of life, make me productive. I want to make my life count for the utmost. To this end take what I have accumulated and touch it into creative love. I turn it over to Thee to be used under Thy guidance and direction. It is no longer mine—it is Thine. We work it out together. Amen.

AFFIRMATION FOR THE DAY: *"Man thinks out many a plan, but 'tis the Eternal's purpose that prevails."* (Prov. 19:21, Moffatt.)

SOME STEPS TO FREEDOM

How can we relate life to the material, so that the material becomes an investment instead of an incubus? The material can be a weight or it can be wings; it can make us sigh or make us sing. A prosperous farmer gave three dollars a year to the church for many years. As he was signing the usual three-dollar check, the pastor remarked very quietly: "I wonder why God doesn't paralyze your arm as you sign that. You ought to give five hundred dollars now as a thank offering." Those blunt words struck straight home. The two men knelt in the barnyard, and the farmer surrendered himself and his money to God. He told his wife what had happened, and she replied, "I've been praying for that for years." He gave three five-hundred-dollar gifts that year. His whole soul was loosed. He was a free man, and happy.

In order to bring the material relationships of life under the control of the Way, perhaps you will decide to take the following steps:

1. *I have decided that God is owner.* "The earth is the Lord's, and the fulness thereof." I have been acting as if I were owner, in other words, as if I were God. But I'm not God; God is God. I abdicate; He takes the throne. God is owner, and I am ower. "The government shall be upon his shoulder"—not mine. I obey. That relationship is pegged down. That is our starting point from which we work out.

2. *I will set aside one tenth of my income as acknowledgment of His ownership.* This does not discharge my total obligation in the matter, but it does set aside a portion as a symbol, a symbol of God's total ownership. Just as one pays rent as acknowledgment of the ownership of the owner, so I pay one tenth as acknowledgment of God's ownership over the remaining nine tenths.

3. *The remaining nine tenths still belong to God and must be used under His guidance.* I believe that His will is always my highest interest, that He is not out looking for a chance to impoverish me, but seeking to enrich me. So I look for His guidance, not grudgingly but gladly.

O God, my gracious Father, Thou who didst make me to live in a body, and who dost will that soul and body may accord well, help me to get my material relations straight, so that I shall make the material not an enemy to be fought but an ally to be sought. Help me to find Thee in my material relationships. In Jesus' name. Amen.

AFFIRMATION FOR THE DAY: *"For the authorities were senseless, seeking no guidance from the Eternal; so they had no success, and all their folk are scattered."* (Jer. 10:21, Moffatt.)

SHALL I TITHE MY INCOME?

4. *I see that the principle upon which God guides me concerning the nine tenths is this: I have a right and duty to use as much of the material as will make me more physically, mentally, and spiritually fit for the purposes of the Kingdom of God.* Need is the criterion. Here I will have to be sensitized, sensitized by His Spirit. Here my conscience will have to be trained to distinguish between need and not need. Yesterday I was on the lake, and I pulled in my oars and let my boat drift. As I looked at the surrounding water, I could see no drift at all. Only as I lifted my eyes to the shore line and watched a fixed point could I see how much I was drifting. In this matter, if I look around me, watch what others are doing, catch their unguided ways, I shall have no sense of drift. Only as I fix my eyes on Christ and watch for His approval shall I know whether I am within need or drifting beyond it.

I know it is possible to pay the tribute of one tenth as a mental license to do what I choose with the nine tenths, to buy God off as it were. In Belo-Horizonte, Brazil, casino grounds were established by the municipality outside the city, where gambling was the chief attraction. At the very center of this one-time Brazilian Monte Carlo is a church put up by the municipality. The church is dedicated to Francis of Assisi, and the central mural depicts him renouncing the world. The mental compensation of the municipality was this: Having paid tribute to the renunciation of the world, as depicted in Francis, we are now free to embrace the world! It did not seem to me just chance that the futuristic spire outside the church had its apex stuck in the ground with its base above! The whole thing was topsyturvy, and always will be, when religion is dragged in to give an air of moral respectability to our vices. I see that. And I must not consider my giving one tenth as a license to be free to do as I like with the nine tenths. My needs must be honest needs, honestly arrived at in the light of other people's needs. For all beyond my actual needs belongs to the needs of others. If I take from their needs, I am guilty of theft.

O Christ, I am coming under the sway of Thy creative Spirit. Thou art sensitizing my inmost being. May there be Thy gentle block when I am about to go beyond my needs. For I know Thy blocks are really Thy blessings. Thou dost take away on one level only to give abundantly on a higher level. So I trust Thee completely. Amen.

AFFIRMATION FOR THE DAY: *My money can be paralyzing or productive. I choose it shall be productive.*

I AM MASTER; THE MATERIAL IS THE SERVANT

5. *Until society takes over responsibility for sickness and old age and makes adequate provision for them, I have a right and a duty to make reasonable provision for both sickness and old age.* For if I do not, then it will fall on charity or on my relatives. I believe that it is the responsibility of society to look after me when I am ill and incapacitated for work, provided I contribute to society to the extent of my ability when I am well and able to contribute. These two principles are inherent in the Christian Scriptures: "To each according to his needs" (compare Acts 2:45), and "From each according to his abilities" (compare II Thess. 3:10). And if one doesn't give to society according to his abilities, he should not get according to his needs. Chrysostom, the church father, says: "The wealth is common to thee and to thy fellow servants, just as the sun is common, the earth, the air, and the rest. To grow rich without injustice is impossible." The only way to take "injustice" out of riches is by dedicating it to the needs of others, keeping only that which is necessary for our own needs.

6. *As I have taken the above steps, I can now live, not on the unblest material, but on the blest.* What I shall keep for myself will have the touch of God's blessing upon it; it will go further and will enrich in the going. Then the material will become the sacramental. Then it will become something to rejoice in instead of something to be afraid of. Besides, I remember this promise: "God is able to bless you with ample means, so that you may always have quite enough for any emergency of your own and ample besides for any kind act to others." (II Cor. 9:8, Moffatt.)

7. *I am no longer afraid of the material. I am master; the material is the servant.* The material is my servant because I am now the servant of Christ. As I belong to Him, so now all things belong to me. I do not belong to them; they belong to me, for I belong to Christ. I am free! A big landowner showed a poet his acres, "Everything you can see belongs to me." "Oh, no," said the poet; "everything I can see belongs to me." It did!

O Christ, I feel emancipation going through my blood. I am delivered from the bondage of the material. It is now my servant. I shall use it in the purposes of Thy Kingdom, shall send it winging its way to heal and bless and create and redeem. Like Mary, Thy mother, each material thing I have can say, "I am here to serve the Lord." Amen.

AFFIRMATION FOR THE DAY: *"But when he attained power, he became haughty, and that ruined him."* (II Chron. 26:16, Moffatt.)

SOME ILLUSTRATIONS OF DEFEAT—AND VICTORY

This matter of our relationship to material wealth is so important that we must continue our meditation upon it.

A rich man, with a streak of meanness, left a very large sum of money for a monument to himself. The shaft was struck by lightning three or four times. Now just a broken shaft is there. Whether God knocked down that shaft with lightning is a question, but if God hadn't done it man would have. For every time anyone who knew the man looked at the monument he would have shattered it by his estimate. That man saved his life and lost it.

Into the section of the country where I am writing two men came. One was a doctor, ill with tuberculosis. But doctors were needed so desperately that he was carried to bedsides to attend people. The doctor became so interested in the people of the Adirondacks that he lived on—and how! A great tuberculosis sanitarium and the Trudeau Foundation came into being. The doctor's name is a benediction. Another man came into this country, made money and lots of it. To add a cubit to his stature he left money for a college to be named after himself. It was never built; lawyers are still squabbling over it. His name has a bad odor. The wealth of Dr. Trudeau is healing, creative wealth.

I sat by the bedside of a beautiful soul, A. A. Hyde, of Wichita. Years ago he gave a subscription to a public project which business reverses made impossible to pay. He might have taken the easy way out. He didn't. He paid his pledge and went "broke" in doing so. Forced to find a way to support his family, he hit upon the idea of a healing salve. He made a compact with God and himself to give a certain large percentage of all his future profits to the extension of Christianity through foreign missions. Today this salve has the largest sale in foreign lands of any American salve. The missionaries used it and introduced it. It spread. The touch of a great dedication was upon it. Hyde and his money live—they are immortal.

O Christ, I know that Thou canst touch me and my earnings and change them from death to life. I offer to Thee all I am and all I earn. Use me and it for the enriching of an impoverished world. Thou hast me. Help me to live under Thy guidance and to be a steward of all Thy entrustments to me. For I would live and live fully. Amen.

AFFIRMATION FOR THE DAY: *"There should be no poor among you . . . , provided that you are attentive to the voice of the Eternal your God."* (Deut. 15:4, Moffatt.)

EMPTY FUTILITY AMID PLENTY

There are two drives in human nature—the self-regarding and the other-regarding. If the self-regarding drive is in the saddle, you are ridden to empty futility, no matter how much you accumulate. One of the richest men of this century arose in a meeting and said: "I've given so much time and attention to the thing I really care little about, namely, money, and so little time to the things I really care about, namely, spiritual things, that I wonder if I've spent my life wisely." Many men "spend the first half of their lives expending health to gain wealth and the second half of their lives expending wealth to gain health."

An American doctor, an expert in hospital construction, was asked by a committee from Montevideo, Uruguay, how much he would charge to plan a hospital for them. He set his fee at $100,000. The committee saw him again, told him of the needs of their great little republic, asked him if he would do it as a contribution to friendship—for nothing. He said he would. He put up one of the most wonderful hospitals in the world and saved millions of dollars for them on their plans. He is loved by Uruguayans, who take their visitors, as they took me, to see the monument to the man. The self-regarding said: $100,000 is the price! The other-regarding said: I'll do it for love! Had the doctor responded to the first motive, we would have forgotten him; but he responded to the second, and we can't forget him.

Twenty years ago Russia was starving. The Middle West had a surplus of wheat. They gave it to the Russians, railroads carried it free, grain elevators handled it for nothing, and ships carried it gratis. It saved the farmers—their prices stayed up—and it saved the Russians. And it left a deposit of good will in the souls of both peoples.

A porter groaned as he picked up my heavy bags, "You carry your gold around with you, don't you?" I could say that I did! My "gold" was within—peace, harmony, God! Obeying God brings *that!*

A proverb puts it thus: "That which I spent I had; that which I kept I lost; that which I gave I have."

O Christ, who didst say, "I am the light of the world," we know that Thou art still the Light of the world, especially the Light of the world of things. Help me today to take the Way, and then I shall walk in the Light. Amen.

AFFIRMATION FOR THE DAY: *"One gives away, and still he grows the richer: another keeps what he should give, and is the poorer."* (Prov. 11:24, Moffatt.)

IN WHICH WE CONSIDER BOREDOM

In a very stimulating book, *How Never to Be Tired,* Marie Beynon Ray lists boredom as Enemy No. 1. She puts fear Enemy No. 2. Considering her particular emphasis on tiredness, it is quite probable that boredom does create more tiredness than anything else. But I have deliberately put boredom toward the last of the enemies of the personality, for it seems to me to be as much a result as it is a cause. We are bored because we feel that our sums are not adding up, that we are not on the Way. Boredom, therefore, is a result of the sense of futile living. It is true that the result turns into a cause. We are bored; therefore we are tired. The boredom produces the tiredness. But the boredom itself is produced by a feeling of out-of-gearness.

This is seen in the words of Edmund Gosse: "You speak of the peace which the years bring. But they have brought no peace for me. Life is pleasant, but I am not without terror at the idea of this sensual sufficiency coming to an end. I have no idea how the spiritual world would look to me, for I haven't glanced at it since I was a child." He was bored and even terrified at life because he didn't know how to live it. He knew instinctively he wasn't on the Way. When one is on the Way, then boredom drops off like a dead leaf. A living interest comes back into life that takes the dullness out of living.

But boredom, though a by-product, can be, and is, devastating. "Boredom with housework," says Marie Beynon Ray, "has made women blind, boredom with a husband has made them cripples, boredom with a mother-in-law has paralyzed them." Many of these people think they are physically ill—and they are! But the cause is not physical but mental and spiritual. This is confirmed by another: "Over fifty per cent of all ills are of a mental nature. More than half the hospital load of the nation is mental cases—and a vast number of these sick people believe their trouble is physical." Boredom slows down the machinery of life; interest makes it run again. The Christian cannot be bored, for he is under "the stimulus of Christ." A living interest works within him.

O Thou living Christ, who didst walk the earth well amid the sick, strong amid the weak, radiant amid the dull, and alert amid the tired, give me of Thy fountain of life. Show me how to live so that I too shall never be tired, never exhausted. For I shall be tapping Thy resources continuously. Amen.

AFFIRMATION FOR THE DAY: *"Drink from your own cistern, drink fresh water out of your own well."* (Prov. 5:15, Moffatt.)

A LONG REST?

We continue our study of boredom by summing up the conclusions of Marie Beynon Ray:

"That mental work cannot cause fatigue.

"That the fatigue we feel may be actual fatigue, an incapacity to do further work; or a feeling of fatigue, which is not actually an incapacity to work nor even a measure of actual fatigue—but in either case it was not brought on by mental work.

"That there is no such animal known to science as a man brought to the point of exhaustion or breakdown by mental work.

"That it is boredom, not work, which is the cause of much fatigue—boredom and other psychological factors.

"That the chronic fatigue of the sedentary worker is 100 per cent due to psychological factors.

"That fatigue that is not wiped out by the normal period of rest is pathological, and that no amount of rest will ever cure this kind of fatigue.

"That the glands do influence energy, but that most people are normal in this respect and need only to apply the proper emotional spurs to stimulate glandular energy."

One of the things psychology and medicine are emphasizing is that no organ works well if attention is paid to it. You can upset the rhythm of an organ by thinking about it. The organ, if it thinks, is not thinking about itself—it is thinking about the whole. It loses its life and finds it. The same is true with the total person. He must think about something beyond himself if he is to be rhythmical and happy and without boredom. The self-centered make themselves tired.

If you get your eyes off yourself and focus them on others, fatigue will drop away. Someone has said: "When we look within we are depressed, when we look around we are impressed, when we look at Jesus we are blessed." Look at Him and others, instead of at yourself.

O God, Thou fountain of life, Thou spring of all energy, I come to Thee with exhausted nerves—exhausted through conflict and fear and boredom. I bring them to Thee. Bathe them in the fountain of Thy calm and peace. Give me a new sense that I live with a purpose, a purpose to do Thy will, and that in Thy will are no boredoms. In Jesus' name. Amen.

AFFIRMATION FOR THE DAY: *"That our God may brighten our eyes and grant us sustenance in the days of our bondage."* (Ezra 9:8, Moffatt.)

STEPS OUT OF BOREDOM

You are probably bored with my talking about boredom without talking of how to get release from boredom! Here are the steps:

1. *Ask this question of yourself and ask it honestly*: *In a world sparkling with novelty and opportunity, why am I bored?* You may answer, "It's because of the dull, stupid people I'm compelled to meet." Or, "It's because of the monotony of my work." Or, "It's because life has let me down; I'm frustrated." All of these answers are outside of *you*. In nine cases out of ten you are on the wrong trail. You are like a fever-tossed man who turns to this side of the bed and then that, hoping vainly for a cool spot, when the fever is within him. If "the kingdom of God is within you," the kingdom of boredom is also within you. Africans have a custom of holding a berry in their mouths so that everything they eat tastes like the berry. You are probably holding the berry of a wrong attitude toward life in your mouth, so that everything you eat tastes bitter or insipid.

2. *You will probably find one of two causes for your boredom: a sense of wrong moral and spiritual attitudes or a sense of frustration in your life plan or work.* The probabilities are that the first is the cause. You are your own hell or your own heaven.

3. *You will probably find that you are thinking of yourself first.* When you are not at the center of things, you are bored and unhappy. You are out of harmony with the great Design, and therefore you are up against it. Dr. Ira S. Wile says: "In one sense, fatigue is a consciousness of time. When we are doing something we don't like to do, we watch the clock. . . . Or fatigue [is] due to a lack of inner harmony, to internal strivings, or even fatigue from sheer habit. All these are forms of neurotic fatigue. Normality is unawareness of the functioning of body and mind. Once we pay attention to the organs, we soon acquire the habit of self-reference. Nothing is more tiring. To enjoy complete freedom from fatigue we must get away from all consciousness of occupation, of effort, time, self."

O Christ, I see that I am bored with myself because I have to live with a wrong self. I need to be set at rights—within. For futility dogs my steps; my futility is ever with me, in me. And now I want to be cleaned out.

"So wash me then without, within,
And cleanse with fire if that must be." Amen.

AFFIRMATION FOR THE DAY: *"Look to him, and you shall beam with joy, you shall never be abashed."* (Ps. 34:5, Moffatt.)

FURTHER STEPS TO VICTORY

We come now to the next step in release from boredom:

4. *The remedy for this attitude of self-reference is self-surrender.* You have been on your own hands, and you are tired of yourself. You deliberately turn over your bored self to Christ.

5. *Since you are fully surrendered to God, now a purpose runs through all you do.* For you are no longer hanging at loose ends; you are going somewhere. You are working out a pattern, His pattern. The commonplace is no longer the commonplace; it too has the golden thread of His purpose running through it. You are living a God-purposed and a God-guided life.

6. *You are no longer dealing with the little and insignificant, for you can show a spirit in everything you do.* You see that it is not so much what you do as how you do it that really matters. Every little thing you do you will do greatly. When you say, "Good morning," the smile of morning will be in your words. When you start your work, you will put harmony into monotony and tune your work to "the music of the spheres." You will live in time and eternity simultaneously, and eternity will make time significant. Every common bush will be afire with God.

7. *You will do everything you do "for the love of God."* You have been doing everything for the love of self. Now you do everything for the love of God. It is said, "On that day the very bells on the horses shall be inscribed with 'Sacred to the Eternal'; . . . indeed, every pot in Jerusalem and in Judah shall be sacred to the Lord of hosts." (Zech. 14:20-21, Moffatt.) The pots and pans of daily use become temple vessels when they are handled "for the love of God." I saw in a chapel in London, Ontario, a carpenter's bench which had been made deliberately into a Communion table. That is as it should be, for every act of the consecrated carpenter working "for the love of God" becomes a reflection of the Carpenter. The Quakers say that all breaking of bread should be a partaking of the Body.

O Christ, I see I am to make dull hours into dancing hours, for Thou art to be with me "always and in all ways." I am no longer a clod, for a divinity stirs my clod; a divine purpose takes all the cells of my being and makes them into "an organism of the Spirit." I am indwelt, inspired, intrigued—with everything. I thank Thee. Amen.

AFFIRMATION FOR THE DAY: *"For life's own fountain is within thy presence, and in thy smile we have the light of life."* (Ps. 36:9, Moffatt.)

RETIRE TO NEW RESPONSIBILITIES

8. *Deliberately take up another task if your present one tires you.*
I mean in addition to it. I know you throw up your hands at that, but
I mean it. "We are tired not by what we do," says Marie Beynon Ray,
"but by what we don't do, by all the neglected interests and excite-
ments out in the world which we are missing. Relaxation, not rest, is
what is needed. And relaxation means constructive activity. The cure
of fatigue is increased activity, either in the form of work or play."

Edgar Guest retired at fifty. In no time he was flat on his back,
calling for doctors, nurses, and medicine. Not a single doctor could
find anything wrong with him, and that made him wild, for he was
a very sick man. Finally his wife told him what was wrong. He was
dying—dying of boredom—and he'd better get out of bed under his
own power before they had to call the undertaker. Guest seemed delighted at this news and got up at once and set to work. He's been
at it and in the best of health ever since.

And don't try the "rest cure." Places where people do nothing but
rest and stuff themselves with food are going out of business. Why?
Because nine out of ten people who come to these places do not need
rest; they need to be delivered from themselves. "I have never seen
a single chronic case of nervous disorder cured by such means," says
Dr. Abraham Brill. Not rest but rescue is needed. These people need
to be rescued from self-attention.

A man retired at fifty-five. He thought he would live on his pension.
Instead, he lived on aches and pains and grouches. His whole mental
occupation was to justify his inactivity—was he not ill; how could he
work? Then he began to work a day or so at a time. Now he is working
full time. "He's a different man," everybody says. He is. Work did it.
Responsibility rested him, because it brought him into harmony with
himself. Dr. C. F. J. Richards said: "I am sixty-eight. I still work
nine or ten hours a day, and I have never in my life been tired. I
used to run a rest cure, and I saw that all these people had one thing
in common—a lack of self-command. It was their minds, not their
bodies, that were sick." She put people to work—and cured them!

O Christ, who didst say, "My Father worketh hitherto, and I work,"
give me Thy passion for creative activity. I do not want to be fussily busy,
but to be calmly creative. For I am made by work and for work. But with
Thee work will be play and all life a vacation. I thank Thee. Amen.

AFFIRMATION FOR THE DAY: *"All the stimulus of Christ."* (Phil. 2:1,
Moffatt.)

PERFECTIONISM OR NOTHING

We come now to another road with a dead end—perfectionism or nothing. There is a brand-new sin in the catalogue of sins—perfectionism.

I am a little afraid of brand-new sins. Anything that is brand new may be a new rationalization. The recent condemnation of "perfectionism" is a cloak to cover compromises. Anyone who wants something radically different from what *is*, is branded a "perfectionist." We are told we must give ourselves to "the discipline of the attainable," meaning we must pare down to a dull average.

When Christians adopt that attitude, they are accepting a defeatist, worldly attitude. For to the Christian the attainable is the obtainable —infinite resources are at his disposal. His spirit is: "The miraculous we can do at once, the impossible takes a little longer." Jesus said, "Be ye therefore perfect, even as your Father which is in heaven is perfect." Our possibility of perfection is based on God's actual perfection. We yield to processes toward perfection. So we give ourselves to "the discipline of the obtainable." "For with God nothing is ever impossible," came the assurance to Mary. "I am here to serve the Lord. Let it be as you have said," she replied. (Luke 1:37, 38, Moffatt.) And she gave the world a Redeemer. I am not afraid of perfection. I'm afraid of accommodation to imperfection.

But having said this, I must now recognize that there is some truth in this charge against "perfectionism." And the truth is this: Many people, because they can't do everything, do nothing; because they can't be perfect, they withdraw. That is a real danger. And many walk into it, often unconsciously. And often it is a sin of very good people. They are so conscientious that, unless they can be perfect in all they do, they won't do anything. Their consciences attuned to the highest will not approve anything less than the highest. Hence they withdraw into troubled inactivity. I made this mistake in regard to language. I set such high standards for myself in English that, when I failed to reach the same in another language I withdrew into the use of interpreters—accepted crutches which lamed me.

O God, Thou who dost love us in spite of our imperfections and sins, help me to love myself in spite of my imperfections and sins. And since Thou dost believe in me in spite of all, help me to believe in myself and others—in spite of all. For I am under Thy redemption. Amen.

AFFIRMATION FOR THE DAY: *"The erring will gain insight, and murmurers will accept the truth."* (Isa. 29:24, Moffatt.)

167

STEPS TO VICTORY OVER PERFECTIONISM

Here are the steps that will bring release from perfectionism:

1. *Fix it in your mind that there is real danger in this attitude.* I know a person with great possibilities who is today a helpless neurotic, unwilling to do little things at hand because of an inability to do the great things.

2. *Make up your mind that you are to be perfect, but perfect only in love, never in the expression of that love.* When Jesus said, "Be ye therefore perfect," the word "therefore" pointed back to the preceding verses which tell of love—love your enemies, love those who do not return the love. A child may love a parent perfectly—as a child—but the expression of that love is imperfect. And the parent knows it, sees through the imperfect expression to the love itself, and rejoices in it.

3. *The perfection in love is perfect but growing.* The bud is perfect as a bud, the flower perfect as a flower, the fruit perfect as a fruit. Each stage is perfect and yet growing.

4. *Primarily you are to "grow in grace"—not in graciousness.* You do grow in graciousness, but it is a by-product of growing in grace. You must never be graciousness-conscious. For if you are, you are not gracious. You can safely be grace-conscious, for that speaks of receptivity, of the taking of a gift. That humbles you and lifts you at the same time.

5. *Surrender your perfectionism into His hands—this perfectionism which is only another name for pride.* Be willing to make mistakes and to stumble, knowing you will always be stumbling forward.

6. *Rejoice not in what you are, but in what you are becoming through His grace.* You are on the Way—not at the Goal. You are "the young green corn divinely springing," and the promise of perfection in being is beating within your pulses.

7. *You are not perfect, and yet you have a perfect Saviour.* That fulfills the desire for perfection. You can be a perfectionist, but not in yourself; you can be a perfectionist in Him. Perfectionism is thus purified and fulfilled.

O Christ, I see, I see. I am gazing and growing, gazing at Thy beauty and growing into Thy likeness. Thy perfection does not paralyze me; it awakens, inspires, beckons me on. And yet I do not strain after Thy perfection. I receive, I take, I absorb, I assimilate, and thus I grow unconsciously. Am I grateful? To the depths. Amen.

AFFIRMATION FOR THE DAY: *I cannot always trust my guidance, but I can always trust my Guide.*

ANOTHER ROAD WITH A DEAD END—JEALOUSY

We cannot end our long list of roads with dead ends without emphasizing *jealousy as a road that leads only into defeat and frustration.*
Strange that I have put off the consideration of it so long, and
stranger still that, after going through about three thousand notes of
materials for this book, I could scarcely comb out a dozen references to
jealousy and envy. And yet it was probably the one thing that crucified Jesus. At least Pilate "knew that the high priests had handed him
over out of envy." (Mark 15:10, Moffatt.) Envy and jealousy are still
crucifying Jesus. But more, they are throwing disruption into many
personalities. If you have jealousy or envy in your life, you are on
not-the-way.

Near where I am writing is a ghost town, once a thriving, prosperous paper-mill town. Two men in the mill became jealous of each
other, and when one man came to the top, he closed the mill to spite
the other man. Hundreds were thrown out of employment, a town
fell to pieces, a community was devastated, to satisfy the jealousy of
one man. "Satisfy"? Hardly. He will have poison in his bosom the
rest of his days. For jealousy is poison.

Two brothers were jealous of each other, and that poisoned their
relationships and upset everything around them. A jealous wife or
husband can keep a home in a nervous hell. "For wherever jealousy
and rivalry exist, there disorder reigns and every evil." (Jas. 3:16,
Moffatt.) Note "wherever." There are no exceptions. Jealousy has
been, is, and ever shall be the cause of disorder and evil. And further
note "every evil." Out of jealousy comes a whole brood of ugly evils.

And yet jealousy can and does invade supposedly Christian people.
A prominent evangelist was jealous of Moody and went out of his
way to discount Moody and his work. Result? This prominent evangelist faded out, his power ebbed away, and soon he was talking hol-
low words. Few remember his name, while Moody lives on immortal.
Jealousy may be green-eyed, but it is brown-souled—seared into
brown devastation.

O Christ, at whom all sorts of shafts of jealousy were thrown, and who
didst, by Thy love and patient good will, turn it back as forgiving grace,
give me the patient good will to deal with jealousy. And save me from the
poison of it. May it never invade me. In Thy name. Amen.

AFFIRMATION FOR THE DAY: *"Put affection into your love for the
brotherhood; be forward to honor one another."* (Rom. 12:10,
Moffatt.)

STEPS TO VICTORY OVER JEALOUSY

We must now look at the steps for release from jealousy:

1. *Fix this in your mind: Jealousy detracts from you and makes you unfit to gain the love of the loved one.* A jealous person defeats his own purposes. You do not gain love by jealousy; you lose it. You cannot love a jealous person—not really, not with the stops out—jealousy is tied up, suspicious, unlovable. You can be jealous or lovable; you can't be both.

2. *Look on jealousy as self-centeredness.* If you are a jealous person, you are a self-centered person.

3. *Go to the root and surrender the unsurrendered self to God, and jealousy will drop away—rootless.* When you surrender yourself to God, you then enter a fellowship where you become "organs one of another." So if we are organs of each other, then a good executive is my organ of executive ability, a good singer is my organ of song. I need not be jealous because that other person is an "organ" of me.

4. *Since you are surrendered to God, now you need not be looking around to see what is happening to this, that, or the other person. Your approvals and your joys come from God.* Peter said to Jesus, "Lord, and what shall this man do?" The reply, "What is that to thee? follow thou me." (John 21:21, 22.) Peter had a little lingering jealousy of John. Pentecost had not yet burned it out, so he looked John-ward instead of Jesus-ward.

5. *Surrendered to God, you now work out a unique plan—a plan which no one else can fulfill.* When the disciples of John saw Jesus was going ahead of their master, they said: "Rabbi, the man . . . to whom you bore testimony—here he is baptizing, and everybody goes to him!" John replied that he was the bridegroom's friend—"Such is my joy, and it is complete." (John 2:26, 29, Moffatt.) In other words: "I know my place. I've found my niche, and I'm happy in it."

6. *Say everything good you can of the person toward whom you are tempted to be jealous.* As you do so, your attitude will turn from jealousy to love—especially if you breathe a prayer for the person every time you hear his name.

O Thou loving Father, help me to rejoice in the joy of all thy children; help me to feel success in the success of anyone; help me to be honored in the honors of others; help me to love with a creative love. Amen.

AFFIRMATION FOR THE DAY: *"When my heart was sour."* (Ps. 73:21, Moffatt.) *But mine is sour no longer, for I wish the best for everybody.*

FASTENING UPON AN IDOL

We must look at another road with a dead end which many are unconsciously taking—*the road of fastening yourself upon an idol.* Fritz Kunkel lays bare the devastating effects in the personality of those who stop short of reality and fasten upon substitutes, fasten upon idols. An idol is a relative thing become an absolute. In its place an idol is a good thing, but its place is not absolute; it is relative. It must be surrendered to and related to something beyond itself.

A great many people fasten themselves upon idols in religion—for instance, a favorite preacher. Faith is pinned upon that preacher. If he stays steady upon his pedestal, then the religion of the idol goes smoothly. But if he wobbles on his pedestal or, worse, if he falls? Then the faith fastened upon him goes down with him. But he doesn't have to go down in a crash. If he turns out to be less than perfect, then faith is disappointed and hurt and bruised. The idol-worshiper nurses a hidden pain.

I came near doing this as a young Christian. The man under whom I was converted was my ideal and came near being my idol. I found myself imitating his rough voice. And then I found that, while he was a good man, he was not a perfect man, and my idol tottered on its pedestal. In that moment Christ said to me: "Are you following him, or are you following Me?" I saw it—he had come between me and Christ. He must be surrendered. He was. Then he was not an idol; he was a good man to whom I owed much and was deeply grateful. I was released from bondage; I was free.

There are those who make an idol of the religious group to which they belong. People have an instinct for belonging to a group, the herd instinct. Within the group they feel secure, they "belong." And in the belonging they glorify the group to which they belong; they put upon it a halo and invest it with saving qualities. Those who belong to the group or denomination are all right, are safe; those who do not are insecure, are unsaved. The group has become an idol.

O Christ, how easy it is to stop this side of Thee and fasten upon something less than Thee. And when we do so, we know that we are doomed to disappointment, to inner hurt. For Thou alone dost not let us down. Everything else does. I would therefore fasten my affections on Thee, and Thee alone, supremely, all else relative. Help me. Amen.

AFFIRMATION FOR THE DAY: *"If you lose your freshness in the land and deprave yourselves by carving an idol."* (Deut. 4:25, Moffatt.) *I too fasten on idols as I lose the freshness of God.*

WHEN THE IDOL CRASHES

We saw yesterday that the group may become an idol.

As long as we can invest our idol with saving qualities—and that is easy in the first days of "belonging," for one has a sense that at last the haven of security has been found—then everything goes well. But if difficulties arise within the group, and the group turns out to be less than perfect, then a sense of "lostness" comes over the devotee. The idol is about to fall. There is such a sense of insecurity that another group has to be formed, minus the less-than-perfect elements. The idol must be re-established upon its throne. In the breakup many are not able to reinvest the new idol with infallibility, and hence they wander spiritually homeless, lost souls. They don't "belong" any more.

In Latin America these orphaned souls can be counted by the millions. They had fastened upon the "Church" as the ark of safety. All in it were safe, for the "Church" was "infallible." And then the modern investigating mind came into being, and the infallibilities fell to pieces. They saw that there was nothing infallible about the "Church" except that it was infallibly fallible. They were set adrift and found no resting place between infallibility and infidelity. So Latin America has produced more infidelity than any other place in the world, except perhaps Russia, and even that is "perhaps." The soul of educated Latin America is a vast moral and spiritual vacuum into which everything is rushing—the worship of Psyche and Cupid, Positivism, the worship of Humanity, Eastern cults—everything. Millions declared themselves Spiritualists in the last census in Brazil. Why is there an anticlerical movement arising in almost every Latin American country? The idol had been invested with saving qualities, and then the devotees found that even the saving idol was not saved, not saved from human frailties and sins. A sense of spiritual orphanage has set in. "What are the three great needs of your country, and in what order?" I asked a Brazilian. He replied: "The first need is Christ, the second, Christ, and the third, Christ." He was right, for this side of the Absolute we fasten upon idols. And idols always let us down.

O Christ, I know that Thou art alone the Absolute, our resting place, for in Thee we find the Absolute God. We would get to Thee and to Thee alone. For in Thee is everything. Thou art the Way. Outside of Thee is not-the-way. So I come—to Thee. Amen.

AFFIRMATION FOR THE DAY: *"They went after false gods to become false like them."* (II Kings 17:15, Moffatt.) *I become like that which I worship.*

STEPS TO RELEASE FROM IDOLS

We now come to the steps for release from idols:

1. *Fix in mind that everything this side of God has the seeds of disillusionment in it if made into an idol.* They may be good things—home, children, husband, wife, a minister, a group, a rite, a ceremony, a denomination—but they are all relative. You can rest only in the Absolute. "Goodbye, dear reader," said Will Durant in his book on his own philosophy of life, "I am going out in the garden to play with my children." In other words, his philosophy of life rested in human relationships. My inner comment was: "And suppose something would strike your family circle—sickness, death? You have built your nest too low. The floods can reach it. You are vulnerable. Only when your ultimate life values are in God are you invulnerable." He was resting on an idol.

2. *Fix in mind that no man, no institution, no creed, no denomination, no group, no rite, no ceremony can be invested with saving qualities without disappointment or letdown.* All of these have to be saved. How, then, can they save?

3. *Fix in mind that no man, no institution, no creed, no denomination, no group, no rite, no ceremony is the issue.* If any of these is made into an issue, it is a false issue, an issue over an idol. Christ and Christ alone is the issue. He is the Dividing Line. If we are in Him, nothing else need divide us. "He that is not with me is against me." But He did not say: "He that is not with this man, this institution, this creed, this denomination, this rite, this ceremony is against me." That would equate Christ with the relative things gathered around Him through the centuries. In other words, it would make Christ an idol maker. One is the issue—Christ. Had this been kept clearly before Christians, then they might have been saved infinite bitterness and division. In Latin America an evangelical denomination was split over the meaning of *aion*—are the sufferings of the damned "eternal," or only "unto the ages"?

O Christ, I see, I see how we have reduced Thee to irrelevancies. We have made Thee the center of an idol worship. Forgive us. Help us to put Thee on the Throne again, and help us to bow our knees to nothing less than Thee. For Thou art the Way. Amen.

AFFIRMATION FOR THE DAY: *"Your Teacher never leaves you now; you see your Teacher for yourselves, and when you swerve to right or left, you hear a Voice behind you whispering: 'This is the way, walk here.'"* (Isa. 30:20-21, Moffatt.)

FURTHER STEPS TO RELEASE

We continue our steps in release from idols:

4. *Be a member of this group or that denomination, but do not belong to it—belong to Christ.* The group or the denomination belongs to you; you do not belong to it. Paul put it in these words: "All belongs to you; Paul, Apollos, Cephas [all great teachers], the world, life, death [all great facts], the present and the future [all time]—all belong to you; and you belong to Christ, and Christ to God." (I Cor. 3:21-22, Moffatt.) You belong to nothing—nothing but Christ. But when you do, then all belongs to you.

5. *Lean lightly on things and men—absolutely on Christ.* When a Negro was taken up in an airplane for the first time, he was asked how he liked it. He replied, "Fine, but I never did let my whole weight down." Let your whole weight down only on Christ. If you let your whole weight down on anything else, on anything other than Christ, it will let you down. Everything surrendered to Christ comes back to you; it belongs to you, forever.

6. *Expect the man and the group to be imperfect and accept them as such.* "Blessed is the man what don't expect nothin', for he won't be disappointed." This can be said of men and things, but it cannot be said of Christ. Here we can let expectation take wings, for in Him we are never disappointed. "He who believes in him will never be disappointed." (I Pet. 2:6, Moffatt.) In everything else you will be disappointed if you do not provide for imperfection.

7. *Follow the man or the group as they follow Christ.* That provides for contact with persons and groups, saves us from cynical aloofness and isolationism, and yet we do it with reservations. We are free to break with them, if they break with Christ. And we can do it without moral and spiritual disaster to ourselves. We have tied ourselves to men and groups with a bowknot. To Christ we are bound by bonds that cannot be untied or broken.

O Christ, it is all clear; I see that I belong to Thee unbreakably. Other things belong to me breakably. They may come and go; Thou remainest. They may wax old as doth a garment, but Thy years are ever the same. I am beyond disappointment. I cannot be reached by the passing show of life. I am in Thee. And Thou art the same yesterday, today, and forever. Amen.

AFFIRMATION FOR THE DAY: *I am through with "the slippery gods of the glen."* (Isa. 57:6, Moffatt.) *My heart is fixed on God.*

JESUS TAKES THE PLACE OF IDOLS

We have one more day's meditation on release from idols.

Men turn to idols because God seems so aloof, un-get-at-able. But for us Jesus takes the place of idols. When we get hold of Him, the necessity for the idol drops away. He is near at hand, tangible, approachable. For He is "Emmanuel—God with us."

We long for the near-at-hand, but we also long for the universal. We cannot be satisfied with the concrete unless the Universal is in that concrete. These two things are put together in this passage: "May Christ dwell in your hearts. . . . May you be so fixed and founded in love that you can grasp . . . what is the meaning of 'the Breadth,' 'the Length,' 'the Depth,' and 'the Height,' by knowing the love of Christ which surpasses all knowledge!" (Eph. 3:17-19, Moffatt.) Here is a fixed faith—"fixed and founded"—and yet unfixed, "able to grasp 'the Breadth,' 'the Length,' 'the Depth,' and 'the Height.' " If Christ dwells in your heart, you are the narrowest person in the world—you are a man of one Person, one Allegiance, one Love—you are One-centric. And yet you are universalized. You "grasp" every dimension of life. You "grasp" the truth in "the Breadth"—the liberals. You are more liberal than the liberals, for truth found anywhere belongs to you because you belong to the Truth, Christ. You "grasp" the truth in "the Length"—the successionists, those who feel a sense of solidarity of the Christian centuries. You are more successionist than the Apostolic Successionists, for you are a Christ successionist—all the Christians of the ages, not only the apostles, belong to you because you belong to Christ. You can "grasp" the truth in "the Depth"—the fundamentalists, those who insist upon the Incarnation, the Atoning Death, the Resurrection. But you are more fundamental than the fundamentalists, for you are "fixed and grounded" in the incarnate, atoning, resurrected Christ. He, and not merely doctrines about Him, is the fundamental center of your faith. And you can "grasp" the truth in "the Height"—the mystics. But you are more mystic than the mystics, for you know "the love of Christ which surpasses all knowledge"—the universal.

O Christ, I put one point of my compass upon the fact of Thee; then I let the other point sweep as far as it will and take in the whole horizon of fact. I am fixed, oh, how fixed! And yet I am free, oh, how free! My center is in Thee—and everywhere! I thank Thee. Amen.

AFFIRMATION FOR THE DAY: *I have given myself to Him who is the "express image" of God. What need have I for any idol?*

GATHERING UP LESSONS LEARNED

We are now entering the last week of the first half of the year. We must gather up the lessons learned before we start on the more positive side of the Way in the second half.

The emphasis of this book is that the Way is not merely the way of salvation. It is that, thank God, but more. The Way is the way to do everything. And everything not-the-way, is not the way. In the Pan-American Airport building in Panama the "seeing eye door" opens as you approach to come in or go out. But when I tried to go out by the door marked "Entrance," nothing happened. The "seeing eye" did not see me, paid no attention to me. I might have become angry or I might have prayed to all the gods that be, but that door would not have opened. Only as I retreated and entered the other aisle did the door "see" me and open. When I obeyed the nature of reality, things began to open. It is so everywhere in everything for everybody. Life is made to work in God's way and only in God's way. If you try to work it some other way, it works its own ruin.

When I arrived back from a two and a half months' tour of Latin America, I was anxious to catch up with events; so I went to the book-stall at the station in Miami, and asked for *Time* and *Life*, and received the reply that there were none, for—so the clerk said—*"Time* and *Life* are on strike." "Yes," I said to myself as I walked away, "'Time' and 'Life' are on strike. We wouldn't use time and we wouldn't live life in God's way, so they are both on strike against us." Time is getting more and more filled with problems, and life is more and more filled with frustrations. Time and life are on strike against us. If we live life as it should be lived, that is, according to the Way, and if we use passing time as it should be used, they will work with us, doors will fling open at the very sight of us, and life will be an open vista—life will be livable, time will tingle with adventure.

Jesus is the Door, not only to salvation; He is the Door to everything. Everything opens when you come in His Way.

O Jesus, I see that Thou art the Door, and when I humbly come Thy Way everything in heaven and on earth is open to me. I live in a wide open universe. Beauty and love and service and joy and redemption are all open to me. I walk everywhere with doors being flung open to me as though I were royalty. I am—in Thee. I thank Thee. Amen.

AFFIRMATION FOR THE DAY: *"I am the Gate; whoever enters by me will be saved, he will go in and out and find pasture."* (John 10:9, Moffatt.)

HEED THE HELM OR THE ROCKS?

We must continue gathering up our thoughts on the Way. When we try to manipulate life and make it work in our way instead of humbly accepting God's way, then we get into trouble.

An outstanding Canadian layman said: "The idealisms of yesterday have become the necessities of today." The substitutes won't work. The psalmist says: "All who swerve from thy will, thou spurnest; their notions end in nothing." (Ps. 119:118, Moffatt.) Notions that end in nothings! "The mountains labor and bring forth a mouse!" We have colossal effort and contemptible effect. We get what we want and then we don't want it. Dorothy Thompson, after visiting Germany, says: "The trouble with our war is that we have got our unconditional surrender. We asked the Germans to give themselves over to our will and they have, and it seems we haven't any will." We should have tried to get the Germans and ourselves to make unconditional surrender to God. Then there would have been an open Door. "He that sitteth in the heavens shall laugh"—shall laugh a sad laugh at our impossible attempts at playing God.

Jeremiah might have been speaking of today: "For the authorities were senseless, seeking no guidance from the Eternal; so they had no access, and all their folk are scattered." (Jer. 10:21, Moffatt.) When you do not seek guidance from God you are not merely bad, you are *senseless.* For the Christian way is just sheer sense—all else is nonsense. "The devil is not only bad, he's a fool," says a very discerning friend of mine, "for if you reap what you sow then look what he reaps. 'The sorrows of Satan' is more than a phrase, it is a fact." I suppose the devil doesn't mind being called bad, but he hates being called a fool; he can't stand being laughed at. And yet life does laugh at our "senseless" ways.

After I had spoken on this subject to an English-speaking audience in Buenos Aires, the pastor asked a woman if she understood what I had said. "Only too well," she sadly replied. What I said was simply a commentary on the text of her own experience.

O Christ, I come to Thee with my wayward, stupid will. I have been afraid of Thy will. I have been afraid of Life. And now I come to Thee with humbled heart, humbled through many a setback and many a blank wall against which I've run. I'm hurt. But wiser. So I come to give Thee my recalcitrant will to have Thee make it over again. Amen.

AFFIRMATION FOR THE DAY: *"Make the Eternal your delight, and he will give you all your heart's desire."* (Ps. 37:4, Moffatt.)

"MANY OTHER WORDS OF THE SAME NATURE"

We must pursue this subject of the Way being the way for everything until it shall no longer be an idea, but an axiom.

The prophet Habakkuk utters the truth we are emphasizing in these words: "Has not the Lord of hosts ordained, that 'the toil of the nations ends in smoke,' and 'peoples wear themselves out for naught.' " (Hab. 2:13, Moffatt.) Is this "ordained" arbitrarily by God by His imposed declaration? Or is it ordained by the nature of reality, written into the nature of things? When nations do not take God's way, does their toil end in smoke? Inevitably? And do peoples who take paths other than God's "wear themselves out for naught"?

The saying, "He who will not heed the helm must heed the rocks," is not imposed on the facts, but coined out of the facts themselves. For if the hand of Christ is not on the helm, then the hand of catastrophe guides you straight to the rocks—inevitably. That is the text of life, all else is commentary.

If you try to cut out the text, it will come back again stronger than ever. When Jeremiah wrote the judgment of God, Jehoiakim, the king, didn't like it, so he cut the scroll with a penknife, cut out the parts he didn't like, and threw them into the fire. "That's that," thought the king. He had settled it. Had he? Listen: "So Jeremiah took another scroll, and gave it to Baruch . . . , who wrote upon it, to Jeremiah's dictation, all the words of the book that Jehoiakim . . . had burned, besides many other words of the same nature." (Jer. 36:23, 32, Moffatt.) Note, "besides many other words of the same nature." Do you get rid of God's laws written into the nature of reality by burning or spurning them? Hardly. They come back, and come back redoubled—"many other words of the same nature." If you don't listen to it from the Bible, then psychology, history, experience will speak "many other words of the same nature."

If we don't listen, then life judges us. Dan Brummitt said in regard to his careless walking at cross streets: "If I'm bumped off an appropriate inscription on my tomb would be: 'Died of looking the wrong way.' "

O Christ, inescapable Christ, how can I run from Thee. If I flee from Thee I flee from life. I cannot do that and live. Then help me to flee into Thy arms, into Thy ways. For I know that Thou hast the words of eternal life, Thou art eternal life itself. Amen.

AFFIRMATION FOR THE DAY: *"Take hold of the Eternal your God and you will keep hold of life."* (II Chron. 20:20, Moffatt.)

WHITEWASHING FLIMSY WALLS

Jehoiakim dramatically burned the laws of God and they dramatically came back. But what about the silent decay which very undramatically sets in when we take ways other than the Way?

Jeremiah depicted the dramatic rejection, now he depicts other undramatic results: "Turning his thoughts from the Eternal, he is like some desert scrub that never thrives." (Jer. 17:5, Moffatt.) Turn your thoughts from the Eternal, think on other ways, and you become "like some desert scrub that never thrives." When you don't think God's thoughts you haven't the key—economists plan for economic ruin; politicians undermine the body politic; philosophers philosophize in the dark; psychologists pick people to pieces, but since they have no great Design they do not know how to put people together again, so leave them more disrupted than before; moralists without God lead to immorality.

Jeremiah changes the figure and puts it thus: "Your footsteps stumble on the twilight hills, before the gleam you look for turns to dense, dead gloom." (Jer. 13:16, Moffatt.) If the Way is "the path of the just" that "shineth more and more unto the perfect day," then those who go on not-the-way are on a path that fadeth more and more unto the perfect night. Men hope for "the gleam," but it ends in "gloom," the "dense, dead gloom."

Ezekiel puts it in these dramatic words: "These daubers whitewash any flimsy wall run up to safe-guard the people . . . till down falls the flimsy wall; and then you will be asked, will you not, 'What about your whitewash?'" (Ezek. 13:10-12, Moffatt.) We are in the vast process of whitewashing flimsy walls run up to safeguard the people—militarism, selfish nationalism, force, balances of power, spheres of influence, leagues, pacts and treaties between sovereign nations. They are all flimsy walls, beautifully whitewashed. But the "deluge of rain is coming . . . and a stormy blast shall break out, till down falls the flimsy wall." (Verse 11.) Life will try our flimsy walls. It will render its verdict, and everything not-the-way will collapse. Christ pronounces; life executes.

O Christ, I see more clearly every hour that Thy way is my way and I cannot have my way unless I take Thy way. So from pure self-interest I would take Thy way. And yet when I take Thy will I am loosed from pure self-interest. I love Thee, I love everybody, I love myself. Amen.

AFFIRMATION FOR THE DAY: *"Why break the commands of the Eternal? Why defeat yourselves?"* (II Chron. 24:20, Moffatt.)

FOR THE EVERLASTING RIGHT

We have seen that the Way is in the nature of Reality.

Ezekial puts it thus: "Your doom appears; your sin has blossomed, your pride has budded." (Ezek. 7:10, Moffatt.) The doom is not imposed from without as punishment—it is inherent. The "doom" is in the blossoming of the sin, in the budding of the pride. The psalmist speaks of the silent laws of God, "their speech has never a word, not a sound for the ear, and yet their message spreads the wide world over, their meaning carries to earth's end." (Ps. 19:1-4, Moffatt.) They are written in us, for each of us

> ". . . ever bears about
> A silent court of justice in his breast,   5½
> Himself the judge and jury, and himself
> The prisoner at the bar . . ."

They are written in the heavens:

> "For the everlasting right
> The silent stars are strong."

"The stars in their courses fought against Sisera"—they fight against any who fight against the Way. We read, "God has prepared all that for those who love him." (I Cor. 2:9, Moffatt.) He has prepared it in the constitution of things. The Way is the warp and woof of the universe. Somebody has said, "The world is vascular—cut it anywhere and it will bleed." It will bleed with the blood of Christ.

The Oxyrhynchus papyri give a striking saying of Jesus: "The Kingdom of Heaven is within you, and whosoever shall know himself shall find it." The first part, "The Kingdom of Heaven is within you," is taken from the canonical Scriptures, but the second part, "and whosoever shall know himself shall find it," sounds Greek—"Know thyself." And yet in the light of modern discovery, it more and more sounds true. The more you discover the laws of your being, the more you discover the laws of God. They are the same. And the amazing discovery is this: The Author of the laws of the Kingdom written in Scripture and the Author of the laws written in us is the same.

O Thou hidden, universal Christ, I cannot turn anywhere without confronting Thee. For I meet Thee on every road, the road of the Scriptures and the road of life. Amen.

AFFIRMATION FOR THE DAY: *Christ is everywhere and He is in me. What more do I want, except more of Him?*

THE OPEN SECRET

We saw yesterday that "the Kingdom of Heaven is within you, and whosoever shall know himself shall find it." "But," queried a thoughtful woman in Latin America, "if the law of Christ is the law of our being, why have we been so long in discovering it?"

Jesus speaks of "the open secrets of the Realm of heaven." (Matt. 13:11, Moffatt.) The Kingdom of God is a secret. It is hidden within the nature of Reality, but it is an "open secret," open to those who pay the price and search for it. All God's great things are "open secrets." Electricity was hidden in the universe before the foundation of the world, but not until Franklin was it discovered. The possibility of being heard around the world was there from the beginning, but Marconi brought it to light. All the laws of God are gradually being discovered.

Jesus is the Key to the meaning of the universe. Follow the clues He gives and you get the answers every time. But the answers are hidden answers, they are an "open secret." The secret is a spirit, the spirit of self-surrendered humility. Everything in the Kingdom is open to those who surrender to and obey the Kingdom. We are in the process of discovering that Kingdom hidden in the nature of Reality. The Kingdom is there, the ground plan of our being.

H. G. Wells says that the psychologist can stand alongside the preacher and say that unless you get free from all preoccupation with self-interest there is a disintegration of personality. That is the essence of the Christian position. We can now say with assurance that there isn't a law of your body which contradicts the Christian faith. Those laws are the Christian faith written in flesh and blood and tissue.

When we surrender unchristian attitudes, life works better, works well. "I had nervous headache and nervous indigestion and no relief. Sunday night I was untied while you were speaking. I surrendered it all to God. Been free of it ever since—it's gone," said a woman. When she took Christian attitudes, health set in. Someday the psychologist is going to say: "Be Christian and be well."

O God, Thy Kingdom is written in us as the Way. We know it and we rejoice in it. How wonderful that at last we have found the Great Design, the Pattern for life, the Way to live, so intimate, so a part of us, so inescapable. And we would not escape it. How can we and live? Amen.

AFFIRMATION FOR THE DAY: *Today I shall find some new footprint of the King in my being and in my relationships—an exciting adventure.*

IN WHICH WE ASK OURSELVES QUESTIONS

We have put our finger on sixteen roads with dead ends. Today ends our six months' quest, so today we will run over in searching thought to see whether we are on the Way—fully. Are we ready for an all-out following of the Way?

Have I surrendered that last lurking fear to Him? Am I now living by faith and confidence instead of by fear? Have I given over to God my resentments? Am I all out for the way of love for everybody? Have I left behind me all negativism and retreatism? Do I belong to the "forward march," not to the "backward step"? Have I given over to God all my inferiority complexes? Am I able for anything I should do? Have I given over to Him myself, so that I am no longer a self-centered person? Am I going to try to correct others by trying to correct myself? Shall I let that be my criticism of others? Have I surrendered this touchy, over-sensitive self to God, released from all over-sensitivity? Am I going to cease to look for slights and look for opportunities to be of service? Have I offered to God my inward divisions, with no civil war anywhere? Have I broken the habit of indecision? Am I able now to decide things because there is only one self to decide things? Is my sex life wholly under His control? Will His guidance, instead of my impulses, decide the use of my sex life? Have I surrendered completely and fully all use of narcotics? Am I through with these crutches? Have I given over to God all my material wealth to be used as He directs? Am I through with boredom, never saying again that I am bored since in Him I am eternally alive and interested? If I can't be perfect, am I willing to be imperfect, and gladly willing, since I can do all things for the love of God? Have I given over all jealous feelings, and do I henceforth rejoice in everybody's success? And finally, have I been weaned from all Idols, so that now I have gone beyond them to Christ and through Him to God?

Your feet are on the Way! Say a quiet hallelujah, or throw your hat in the air!

O Christ, why shouldn't I rejoice with joy unspeakable for I've found the greatest thing that life can hold—the Way to live! Can anything be greater than that? So I rejoice, with all the stops out! And now, Father, Thou hast all my ransomed powers. Use them, for they are made to be Thine. Amen.

AFFIRMATION FOR THE DAY: *"The full joy of thy presence."* (Ps. 16:11, Moffatt.) *Yes, in Christ I have a joy without alloy.*

IN WHICH WE SHARE NEEDS

After asking ourselves searching questions, this week we are taking the next step sharing the open frankness of those who have "exteriorated their decays."

Each summer groups come together, not merely to find the answer, but to *be* the answer. They try to become the kind of society they would like to see universalized—the Kingdom of God in miniature. It is imperfect, of course, because made up of imperfect people, but it is in some real way being the new order. They begin by letting down barriers between classes in society, between races, between those who work with their hands and those who do not, between the titled and the titleless, between the leaders and the led; and, most of all, they let down the personal barriers within one—barriers of fears, inhibitions, inferiorities, superiorities, moral conflicts, and guilts.

We ask, Why have you come? What do you want? What is your deepest need? And we spend hours simply talking about our needs. This doesn't become morbid introspection, for we pass straight on from seeing the need to seeking the solution. Within the group we do not have an inner group who have attained, working on those who have not. We are all in a fellowship of need, and God works on us all. This saves us from spiritual Pharisaism.

These are some of the things men and women, lay and clerical, young and old, said were their needs: (1) "I have come here to get back on a right footing with God." (2) "I want to know how to live the abundant Christian life." (3) "I am a victim of my own ego." (4) "As a human race we have flopped. I'd like to get a wallop out of life as Francis of Assisi did." (5) "I am just stale." (6) "I am a church member without power." (7) "I want to get rid of myself." (8) "I am the pastor of a great church. There is the temptation to pride. My official board has given me full rein. But there is no spiritual power. The altar is no longer filled with penitents. I'm barren." (9) "I am a native African. I came to America to get spiritual power. But I have a bitterness. I have been losing since I came." (10) "I am a walking skeleton spiritually."

O God, Thou seest our needs, and seeing them Thou dost not despise us; Thou lovest us still. Love me still. Love me out of my barrenness into Thy fulness, out of myself into Thyself. Amen.

AFFIRMATION FOR THE DAY: *God is not baring my needs to shame me, but to save me.*

"TO GET RID OF THE SENSE OF FUTILITY"

We continue the statements of needs as told to us in our group:
(11) "I am a Negro, and I want to live with a group which it is
so easy to hate if you live where I live." (12) "I have had to pump
my own spiritual well so hard in preaching. I want to preach from
the overflow. I wonder how people can come to hear me week after
week." (13) "I want to have the stops taken out." (14) "Four fifths
of my life, the subconscious, is not surrendered, hence I have no
power." (15) "You would think that in one as old as I am the self
would sit down discouraged in being beaten down, but I don't find it
so." (16) "I have come here to hang myself." (17) "To get rid of
physical, moral, and mental tensions. I want to get rid of fear." (18)
"The shrine is gone and I want it back." (19) "I am a pastor and my
job has me licked." (20) "I belong to the Order of the Quaking
Knees." (21) "I come from the people who are always telling what's
wrong with their husbands." (22) "I have a large ego that needs to
be pulverized." (23) "I am shallow and I need to be deepened." (24)
"I have the same conflicts in me that I find in the world situation."
(25) "I have been pushed around all my life." (26) "To get rid of
a sense of futility." (27) "I want God to save me from talkativeness.
This is the first time I've ever confessed it." (28) "I've been like a
jellyfish just floating around with no direction." (29) "I've been
selfish in my unselfishness." (30) "I want to make my ideas walk."
(31) "My faith in a new world is tottering." (32) "My Christian
foundations have been rocking." (33) "I want freedom from inner
conflicts, tensions. I stumble over myself." (34) "I want the dimness
of my soul taken away." (35) "Would like to lose the negative charge
of self for the positive charge of Christ." (36) "I am the head of a
New Thought movement but I've been on the basis of myself. I've
told people what to do, but from the basis of myself." (37) "I'm in
hell, my wife is in hell, our home is hell, and it looks as though we
are going to stay there." (38) "As a pastor, I thought my trouble was
in the Church and I see it is in me."

O God, we thank Thee for this basic honesty. We know that when we
get a good look at ourselves we may then get a good look at Thee. For as
we see Thee, really see Thee, our chains fall off and we are free. Make me
free, wholly free. Amen.

AFFIRMATION FOR THE DAY: *Today I shall be free from all subterfuge,*
all trimming, all falsity—that I may be free indeed.

IN WHICH WE SHARE OUR VICTORY

When men expressed these needs did anything happen? Did release come? To some, no. They couldn't get beyond themselves. But they were very few. For the most part, those who honestly faced their needs and turned them over to God found release and power and were transformed.

Listen to some of them: (1) "I came here with a chip on my shoulder, cynical, an exhibitionist, but I've found Christ and I'm released and happy." (2) "I have been anti. I have been against things, fighting all the time. Now I see I can't live that way. I've learned how to be positive and constructive." (3) "I haven't preached on being sweet-tempered, for my wife was always present. But now I've buried my temper in the lake." (4) "I'd rather see a sermon than hear one. I've seen a sermon here and now I'm going to be one." (5) "I feel very young again and I'm ready to go." (6) "I was about to give up, everything was so dark, but I surrendered it all to God and I am free from this inner discouragement." (7) "My husband is so good. I have lived with him for twenty-three years and can tell you that his every instinct is Christian—courteous, kind, self-forgetting, noble. He is a lawyer and he carries the Sermon on the Mount into his profession. He could not do an unchristian act if he tried." (8) "People said I shouldn't come here. I should go to a museum! I've been a fossilized soul. But now my eye is single and my whole body is full of light." (9) "I have learned here not only the peace that passeth understanding, but misunderstanding." (10) "I left my fears, my worries, and my self-consciousness down at the lake." (11) "I've missed ecclesiastical phrases. There has been no sense of race, of class, no pious phrases. It's all been so natural. I've discovered the naturalness of the Christian way." (12) "My problem has not been solved, in this atmosphere it has been dissolved." (13) "If this spirit we have here were universalized we would have the Kingdom of God on earth." (14) "I thought I had lost the new life, and I had only mislaid it."

O Christ, we thank Thee that Thou art the answer. For when men touch Thee then the answer comes. We thank Thee that Thou art open to the approach of need. No one need turn away empty. I thank Thee, thank Thee. Amen.

AFFIRMATION FOR THE DAY: *Freely have I received, freely now must I give—to everybody, everywhere.*

"I WOKE UP GRINNING"

We continue these glorious statements from glad and released hearts:

(15) "I came up here with a jumping heart. I surrendered it to God and I'm going back well." (16) "I have been attending conferences all my life. They fall down. This one doesn't, for it is a colony of heaven." (17) "I've lived on the doorstep of Abundant Living, not in the living room. Now I've moved in." (18) "I've been a lover of causes instead of a lover of people. I've learned now to love people as well as causes." (19) "I never knew what prayer was. It is a great thing to talk with God instead of praying to him." (20) "I came here for repose and found something better—security." (21) "I'm leaving my cigarettes behind me." (22) "I've been serving my people a diet of thin soup. I've been serving myself to them, throwing myself at them. Hence their vitality got very low. I'm taking something more than myself back to them—I'm taking God." (23) "I never thought I would see the gospel lived out in society but I have—here." (24) "God and I can now go through anything." (25) "My resentments have all been dissolved into thin air, they're gone." (26) "I've been a watch with a broken mainspring. It's mended and I'm going again." (27) "Here is the least strain of any group I've ever been in. Even the cat moves around so relaxed. The children do too." (28) "I've been directing God and now God has begun directing me." (29) "I wanted to do something for God, now I want God to do something for me and through me." (30) "I was at war—with myself. I surrendered to God and the war was over." (31) "I lost all my property, but now I feel it's all right. I won't have to pay any taxes on it." (32) "The most important thing to me has been this: Don't seek a solution, be a solution. I'm going back to be a solution." (33) "A great tension has been let down. All my life I've thought I had to succeed. I've been in bondage to success. Now I see that my one business is to be true to the highest I know—success and failure are in the hands of God." (34) "This morning for the first time I woke up grinning."

O Christ, Thou dost put laughter in our hearts. For Thou dost free us from inhibiting fear and self-preoccupation. Thou dost make us free from everything, so we are afraid of nothing. Help me to share the good news of freedom, of freedom. Amen.

AFFIRMATION FOR THE DAY: *"If the Son sets you free, you will be really free."* (John 8:36, Moffatt.)

"MY CHILDREN WILL HAVE A NEW MOTHER"

We continue the glowing words from glad hearts: (35) "My children will have a new mother. I talk too much. Here I've learned how to be silent." (36) "This is a pattern that fits everybody. I know that the one who will get the most out of this will be my mother, for she has to live with me." (37) "I've come here to get in touch with convincing Christians. I've had a bigger dose than I dreamed of. Laughing is so easy here."

(38) "I have had phlebitis, but I've found myself going up the steps two at a time." (39) "This has been an eye-opener, mind-opener, soul-opener. Everything has been so natural that it has been inevitable." (40) "This is the place where we played like we were in heaven—and were!" (41) "I was pleasure bent, but didn't expect to have a good time. The good time found me." (42) "You certainly are kind, being white folks." (43) "I've received here my greatest spiritual renewal." (44) "Here I've undergone a spiritual face lifting." (45) "I felt my business in life was to comfort the afflicted and afflict the comfortable. I was not only under the juniper tree, I brought the juniper tree with me. Now I'm through with the religion of a juniper tree." (46) "This experience has put an exclamation point behind every Christian duty. It's been a week of spiritual perception."

(47) "I have been learning how to spell J-o-y, Jesus first, others next, yourself last." (48) "All my life I've had a sore spot and God has healed it." (49) "I'm being unpaganized." (50) "I have had such fellowship here that I'll be liable to say to the people in the subway, 'Hello, brother,' 'Hello, sister.'" (51) "I have hold of a growing answer." (52) "I'll have to change the tone of my voice, for it hasn't had much love in it." (53) "I have had fears and I got rid of them and then I felt afraid that I wasn't afraid!" (54) "I thought I was a sponge being filled up, but I saw I was filled with myself." (55) "I've been a crank among many wheels. But now I am different." (56) "I've come from a church trying to be God, doing everything for itself. Now I have surrendered and am released and happy."

O God, we thank Thee that those who knock at the gates of life find that it opens to them. For they would not have sought Thee unless in a measure they had found Thee. We thank Thee that the lesser finding is to get us to seek the larger finding. Amen.

AFFIRMATION FOR THE DAY: *"Every one that asketh receiveth; and he that seeketh findeth; and to him that knocketh it shall be opened."* (Luke 11:10.)

"IN SOMEONE ELSE"

This week has been a week of testimonies—people telling out of glad hearts what it meant to them when they tried the Way. So far they have all been out of our Ashram groups. Now we must go farther afield and gather up statements from here and there.

A father was gruff and apparently unsympathetic. When his two girls talked of becoming Christians and joining the church and they came to him to talk it over, he gruffly said, "Well, if you do get converted be sure you're converted like your mother." Hers was real. A girl who had gone through a very tragic experience—nothing worse could have happened to her—surrendered herself and her tragedy to God and with a radiant face said, "I really found God last night and it's all different now. My tragedy is dissolved."

A teacher said this: "I wanted to test your statement, that when one is awakened spiritually he is awakened mentally, becomes more mentally alert. My class was dull, retarded a year or more, 'queer-looking,' said other teachers. I got my pupils to listen to God ten minutes each day. They began to be changed morally and spiritually and their faces changed. 'Never saw such a change in faces,' said the same teachers." The Way is the way of the shining face.

A college professor writes: "As you closed your address God's voice spoke clearly to me: 'Gertrude, I'm going to touch your back at this time and you will never have any more trouble with it.' Something so wonderful was experienced at that moment that I was afraid to move. Asking God for healing had never occurred to me. . . . My healing led to an intimacy with God's unlimited interest in all phases of living. I have tried to pass this on to others. One young minister was healed of stuttering in one of my speech classes."

A brilliant young woman was persuaded to take a class of boys, though she herself was not a professing Christian. She worried about it, was persuaded to give herself to Christ and did. She won all nine boys to Christ. On the Sunday they made their profession, a friend said to her, "Bess, I'd give my life to do what you've done." Bess replied, "That's what it takes, but it's worth it."

O Christ, I thank Thee that Thou hast touched others into wholeness. Now touch me. For I am in the same need. I bring to Thee nothing less than myself. I withhold nothing. Take me, make me what I ought to be. Thou hast my full consent. Amen.

AFFIRMATION FOR THE DAY: *"Now in the Lord you are light; lead the life of those who are children of the light."* (Eph. 5:8, Moffatt.)

"HE'S GOT THE WORLD BY THE TAIL"

A great many people think that the Way is hard. The fact is, the way of transgression is hard.

A young man prayed: "O God, here I am. You know all about me. You know my good points and my bad points. I know what you did for Dad, and I know what you did for Quinten Warner. If you can do anything for me, it's about time." The time was then—he found.

You don't have to fight yourself and your sins. Change the inner climate by surrender to love, and these things will drop away. I was on board an ice- and snow-covered ship about to leave New York. Why didn't they clean it off? They didn't. Two days later the Gulf Stream melted it all away. The changed climate did what fighting the ice and snow would not do. Change your inner climate.

The vice-president of a company was irritable, sick, and hadn't a real friend in the world. "I have no philosophy of life," he said sadly. He began reading *Is the Kingdom of God Realism?* and got a philosophy of life, in fact, got life itself. A friend described him thus, "He's got the world by the tail."

A young man said in a meeting for witnessing: "God said to me, 'My child, you need a good going-over,' and, boy, I've got it." But God only cleansed away the rubbish to give him the real. "There is much rubbish, so that we are not able to build the wall." (Neh. 4:10.) When the rubbish was taken away, walls began to rise.

Starr Daily is probably the outstanding remade criminal in the United States. He spent twenty years in the underworld, a hardened criminal. In prison he lived on hate in solitary confinement. For rebellion he was strung up twelve hours a day for fifteen days, his feet and hands in rings. He was only skin and bones. In that condition Christ met him, and the glory poured over him and through him. His whole being was awakened and changed. He was afraid they would let him out of the cell—afraid this would fade. His keepers were awed, slipped things to him from the officers' table. He said he couldn't take them, it would be dishonest. They had to let a man like that out. His brain was awakened, and he has written a number of books. He is now a glowing, contributive, useful Christian citizen.

O Christ, I know that the Way works and that nothing else will work. I know that life approves of this Way. I too approve and give my life entirely and wholly to it. For what can I withhold? Amen.

AFFIRMATION FOR THE DAY: *"Anything that is illuminated turns into light."* (Eph. 5:13, Moffatt.)

THE WAY IS THE WAY OF GRACE

In the opening weeks we talked about the fact that there is the Way and not-the-way. We looked at roads with dead ends and at some who had found the Way. We now turn to look at the various ways within the Way.

While we do this we must remind ourselves that the Christian way is not a patchwork of ways, it is not an eclecticism, a lot of truths brought together from everywhere. The Christian way is Christ, and Christ is the Truth. While Christ being the Truth is the Way, nevertheless within that Way are many ways.

The Way is the way of Grace. I put that first, for it is first. What do we mean by grace? It is usually defined as "God's unmerited favor." "Grace is shorthand for God's redeeming love."

The Gospel starts with God's redeeming love, with grace. It is God's initiative that redeems us. Deissman says: "All the religions of the world begin with man's initiative—man searching for God. In Christianity God takes the initiative." In other religions we have man's search for God, in the Gospel we have God's search for man. "We love him, because he first loved us." I once listened to an address in India by a visiting lecturer on "Man's search for God," and at the close a Scotch missionary quietly said, "Have you read *The Hound of Heaven?* If not, go sell your coat and buy it." *The Hound of Heaven* depicts the Love of God pursuing us down the years. We speak of "the Initiative and the Referendum" as belonging to us. The Initiative belongs to God, the Referendum belongs to us. He initiates and we decide what is referred to us, we decide whether we shall respond to that Initiative. We do not find God, we put ourselves in the way of being found by God.

But the first thing is grace. "The Gospel is not good advice, but good news." It is not primarily a teaching us how to live, but an offer of Life. Jesus did not come to show us the Way, but to show Himself as the Way. "He did not come to preach the Gospel, but that there might be a Gospel to be preached."

O Christ, I bow my head and heart in deepest gratitude that I am responding to Thy Initiative. For I am being pressed upon, gently pressed upon, by Grace. It invades me, awaiting the dropping of barriers that Love might possess me, redeem me, fill me. Amen.

AFFIRMATION FOR THE DAY: *"The grace of God has appeared."* (Titus 2:11, Moffatt.) *My eyes have been open to see it. I'll see more today.*

190

THE PROCESSES OF KARMA OR GRACE

We must continue our meditation of the Way as the way of Grace. We can live by Grace or we can live by Law. Peter speaks of "heirs equally . . . of the grace of Life." (I Pet. 3:7, Moffatt.) If you will not take the grace of Life, then you must take the law of life. You can live by the grace of Life—you surrender to, and are ruled by, the processes of Love. You are receptive to this invading Grace. You do not struggle and try, but surrender and trust and obey. Your little life is caught up into the purposes of Life, you are redeemed by Life, replenished by Life. Faith is a yieldingness to Love.

But if you do not live by the grace of Life, then you live by the law of life. You sink back into the processes of karma, you reap what you sow. You get back from life what you give to life. You are under law. Life becomes a give and take, a very strict bargain. You have to watch each deed, for you know you will get back an exact equivalent. Life therefore works on a strictly "cash and carry" basis—you lay down the cash of your deed and carry away the result or the consequences of that deed. There are no surprises in life, no going beyond on either side. It is all very just and all very dependable, and all very dead.

That is the gospel of the market place religion. You bargain with life and life bargains with you, and it holds you to the bond. There is no Good News in it, for life is grim-faced and so are you. Religion based on give and take has no spontaneity in it, no bubbling joy, no freedom. It plods—it cannot soar. It sighs—it cannot sing. It is the religion of the elder brother: "Thou never gavest me a kid, that I might make merry with my friends." (Luke 15:29.) How could he? The elder brother was living by legalism, so when the scene closes he was on the outside, living by law, and the younger brother was on the inside, living by Love.

In a home, if life were lived on the law of each insisting on getting what he gives, what a deadly, dull house—I cannot call it a home—it would be. In a real home, love reigns. You go beyond law and spontaneously expressed love in a thousand beautiful little ways, never thinking of anything in return.

O Christ, I want to live by the grace of Life, instead of the law of life. I want the gaiety of a life fully surrendered to Love. I surrender all my Pharisaic legalism and become a little child in Thy house. Amen.

AFFIRMATION FOR THE DAY: *"Never think, 'I will treat him as he treated me. I will pay back the man for what he did.'"* (Prov. 24:29, Moffatt.) *God thinks grace—so shall I.*

A DANGEROUS LIBERTINISM?

We considered yesterday living by the grace of Life or by the law of life. One produces the Christian, the other produces the Pharisee. One surrenders and trusts, and the other struggles and struts. One lives by an obtainment and the other lives by an attainment. The one is an artesian well, the other is force pump. The one is based on Christ, the other is based on self. One says, "Love God and do what you like." The other grimly says, "I must do what I don't like."

Yes, God has two hands: the hand of Grace and the hand of law. If you won't take from the hand of Grace, you must take from the hand of law. You can rise into a kingdom of freedom by the hand of Grace, or you can sink back into the fatalities of the law of karma. Life can be a play-spell, or life can be pay-spell.

Isn't this dangerous libertinism? Where is this discipline of life which modern discovery is so insistent upon? It is a universe of law and you have to obey it or break. True. But in the grace of Life you fulfill the law—plus. The law becomes your runway from which you take off to soar in the heaven of freedom.

But this grace of Life is the most exacting discipline. It disciplines you far more deeply than any law could discipline you. When you keep a law, it's kept—kept in the outer conformities. But when you keep a love, it's not kept by outer conformities—it's kept only in the inner conformities. Love is ten times as exacting as law. When you fulfill a law you are off duty, but you are never off duty from love. It's got you every moment, impelling you to go beyond. Consider this passage: "The grace of God . . . schools us to renounce . . . and to live a life of self-mastery." (Titus 2:12, Moffatt.) The grace of God schools us! Here free grace puts us to school! And the severest of schools. It disciplines the inmost thought and the outmost act and everything between. You accept the grace of God and by that very act you accept self-control, rather, self-control through God-control. You are free to act within His control. His control is perfect freedom.

· O Christ, I know that Thy will is my deepest will and when I do Thy will I do my own. For in Thee I come to my full stature. Out of Thee I'm stunted. I want to grow in the grace of surrendering to Grace, and in the love of surrendering to Love. For then I grow—and only then. Amen.

AFFIRMATION FOR THE DAY: *Today I shall walk in "the perfect law of liberty"—a liberty which is a law.*

GRACE AND REALITY

"But," says the questioner, "is this matter of Grace something imposed by religion on life, or is it inherent in life itself?"

If the Christian faith were something imposed instead of something inherent, then, of course, we could not take it. But the Gospel says that grace is rooted in reality: "We have seen his glory, . . . seen it to be full of grace and reality. . . . Grace and reality are ours through Jesus Christ." (John 1:14, 17, Moffatt.) Here "grace and reality" are connected. Is grace part and parcel of the make-up of reality? It is. If grace exists in certain stories about life, instead of being woven into the warp and woof of life, then it is precarious.

Jesus "brought life and immortality to light by the gospel." (II Tim. 1:10, Moffatt.) Life and immortality were inherent in the nature of Reality, but they were "brought to light," lifted up out of the nature of things, made overt where they were covert. He brought them to light in His own person. So He brought grace to light again in His own person. "The grace which he gave us ages ago in Christ Jesus and has now revealed in the appearance of our Saviour Jesus Christ." (II Tim. 1:10, Moffatt.) This grace was "given ages ago." It was written into the structure of Reality, but has now been "revealed" in the appearance of our Lord Jesus Christ. Jesus was the revealer of the nature of Reality, and in that Reality the most beautiful thing revealed is Grace. We can see intimations, outcroppings of that grace amid the laws of nature. Parent birds grow lean in foraging for food for their little ones, and they will unhesitatingly sacrifice themselves to save them. The human mother goes down into the valley of the shadow of death to bring her child into the world, and then will do everything that love can do for that child. We see it in scientists who inoculate themselves with disease germs in order to find a way to relieve others of the danger. Life is shot through and through with this spirit. Someone asked a very successful chaplain how he achieved his success. He pointed to the cross on his lapel, saying, "I work by this, instead of this," pointing to the military insignia on his shoulder. He worked by love, rather than by law.

O Christ, I know that Thy power over me is the power of grace, for in Thee I am beaten to my knees by love. I can stand up to law, but I melt before Grace. Here I find Thee irresistible. For love gets behind my armor and I am defenseless before it. And I'm glad to be conquered by love. Amen.

AFFIRMATION FOR THE DAY: *Today God's grace toward me will make me gracious toward others.*

THE CROSS INHERENT

We saw yesterday that "grace and reality" were connected—inherently so. "The Lamb slain from the foundation of the world." (Rev. 13:8.) What does this mean? Is the cross built into the structure of things, built "from the foundation of the world"?

We have been taught that Christ died once and for all. He was "once offered." It was a finished fact in a certain point in history. We agree. Something did happen there at the cross that doesn't have to be done over again. But if the cross were suddenly imposed on history at a given point, something extraneous, then it would lack a cosmic validity. But if the cross is the scarlet thread that runs through the whole garment of existence, then it would have inescapable meanings. "The Lamb slain from the foundation of the world" points to the cross as inherent.

"The cross is the ground plan of the universe." If so, we would expect to see intimations of that ground plan everywhere. We do. Some of them crude, all of them unmistakably pointing to the cross. The foundations of houses and cities were often laid in ancient times in the blood of the first born. Life was laid in sacrifice. When the gods of Mexico had created everything except the sun, they sat around a fire trying to figure out how to create the sun. It couldn't be done. They were in despair. Then one of the gods threw himself into the fire, and out of his sacrifice the sun was created. Siva, one of the gods of India, is depicted with a blue throat—"he drank the poison that we might ambrosia taste." The seed dies that the plant may live. The mountains are barren that the valleys may be rich. The white corpuscles circulate through the blood stream watching for infection. When they find it, they absorb it if possible; but when they cannot, they fling themselves upon the intruder and die that the rest may live. The cross is in our blood. In the building of Boulder dam ninety-two men died and the tablet says: "They died that the desert might blossom as the rose." An American boy seeing a live bomb about to explode among his buddies, picks it up, holds it high above his head, and lets it blow his own hand off that the others might be saved.

O Thou Lamb slain from the foundation of the world, suffering in the sufferings of men, taking eternally upon Thy heart the sins and sufferings of men, we see Thee everywhere. "We see Thy blood upon the rose," and we see it on the lintels of our beings. We thank Thee. Amen.

AFFIRMATION FOR THE DAY: *"When I am about to run away from my tasks, that Strange Man upon His Cross brings me back again."*

GRACE DID MUCH MORE ABOUND

The cross is inherent, lifted up in history that we might see in a point of time something that is timeless. If a spotlight from Mars were to be pointed at the most important place on our planet it would fall upon a hill called Calvary. But there are lesser calvaries everywhere. Everywhere Christ is hungry in the hunger of the hungry, sinful in the sin of the sinner, He takes it all on Himself.

That means that grace is everywhere, healing, redeeming, saving. "Where sin abounded grace did much more abound." Where disease abounds the grace of health doth much more abound. "The grace of . . . Jesus Christ overflowed far more richly." (Rom. 5:15, Moffatt.) The grace was unrestrained, it overflowed. Or, as Paul puts it again, "The grace of our Lord flooded my life." (I Tim. 1:14, Moffatt.)

A little girl, a refugee from bombed England, wistfully asked her American hostess, when a full glass of milk was placed before her, "How deep may I drink?" She wasn't sure it was *all* for her. How deep may we drink of grace? Is it *all* for us? It is! "Take what you want," says God, "and pay for it." And the paying? It is not our goodness, but our gratitude. Not our worthiness, but our willingness.

The Way is not the way of karma, but the way of grace. And yet there is a truth in karma. The fact is that grace is in karma too. Karma says that you reap what you sow. This is true, but only partly true, for other people reap what we sow. Bound up in a bundle of human relationships, we pass on to others the good and evil results of our sowing. The good results? Yes! So Jesus, standing at the center of existence, passes on to all of us His good karma—His deed of the cross lets grace overflow to everybody. The fact that others reap what we sow opens the way to the vicarious. So "the Lamb [was] slain from the foundation of the world." He is everywhere, even in the hard doctrine of karma. I see His cross in every telegraph pole with its crossbeam. And the message of grace is coming over every wire to us. Many wires but one message: "Grace." Grace is written in the Scriptures, but also in the texture of reality. It is written everywhere, in everything.

O Christ, I find Thy grace seeking, searching, saving. I open my heart, my inmost heart, to its gentle intrusion. I breathe deeply of Thy grace, take it into every fiber of my being, and I am healed and released. I am grateful— so grateful. Amen.

AFFIRMATION FOR THE DAY: *Grace sought me, Grace bought me, Grace taught me, Grace caught me—now Grace has me.*

GRACE PRODUCES SPONTANEOUS GOODNESS

There is a fear, a lingering fear, that this emphasis on grace weakens one. Said a Western missionary, turned Hindu: "I preferred to have my children grow up under karma rather than under grace." He had the notion that grace weakens, and that karma puts iron into you.

But this notion is deeply mistaken. Paul puts it this way: "Much more shall those who receive the overflowing grace and free gift of righteousness reign in life . . . through Jesus Christ." (Rom. 5:17, Moffatt.) Those who receive this grace "reign in life." They reign not only in this little marginal victory or that side line accomplishment, but they "reign in life." Life centrally and fundamentally is under their control. They know how to live, life is theirs. Just as the airman reigns over the sky because he obeys the laws of flying, so the Christian reigns over life because he obeys the laws of life.

Grace binds you with far stronger cords than the cords of duty or obligation can bind you. Grace is free, but when once you take it you are bound forever to the Giver, and bound to catch the spirit of the Giver. Like produces like. Grace makes you gracious, the Giver makes you give.

Karma weakens you, makes you legalistic, bargaining. It produces the Pharisee and the proud Brahman. Both are discredited—life can't use them. Grace strengthens you. "Be strong in the grace of Christ Jesus." (II Tim. 2:1, Moffatt.) The grace of Christ Jesus produces strength, strength of character and strength of love. Those who are swayed by grace do ten times as much as those who are swayed by karma. They have no limitations and no inhibitions. Their grace overflows to everybody.

Grace is not only the key to strength, it is the key to knowledge. "Growing in the grace and knowledge of our Lord and Saviour Jesus Christ." (II Pet. 3:18, Moffatt.) Grace is first, and knowledge is second. You don't know unless you know grace. Knowledge without grace is ignorance, you haven't the key to unlock the mysteries of the Kingdom. But when you start with grace, then everything is open to you. Life is one glad, glorious, opening surprise.

O Christ, I thank Thee that Thou comest to me not as the teacher first of all. Thou comest with grace, grace for my sins, for my weakness, for my health, for my lack of resources, for my ignorance—for everything. Now since I accept Thy grace I can be taught. Teach me. Amen.

AFFIRMATION FOR THE DAY: *Where sin has abounded in me Grace now much more abounds in me. I live by that "much more."*

THE WAY IS THE WAY OF PRAYER

We said in our last week's meditation that the Way was primarily the way of grace, that this grace was invading us, trying to get to us in every possible way short of breaking down our personality. There, grace pauses and awaits consent and co-operation. A lack of consent and co-operation ties God's hands. The giving of consent and co-operation looses God's hands so that God who is "perfect everything can give us perfect everything."

We come now to the method by which we allow grace to invade us and work with us. *The Way is the way of prayer.* Many definitions of prayer have been given. I add another: *Prayer is co-operation with God.* In prayer you align your desires, your will, your life to God. You and God become agreed on life desires, life purposes, life plans, and you work them out *together.* That is prayer. Prayer, then, is not trying to get God to do our will. It is the getting of our will into line with God's will. But the will is not a separate portion of us—the will is the self in action. So prayer aligns the whole self to the whole Self of God. Prayer is therefore attunement. Just as when a note on a well-tuned piano is struck, the corresponding note on a well-tuned violin will vibrate in unison, so when God strikes certain notes in His nature, we find our heartstrings vibrating in unison, provided prayer has attuned us. We quoted in another connection this definition of prayer: "To bring the whole of life into the presence of God for cleansing and decision." "For cleansing and decision"—prayer cleanses, it chastens our desires, realigns them so that you cannot tell where your desires end and God's desires begin. They are one. Since the desires are one, the decisions are one, and the power is one. You lay your impotence alongside of God's potence and lo, your impotence has merged into potence, yes, into omnipotence. When you learn how to pray, you learn how to live—vitally, vibrantly, victoriously. "We can't account for you," said some sociology students to a Christian, "there's nothing in your background to account for the things you do." Nothing—except prayer. That Christian was an ordinary man doing extraordinary things—through prayer.

O Christ, my powers are no longer what they are, but what they can be —in Thee. Heighten them so that I shall be weakness made strong, ignorance made wise, evil made good. I thank Thee. Amen.

AFFIRMATION FOR THE DAY: *"Wait for the Eternal; be strong, my soul, be brave; yes, wait for the Eternal."* (Ps. 27:14, Moffatt.)

LORD, TEACH US TO PRAY

When Jesus was "alone praying, His disciples were with Him." (Luke 9:18.) "Alone" and they "with him." Physically they were together but actually they were poles apart. He had a secret they didn't share, and the secret was prayer. He prayed and He was power; they didn't pray and they were powerless. He was always well; they were always sick of themselves and others. He was masterful as He moved from task to task; they fumbled over the simplest tasks. The afflicted boy "had a better case of demon-possession than the disciples had of God-possession so they couldn't meet the situation." They weren't God-possessed because they weren't prayer-possessed. So they asked Him to share His secret: "Lord, teach us to pray." And He taught them the Lord's Prayer, which might be better named "The Disciples' Prayer." It is the essence of right prayer.

The prayer breaks up into two parts—the God-side and the man-side: (1) "Our Father, Thy name, Thy Kingdom, Thy will." (2) "Give us, forgive us, lead us, deliver us." The first side is Realignment and the second side is Result. In the first side we realign life to our Father, to His name, to His Kingdom, to His will, and in the second we get the result—He gives us, forgives us, leads us, delivers us. These are the alternate beats of the heart of prayer: Realignment—Result, Realignment—Result. And each side of the heartbeat is equal—four things in the Realignment and four things in the Result. In other words, you get as much Result as you have Realignment, and only that much. The more you realign your purposes to God's purposes, the more results you get. The emphasis, then, should be on the Realignment, and the Result will take care of itself. If you are always looking at results you're on the wrong side of things. Look at the means, and the ends will take care of themselves. "You have one responsibility," said God to a modern saint, "and only one responsibility, and this is to live in union with me." When he lived in union with God, then God undertook to look after all the rest. "He has a Christlike indifference to results," was said of a Christian who looked after the means. The results took care of themselves. Learn the first part of the Disciples' Prayer, and the second part takes care of itself.

O Christ, how tenderly wise Thou art. Thou dost always get first things first and therefore results always come out right. I am nervously looking after results and nothing comes out right. Forgive me, and help me. Amen.

AFFIRMATION FOR THE DAY: *"Leave it all quietly to God, my soul."* (Ps. 62:1, Moffatt.)

OUR FATHER

We saw yesterday that the Disciples' Prayer has two heartbeats—Realignment and Result. Today we look at the first. We must align ourselves to: Our Father, Thy name, Thy Kingdom, Thy will.

The first is: Father. In the conception of "Father," a new conception of God, there are two things: Love and Rulership. And these two are one: His rulership is through love. No matter how apparently stern that rulership may be, the animating motive behind and through it is love. God cannot do anything other than the loving thing. In everything that happens to you God will do the best thing that love can do in those circumstances. God doesn't love, "God *is* love." He acts according to love, for He could not act against His own nature.

When you pray then to the Father, you may know that love is going to do the best that love can do for you, in the long-range and short-range purposes of life. Love will always respond either with "Yes" or "No," but whichever one it is, it is always love.

But there is a qualifying word to Father, the word "Our." That determines the nature of religion. Suppose it had been "My"? That would have changed the nature of religion. Instead of being social and we-centered, it would have been individual and I-centered. That would have started us off wrong, the whole prayer would come out wrong. That word "Our" means a shifting of the emphasis from me to the Father and to my brothers. In other words, it means a renunciation, a renunciation of myself. It is the same thing we run into straight off in the first Beatitude, "Blessed are the poor in spirit [the renounced in spirit]: for theirs is the kingdom of heaven." All the resources of the Kingdom belong to the renounced in spirit. So in this first word "Our," we find a hidden but positive demand that we start off self-surrendered to the "Father" and to "Our." If so, then everything is open. If not, everything is closed. The rest of the prayer turns dead if the "Our" isn't alive. And what would "alive" mean? It would mean that "Our" must stretch beyond family, class, race, color, religion, reach to everybody, everywhere. For the word "Our" is unqualified and is therefore without restrictions or limits.

O Father, I come to Thee wearing within my heart the word "Our," and that word is now being cleansed from all limitations. Make it truly "Our" with everybody in, those of my race and those of all races, those I like and those I dislike. In Jesus' name. Amen.

AFFIRMATION FOR THE DAY: *"The Eternal listens to a life in need."* (Ps. 69:33, Moffatt.)

THE LORD'S PRAYER UNFOLDED

We saw yesterday that the word "Our" is a key word. Leave it out and the prayer won't open, for the prayer would then read, "Give me, forgive me, lead me, deliver me." The very nature of the prayer would be changed from social to solitary. The whole development of religion is the development of the word "Our." When that word "Our" is truly Christianized, it takes in everybody of every race and color, including enemies. The high priest, when he went into the Holy of Holies, wore upon his breast the names of the twelve tribes of Israel. When we go into the Presence of the Father, we wear a simple word, a word that goes beyond the tribal relationship, the word "Our." So when we say "Our Father," in those two words are the Fatherhood of God and the Brotherhood of man. Two worlds revealed in two words.

We come now to the second step: "Thy Name." The word "Name" stands for the character in Scripture. To pray "In Jesus' name" means to pray "in Jesus' character." In other words, we pray a prayer consistent with the character of Jesus, the kind of prayer Jesus would pray. This is the thing that determines whether the prayer is Christian. "Hallowed be thy name." ("Thy name be revered"—Moffatt.) In other words, "Thy character be revered" is my first consideration. Jesus put first the determining thing—God's character—while we put the determining thing—Jesus' character, "in Jesus' name"—last. Perhaps it would be better if we started our prayers by saying, "Father, I'm praying this prayer in Jesus' character. He would approve it. It squares with His character." That would cause many prayers to die on our lips unuttered. Like the Mohammedan who washes his feet before going into the mosque, this would wash our mouths, our hearts, our motives. "Thy character be revered as first, before my desires, my petitions." That puts God's character first and my claims second—puts us both in the right place. It also clarifies the next two items: "Thy Kingdom, Thy will." The "will" of God, as expressed in the "Kingdom" of God, is not arbitrary and whimsical. It is an expression of the character of God. A thing is not right because God says so. He says so because it is right.

O God, I see that Thy laws and decrees are not the arbitrary rulings of an omnipotent potentate, but the very expression of Thy nature—a revelation of Thyself. Amid them we feel a heartbeat, the heartbeat of Love. Amen.

AFFIRMATION FOR THE DAY: *"Thy kingdom is an everlasting kingdom, and thy dominion lasts from age to age."* (Ps. 145:13, Moffatt.)

THY KINGDOM COME

We come to the third petition: "Thy Kingdom come." Here Jesus put the Kingdom the first consideration after establishing the fact of the prayer as being according to God's character. Any prayer or program or creed that does not put the Kingdom first is not a Christian prayer, a Christian program, or a Christian creed. For Jesus said, "Seek ye first the kingdom of God . . . ; and all these things shall be added unto you." If you seek something else first, all these things shall be subtracted from you. In a town in Alaska I found all the electric clocks "off." I was told that the fault was in the power plant. It didn't run with systematic regularity, and its irregularity threw all the clocks "off." When your loyalty is not the Absolute, then everything is "off."

Judged by that standard, is it any wonder that the Church has had nothing but problems through the ages? When it drew up its creeds, the Apostles', the Athanasian, the Nicene, it mentioned the Kingdom of God once in all three of them, and then only marginally, beyond the borders of this life, a heavenly Kingdom. No wonder the Church has stumbled from problem to problem when its supreme value was lost or only marginally held. The Church will never get straightened out until it puts the Kingdom where Jesus put it in this prayer—the first consideration and the first allegiance.

I read a very scintillating commentary on the Acts of the Apostles, and after I had read through the comments of the first two chapters covering some sixty pages, I woke up to the fact that something was missing—the Holy Spirit had not been mentioned, not been mentioned in commenting on the chapters where the Spirit was given! It was a Holy-Spiritless Christianity. Hence anemic. The same strange omission has taken place in regard to the Kingdom of God. It is the motif running through everything Jesus taught. But I pick up a Confession of Faith drawn up by a denomination, and the Kingdom of God is not mentioned. The Kingdom of God and the Holy Spirit are the two missing notes in much of our Christianity. And Jesus made both of them central—one the pattern, the other the power.

O Christ, I thank Thee that Thy Kingdom may come through me now. My channels are open. I know the Kingdom is the answer, the answer to all our needs. So may Thy Kingdom come through me this day in everything I do and say. Then I shall be the agent of the Answer. I shall be the Kingdom—in miniature. Amen.

AFFIRMATION FOR THE DAY: *I live and move and have my being in the Ultimate Reality—Thy Kingdom.*

THY WILL BE DONE IN EARTH

We come to the last of four petitions on the God-side of the Disciples' Prayer: "Thy will be done in earth, as it is in heaven."

This last portion explains the previous portion: the coming of the Kingdom of God is the doing of the will of God in earth as it is done in heaven. So "Thy will be done in earth *as* it is in heaven" means a complete totalitarianism for us.

And this is to be "in earth." Perhaps the phrase "in earth" more nearly expresses the meaning than "on earth," as sometimes used. The Kingdom is not to come "on earth," as something imposed; it is to come "in earth," as something inherent. The earth and all it contains has a single law of its being, that law is the Kingdom of God. That law is the law of its life, the way life is made to work. When that law is lived, then the being is fulfilled, it finds the Way. When that law is not lived, then the being is frustrated, it finds not-the-way. There isn't a law of your body that contradicts the laws of the Kingdom. They are the laws of the Kingdom, they are "in earth" and in everything on the earth. When the psalmist says, "Thy rule and order last to-day, for all things are thy servants" (Ps. 119:91, Moffatt), he stated not an idea, but a fact. When "all things" serve God, they serve themselves. When they serve themselves apart from or against God, they lose themselves, they go to pieces. Again, when the psalmist says, "Only the rebels have to live forlorn" (Ps. 68:6, Moffatt), he was lifting up an inherent fact, for those who obey the Kingdom are not forlorn, they are fulfilled. The kingdoms of this world will be secure only when they become "the kingdom of our Lord, and of his Christ." "Your kingdom shall be secured for you, after you have learned that it is the Heavens who reign." (Dan. 4:26, Moffatt.) That is our world security, and only that. "I see a limit to all things, but thy Law has a boundless range." (Ps. 119:96, Moffatt.) A boundless range? A universal range. For the will of God is the life of all beings; "outside of God there is only death." For "Thy hands made and moulded me, to understand thine orders." (Ps. 119:73, Moffatt.) We are made to understand the Kingdom. All other knowledge is ignorance.

O God, our Father, Thy hands fashioned me for Thy ways and Thy Kingdom. When I take my ways I am attempting the impossible—to live against the laws of my being. How can I do that? I cannot. Amen.

AFFIRMATION FOR THE DAY: *"Right well they fare who love thy law; their road is clear."* (Ps. 119:165, Moffatt.)

"GIVE US THIS DAY"

We turn now to the second half of the Prayer. We saw that our kingdoms, whether within or without, whether in the individual or in the collective, are only secure as we have learned that it is the heavens who reign. We turn to the earth only after getting our heavenly bearings. Just as the mariner on the sea has to get his bearings from the stars to be able to put into the right earthly port, so we have to get our eternal values straight before we can get our temporal values straight. Nebuchadnezzar, lifted in pride, was humbled and ate grass like cattle until he realized that not he but the heavens rule. Then he was restored to reason and to his throne. We will continue to eat our words, to eat our plans, to eat our very dung until we too shall learn that the heavens rule and the Kingdom has the last word.

If we get the Kingdom values straight, then we can pray this prayer with some assurance: "Give us this day our daily bread." If we seek "first the Kingdom of God," all these things—food, clothing, all we need—"shall be added." The coming of the Kingdom of God would be the answer to the economic needs of men. For we would then pray, "Give us." Now we are saying, in an individualistic, selfish age: "Give me." If we continue to look after none but ourselves, think of No. 1, then we ourselves will become Enemy No. 1. And we'll have to think of ourselves so much that we will become sick of ourselves, our complexes, and our obsessions. That will be our punishment. We asked for ourselves, and we got ourselves a problem. For the first time in history, man has become a problem to himself. Why? Because he has said, "Give me." Note that "Give me" was the first request that sent the prodigal to hunger amid swine. We have become a prodigal generation for the same reason. And we will get out of this alien "far country" and beyond "poverty amid plenty" only when we pray the prayer, "Give us." For to say, "Give us" would mean the following out of the opening words, "*Our* Father." It would mean a co-operative order instead of a ruthlessly competitive one. Nature would work with us.

O God, our Father, Thou hast made the earth and hast made it bountiful and hast made it so that it would respond to "Give us." Help us to pray that prayer and to pray it not with our lips, but with our plans and our purposes. Help us to build Thy co-operative commonwealth. Amen.

AFFIRMATION FOR THE DAY: *"We who are strong ought to bear the burdens that the weak make for themselves and us."* (Rom. 15:1, Moffatt.)

FORGIVENESS FOR ECONOMIC SINS

We continue into this week our meditation on the Prayer. We come to the second petition on the man-side of the Prayer: "And forgive us our trespasses, as we forgive those who trespass against us." I use the word "trespasses" instead of "debts." The word "debts" has now a monetary significance that has narrowed it, while trespasses has the wider significance of anything we have done against another—any trespass we have made upon the rights, upon the soul of another, any hurt inflicted.

But the prayer connects the forgiveness of trespasses with the getting of daily bread by an "and." Are most of the trespasses we need to have forgiven connected with the economic side of life, connected with the getting of our daily bread? Yes. Our greatest sins are economic sins, sins so hidden under respectability and under custom that we are scarcely aware of them. "Luxuries are the things which make others do without necessities." That bites into the consciences of us all. When we see how few produce and how little they get for the production, and how many, as nonproducing middlemen, rake off exorbitant profits as production passes through their hands on its way to the consumer, then we realize that there is a lot of trespassing both upon the producer and the consumer. And trespassing that hurts. And when we see producer in turn deliberately keep down production to keep up prices though in doing so he may cause children to starve, then we know we must pray this prayer, "Forgive us our trespasses."

We will have to continue to pray that prayer until we come to a co-operative order where when I work for myself, I work for others, and when I work for others, I work for myself. That would be an order in which I love my neighbor as I love myself. That would be the Way. Until then we will stumble from depression to depression. These depressions are God's goads, goading us to the Way. If we won't learn from the Way, we have to learn the hard way. If we won't take from God's hand of grace, we have to take from His hand of judgment.

O God, Thou art teaching us Thy Way, teaching us through Christ and through catastrophe. Help us to take the way of Christ instead of the hard way of catastrophe. For we are stupid and blind and we hurt ourselves. Full of self-inflicted bruises we come to Thee for forgiveness. Amen.

AFFIRMATION FOR THE DAY: *"It is good for me to have been in trouble —to learn thy will."* (Ps. 119:71, Moffatt.)

FOR THINE IS THE KINGDOM

We are to ask God to forgive us on condition that we forgive others. If we do not forgive others, then we can never, never be forgiven. We have broken down the bridge over which we must pass. This necessity for giving forgiveness if you are to get it, is the only portion of the prayer upon which Jesus turns and comments. He thus showed the importance He attached to this matter, vital importance. And note that the forgiveness we are to give others is past, not future—as we "ourselves *have* forgiven." (Moffatt). The basis of expectancy of forgiveness is the fact that we *have* forgiven others.

Consider the next item in the Prayer: "And lead us, not into temptation, but deliver us from evil." I have inserted the first comma, which is legitimate, since there was no punctuation in the original. That changes the sense. The prayer is for leading—"Lead us." The rest points to where the leading should be—"not into temptation, but deliver us from evil." This portion of the Prayer is hardly morally intelligible without the punctuation, for God cannot lead into temptation. At first sight the Prayer seems to end on a low note. We would have expected some high exultant note. And yet I wonder if the petition itself is not the highest: "Lead us, so that evil is not a temptation to us any longer." We are to get to the place where we are beyond temptation. That is victory.

The last portion is actually a prayer for deliverance from evil. Not a deliverance from this, that, or the other evil, but from "evil" itself. To Jesus evil was evil in whatever form it came—whether in the evil of the flesh or the evil of the disposition, whether in the individual will or in the corporate will. Evil was never good and good was never evil.

The Prayer ends with an assertion: "Thine is the Kingdom, and the power, and the glory." Note, "Thine *is* the Kingdom"—now. God has never abdicated. He still rules. The "power" and the "glory" are "Kingdom power" and "Kingdom glory"—the unworthy type of "power" and "glory" Jesus rejected in the wilderness struggle. The "Kingdom power" and the "Kingdom glory" are the only "power" and "glory." All else is decaying power and fading glory.

O Christ, Thou art not only purifying us through prayer, Thou art purifying our very prayers. When our prayers have a bath of Thy mind these rise up how pure, how simple, how real! Purify our prayers. Amen.

AFFIRMATION FOR THE DAY: *"Thinking on how to live, I turn to thy directions."* (Ps. 119:59, Moffatt.)

PRAYER IS REALITY

We are now ready to consider prayer in more detail.

1. *Prayer is Reality.* There are some who feel that prayer is good exercise, good autosuggestion, but that it is not Reality. Suppose it were only autosuggestion, then it would be worth while, for it would be good autosuggestion. It would suggest to us the highest, namely, that there is purpose in the universe, that it is a good purpose, that you can ally yourself with that purposeful goodness and live by it. This is far better in its psychological results than if you were to suggest to yourself that there is no purpose behind the universe and the whole process is leading nowhere except to ultimate despair. That is bad autosuggestion with bad results. If prayer were only autosuggestion, I would still pray. It's a better hypothesis with better results. But I would find it difficult to pray for long, for we cannot give ourselves to an unreality. I do not want to live in a paradise if it turns out to be a fool's paradise. But how could prayer be unreal if its results are so real? "His face shows he is a man of prayer," was said of a Christian. Those who pray not only have better faces; they have better lives behind those faces—more power, more purity, more peace, more poise.

"To talk with God,	"To walk with God,	"To wait on God,
No breath is lost—	No strength is lost—	No time is lost—
Talk on!	Walk on!	Wait on!"

"I've let down in my quiet time and I've suffered defeats," said a returned missionary from China. Defeat in prayer meant defeat in practice. On the other hand, Mackenzie King, long-time prime minister of Canada, says: "I am able to meet my files with confidence and poise when I have spent a quiet time each day with God." A young woman had several breakdowns and was on the verge of another, went to her doctor and was surprised at his words: "Jane, I don't know what to do for you. You had better go home and get on your knees and pray." She did—and arose a new person. "Mother, wasn't that strange for him to say that to me?" she remarked. No, it wasn't, for experience had shown the doctor, skeptic though he was, that something happens in prayer—something very real.

O Christ, I know that Thou art the finest character who ever lived and Thou didst pray. Could unreality have created Thee, the only Real? Then teach me Thy secret, help me to know how to pray—really. Amen.

AFFIRMATION FOR THE DAY: *"Wait, wait for God; I shall again be praising him, my saving help, my God."* (Ps. 43:6, Moffatt.)

TO RISE AS ONE IMPERISHABLE

We continue regarding prayer as Reality.

A sailor, writing to his family, described the evening prayer time when he and two or three of his mates gathered: "We offer a prayer of thanksgiving for all His wonderful gifts and loving care, and ask for new strength to meet each day. It is these experiences that we will remember when the war is over, the rest is better forgotten." Those sailor lads on the deck of that ship knew when they touched Reality.

They knew what this German Christian, Van Meysenburg, knew: "To kneel as one that passes away, and to rise as one imperishable." I know that when I pray, I'm better; when I don't, I'm worse. I touch life with a perishable touch when I touch it without prayer, but when I do pray then I touch life with an imperishable touch. If you don't have a quiet time in the morning you'll probably have an unquiet time at night. A member of the House of Representatives said: "After a quiet time of prayer in these breakfast groups my desk is cleared more easily." His desk was cleared for he was cleared—by prayer.

After four weeks of failure by the Constitutional Convention to write one word of a constitution for the United States, Benjamin Franklin addressed George Washington as follows: "I have lived, sir, a long time; and the longer I live, the more convincing proofs I see of this truth, *that God governs in the affairs of men.* . . . And I also believe that, without his concurring aid, we shall succeed in this political building no better than the builders of Babel; we shall be divided by our little partial, local interests, our projects will be confounded, . . . and mankind may hereafter, from this unfortunate instance, despair of establishing government by human wisdom, and leave it to chance, war, and conquest. I therefore beg leave to move, That henceforth prayers, imploring the assistance of Heaven and its blessing on our deliberations, be held in this assembly every morning." From that moment they began to make progress and produced the Constitution, which Gladstone said was "the most remarkable work known to me in modern times to have been produced by the human intellect, at a single stroke." Prayer turned the tide.

O God, I know that Thou art putting prayer into my heart, not to mock me but to make me. I know that Thou art inspiring prayer to answer it. I know that my prayer moment is my most real moment. Amen.

AFFIRMATION FOR THE DAY: *"Yet I am always beside thee; thou holdest my right hand, guiding me with thy counsel."* (Ps. 73: 23-24, Moffatt.)

PRAYER IS RECEPTIVITY

We studied yesterday the fact that Prayer is Reality. During a meeting of the National Bankers' Association, the man who was elected president of the association made the following statement: "In all of the great moments of my life I have always prayed, and I would like at this time to ask the members of this association to bow with me in prayer." When he finished there was hardly a dry eye in that large meeting. That group had touched Reality—touched it through prayer.

We come now to our next step:

2. *Prayer is Receptivity.* To put the first two together: Prayer is Receptivity to Reality. God the infinite Reality is pervading us and invading us. The pathway over which He comes to the center of our beings and purposes is receptivity. I am tempted to put it "relaxed receptivity," but perhaps that would be unnecessary for receptivity, to be receptivity, must be relaxed. You cannot inscribe anything on a tense conscious mind. Receptivity is the surrendering of all fears, all doubts, all inhibitions, especially all self, for the ego even in God's presence asserts itself, wants to be God. It must be surrendered.

That surrender does not mean collapse. It does not mean that we become mushy meaninglessness in His presence. It means that we offer to God an alert self, not now eager for its own way, but for the Way. A self that, knowing its place as second, is eager to serve the First. A surrendered self is not pulp. It is a person, and now a person with a controlling purpose, a purpose to follow the Person wholly.

A shop assistant puts it this way: "I just go quiet and empty into His presence and give myself time for His loving counsel to come through." "Time for His loving counsel to come through"—time and receptivity. Time alone would not be enough unless along with it were the alert receptivity. A schoolgirl of fifteen told of her plan: "I get into bed and think prayers, and then I relax my mind and body and something comes to me. I feel as if I were in a different world and am so happy." She *was* in a different world—the invading Love of God took possession of the center of her being thrown open through relaxation and receptivity. Receptivity is faith, no longer struggling but serene and securing.

O Thou Living Christ, who dost come to my heart amid the silences, and who dost heal every hurt in Thy coming, I throw open every pore of my being to Thee, to Thy healing. Thou alone art all I want. Amen.

AFFIRMATION FOR THE DAY: *"Leave all to the Eternal, who loves you."* (Ps. 55:22, Moffatt.)

PRAYER IS RESPONSE

Prayer is Receptivity, we said yesterday. A further step today:

3. *Prayer is Response.* If prayer were only receptivity it would leave us leaning too much toward the passive side. It would leave us in an attitude of taking without undertaking. The taking of God must produce undertaking for God. The quiet must quicken. And it does.

Prayer is creative. When our lesser life touches Life it becomes alive —alive to the fingertips. The account says: "In the early morning, long before daylight, he got up and went away out to a lonely spot. He was praying there when Simon and his companions hunted him out and discovered him; they told him, 'Everybody is looking for you,' but he said to them, 'Let us go . . . that I may preach . . . That is why I came out here.'" (Mark 1:35-38, Moffatt.) He came out to this lonely spot—to preach! "That is why I came out here." The praying was preaching, at least, preaching in incubation. The praying stimulated the preaching, the receptivity became response. The impression of the prayer hour became the expression of the preaching hour. The most active persons in the world are the people who become inactive in the Silence. There they learn to live in the passive voice that they might live more effectively in the active voice. Alexis Carrel says: "Prayer is the most powerful form of energy one can generate." Prayer *is* a form of energy, for those who pray do not waste energy in fussy activity, a running around in circles, getting nowhere fast. The poised prayerful heart is sure of its directions, is sure of its resources, and moves from task to task with calm confidence. The prayerless are hurried, flurried, worried. They wear themselves out with frictions.

A student in a theological seminary told me of the profound effect upon him and others when Kagawa stood up and prayed a prayer of a single sentence, "O God, may we wake up to Jesus." Prayer does wake us up to Jesus—does give us His awareness and His energy.

> "You must use your hands while praying, though,
> If an answer you would get;
> For prayer-worn knees and a rusty hoe
> Never raised a big crop yet."

O God, wake us up to Jesus. Give us His passion for prayer and His passion for people. May our needs drive us to Thee and the needs of others drive us to them. For we have discovered a working force. Amen.

AFFIRMATION FOR THE DAY: *"The Eternal was on your side, because you were on his side."* (II Chron. 15:2, Moffatt.)

PRAYER IS RENEWAL

We come now to the next fact of prayer:

4. *Prayer is Renewal*. Like a watch, life has a tendency to run down. It needs rewinding. Prayer rewinds the springs of life. You don't have to tinker with the hands to make them go by shoving them around, not if the spring is sound and wound. Prayer brings resources.

John Burroughs suggested a sentence for one of the rooms of the Bok Singing Tower: "It is so easy to get lost in the world. I come here to find myself." It *is* so easy to get lost in the world. I come to the prayer hour to find myself and my directions again. Prayer is the period of circling, like the homing pigeon, circling to gain a homeward direction. To prayer we come, turning round and round on ourselves. From prayer we go with the homeward direction in the heart. The wings no longer hesitate for the heart is sure.

And in prayer we not only find our directions, we find our resources to go the directions we know. It was said of Jesus: "The news of him spread abroad more and more; large crowds gathered to hear him and to be healed of their complaints, while he kept in lonely places and prayed." (Luke 5:15-16, Moffatt.) He ran away from the crowds— to pray. We run after the crowds—and don't pray. Hence we don't get the crowds, for the crowds see we have nothing to give. We preachers are often primarily crowd-conscious and secondarily prayer-conscious. Jesus was primarily prayer-conscious and secondarily crowd-conscious. He got both. We get neither. And when the crowds got to Him, He had something to give, for the next verse says: "Now the power of the Lord was present for the work of healing." Those two things were cause and effect: "He kept in lonely places and prayed. . . . The power of the Lord was present." These two things are also cause and effect: "He kept in public places and was prayerless. . . . The weakness of man was present."

Prayer is a lift-up with no let-down, for it is no mere shot-in-the-arm, a stimulant. It is a renewal, a renewal of resources. For in prayer you have a life transfusion. You are God-infused.

O God, give me a transfusion of Thy blood. Put within my withered veins Thy life so that I shall live, live abundantly and vibrantly and vitally.

> "'Tis life, whereof our nerves are scant,
>   O life, not death, for which we pant;
>   More life, and fuller, that I want." Amen.

AFFIRMATION FOR THE DAY: *"Never shall I forget thy laws, for they put new life into me."* (Ps. 119:93, Moffatt.)

PRAYER IS REVISION

We come to our next step in our thoughts about prayer:

5. *Prayer is Revision.* A revised version of your life is put out every time you pray, really pray. For in the silence before Him, you bring more and more areas of life under His control, more and more powers are put at His disposal, more and more channels of receptivity are opened, more and more alignments of our wills are made to the will of God. Someone has defined education as change. Then prayer is life's deepest education, for in prayer you are being educated at the place that counts—at the center of life. You are being educated in being.

> "Dear Lord, three things I pray:
> To see Thee more clearly,
> Love Thee more dearly,
> Follow Thee more nearly,
> Day by day."

If prayer is revision, then prayer means pruning. "He . . . cleans every branch which does bear fruit, to make it bear richer fruit." (John 15:2, Moffatt.) Cleans it of what? He cleans it of sucker branches that sap the life of the branch, suckers that bear no fruit, only keep the branch from bearing fruit. These sucker branches are not bad, they simply take life that should go into definite fruit bearing. Many of our lives are overgrown with the unimportant. We are busy with the nothings. Prayer brings the important to the center of consciousness and pushes the unimportant to the edges. An artist had beside him as he worked a collection of precious stones of many colors. When asked why, he replied, "I have to wash out my eyes constantly in the colors of nature." These colors clarified his colors. I look at Jesus and a sense of the worth-while comes upon me. I wash out my eyes in His colors. Someone tried to get slum children to clean up. They didn't respond to these appeals until another method was tried —a child with clean face and clothes was brought to them. Then they went off one by one and washed their faces. I look into the face of Jesus and I know when I do that, that I must wash my own face, my heart, my life. Prayer prunes out purposes and our persons.

O Christ, I look into Thy face, hear Thy voice, and I go away feeling as though I wanted to throw away something. I want to empty my hands to grasp a whole Christ, I want the eternally Worth-while. Amen.

AFFIRMATION FOR THE DAY: *"How can a young man keep life clean? By keeping to thy word."* (Ps. 119:9, Moffatt.)

PRAYER IS RELAXATION

6. *Prayer is Relaxation.* After Jesus had given the Disciples' Prayer, He told of the man at midnight going to a friend and asking for bread because someone had come in his journey and he had nothing to set before him. If I were an artist painting the picture of "The Christian," I would paint this man at midnight stretching out one hand toward the Friend asking for bread, and stretching out the other hand toward the man in need. We might call him "The Mediator"—mediating between Fullness and emptiness. We might call him "The Pray-er."

Jesus gave this picture to stress the importunate side of prayer. The man hung on and got what he wanted. Prayer creates persistent personality. But lest this parable should create tense, anxious personality, Jesus corrects this in the verses following by stressing relaxed receptivity. Three times he stresses the active: "ask," "seek," "knock"; but ten times He stresses the relaxed receptive side: "shall be given you," "shall find," "shall be opened unto you," "receiveth," "findeth," "it shall be opened," "will he give him a stone?" "will he give him a serpent?" "will he offer him a scorpion?" "give the Holy Spirit." (Luke 11:5-13.) Here Jesus gave an emphasis of ten to three on the accepting side of prayer. But we cultivate the asking side, not the "shall be given you"; the seeking, not the "shall find"; the knocking, not the "shall be opened." We are active instead of active-taking.

In breathing, the outbreathing and the inbreathing are equal. But suppose it were all outbreathing and no inbreathing? You'd die—on a half emphasis. In prayer, you must breathe out, remind God of your need; but you must also breathe in, receive from God for your need. The rhythm of prayer: Outreach—Intake; Outreach—Intake.

> In the heart of man—a cry;
> In the heart of God—supply.

This, then, is another rhythm: Cry—supply; cry—supply. But the "supply" depends not merely on the supplication, but upon the relaxation, upon relaxed receptivity. Plead the petition, pay the price, pick up the gift, and go away rejoicing. Talk faith to God and yourself. But the faith must not be talking faith. It must be a taking faith.

O Christ, I have asked Thee and now I must go a step further. I must take from Thee. I grow bold in Thee since I am surrendered to Thee. So everything is mine. I take it. Amen.

AFFIRMATION FOR THE DAY: *"We are being transformed into the same likeness as himself."* (II Cor. 3:18, Moffatt.)

PRAYER IS RELEASE

We saw yesterday that prayer is relaxation. It is opening the depths to God, learning the art of listening. Hearing comes through attention. You can shut off your attention and thereby shut off the hearing. On the other hand, you can turn on the attention and hear when others hear nothing. You can cultivate attention and therefore cultivate hearing. Relaxed attention to God—that is prayer.

We come to the next step:

7. *Prayer is Release.* First of all, it is release from ourselves. Prayer is the most self-transcending attitude and act of which we are capable. It is a flight from the alone to the Alone. And then we are not alone —we are with Another. And being with that Another, we lose our aloneness, we become merged in Him. We cannot tell where our thoughts end and His thoughts begin, and where our acts end and His acts begin. For we are merged. Merged, not submerged. We are not swamped by God. We retain our sense of identity, and we are never so much ourselves as when we are most His. Someone, surprised at a famous surgeon pausing to pray as he began an operation, asked about the habit. His reply: "When I am operating I feel the presence of God so real that I cannot tell where His skill ends and mine begins." There was no ending and no beginning. They were one.

On the wall of a room of a church school I saw this placard: "I can do very little, *we* can do anything." That is pertinent to prayer. "I can do very little alone; we can do anything together." Prayer is working out life's solutions together. Here is a striking example: "My husband had an attack of angina pectoris. The heart specialist said that he could not live through the night as the artery leading to his heart was closed and hardened. When I asked him how long it would take to open he said: 'It will never open again.' I called our group to prayer. He lived on, is back to his office again, and has never had a return of it in any way. He really works harder than ever before, but the more intense part of his activities is for others and he uses God's strength rather than his own. This attack was ten years ago." If God and she handled that desperate situation together, cannot God and you handle your lesser situations? Prayer unties knots everywhere.

O Christ, in myself I am a mass of festering weaknesses. In Thee I am able for anything. So I shed my weakness and take Thy completeness. I am no longer little, I am in Thee. That suffices. Amen.

AFFIRMATION FOR THE DAY: *"Leave all to him, rely on him, and he will see to it."* (Ps. 37:5, Moffatt.)

PRAYER IS REJOICING

We come to our final consideration:

8. *Prayer is Rejoicing.* There is a rejoicing at the heart of prayer—a rejoicing that you have the answer to anything that may come. The prayerful heart is the confident heart, not confident with a self-hypnosis, but with a realization that anything that happens can now be overcome, mastered, and used. An alternate translation puts the familiar verse (Ps. 91:1) thus: "He that chooseth as his permanent abode the secret place of the Most High shall always be in touch with the almightiness of God." This is the secret of our inward hilarity. You can laugh at life, for you are more than a match for life.

Someone asked a joyous modern saint if Jesus ever laughed and his reply was: "I don't know, but I do know that he has fixed me up so that I can laugh." And this laughter is not merely at jokes, but a deeper laughter, a laughter at life itself, a triumphant laughter that knows that now in God you can meet life whatever happens.

There is this passage: "The full joy of thy presence." (Ps. 16:11, Moffatt.) The joy of the presence of God is a "full joy"—not a joy of a part of life that leaves you in conflict with the rest of life, but a joy which brings harmony to the whole of life, body, mind, and spirit. The trouble with prayerless joys is that they leave a conflict, a satisfying of one portion of the person, for instance sex, and then leave the rest of the person frustrated and in conflict. But this joy is a "full joy." It is unalloyed joy. An hour spent in the presence of God brings the purest joy known to man. "The joy of elevated thoughts," of which Wordsworth speaks, is good, but this joy in the presence of God is a joy not merely of elevated thoughts, something from us up, but a joy of descending thoughts, thoughts poured in from above. That is "the full joy" of His presence. Prayer creates the singing heart. A friend speaks of how "heaven lit upon my lips," and we think we can understand—he spoke heavenly words. But heaven not only lights upon our lips. It settles in our hearts, runs along our nerves, thrills in our bodies, and permeates our beings. Joy, joy, joy—the full joy of His presence.

O Christ, I thank Thee from the depths of my being that I have found in Thee a joy that knows no recoil and from which I do not have to recover. This joy is recovery, is health, is life. I kneel in speechless adoration at the wonder of it. Amen.

AFFIRMATION FOR THE DAY: *"Wait, wait for God. . . . I shall again be praising him, my saving help, my God."* (Ps. 42:5, Moffatt.)

STEPS TOWARD A REAL PRAYER LIFE

We come now to the steps we may take to establish a real prayer life. I give these suggestions as scaffolding that may be taken down when the building of real prayer has been established.

A Negro student said to me: "I go to these socials with these girls, but I don't know what to say to them. Can you help me?" I asked him whether he was in love with any of them, and he replied that he didn't think he was. I replied: "Then, that's your trouble. If you fall in love with one of them you'll know what to say." It is so in prayer. Fall in love with God and you'll know what to say. "Religion is a long falling in love with God." But love needs to be cultivated. It is not always "love at first sight." Love often comes through insight, insight gained over a long period of contact. So these suggestions are in order to let love through.

1. *Breathe a prayer for help as you begin life's most important exercise.* You are beginning something which will make the difference between weakness and strength, between defeat and victory.

2. *Remind yourself that God is more anxious than you to set up this relationship of two-way prayer.* You do not have to overcome God's reluctance. You have to lay hold on His highest willingness. All His barriers are down. All you have to do is to take down your barriers. Prayer lets God's love in.

3. *Determine that a vital prayer life is worth while—the most worth-while thing in life.* If patience in failure is necessary to learn any worth-while thing, then you must determine to be patient with your failures here. But remember they will be your failures, not God's.

4. *Decide how much time you can give to this prayer exercise.* Begin in a small way and then increase the time. I find I cannot get along with less than an hour and a half a day as a minimum. You may begin with ten minutes.

5. *Organize the rest of the day around this prayer time.* Don't let the rest of the day decide this prayer time. Let this prayer time decide the rest of the day. Fix that time and let it stay fixed so that each day you do not have to debate the question.

O God, I'm beginning life's most important lesson. I shall stumble and I shall fall, but if I stumble I shall stumble in Thy direction, and if I fall I shall fall on my knees. For in this are the issues of life and death. Help me. I believe that Thou wilt. Amen.

AFFIRMATION FOR THE DAY: *"Those who turn to the Eternal lack no good."* (Ps. 34:10, Moffatt.)

FURTHER STEPS TOWARD A REAL PRAYER LIFE

We continue our steps in the ladder of prayer:

6. *Fix the time in the morning, if at all possible.* If you fix your prayer hour at night it will be backward-looking. If you fix it in the morning it will be forward-looking. After Gethsemane, Jesus said, "Rise, let us be going"—be going to meet life's tragedies. Prayer should end in "Rise, let us be going"—to meet anything, anywhere. The psalmist says, "My prayer comes to thee in the morning." (Ps. 88:13, Moffatt.) Again, "I sing of thy strength, a morning song to thy love." (Ps. 59:16, Moffatt.) And again, "Morning by morning he awakens me to learn my lesson." (Isa. 50:4, Moffatt.) You are fresher in the morning and can learn better. "A vision of the Eternal's goodness in the temple at the morning-hour." (Ps. 27:4, Moffatt.) "I am up before the dawn to pray, waiting for thy promises." (Ps. 119:147, Moffatt.) Wait for God in the morning "when the soul of the day is at its best."

7. *Prime your prayer pump by reading from the Scriptures.* Let God speak to you through the Word, before you speak to Him through your words. It gives a climate to the prayer hour, starts your thinking in the right direction. Take a pen with you and note down what comes to you. That is an act of faith—something is going to come!

8. *Still the mind after reading the Word.* In that stillness God and your deepest desires can meet.

9. *If the mind wanders, do not be dismayed. Pray for the thing to which the mind wanders.* In that way you can redeem the wandering. It will be a prayerful wandering. So you need not worry about mind wandering.

10. *Pray for yourself.* If you are purified, then your prayers will be purified. I find myself praying less and less for things, and more and more for right relationships. For if I get the right relationships, then the things needed will come as a corollary. The purification of the loyalties is the essence of purification. If there is anything in your life about which you cannot pray, bring it up relentlessly and expose it to God's presence and to His suggestions.

O Christ, search me and see if there be any hidden sin in me, anything about which I do not want to pray. Bring it to Thy light and let me decide it there, there in the Light. And help me to decide it decisively and forever. For Thy mind is my healing and my health. Amen.

AFFIRMATION FOR THE DAY: *"Make the Eternal your delight, and he will give you all your heart's desire."* (Ps. 37:4, Moffatt.)

PRAYER AS THE CLIMATE OF THE DAY

We come to the remaining steps in learning to pray:

11. *Pray first for yourself, and then go out into concentric circles reaching out into ever-widening spheres.* You will grow with the reach of your prayers. Hold these objects of your prayers up to God in loving thought.

12. *Pray for people whom you dislike and who may dislike you.* That will sterilize any thought that may infect you.

13. *After you have prayed for others, ask if there are any "orders of the day" and then listen.* God has purposes and plans He would unfold through you. Listen for specifications. "Every morning I stand at attention before God to receive the orders of the day."

14. *Pray these prayers "in Jesus' name."* That is, in His character. That is the sieve through which the unworthy prayers drop. The Christian prayers remain.

15. *Believe that He hears your prayers and will give what you need, at the time needed.* Not necessarily what you ask, but what you need. God will supply "all your needs," not all your requests. He may give you something better than you ask. It will be as good as you ask, or better.

16. *Do everything that comes to your mind that would help answer the prayers.* God may answer the prayer through you.

17. *Drop it into the subconscious mind, and let it there be a prayer-attitude running through both the conscious and the subconscious attitudes.* It will not be a strained attitude, but prayerfully expectant.

18. *Let prayer be the climate of the day.* "Prayer is the melody you sing as you go about your work." Let it be an undertone as well as an overtone. It will then tone up the day.

19. *If you have to wait for anybody or for anything, such as a train or an elevator, fill in that waiting time with prayer.* That saves you from fretful frustration and makes your vacant spaces victorious spaces. You are never nonplused and you waste no time. In any case, "prayer is a time exposure to God," and in every moment of exposure to God you are better. You are the answer.

O Christ, in Thy presence I am made over again into Thy likeness. I would emerge from every prayer moment more alive to Thee, more alive to life, and more alive to others. For I know that the praying itself is the success, whatever comes out of it. Amen.

AFFIRMATION FOR THE DAY: *"For the Eternal delights in his people, adorning the afflicted with a victory."* (Ps. 149:4, Moffatt.)

A DISCIPLINED LIFE

We turn now to the truth that must be set over against the one we have been considering. We have been saying that the first law of life is receptivity, to know how to accept what Life offers to us.

A soldier asked Lilian Eubank in a U.S.O. club, "What kind of vitamins do you take?" He explained: "I have watched you for a month, and it does not matter how confusing a situation you are in, how disagreeable the people you are with, you always have a smile and a cheery word. I can't understand it." She said: "It isn't a vitamin at all, but a philosophy of life, that one has to smile when he or she really believes basically that everything works together for good—if you *let* it." That is the point—if you let it. If you know how to be receptive and responsive to God and let Him work things out for you.

But to do that we must learn to be disciplined persons. While the Way is the way of dependence, drawing strength from Another, nevertheless, in order to do that we must be disciplined. Very often "free grace" has been preached in such a way that it has weakened character. Paul warns against this in these words, "Do not make your freedom an opening for the flesh." (Gal. 5:13, Moffatt.) Here, liberty had become license. Discipline was needed.

The acceptance of grace is a privilege, a blessed privilege, provided it is permeated with discipline. Dependence plus discipline equals dependable disciples. This combination was shown in this incident in which God apparently showed a sense of humor. A woman writes that she had been healed, gloriously healed of paralysis in the legs and arthritis when she surrendered it all to God. Then she said: "Now Lord, you've healed me, what are you going to do about my overweight?" The answer: "This kind goeth not out save by fasting." Where only dependence could heal, that was the answer. Where only discipline could heal, that was the answer. The balanced life is the Way. The Christian is blessedly balanced.

Discipline, then, is not a turning into an unnatural, screwy type of person, but it does mean that the forces of life are not unharnessed forces that roam everywhere and get nowhere, except into trouble. They are harnessed to God's ends; they are disciplined.

O disciplined Christ, so disciplined and yet so free, teach me Thy secret. For only as I am disciplined can I dance the dance of freedom. I want my powers to be at the disposal of the highest. Amen.

AFFIRMATION FOR THE DAY: *"Happy are they who follow his injunctions, giving him undivided hearts."* (Ps. 119:2, Moffatt.)

THE WAY IS THE WAY OF DISCIPLINE

The Way is the way of discipline. Yesterday I saw a beautiful elm tree which had been blown over in a storm because some of the roots had strangled the tree. They had twined themselves around the base of the tree underground, so that the very things which were intended to sustain the tree had strangled it.

Our natural urges are given to sustain us, but if they get out of place they can strangle us. Sex dedicated is sustaining. But sex out of place, an end in itself, coils about the rest of life and strangles it. Self dedicated is sustaining, but if the self becomes the center of life it can strangle the personality. The trouble with the roots of that fallen tree was that, instead of reaching out beyond themselves, they turned back on themselves and the trunk. They were not disciplined to their original purpose. The natural became the unnatural.

Dr. Charles Mayo, one of the greatest surgeons of the world, came into a room dragging one of his legs clumsily. A friend of mine asked him about it. He replied: "There is a passage in the Bible which says, 'They made me the keeper of the vineyards; but mine own vineyard have I not kept.' I saw this coming on, but I would not pay heed." He had not disciplined himself to the advice he gave to others, and he dragged a lame leg through life as the result. Many of us are dragging ourselves lamely through life because we would not be disciplined to what we knew. They tell us that civilization depends upon the nine inches of topsoil on the earth; if that goes, we go with it. And yet we have wasted those precious nine inches with the result that millions languish upon eroded, impoverished lands, and gain a precarious living in dust bowls. The lack of discipline strikes back in undernourished bodies and decaying civilizations. Our personal lack of discipline strikes back at us in impoverished souls and bodies and in a decaying spiritual life. Be disciplined or be decadent.

I glanced up from my writing on a train and saw on a lever these words, "Lift up to release." We have to lift up to release. If we think we can turn our powers to lower purposes and be free, we are mistaken. You have to lift up to release.

O Christ, help me to lift up my powers to Thy purposes and Thy plans; then I shall be released and free. I am blinded by local clamorings. Give me the long look and the far-seeing purpose. Amen.

AFFIRMATION FOR THE DAY: *"I am the Eternal . . . training you for your good."* (Isa. 48:17, Moffatt.)

DISCIPLINE PRODUCES SPONTANEITY

The Way has been called "The Christian discipline." "The aim of the Christian discipline is the love that springs from a pure heart, from a good conscience, and from a sincere faith." (I Tim. 1:5, Moffatt.) Strange that the end of discipline is defined as spontaneity—"love that springs." And that is the end of discipline, to make you free.

There is a false idea of freedom prevalent in modern civilization: "You are free to do as you *like*." The Christian answer is, "You are free to do as you *ought*." Said a high-school boy to his principal: "Sir, they say that this is a free country. But where's my freedom? They tell me to go to school, and I have to do it; to study or to go home, and I have to do it. Where's my freedom?" He was serious—and in serious trouble with himself. A returned soldier, rebuked for something he said, replied, "I have fought over there to say and do exactly as I please." In both cases life did not approve; both these persons were in trouble with themselves and others. Liberty comes through obedience to law. A man who had lived a defeated life told how he became victorious: "It is silly for a poor mortal to buck the stream of life. I have always sought out its currents and have sought to flow with it."

Love can "spring," be spontaneous and free, only if it comes "from a pure heart, from a good conscience, and from a sincere faith." In other words, from a disciplined life. Any supposed freedom that leaves you with an impure heart, a bad conscience, and an insincere faith ends not in springing and singing, but in sighing and dying.

Another passage puts discipline as the result (the first passage puts it as "the aim"): "God has not given us a timid spirit but a spirit of power and love and discipline." (II Tim. 1:7, Moffatt.) The aim of discipline is to produce discipline. The first result of that discipline is courage—"not a timid spirit." A disciplined person has a sense of courage. He is afraid of nothing for he knows that the sum total of reality is behind him. He has a sense of "power" for he knows he is working with God, and God is working with him, and he has a "love" that springs and sings.

O Thou singing Christ, teach me Thy way, the way of discipline. For I too would sing. I too would be free. For Thy will is freedom; my will is bondage. When I take my way I end in a mess. When I take Thy way I end in courage, power, and love. Amen.

AFFIRMATION FOR THE DAY: *"My son, spurn not the Eternal's schooling."* (Prov. 3:11, Moffatt.)

DISCIPLINE PRODUCES LIBERTY

Discipline is not something that is imposed on us. It is discovering the laws of our being and finding that they are the laws of God. "Happy are they who follow his injunctions, giving him undivided hearts." (Ps. 119:2, Moffatt.) The opposite could be this: "Unhappy are they who follow their own inclinations, giving themselves a divided, conflicting self."

Again, the psalmist puts it thus: "Thy statutes are my songs, as I wander through the world." (Ps. 119:54, Moffatt.) Statutes become songs! Laws become a liberty—to sing! The idea of the disciplined person as a disagreeable person is false. The disciplined person is full of rhythm and song, for he is attuned to Life. It is true that Jesus said: "Everyone has to be consecrated by the fire of the discipline" (Mark 9:49, Moffatt), but this "fire of the discipline" only burns away the fetters. When the three Hebrew children fell bound into the fiery furnace, the fire did nothing to them except to burn their bonds. They walked around free in the fire. And the form of the Fourth was with them. The fire of discipline does nothing to you except to burn every clinging fetter and make you walk free with the Fourth. You are *consecrated* by the fire of the discipline." The fire frees you to be dedicated to the worth-while.

Someone has said that "beauty is the purgation of superfluities." Discipline takes away superfluities, confines us to the essentials, and makes life beautiful, for nothing clutters up the picture. We must so discipline our lives that nothing remains except that which counts and contributes.

"Miss America of 1945," addressing high-school students, said: "You cannot hate and be beautiful." They don't jibe. For hate is undisciplined love. Lust is undisciplined sex. Worry is undisciplined foresight. You cannot have an undisciplined life and be beautiful. For beauty is the harmony of lines. Discipline brings life into central harmony by directing it toward great ends. Discipline is development —development in harmony.

O Christ, I know I shall surrender myself to the discipline of something, to the discipline of the pressures around me, or to the discipline of Thy will and purposes. If I do the first I shall pass away, if I do the second I shall remain forever. Help me. Amen.

AFFIRMATION FOR THE DAY: *"Happy is he who has thy discipline and thine instruction, training him calmly to wait on, in adversity."* (Ps. 94:12-13, Moffatt.)

STEPS TOWARD A DISCIPLINED LIFE

Many people accept grace and rise to a new life and then it leaks out because of a lack of discipline. A brother prayed very often, "Fill me, Lord." A man near by was overheard to say, "You can't, Lord. He leaks." Many of us are not "filled," because if we were we would leak out. God isn't going to pour the water of His grace down the rat-holes of undisciplined living.

We must now take these steps in becoming a disciplined person:

1. *Let discipline begin at the center, not at the margin.* The center is you. You must be undivided in affection. It was said, "Asa's mind was undivided all his life." (II Chron. 15:17, Moffatt.) That is at the basis of all successful, effective character. "A double minded man is unstable in all his ways." (Jas. 1:8.) "Purify your hearts, you double-minded." (Jas. 4:8, Moffatt.) "Keep, then, an undivided mind for the Eternal our God, to live by his rules and to obey his orders." (I Kings 8:61, Moffatt.) One of the greatest tragedies of history is this: "When he grew old, he had no undivided mind for the Eternal his God. . . . His wives seduced him to follow foreign gods." (I Kings 11:4, Moffatt.) Solomon was a wise man turned foolish because of a lack of inner discipline—discipline at the place of his affections. He wanted mutually incompatible things and fell between stools. Listen to this sound advice: "To those who find them, they are life, and health to all their being. Guard above all things, guard your inner self." (Prov. 4:22-23, Moffatt.) Solomon must have said that with a wistful sigh, for it was the very thing he did not do. He did not guard his inner self, so his outer life came down in ruin around him.

Discipline the inner self by a complete self-surrender to God. Don't give up this thing, that thing. Give up the self and that carries everything else with it. God has *you*—and that means all you've *got.* I know of a man who is a marginally surrendered person. He is centrally unsurrendered, the self sticks out through all he does for God. A very discerning friend commented, "He came near being a great man." He surrendered the marginal, kept back the central.

O Christ, I know Thou art relentless, for Thou art love. Thou canst not be satisfied with my marginal allegiances. Thou art asking for me. And I give Thee that—now and forever. I am disciplined through self-surrender. The inner tension is gone. Thou hast me. I'm glad. Amen.

AFFIRMATION FOR THE DAY: *"The Eternal's law is in his heart, his footsteps never falter."* (Ps. 37:31, Moffatt.)

DISCIPLINE YOUR HABITS

We are now on the discipline of the center. Of one man someone said: "He cared little for his character and everything for his reputation." He tried to discipline a reputation, leaving an undisciplined character untouched.

Someone has said that "there are Seven Deadly Sins: The first is dishonesty, the other six are selfishness." But dishonesty too is a species of selfishness, so the seven are one—self-centeredness. The first discipline, then, must strike at the first sin—egocentricity.

2. *Discipline your habits.* Having surrendered the center, you may now deal with the margin. Go over your life and see if there is anything that is incompatible with that fundamental surrender of the self. Someone has defined a preacher as "one who preaches a whole gospel and wholly lives it." Evelyn Underhill speaks of "a willed correspondence to the world of spirit." Would it not be more Christian to speak of a willed correspondence to the will of God—in everything? A very intelligent woman who had gone through many cults in her quest writes: "After reading your chapter on discipline in *Abundant Living,* I finally stopped smoking after twenty years of consuming twenty cigarettes a day. I prayed God to replace my will with His will, as you teach, and really, it was not difficult." Perhaps your experience will.be like this pastor's: He battled with cigarette smoking, gave it up several times, would go back to it. One day he really prayed and these words came: "I can do all things through Christ who strengtheneth me." The desire left.

Perhaps the habit may be of another type: a sex habit that saps the lifeblood from the central purposes of life; or a habit of taking the line of least resistance instead of standing up for your principles; or a habit of evading responsibility, excusing yourself when opportunities are presented; or a habit of negativism, of always raising objections to positive plans; or a habit of criticism and faultfinding, of picking flaws in others; or a habit of living in a state of self-reference—"How would that affect me?"—or a habit of comparing yourself with others instead of with the will of God. Discipline all these.

O Christ, Thou art making me a disciplined person and I am glad. I feel that these barnacles which have accumulated through the years and have slowed down the progress of my ship are being sloughed off. I'm getting ready for action. I thank Thee. Amen.

AFFIRMATION FOR THE DAY: *"Happy are they who hold to what is right, who do their duty at all times!"* (Ps. 106:3, Moffatt.)

OUT OF GOOD AND EVIL STORES

Before we leave the disciplining of our habits we must turn to the positive side—replacement of the old by the new. Habit can work with you as well as against you.

Someone said to the exuberant Billy Bray, who was always praising the Lord: "Isn't it possible to get into the habit of praising the Lord?" "Yes," replied Billy, "and it's a very good habit, and so few have it." You can build up a set of good habits so that you habitually take the Christian way without thought. Every act repeated drops into the subconscious mind and becomes an attitude that easily repeats itself. Jesus says, "The good man brings good out of his good store." (Matt. 12:35, Moffatt.) The good which he brings forth is out of his good store, which is the sum total of accumulated good habits which have passed into attitude and character. No good action, therefore, is lost. Even though it seems to have no effect on the other person, it does something to you, becomes a part of your good store. This becomes a part of inevitable goodness. You are fated in the direction of good.

On the other hand, Jesus says, "The evil man brings evil out of his store of evil." (Matt. 12:35, Moffatt.) Every evil thought, every evil act or attitude becomes a part of the "store of evil." The "store of evil" becomes fate, destiny. Every temptation yielded to makes inevitably easier the yielding to the next temptation, until the character is fixed—in evil. Only the power of God can break it.

But to return to the "good store." You can add to the good store of your children by your example and your teaching. A magazine editor told of his boyhood days when his Irish father would say to him as he came back from work, "Have you told the truth? Have you fought square? If so, then begorra, you're all right. But if you haven't, I'll break every bone in your body." Rough teaching; but years later, when the editor was offered a half-million-dollar bribe to print certain things, he wouldn't accept it. There was his father's teaching—the "good store" held him in the crisis.

We speak of a man "making his pile." The "good store" is the pile that counts when you most need it.

O Christ, the simple thought, the simple act, the simple habit becomes a part of my store, a part of me. Teach me to watch day by day the little things that make me inevitably. I want to be a truly disciplined person, to be good inevitably. Amen.

AFFIRMATION FOR THE DAY: *"I know that his orders mean eternal life."* (John 12:50, Moffatt.)

DISCIPLINE YOUR COURAGE

We continue into this week our emphasis of the Way as the way of discipline. There are some who would say that "salvation is by character." We do not accept that. Salvation is by grace through faith—salvation is by Christ. It is a gift. But if it is a gift, it is also a growth, a growth in character. And character is developed through discipline.

That leads us to this step:

3. *Discipline your courage.* Every time you refuse to face up to life and its problems you weaken your character. Character needs courage to make it real character. If we have no courage, we are what Nietzsche called "moral cows in our plump comfortableness." Present-day civilization is suffering from a lack of moral courage. So many people are in the inglorious business of keeping their heads stuck in. If you do that long enough there won't be an idea left in that head when you do get it out. We are in the process of being standardized morally—and at a very low level. "Everybody does it," is the new moral code to which we bow and which we obey. A woman was losing her husband's affections over a lot of little things, among them his dislike for highly painted fingernails. When a counselor advised her to let this go for the sake of holding the family together, she replied in dismay: "But I couldn't face society if I did—everybody does it." She lost her husband because she had no courage to get out of step with an imperious but senseless custom.

Many of us lose our souls for lack of courage. We will not stand up and take it, so we crawl—become worms. If you are on the Way you must get used to the sight of your own blood. Paul speaks of four steps in development: "Knowing that trouble produces endurance, endurance produces character, and character produces hope—a hope which never disappoints us." (Rom. 5:3-5, Moffatt.) Note the steps: (1) trouble leads to (2) endurance; endurance to (3) character; and character to (4) hope. Character is formed out of endurance which is formed out of trouble and character brings forth hope—the only hope that will never let us down, will not disappoint us.

O Christ, I see that the trouble that comes from courage is strengthening my fiber, strengthening me, giving me hope, a hope that holds up. Then give me that gentle courage that will be disciplined to face life bravely and cheerfully. Amen.

AFFIRMATION FOR THE DAY: *"The Eternal is my light and aid; whom shall I fear?"* (Ps. 27:1, Moffatt.)

DISCIPLINE YOUR BEGINNINGS

We continue our meditation on discipline.

4. *Discipline your beginnings.* When Jesus spoke of the fire of discipline, He did so after mentioning three possible hindrances—hand, foot, eye. If any of these offends, that is, cuts across the purposes of your life, cut it off or pluck it out. We are to be disciplined at the place of the hand, the foot, the eye.

The hand is the thing that takes hold, the thing that grasps what we want. Don't take hold of a thing unless you want that thing to take hold of you. For your possessions often end in possessing you. Be careful of what you grasp. Grasp it only if you are willing that the thing shall grip you. The hand must be disciplined.

The foot approaches the thing desired. Don't walk toward a thing unless you are willing to take hold of the thing and have the thing take hold of you. Discipline your approaches to life. Many people think they can walk up to a thing and enjoy the anticipatory thrill of approach, but turn back this side of the deed. This is deadly, for it is destiny. You destine yourself to the deed when you decide to approach it.

The eye looks at the thing which you may approach and then may grasp and possess. Watch what you see. You first see, then seek. For seeing creates desire and desire creates emotion, and in the battle between the emotion and the will the emotion nearly always wins. Jesus put His finger on the necessity of the disciplined eye in these words: "Anyone who even looks with lust at a woman has committed adultery with her already in his heart." (Matt. 5:28, Moffatt.) The look leads to adultery in the heart, and adultery in the heart leads to adultery in the act, so quench adultery at the place of the look. Those who think they can indulge at the place of seeing and can pull back at the place of seeking, are putting their feet on a slippery bank. Discipline the beginnings and the ends will take care of themselves. In temptation, flight is better than fight. To avert the eye is easier than to avert the destiny that comes from approach to and handling of the desired thing.

Discipline the beginnings. The ends are in the beginnings.

O Christ, how wonderfully true Thou art to life. Thou dost lay it bare before our eyes. Through Thine eyes we see, really see. Help us to see and to seek what Thou didst see and seek. Then we shall be safe. Amen.

AFFIRMATION FOR THE DAY: *"When I think my foot is slipping, thy goodness, O Eternal, holds me up."* (Ps. 94:18, Moffatt.)

DISCIPLINE YOUR PERSISTENCE

We look at another place of discipline:

5. *Discipline yourself at the place of carrying through.* A great many good but ineffective people discipline their beginnings. They take up good things, but they don't carry through. Their lives are strewn with the wreckage of good beginnings and poor endings.

Don't take up everything that comes along. Save yourself for the best. "Beware of sacrificing your burnt-offerings at any sacred spot you see." (Deut. 12:13, Moffatt.) Save yourself to sacrifice your life offering on the Altar of the Worth-while. Louis Untermeyer prays:

> "From compromise and things half-done,
> Keep me, with stern and stubborn pride."

"You must not swerve to the right or to the left, but always follow the straight road of life which the Eternal your God has laid down for you, that you may live." (Deut. 5:32-33, Moffatt.) Get guidance from God, know your call, and then stay by it till you hear the recall. That doesn't mean that you may not have to retrace steps, change tasks, and callings—you may have to. But it does mean that once you know your call and your task, stay by it with the persistence of a puppy with a root. In a long-distance race the little man who finished last *finished*, though he was several laps behind, and the winner was already across the tape. Instead of dropping out as the rest had done when they saw they were beaten, he kept doggedly on. The crowd laughed at first, then applauded, and he got an ovation at the close.

"I am staying on. . . . I have wide opportunities here . . . , and there are many to thwart me." (I Cor. 16:9, Moffatt.) Many of us would have said: "I am quitting. . . . I have wide opportunities here, but there are too many things against me."

"The Lord said: 'Well, where is the trusty, thoughtful steward whom the lord and master will set over his establishment?'" (Luke 12:42, Moffatt.) Note two things: "trusty" and "thoughtful"—honesty and intelligence. Honesty without intelligence, or intelligence without honesty are both inadequate. But the "trusty" means not only honesty, but that he can be trusted to go through to completion.

O Christ, I know you want to use me. But I cannot be used unless I am trusty and thoughtful. Help me to be trusted to go through—clear to the end with unwavering persistence. Amen.

AFFIRMATION FOR THE DAY: *"Never will he let you slip; he who guards you never sleeps."* (Ps. 121:3, Moffatt.)

DISCIPLINE YOUR TIME

We look further at discipline:

6. *Discipline your time.* If, in discussing the last point of disciplining yourself to carry through to completion tasks taken up, your rationalization is, "Well, I haven't the time," then the answer must be: Discipline your time. If you actually haven't time for it, then you ought not to do it; it isn't your task. You must exercise the duty of refusing to do good. You must not take too much on your plate with a lot of leftovers.

But perhaps the real difficulty is that you don't use to best advantage the time you have. Your time is undisciplined. You carry on conversations long after they have run out of intelligence, for most conversations run out of intelligence in half an hour! You do not tackle your tasks decisively and get them done and out of the way. You daydream instead of think; you dawdle instead of do. You waste hours of time at games which are supposed to be recreation, but which wreck time and you.

Time is distilled opportunity. Don't waste it, for in doing so you lay waste yourself. Every wasted moment is so much wasted man, that man you. Budget your time. Plan your work, and work your plan.

Don't be always running to try to keep up with your tasks, keep them in hand, anticipate them. A sign says: "Don't write—wire." I'd like to reverse it: "Don't wire—write." For that means that you have looked ahead, have seen the thing coming, have met it ahead of time, instead of waiting till the last minute and then fussily wiring, feverishly telephoning long distance. That kind of person is upset and upsetting. He demands that people atone for his procrastinations by answering his feverish requests with feverish response.

The Man who influenced the world most was the Man with the leisured heart.

A little boy, late for school, asked God to help him to be there on time. He ran, stumbled, and breathlessly said, "God, I asked you to help me, but don't push me." Don't let your jobs push you; you stumble if you do. Discipline your time.

O Christ, when I look at Thee I see that Thou wast never in a hurry, never ran, but always had time for the pressing necessities of the day. Give me that disciplined, poised life with time always for the thing that matters. For I would be a disciplined person. Amen.

AFFIRMATION FOR THE DAY: *"He that believeth [in Him] shall not make haste."* (Isa. 28:16.)

DISCIPLINE YOURSELF TO "WHAT IS"

We look at another place of discipline:

7. *Discipline yourself to "What is."* There are many who are uselessly beating themselves upon the bars of life, beating their wings out, because they cannot fly. "If I were only there, or anywhere but here, I'd be all right." They dream of what they would do if they were not here.

But we've always got to live on what is. The children of Israel lived on manna in the wilderness as they journeyed to the Promised Land. Manna means, "What is." They didn't know what it was, so they called it "What is." They lived on "What is." You and I must live on "What is," no matter if we hope to live on "What will be." The children of Israel got tired of manna, but it sustained them till they got to the Promised Land. You and I may get tired of "What is," but we must learn to live by it till we get to our Promised Land.

I was off-loaded in Trinidad on my journey back from South America, off-loaded by two local passengers. I was a "through" passenger. It meant my missing important mass meetings in Miami, long planned. The priority officer agreed that I had had "a raw deal." But these words came to me as clear as crystal: "Lord, I do not ask for special treatment; I ask for power to take any treatment that may come, and use it." Peace settled within me. That sentence itself has lingered like a benediction within me ever since. I lived by it during that waiting period, lived by "What is," and have lived by it in many a situation since. To get that sentence was worth the delay. You can rescue out of every unjust, impossible situation something that makes that situation not confining, but contributing. You can live on "What is." And the manna will feed you, sustain you till you get to God's better thing—to God's Promised Land.

A letter carrier at fifty had a stroke which impaired one arm and made one leg drag helplessly. His letter-carrying days were done. Not so. He still distributes letters, all of them of good cheer. He sits in front of his house, waves a cheery greeting to everybody who goes by—the center of the city's good cheer. He is living on "What is" and is helping a city to do the same.

O Christ, I thank Thee that Thou didst live on the manna of the silent years of obscurity in Nazareth—and live on it gloriously. Help me to live on what comes, good, bad, indifferent. Then I shall live. Amen.

AFFIRMATION FOR THE DAY: *If I don't get what I like, then I shall like what I get.*

DISCIPLINE YOUR TONGUE

We must look at a discipline that is needed by all:

8. *Discipline your tongue.* The expression of a thing deepens the impression, so a word uttered becomes a word made flesh—in us. We become the incarnation of what we express. Jesus said: "By thy words thou shalt be justified, and by thy words thou shalt be condemned." This always sounded superficial until I saw that you become what you say. If you tell a lie, you become a lie. The deepest punishment of a lie is—the liar. He has to live with a man he cannot trust. That is an uneasy hell. There are therefore no "white lies," for they leave a black mark—on the soul. "Isn't a lie ever justifiable?" No, absolutely no. Evil means produce evil ends always. Let it be said of you as was said of Sara Teasdale: "Her later lyrics grew more and more straightforward, more dependent on an inner authority and less upon clever manipulation of facts."

Discipline your tongue not only to the truth but to the relevant truth. Discipline yourself to concise, straightforward speech. A speaker introduced by a very flowery, verbose chairman arose and said, "The adjective is the enemy of the noun." It is. Sometimes it is the speaker himself who weakens his nouns by his adjectives. A speaker sat down sadly after a wordy discourse and remarked: "I couldn't have said less, unless I had said more." He had preached his own funeral. Discipline your tongue to the relevant, to speech that is straightforward, that says what it means and means what it says.

Discipline your tongue to the loving. When in doubt, say the most loving thing and you will not be wrong. I asked the Western Union clerk if I could put the word "love" into a tourate telegram, telling of arrival, without de-tourating it. She replied: "Yes, for if 'love' weren't allowed to be put into tourate telegrams, it might cause trouble in homes." If we don't put "love" into everything we say, it may cause trouble anywhere. Paul says: "This is how I write. 'The grace of our Lord Jesus Christ be with you all.'" (II Thess. 3:18, Moffatt.) Is that how we write and speak: "grace . . . all"?

O Christ, nothing but gracious words proceeded out of Thy mouth. Discipline my tongue to the truthful, to the relevant, and to the loving. For my words will condemn me to be what they are. Then help me. Amen.

AFFIRMATION FOR THE DAY: *"Set a watch upon my mouth, O Thou Eternal, guard thou the door of my lips; may I have no mind to evil."* (Ps. 141:3, Moffatt.)

DISCIPLINE YOUR DISCIPLINES

Today we sum up our meditations on discipline. Discipline is not something imposed on a reluctant human nature by an arbitrary God. True, it is said, "He let you hear his voice out of heaven, for discipline." (Deut. 4:36, Moffatt.) But the "voice out of heaven" is exactly the same as the voice out of our needs. For the voice out of heaven only voices what we need, but often cannot voice. God's voice and our needs are one. Our choosing of disciplines is the choosing of the laws and demands of our beings. If this is true, then we must:

9. *Discipline our disciplines.* We must not allow them to become too obvious, too much a living by rule of thumb, too stilted. A person who is obviously trying to be disciplined is not rhythmical and winsome. The disciplines must be buried in the subconscious where they work naturally as a part of you. In the beginning you may have to impose them until they take root within you. But the end is to make them artesian instead of artificial. The disciplines must be as hidden as the art of the violinist who obeys rules, but seems not to be obeying anything except the creative urge within him. The rules have become a regularity, the laws have become a liberty.

Jesus said to His disciples, "Take heed to yourselves" just after He had said: "That will turn out an opportunity for you to bear witness." (Luke 21:34, 13, Moffatt.) The connection was obvious: Keep yourselves spiritually fit and ready, so that when you are suddenly brought by circumstances before an opportunity for witnessing you may not be nonplused. Your disciplines will then function as spontaneous habit. For the disciplines have become *you.*

The end of the discipline is not merely to make you, but to make you a Christlike you. "If he [the disciple] is perfectly trained, he will be like his teacher." (Luke 6:40, Moffatt.) The end of the discipline is to make you "perfectly trained" so that you may be like your Master. You are being disciplined into Christlikeness.

O Christ, I thank Thee that Thy disciplined heart didst sing its song of freedom, give me the song of freedom through discipline. Bring every desire into captivity to the obedience of Thy will. Then I too shall sing the song of freedom. Amen.

AFFIRMATION FOR THE DAY: *"The Eternal your God disciplines you as a man disciplines his son."* (Deut. 8:5, Moffatt.)

THE QUESTION OF UNMERITED SUFFERING

We come now to another type of discipline—*the discipline of circumstances and unmerited suffering*. We have been considering a chosen discipline, something that we impose on ourselves. But what about disciplines which we do not choose, things we are compelled to bear without our choices?

A discerning friend, after listening to the message on the Way—how it fitted into life and life fitted into it—said, "The message of the Way is too neat. What about the tragedies of life, when life doesn't come out so neatly?" He did well to call our attention to this phase. For our answers cannot be too neat, for life isn't too neat. You find stark tragedy that doesn't make sense, doesn't add up.

This is one answer: the way of refusing to recognize anything as evil. Meet suffering and pain and catastrophe with a barrage of mental affirmation of the good. This method has a very great truth in it. It is better than affirming evil as evil, suffering as suffering, and letting it go as that. You can get rid of a great deal of suffering and evil by simply affirming them away—"a great deal," but not all. And that residue that cannot be affirmed away is the rock upon which many go to pieces, physically and spiritually. The Way must be able to answer everything, including that residue. Can it?

Yes, for the Way nowhere asks you to affirm away all evil. You can affirm away a great many physical and spiritual evils that are rooted in wrong mental attitudes, but there are structural diseases which are facts, and no amount of mental suggestions can change those facts. Functional diseases can be removed by affirmation, but structural diseases can only be alleviated by affirmation.

What, then, is the answer of the Way? It is this: God wills to heal all diseases—they are not the will of God. He is healing through surgery, through medicine, through climate, through mental suggestion, through deliverance from mental attitudes that produce disease, through the direct operation of the Spirit upon our bodies and through the final cure—the resurrection.

O Christ, I know, I know that disease and evil are not Thy will. They do not fit into Thy Kingdom. They cannot be a part of Thy final purpose. Show me the Way to overcome them. Amen.

AFFIRMATION FOR THE DAY: *"Though I must pass through the thick of trouble, thou wilt preserve me."* (Ps. 138:7, Moffatt.)

YOU CAN USE SUFFERING

The Way recognizes that some diseases can be gotten rid of now, but some will have to wait the final cure in the resurrection. The Way would abolish all evil of the body and mind. But there is a residue which must await the final cure. The mortal frame breaks down finally in a mortal world; we are not constructed to be eternally here.

But the Way offers this possibility for the residue that cannot now be remedied: *You can use it. You can take it up into the purpose of your life and make it contribute to the rest of life.* There is no pain, no suffering, no frustration, no disappointment that cannot be cured or taken up and used for higher ends. In either case you have a way out. You are relieved of it or enriched by it. You are not nonplused —the Christian never is. He *always* has a way out. He is never stymied, for if he can't do this, he can do that, both equally good in the *final* results. The Way always has a way.

This is one of the essential characteristics of the Way, and here it is unique. Hinduism and Buddhism explain everything, and leave everything as before. The Way explains little and changes everything in sight, for its answer is not a verbal answer; it is a vital answer.

An architect who made a beautiful city in an Arizona desert told me that the architecture of an area is determined *by the lack of materials.* Because they can't get those materials, they have to take others, and these determine the architecture. The lack produces the constructive type—they make their lacks work. You can make your lacks work; you can make them drive you into new directions.

A lack of beauty drives many a woman into constructive usefulness, for if she had beauty she would be caught at that level and never get beyond it. But, lacking it, she decides to turn her energies into accomplishment—and does. Many a man lacking talents decides to make the most of what he has, offers them to God, has them heightened, and goes beyond other people more richly endowed. His lacks determine his architecture. Japanese Christians in desert camps made artistic things out of cabbage leaves, and Christmas cards were beautified by sage brush—all they had.

O Christ, Thy lacks too were made into beauty. Thou didst glorify a carpenter's shop, made the commonplace into the sacred, made of the hillsides a temple and a home, and finally on a cross didst make the place of a skull into the pilgrimage place of the world. Help me. Amen.

AFFIRMATION FOR THE DAY: *"The sufferer is saved by suffering"*— but only if he uses it.

LIFE IS DETERMINED MORE BY REACTIONS

We saw yesterday that the lacks of life can determine the architecture of life. A young army officer said this: "Weather, in war, is always favorable, if you know how to use it." That is the point—*if you know how to use it*. The fact is that everything that comes to you in life is favorable—if you know how to use it. Everything, except one thing: your own personal sin. That is never favorable; its results are always evil. And yet even that can be made into usefulness. God can help you to use even your sins, now forgiven and conquered, to help others in their moral battles.

Life is determined perhaps more by reactions than by actions. Life comes to you without your acting, it forces situations upon you without your asking or your acting. It is then that the reaction counts. You can react in self-pity and in frustration. Or you can react with confidence and courage and can make the evil thing make you better. Its origin may be evil, but by the time it gets through you its destination is good—you have turned evil into good. A woman of culture surrendered herself to God, and then troubles began to pile in: her husband was more and more unresponsive, and her daughter, a brilliant girl, went to a mental hospital. She brought them both back through her marvelous spirit. The daughter, restored by her mother's love and faith, said: "Mother, everything is poured on you. You get over one thing, and then it's another. But you sit there and smile. You're wonderful." She is. This is how she sums it up: "Nothing hurts me now. I have power to come back from anything." Her teeth were falling out; the dentist said nothing could be done. She surrendered the matter to God, prayed, and her teeth tightened up. "You'll die with them," said the dentist in astonishment. It was this woman's reactions that made all kinds of weather serve her. Nothing hurt her, everything helped her.

Edwin Markham says that "sorrow stretches our hearts for joy." It does, and more—it stretches our hearts for new achievements, for new usefulness. Sorrow plows the field for God's sowing and our harvest.

I thank Thee, O Christ, that I can be saved from all self-pity and all frustration. I shall react to whatever comes in Thy way. And Thy way is the way of making everything serve. Even a cross serves, and the worst becomes the best. I follow for I see. I am unafraid. Amen.

AFFIRMATION FOR THE DAY: *"Who turns a rock into a pool, flint into fountains!"* (Ps. 114:8, Moffatt.)

BLOCKS BECOME BLESSINGS

We said yesterday that not what happens to you but your reaction to what happens to you determines the result. The same thing may happen to two people. One reacts in one way, the other in another. The results are entirely different.

Jesus planned for quiet with God, but the crowds broke into His plans for quiet. "He welcomed them" (Luke 9:11, Moffatt)—welcomed them when they broke into His plans. And more, He "spoke to them of the Reign of God, and cured those who needed to be healed," and He fed them. The greatest thing there was not the preaching of the Reign, nor the healing, nor the feeding—it was the spirit through it all, the spirit that could take an interruption and make it into an interpretation. That spirit lives on after the immediate actions die away. He got back to His prayer hour—He didn't allow the local interruptions to interfere permanently with His long-range purposes. And then the prayer hour carried within it the victory of the interruption. The reaction was the reward.

The account again says: "The Pharisees . . . plotted against him. . . . But as Jesus knew of it he retired from the spot." (Matt. 12:15, Moffatt.) He could beat a strategic retreat and bide His time. The Way is not the way of the bulldozer plowing roughshod over everything, but of the stream that runs around obstacles and always gets there.

A detour is the shortest way around an impossible block. A detour can be made into a period of fretfulness or of fruitfulness. You and I received the gospel because of a blocking: "The holy Spirit having stopped them" (Acts 16:6, Moffatt), Paul turned from Asia to Europe, and as a result the gospel came through Europe to us. We are the result of a blocking. You can make all your blockings a blessing to somebody and most of all to yourself. Paul again said, "My affairs have really tended to advance the gospel" (Phil. 1:12, Moffatt), and yet he wrote that from prison.

The Christian under trouble doesn't break up—he breaks out.

O Christ, I thank Thee, for this victorious way of life. Nothing stops it—permanently. For it has an incorrigible victory within it. Help me to take this way of meeting life. Then I too shall be incorrigibly victorious. Amen.

AFFIRMATION FOR THE DAY: *"At the Flood the Eternal was enthroned as King, . . . bestowing strength upon his people."* (Ps. 29:10-11, Moffatt.)

HE BORE ME AWAY INTO A DESERT

We continue our study of the Incorrigible Way.

John says: "I . . . found myself in the island called Patmos, for adhering to God's word and the testimony of Jesus. . . . I found myself rapt in the Spirit, and I heard . . ." (Rev. 1:9-10, Moffatt.) He was isolated because he was true, but that isolation brought revelation. Shut off from men, he was open to God. He couldn't see any future for himself on a lonely island, and yet he saw the whole future of mankind. Islands of isolation are good listening posts. Shut off from the presence and the voices of the world, you can hear God more easily. When the present offers you little on your island isolation, the future will offer you everything.

Again John said: "So he bore me away rapt in the Spirit to the desert, and there I saw . . ." (Rev. 17:3, Moffatt.) John was not only on an island now; he was *in a desert* on the island. Within the isolation there was barrenness. Sometimes our isolations are hard to bear, but the apparent barrenness that also comes with the isolations is harder to bear. Often isolations seem to get us nowhere and bring us nothing. But there John "saw"—what? The downfall of the empires of the world! In the barren periods we may do little, but we can see God do much, everything. And what does it matter whether we do things or see God do them? We sometimes think we and our work are indispensable. Our work is dispensable. Our union with God is the one thing that matters. If you are "in the Spirit," in the will and purpose of God, then you are fulfilling your life purpose whether you are "in a desert" or elsewhere.

The hymn "Lord, We Are Able" is translated into an African language as "Lord, We Can Take It." That's it—"we are able" to do things, or "we can take it" when we can't do things and life does things to us, for instance, sets us down in a desert. For "we can take it" and use it. The Chinese have a saying: "I can eat bitter." We can eat the bitter, assimilate it, make it contribute. When you are on the Way, you can "eat bitter," for the "bitter" is often the disguised better.

O living Christ, Thou too didst eat bitter, even the bitterness of the cross. That bitterness in the root became sweetness in the fruit. That Calvary became an Easter morning. I want to make all my "bitter" into the better, for me and others. Then shall I live abundantly. Amen.

AFFIRMATION FOR THE DAY: *"His feet were forced into fetters . . . till the promise of the Eternal came true, the promise that tested him."* (Ps. 105:18-19, Moffatt.)

IN THE DARKNESS

Let us look at another passage: "I will grant him [the conqueror] to see the Morning-star." (Rev. 2:28, Moffatt.) The conqueror sees the Morning Star—Christ—in every dark situation. Kagawa, the great Japanese Christian, said, "In the darkness I found God face to face." "Come into the valley," said God to an ancient prophet, "and I will speak to you there." God speaks to us in dark valleys; there we find Him face to face. So "whoever is walking in the dark, without a ray of light, let him have confidence in the Eternal, and lean upon his God." (Isa. 50:10, Moffatt.) You can see the stars, even in the daytime, from the bottom of a well.

Nitrates come out of the most barren part of Chile—the barrenness enriches the world. The dark clouds hold the rain that makes things grow. Incidentally, the clouds are dark only to you. In an airplane above the clouds there are no dark clouds; all clouds are white clouds from above. There are no dark happenings when viewed from above.

From an airplane I saw a river boat twisting here and there going down a broad river in Brazil. I supposed the people on board wondered why this unnecessary waste of time in twisting to this side and that. But from above I could see where the sandbanks and where the deep waters were, and that the pilot was picking out deep waters for safety. So he had to twist back and forth. And so "the long way round was the short way home." Your frustration may be a guiding past a sandbank. You will see it all clearly someday—from above.

The South American Indians like bitter medicine. They don't think that sweet medicine is beneficial. They like iodine to be put into wounds though it smarts. "It hurts good," they say. You can make your hurts "good" or bad by the way you take them. If your hurt makes you nourish self-pity, then it "hurts bad"; but if your hurt drives you to dedication, then your hurt "hurts good"—it is healing you. To put it in other words: "Your pain is the breaking of the shell that encloses your imagination." Your imagination is now free to understand and sympathize with others.

O Christ, Thou art teaching me to understand, to understand by undergoing. I could never learn otherwise. So let it hurt—good. For I would have my imagination trained to understand, and to enter into the pain of others. So give me my lessons and help me learn. Amen.

AFFIRMATION FOR THE DAY: *"Before my trouble I went wrong, now I do thy bidding."* (Ps. 119:67, Moffatt.)

MAKING GRIEF GLORIOUS

Jesus said, "Better get into Life a cripple." (Mark 9:45, Moffatt.) Here Jesus describes those who limp into Life. But the point is they get into Life.

There are those who, made for love, are denied a home and children. They are inwardly bitter and frustrated. They limp into life, and then death. On the other hand, there are those who, denied the expression of sex creation and a home, sublimate their sex activity into creative work, mothering the orphaned and creating newborn souls. They are fruitful on another level. I quoted before: "I am one of those old maids you have helped to see the way to take life and love it!" This woman is entering "into Life a cripple"; she is limping into Life. But she is doing it joyfully and richly. And when you look at that life, you find the limp is gone! And she is no "old maid"; she is eternally a mother, mothering hopes and love and newborn souls. Motherhood, on the physical level, lasts for about twenty-five years, but this larger motherhood lasts throughout life and eternity!

A mother lost her son, turned inwardly on herself in self-pity. This self-pity produced pains, and she's a chronic invalid with everybody babying her. She is a festering place in the family.

> "Two men look out through the same bars:
> One sees the mud, and one the stars."

Two people face loss. One limps into Life, and the other limps into death. A pastor lost a loved daughter, and his reaction was: "I'll now have to laugh enough for two." And he did.

Dr. Lincoln Ferris grieved over a beloved wife who was infected by a doctor who had just come from a childbirth. He spent $30,000 to bring her back to health, nearly lost his faith, and was almost demented: "O God, why didn't you stop that doctor at the door?" As he walked along the street one day, the Spirit said: "Can't you say what Jesus said: 'Father, into thy hands I commend my spirit'?" He did, right then and there. His despair was taken away, and he was released and happy. He entered into Life—without a limp!

O Jesus, we feel that Thou didst do just that. Without a home, Thou art at home everywhere. And we all feel at home with Thee. For Thou art at home in our sorrows and frustrations, at home there to release and give victory. Thou art touching everything and changing everything. Amen.

AFFIRMATION FOR THE DAY: *"I render thanks to Christ Jesus our Lord, who has made me able for this."* (I Tim. 1:12, Moffatt.)

USING CYCLONES

We continue this week our meditation on unmerited suffering.

The war has left a harvest of devastated homes, hearts, and hopes. "Why didn't God stop the war?" is the anguished cry. How could He, without taking away our wills, depersonalizing us, making us things? The war was of our making. We produced the conditions out of which Hitler, Mussolini, and Tojo grew. The boys at the front were not dying for us; they were dying for our sins. The only good that will have come out of this war is what we rescue in making a new world for everybody.

"Well, what is God doing?" He is doing what He has always done. He is helping us to rescue a good out of a bad, to make a new world out of an old one. He did that at the cross. Jesus took the worst thing that could happen to him, namely, His death, and made it into the best thing that could happen to the world, namely, its redemption. God is doing that now. He is helping us make the worst serve the best.

Jesus said: "He [Satan] has no hold on me; his coming will only serve." (John 14:30-31, Moffatt.) He made even Satan serve. When Satan has no hold on you in self-pity, self-centeredness, or bitterness, then his coming will only serve you, make you better and more useful. So the very efforts of Satan contribute to Christian ends. There is "a teleology of suffering"—suffering can have purposive ends. Ten years ago Paul Ware was so badly injured in the legs by fire that the doctors said he would never walk again. He determined he would. He exercised his legs at night when free from observation. He learned to walk again—not only to walk, but to run. He won a national championship in the 440-yard dash. He made his impediments into instruments.

I asked a pilot what was the worst difficulty in flying through the Caribbean. Was it cyclones? He replied: "No, we can even use cyclones, they move slowly at the center, so we get on the edge and get a hundred-mile-an-hour wind behind us, and then coming back we get on the other edge. We use them going and coming." Using even cyclones! Going and coming!

O God, I know I can use everything when I am in Thee. Nothing can hurt me, nothing can make me afraid, nothing can stop me. I thank Thee that I'm unbeatable and unbreakable—in Thee. Amen.

AFFIRMATION FOR THE DAY: *"Thou are on every side, behind me and before, laying thy hand on me."* (Ps. 139:5, Moffatt.)

GOD AND MAN WORKING TOGETHER

Yesterday we saw that God could not arbitrarily do away with suffering without depersonalizing us. But He can and will do away with suffering *with our co-operation*. God has left us "unfinished masters of an unfinished world."

A gifted horticulturist has spent a lifetime in developing what many horticulturists believe to be the most beautiful rose in the world. A friend admiring it said, "What a wonderful rose God has made." The man replied, "God did not make this rose. God and I made it." In the end, when we look upon the new creation, we will be able to say, "God and I made it." God has furnished the raw materials, has shaped them into beginnings, and now invites us to co-operate in shaping them into His ends—His ends which are really our ends too.

In the meantime, we have an unfinished world full of mistakes and sins, and these cause suffering, much of it unmerited. Almost all of our sufferings are man-made. The residue of suffering which comes from so-called "acts of God" we will find in the end has a purpose in the sum total of things. Earthquakes will be found to serve some purpose. Floods are now being discovered as very often the result of man's greed and folly in cutting down the forests from the mountains. They call the Yellow River "China's Sorrow," but it should be called "China's Folly," for the mountains have been denuded of trees and cannot hold the moisture, and so the Yellow River floods its banks because of that folly. But we are learning how to control floods, and in learning how to control floods we are learning how to control ourselves. In the making of the world we are making ourselves. God has made the world and ourselves interdependent. As we go down in character, the world around us falls into wrack and ruin. As we go up in character, the world around us goes up with us. No wonder Paul says: "Even the creation waits with eager longing for the sons of God to be revealed." (Rom. 8:19, Moffatt.) When we are Christian, the world will be creative—to the full.

O Christ, I come to Thee, for Thou hast made the world and me, and Thou art trying to make us—together. Help me to co-operate this day in creation, in creating things and myself and others. I love the adventure of it. Thank Thee for giving me a share. Amen.

AFFIRMATION FOR THE DAY: *"The Eternal is good to all who look to him, and his compassion covers all that he has made."* (Ps. 145:9, Moffatt.)

IF FATE THROWS A DAGGER

God has made the world unfinished, and the unfinished part of it sharpens our souls. There is enough resistance in things to make the world an emery wheel upon which to sharpen our wits.

A friend with whom I talked in Cuba was ruined by a freeze in Florida in 1895. He went to Cuba to begin over again, developed a new orange out of a native sour orange, a tree that bears all the time. He was decorated by the Cuban government for his contribution to Cuba. But it was a calamity which started him over again, a freeze which froze him out to better things.

Ruskin says: "There is no bad weather; there are only different kinds of good weather." There is no bad weather, except as you take it badly. Adverse weather is only perverse weather as we fail to harness it to our purposes. Adverse winds can blow you forward if you know how to manipulate the sails.

"If Fate throws a dagger at you, there are two places to take hold of it—by the blade or by the handle." If Fate throws calamity at you, you can take it by the blade of self-pity and it will cut you, wound you deeply. But if you take it by the handle, you can make it make you. Bishop Angus Dun, of the Episcopal Church, stood in the midst of a Washington hospital ward filled with disabled soldiers, the wreckage of war. He deliberately undressed before them to show the braces he had been compelled to use all his life. He had worn them so well that few suspected that he was wearing them, living against constant resistance. It's the inner spirit that decides whether the pain shall be a goad to desperation or a goad to doing. A woman was in a hospital for ten years because of an accident which broke her spine and severed the spinal cord. She said to Bishop Schuyler Garth: "They say that life begins at forty. I was forty the day after the accident. Life began for me then." It really did. People flock to her bedside to learn how to live, for she is living abundantly and radiantly. "There is no such word as 'difficulty' in the dictionary of God," said a missionary to Mexico. For difficulties can become doors.

O God, I'll have to change my vocabulary, for I am changing my attitudes. The things I've called stumbling blocks I'm now seeing as steppingstones, the resistances are becoming resurrections. All things serve. I thank Thee. Amen.

AFFIRMATION FOR THE DAY: *"The Eternal delights in his people, adorning the afflicted with a victory."* (Ps. 149:4, Moffatt.)

THE WAY MAKES A DIFFERENCE IN DEATH

There is no "Wailing Wall" in the Christian way. An undertaker said to a friend of mine: "I have noticed that Christianity makes a difference in death. Christian people know how to take it better."

I almost dreaded to go into a home where the son-in-law was killed as a pilot in the South Seas. There was the daughter, a young mother and her baby. What could one say in the presence of this immense sorrow? But they talked about it so naturally, so altogether victoriously, that I found there wasn't anything to say. They had the answer! The service was not a memorial service, but a dedication service. One looks back; the other looks forward. They would dedicate themselves to the unfinished tasks of the young pilot, tasks he had never got to, tasks of doing away with war, for he hated the thing he felt compelled to do. As a life dedication they would do what he couldn't.

When friendly neighbors saw Mary leave the house, they supposed that she was going to the tomb of her dead brother. "They imagined she was going to wail at the tomb." (John 11:31, Moffatt.) They could see nothing to be done except that—wail at a tomb, the picture of hopeless despair. But Mary did not go to a tomb. She went to a Person. And that Person knew what to say: "I am the resurrection and the life." He was the answer.

A friend of mine, a layman, was asked to conduct a funeral, so he went to the New Testament to see how Jesus conducted funerals. He discovered "that Jesus didn't conduct funerals—He conducted resurrections." Jesus never conducts funerals of anything. He conducts resurrections of everything! For everything *in His hands* lives! Turn over your sorrow, your frustration, your disappointment to Him, and in His hands it will live. Hosea saw this: "I will . . . make the dale of Trouble a door of hope." (Hos. 2:15, Moffatt.) A woman, not seemingly pious, lost her only child and said, "This is the time I am religious." Her dale of Trouble had become a door of hope. She didn't go to a "Wailing Wall"—she went to Jesus.

O living, saving Christ, I come to Thee. For Thou art not a road with a dead end. Thou art the Way, the Way for me now in my trouble. For through Thee I am invincible. I can't be beaten, except beaten into shape. I am in Thy hands, and so is my sorrow. Amen.

AFFIRMATION FOR THE DAY: *"My road may run through a glen of gloom, but I fear no harm, for thou art beside me."* (Ps. 23:4, Moffatt.)

THE DALE OF TROUBLE BECOMES A DOOR OF HOPE

Carlyle said of Tennyson: "He carried around a little bit of chaos, and he was always turning it into a cosmos." Jesus was always doing that. "He will fix it for you, for He knows just what to do," says the Negro spiritual.

And often He saves us not from the pain, but through the pain. A guide and an inexperienced climber had to stay all night in the Pyrenees; they couldn't make it back. Toward dawn there was a tempestuous wind that twisted trees, started rocks rolling down the mountain sides and the inexperienced climber was terrified. The guide reassured him: "This is the way the dawn comes in the Pyrenees." And sometimes our dawns come through storm and tempest. A doctor said to a member of one of our Ashrams: "You are not going to live long; your disease is incurable." "All right," the man replied, "whether by life or by death I want to glorify Him." He is simple and happy, making the most of the passing hours. He is now living in the Dawn even though the storms of dissolution are blowing fiercely around him. Someone has said that "spikenard when jostled lets the perfume out." The jostling of approaching death has served only to let the perfume out.

I said to a very dear friend one day, "Yes, but I always come up smiling." "Yes," said the friend, "and more, you go down smiling." I have laid this compliment at the feet of Another—I learned it from Him. He not only came up smiling; He went down smiling: "My peace I give unto you." This in the shadow of the cross.

Sometimes the ability to go down smiling heads off the going down. A missionary in China was taken out to be beheaded. When she got to the place of beheading, she burst out laughing. Her captors asked her why—it was no laughing matter! She replied, "I was just thinking how funny it would be to see my own head rolling down the hill, for as my head would roll down the hill I'd be on my way to Glory. That makes me laugh with joy." "Well," said the bandits, "if it's going to make her happier, why should we please her that way?" And they let her go!

O Christ, Thou dost give us the power to smile going down and coming up. For there is no loss in Thee. Everything is sheer gain. For whatever happens turns out through Thee to contribution. I thank Thee. Amen.

AFFIRMATION FOR THE DAY: *"Thou didst bid me hope; this comforts me in trouble, thy promise puts life into me."* (Ps. 119:49-50, Moffatt.)

"I CAN TAKE IT—CAN YOU?

Someone asked a woman who had been on her back for eight months how she was. The reply: "I have pain in my back, in my head and arms, but outside of that I'm fine." In other words, if you have an area of pain, think of the areas without pain! If you have one sorrow, look at your joys.

William L. Stidger tells of being asked by a train porter to take charge of a blind soldier on his way home. When they walked on the porch, the father and mother knew of the boy's blindness for the first time. The mother burst into tears; the father was shocked and shaken. But the boy, his head held high, said, "I can take it." The father recovered himself and said, "Son, if you can take it, so can we." They had the spirit. "Rust will crumble a metal, while hammer blows will only harden it." The rust of continuously placid, untroubled living may crumble your spirit, but the hammer blows of trouble may harden you.

Paul speaks of "this pain divine." Pain is divine if it leads you to finer character and contribution. But "this pain divine" comes only from what Paul calls "this pain God is allowed to guide." (II Cor. 7:10-11, Moffatt.) If resentment and self-pity and complaint are allowed to guide your pain, then you are guided into frustration. But if you turn it over to God and allow God to work out the matter with you and for you, then it ends in exactly what Paul says, "ends in a saving"—a saving of you and others.

In India the farmers winnow wheat by holding up a basket of wheat and chaff and letting it slowly fall so the wind can blow through it, driving the chaff away and leaving only the wheat to fall to the ground. The winds of sorrow and trouble blow through your spirit, but they do nothing except to separate the chaff from the wheat. You become a sifted soul, sifted of everything except the worth-while. The Brazilians have a saying: "God can write straight even on a crooked line." The lines of your life may be crooked, not make sense, but God can write straight, can bring good out of crooked events. The outer events of Jesus' life were crooked, but God wrote redemption on them.

O God, I surrender to Thee the crooked lines of my life. They don't make sense. But I know Thou canst write straight even on a crooked line. So they are at Thy disposal. Everything good out of everything bad—that's it. Amen.

AFFIRMATION FOR THE DAY: *"Rock, rescue, refuge, he is all to me, never shall I be overthrown."* (Ps. 62:2, Moffatt.)

STEPS IN USING SORROW

We come to our day of summing up the steps to meet sorrow and frustration.

The psalmist says, "A deadly trouble courses in his veins" (Ps. 41:8, Moffatt.) But no trouble need be "deadly"—unless you allow it. Again he says, "My soul is melting with secret sorrow." (Ps. 42:4, Moffatt.) But the sorrow need not melt the soul, need not if you no longer make it "secret." Bring it up and face it.

Take these steps: (1) *Bring the sorrow into light and face it frankly.* To bring it up and out sterilizes it. (2) *Do everything you know to remove it.* Listen to God; He may tell you what you can do. (3) *Surrender the sorrow into the hands of God and let it stay there.* In your heart it festers; in God's hands it becomes useful. Don't give it to God today and take it back into your heart tomorrow. Say to yourself, "God has my sorrow." (4) *Talk it over with some friend, but "don't syndicate your sorrow."* "A sorrow shared is a sorrow halved." But having shared it, don't talk it over with too many people. You are liable to become morbid. (5) *Don't consciously or unconsciously wear a martyr's crown.* Don't bid for sympathy. You are liable to exaggerate your trouble to get more sympathy. Even wearing the martyr's crown for a short time may open the door to a martyr's complex. (6) *When you are beginning to feel sorry for yourself, go to the looking glass and burst out laughing—at yourself.* When you can laugh at yourself, you're safe. (7) *Smile before the world, even when you don't feel like it—smile on principle.* (8) *Don't pray for release, but pray for power to use the sorrow, and release will come as a by-product.* Brother Lawrence said that when he prayed for release he didn't get it, but release came when he prayed for power to stand things. (9) *But don't pray for power to stand things—pray for power to use things.* Go on the offensive. (10) *Your greatest contribution is to show a spirit through everything that happens.* It's not what happens but the way you take it that counts.

O Christ, I know Thou art my way out, for Thou hast gone through everything and hast overcome everything for Thyself—and for me. In Thee I cannot go down. I'll come up and come up smiling. My joy is not in my circumstances. My joy is in Thee. Amen.

AFFIRMATION FOR THE DAY: *"That I might live, ever mindful of God, in the sunshine of life."* (Ps. 56:13, Moffatt.)

A SECRET SOCIETY

We come this week to consider "A Secret Society." It is based on this statement of Paul: "I have been initiated into the secret for all sorts and conditions of life, for plenty and for hunger, for prosperity and for privations; in Him who strengthens me, I am able for anything." (Phil. 4:12-13, Moffatt.)

People, especially in America, dearly love secret societies. It gives them a sense of security and superiority to know they are "in on a secret." Well, here is a secret society which guarantees absolute security. No matter what happens, prosperity or privation, you are safe—secured against anything and everything. The "secret" seems to be that you can live "on account of" or "in spite of." You do not despise "on account of"; you can get joy out of surrounding life, home, beauty, friendships, love; you are healthy minded, rich in everything around you. But you do not depend on "on account of." You can take it, but you don't lean on it. You can live "in spite of."

Some people cannot live "on account of." They cannot take the joys of life and assimilate them and make them a part of their Christian lives. They are afraid of them. They are not happy unless they are unhappy. If they put on a good and useful outer garment, they always wear a hair shirt under it. That hair shirt saves them, for they believe in the gospel of being unhappy. The Hindu ascetic cannot live "on account of." He can live only "in spite of." I sat beside a former high court judge who had renounced the world and sat among ashes meditating on the banks of the Ganges. "Please leave me alone. You disturb my meditation," he said. Conversation, friends, comfort—all were ruled out. He could live "in spite of" but not "on account of." Another sadhu told me he had been in his monastery for thirty years and during that time he had not seen a woman. He was afraid.

But the purest Man that ever lived, and the most emancipated, was not afraid. "Jesus loved Martha, and her sister, and Lazarus." That statement would have "killed" any religious teacher in India. But Jesus could live "on account of," for at its center was a renunciation.

O Christ, I thank Thee that Thou art of the healthy mind and attitude. Thou didst not despise love for man, for woman, but Thou wast not tripped up by it. Emancipation amid participation. Oh, give me Thy secret, for I too would be free. Amen.

AFFIRMATION FOR THE DAY: *I can live on compliment, for I love something more than compliment—Christ.*

A GOSPEL FOR THE HAPPY?

Some people can live "in spite of" but not "on account of." They feel it their duty to be unhappy as a protest against a world of this kind.

A woman asked one day: "You have a gospel for the hurt; do you have one for the happy? I have a happy home; my husband, my children love me and I love them, and we haven't any particular financial worries. Have you any gospel for me—a happy person?" I could say that I had, and that gospel is just this: "I have been initiated into the secret . . . for plenty . . . , for prosperity." When we are Christian, we can make "plenty" more plentiful and "prosperity" more prosperous by dedicating them and making them an instrument of the purposes of God. Without that dedication, then plenty and prosperity have a worm—the worm of selfishness—eating at their hearts. But dedicated plenty and prosperity are sound and singing.

Take love. The Christian, with central loyalties to God and people to whom he is bound by ties of marriage intact, is free to accept and give love. The home in which I write this is a beautiful home with a deep and beautiful attachment between husband and wife. With their loyalties and mine intact we are free to give each other a very deep affection. The Way is the way of healthy-mindedness. The God who made sunsets and sunrises, who painted the lily, put a smile on a baby's face, and laughter in our souls is not happy when we are unhappy. He made us for positive appreciation and love and enjoyment. Someone imagining what an Ashram would be like wrote: "Brother Stanley goes around with long black robes, and the rest follow him weeping." Nothing could be further from the truth. The people do not follow "Brother Stanley," but Christ, and as a consequence there is gaiety not gloom, laughter not weeping. "All things belong to you, . . . the world." The world of beauty and art and friendship and growing things and the sheer zest of living—all belongs to you. For the Way is written in them, and when we take them we find the Way. "Thou wilt keep my footing upon the heights." Yes, upon the heights of love and life.

O Christ, Thou dost give me everything. I'm beautiful in every flower, rich in every friendship, happy in every baby's smile, and gay in the laughter of the truly gay. I thank Thee, I thank Thee. Amen.

AFFIRMATION FOR THE DAY: *When things go my way, I can take them; and when things go against me—I can take it!*

THE ULTIMATE SECURITY

We saw yesterday that we can be initiated into the secret for plenty. Today we pause upon the secret of initiation for privation.

In one of my books I told the story of Dr. Robert Blair. He went to China on an adventure of love and there caught an eye infection that left him blind. His wife died of a painful cancer; one son died of Addison's disease, another from an infection; his daughter caught infantile paralysis and can walk only on crutches. Between them they had a pair of crutches and a Seeing Eye dog to begin life over again. Was that all? Oh, no. They had an unconquerable spirit. Dr. Blair was pastor of a church, and the daughter ran the home—on a pair of crutches—and they were radiant. And now the sequel. The remaining son was killed on Okinawa, and the father became ill with a painful skin disease and had to resign his church. But father and daughter are both still on top—still radiant. They have been initiated into a secret. They can stand privation because they can use privation.

If you can stand only prosperity you are weak, and if you can stand only privation you are weak. You are strong only if you can stand anything—good, bad, and indifferent. Josiah Royce says that "no man is safe unless he can stand anything that happens to him." Then the Christian is safe, for he not only can stand anything that can happen to him but can use it.

The securities promised by insurance societies, by governments, by bank accounts are all partial securities. They are vulnerable. You can find the Achilles' heel in every one of them. But here is the ultimate security, for life can hit you from either side—privation or prosperity—and you can not only stand it, you can smile it, and not only smile it, you can sing it. Doubt it? Listen to this: "After ordering them to be flogged . . . , he put them into the inner prison and secured their feet in the stocks. But about midnight, as Paul and Silas were praying and singing . . ." (Acts 16:22-25, Moffatt.) "Praying and singing." Praying is obvious and natural in such a situation, but singing is different. They knew "the secret."

O Christ, I thank Thee that Thou hast taught my heart to sing as well as to pray. For I've learned life's deepest secret, and now I am secure. The wind can blow from any direction and it will only drive me to my goal. Glory be! I thank Thee. Amen.

AFFIRMATION FOR THE DAY: *I am safe, for I can stand anything that can happen to me—stand everything, for I can use everything.*

THE PASSWORD

We have seen the fact that we can learn how to live by prosperity or by privation. Now look at the initiation fee and the password.

This secret society is an open secret society. Jesus speaks of "the open secrets of the Realm of heaven." (Matt. 13:11, Moffatt.) It is a secret secret—you have to know the combination. But it is an open secret—anyone can join. Provided you are willing to pay the price. And the price is commensurate with the security provided. Other secret societies give a partial security and demand a partial price. This one offers a total security for the total person, in total situations, for a total length of time, time and eternity, and therefore it demands a total price—the price of yourself and all you have.

If God has you partially, He can secure you only partially; you are still vulnerable. But if He has you wholly, then you are wholly secure; you are invulnerable. Everything now "works together for good" to those who love Him. When God has all of you, then you have all of Him, and in Him there is perfect security. Anything can go, but if you have God, you have everything.

A young bride reading a telegram over the shoulder of her husband—a telegram telling that their newly founded home had burned—looked at him and said: "But, dear, we've still got one another." When the Christian has his central relation with God intact, he can come back from anything.

The "password"? The password into this secret society is in the last portion of that verse: "In him I am able for anything." The password is "anything." Repeat the password to yourself until it becomes not a word which you possess but a word which possesses you. You are ready for "anything," from anywhere. You march forth panoplied behind and before, and the slings and arrows of fortune cannot find an opening, and the atomic bomb could blow you only into perfect wholeness—forever.

So whisper the password "anything" to yourself as you awaken and as you fall asleep, and say it during the day, and you will become "able for anything."

O Christ, Thy secret society is open, I know, to even me. For there are no snobberies there. It is free to everybody who will pay the price and take the gift. I am so glad it is a gift. I can take it, holding in my hands my all, as I do. I'm in, I'm in. Amen.

AFFIRMATION FOR THE DAY: *I have the ultimate security, for I can make good, bad, and indifferent serve the ends for which I live!*

THE MEANING OF FAITH

We study together for the rest of the week the place of faith in all this. Many sigh and say, "I'd like to be initiated into this secret society, but it is a step of faith, and I just haven't the faith."

Faith is not trying hard to believe. That is anxiety trying to look like faith. There is a humorous touch to Paul's saying: "Salute Tryphaena and Tryphosa, who work hard in the Lord." (Rom. 16:12, Moffatt.) They might be called "Brother Try" and "Sister Try," sweating Christians "who work hard in the Lord." They exhaust themselves; they are under the gospel of trying. I would like to change their names to "Trustphaena" and "Trustphosa," "who accomplish much in the Lord." The passing from trying to trusting is the change of the basis of your life from yourself to God.

Here was a young minister, sick with tuberculosis, who was told by doctors that his lifework was finished. For seventy-two hours he struggled in the dark, and then God spoke to him, "I will take care of you and your future." He surrendered the whole matter to God, ceased to struggle, became joyous, and got well. He says: "I'm grateful it came. Up to that time I was depending on myself and my preparation; after that I was depending on God. I'm a new man and have a new ministry." He has passed from fighting to faith, from trying to trust.

What, then, is faith? The best definition I know is this: *Faith is welcoming that which you believe in.* Faith, then, has gone beyond belief. It welcomes now as fact what you have believed in as idea. "Faith is an affirmation and an act that bids eternal truth be fact." It is "an affirmation *and an act.*" You must act faith as well as affirm faith. Peter Bohler said to the seeking John Wesley: "Preach faith until you have it, and then, because you have it, you will preach it." You must affirm faith, talk faith to God and man and yourself, and then act faith. The ten lepers leaped over the stage of affirming faith and acted faith: "'Show yourselves to the priests.' . . . And as they went they were cleansed." (Luke 17:14, Moffatt.) In the act of obeying faith turned to fact—healing ensued.

O Christ of God, help me to act upon the things I believe. Help me to welcome them now as working facts within me. Let me have more than a faith affirmation and a faith act. Let me have a faith attitude. Amen.

AFFIRMATION FOR THE DAY: *"Though I cried out, 'I am crushed,' thinking . . . , 'All men are a failure,' yet I had faith."* (Ps. 116:10-11, Moffatt.)

AN OPEN UNIVERSE

We continue our meditation on faith. We saw yesterday that faith is not struggling and trying; it is letting go and trusting. The oft-repeated statement, "Let go, let God," someone suggests, should be put this way, "Let go, let God, let's go." But "Let's go" is last—and rightly. Peter says, "Furnish your faith with resolution." (II Pet. 1:5, Moffatt.) Note that faith is first and resolution second. Our gospel is not primarily resolution—a whipping up of the will. It is primarily faith, a surrender of the will to the will of God. Then linked with Almighty Resources you can now add resolution, for the resolution now is not an anxious fretting, trying in one's own strength and power, but a restful, confident resolution to take infinite Resources.

This is an open universe, open to faith. But there is a legitimate catch in the words of Jesus, "All that ever you ask in prayer you shall have, if you believe" (Matt. 21:22, Moffatt), for in saying that anything is possible to those who believe, the catch is in the fact that you cannot have faith unless you are committed to God, in which case you will ask only the right thing in faith. It is self-correcting.

Moreover, it is self-developing. Jesus said, "Regain your sight, your faith has made you well." (Luke 18:42, Moffatt.) Suppose He had said, "My power has made you well." That would have left no incentive in the person healed, for someone else had done the whole thing. But this putting of it—"Your faith has made you well"—left the man with a sense of self-respect. Jesus develops people as He gives to people. "It is the faith He inspires which has made the man thus hale and whole before you all." (Acts 3:16, Moffatt.) He inspired the faith, and then answered the faith. Jesus faithed faith out of the faithless.

We often say, "Seeing is believing." But here, "Believing is seeing"—seeing things come to pass. Jesus said, "As you believe, so your prayer is granted." (Matt. 9:29, Moffatt.) These two words "as" and "so" are the smallest and greatest words of life: "As"—faith; "so"—result.

O God, I come to Thee with the smallness of my faith—it is a grain of mustard seed. But it is a seed, and in it is everything, everything I want to be and do. Water it with Thy faith and I know it will spring up and be adequate for anything. In Jesus' name. Amen.

AFFIRMATION FOR THE DAY: *"As for me, I hope on and on, I praise thee more than ever."* (Ps. 71:14, Moffatt.)

FAITH IS ALERT RECEPTIVITY

We continue our meditation on faith. Faith brings things into the now, but it can wait till the morrow. It is timeless. A little girl praying for her father's recovery said: "O God, make my daddy well. One, two, three—go!" We can understand the child's impatience, but the surer faith is this: "So, when he heard of the illness, he stayed where he was for two days." (John 11:6, Moffatt.) Here was a divine pause. He was working out purposes too great for haste. Suppose Jesus had rushed to Lazarus' side. Then we should have had a rising from illness, or a rising from a very recent death—a swoon they would have called it. This pause brought a miracle that was a miracle! God only pauses to make us of tougher fiber through the waiting, or to work a greater miracle. His pauses are always purposeful. The pause often lets us settle more deeply "in His name," "in His character," and thus assures that the prayer be answered.

Here are the steps: "By faith . . . we wait in the Spirit for the righteousness we hope for." (Gal. 5:5, Moffatt.) (1) By faith. (2) We wait. (3) In the Spirit. (4) For the righteousness we hope for. Here is pure receptivity, an attitude of open acceptance. But it doesn't end in passivity. It ends in activity, for the next verse speaks of "faith active in love." Suppose we put it in terms often preached as Christianity: (1) We fight. (2) We struggle. (3) In the spirit of determination. (4) For the righteousness we expect to attain. That would be pure self-endeavor. The end of this would not be "faith active in love," but "fighting active in frustration." This latter would be strain, hence drain, and the end would be bankruptcy and frayed nerves. "Faith active in love" is creative and healing and filling. Of someone it was said, "She took life on tiptoe." The person of faith takes life on tiptoe, and the person of self-centered trying takes life on leaden feet. Moody once said: "A little faith will bring your soul to heaven, but a lot of faith will bring heaven to your soul." It will.

Jesus said, "You believe—believe in God and also in me" (John 14:1, Moffatt.) "You believe" in something—chance, your own effort. Everybody believes in something. Then believe in the highest, God, and God as shown by Me.

O God, help me to take this belief which I am bound to fasten on something and help me to fasten it upon the highest—upon Thee and Thy purposes. Then faith will not be barren, but will blossom. Amen.

AFFIRMATION FOR THE DAY: *"In God I trust without a fear: what can man do to me?"* (Ps. 56:11, Moffatt.)

HOW NEVER TO BE TIRED

We have been considering the fact that the Way is the way to meet "anything." Does this "anything" include the fact of physical and mental tiredness? Is the Way the way never to be tired?

It is very interesting and important to realize that a great many people don't carry their religion over into their bodies and minds. Their religion doesn't get across to the nerves and tissues the renewing power of God. Such people expect to rest in heaven, but here they must put up with exhaustion and weariness. "Come unto me . . . , and I will give you rest," is interpreted as spiritual rest only. Their faith is compartmentalized and cramped. It ought to contribute to the total life in a total way; instead it contributes to a part of life in a partial way. "The body is . . . for the Lord; and the Lord for the body." (I Cor. 6:13.) Are the Lord and the body affinities? Is an unfit body out of tune with the Lord?

"How never to be tired," obviously needs some qualification. There is a good healthy tiredness that comes as a result of heavy physical exertion. "Jesus, . . . wearied with his journey, sat thus on the well." (John 4:6.) There is the tiredness that comes from structural disease. There is the tiredness that comes from old age. Apart from these three qualifications, it is possible never to be tired.

In regard to the first—bodily weariness through hard physical labor—that can be balanced and balanced quickly. Marie Beynon Ray says: "This sort of fatigue cannot pile up. There can be no fatigue debt. The energy lost during the day is made up by a night's sleep. It cannot be carried over to the next week or the next day, not with proper food and rest. A man may die of physical overwork, but if he does, it is right there on the job, with hammer raised for the next blow." (*How Never to Be Tired,* pp. 80-81.) I find by experience that I can go to bed after speaking from three to five times a day and wake up refreshed and ready and can keep this up for years. A night's rest balances the accounts and throws off fatigue toxins. Ten minutes' vigorous exercise before going to sleep relaxes me, distributes the blood through my system. I usually go to sleep at once and awake with the accounts balanced. I've learned to let God into the bodily processes.

O Christ, I thank Thee for Thy boundless energy. Night and day men thronged Thee, and yet they did not exhaust Thee. Give me Thy secret; help me to tap the Resources Thou didst tap. Amen.

AFFIRMATION FOR THE DAY: *"He gives you all your heart's desire, renewing your youth like an eagle's."* (Ps. 103:5, Moffatt.)

CONCERNING NERVOUS BREAKDOWNS

We saw yesterday that if you are still tired after twenty-four hours of complete rest, then the tiredness is in the mind and spirit—it is mental and spiritual, not physical. To take a six-months rest to get rid of physical weariness is folly. You get tired resting. For after the first twenty-four hours, if you are not rested, you become worried that you are not rested, and the more you worry the less rested you are. So the more you rest the more weary you become. The cause of the exhaustion is not in the body. Dr. A. A. Brill says: "Absolutely 100 per cent of fatigue of sedentary workers who are in good health is nervous fatigue."

That leads to the question of nervous breakdown. We are told by those who know that nervous breakdown is never caused by overwork. Dr. Austin F. Riggs: "Hard work, plenty of it, whether physical or mental, never in itself produced one single case of nervous exhaustion." Dr. A. A. Brill: "No one ever suffers a nervous breakdown from overwork. These maladies simply do not exist." Dr. Paul Dubois: "Of all my nervous cases, I never found one which could be traced to overwork." Dr. Ira Wile: "Unconditionally, there is no such thing as breakdown from overwork."

Then nervous breakdowns come from what? Two things: (1) Too much thinking about them will produce them. A famous preacher delivered ten consecutive sermons on how to avoid a nervous breakdown and ended up with one! His psychology was bad—he thought too much on nervous breakdowns. "Whatever gets your attention gets you." He could have stated his truth positively without emphasis on breakdowns. (2) There is some conflict at the root of every nervous breakdown. The cause of the conflict must be found and adjusted.

But a word must be uttered regarding the calling of these tirednesses and breakdowns and pains "imaginary." They are not imaginary—they are very real. To tell the sufferer that his troubles are imaginary is to add insult to injury. They are real, but are produced by wrong mental and spiritual attitudes.

O living, healing Christ, I come to Thee for rest. I want the roots of my weariness to be removed. If they have been covered up by excuses and rationalizations, then help me this day to uncover them. For I would be whole—perfectly whole. In Thy name. Amen.

AFFIRMATION FOR THE DAY: *"The Eternal's law is a sound law, reviving life."* (Ps. 19:7, Moffatt.)

THINGS THAT PRODUCE TIREDNESS

We come now to the causes of tiredness. From my own experience I would list them as follows: (1) Self-centeredness. (2) Boredom. (3) Worry. (4) Fear. (5) Inferiority feelings. (6) Resentments. (7) Indecision. (8) Oversensitivity. (9) Inner Guilts. Let us look at them briefly.

1. *A self-centered person is usually an exhausted person.* Self-centered persons have themselves on their hands all the time. Preoccupation with yourself will leave you tired, especially of yourself. The self-centered are trying to live in an impossible way, namely, as though they are the center of the universe, and they are not. God is. And they are breaking themselves on that fact. They must surrender themselves to God or else be a problem to themselves. No amount of rest can rest a self-centered person. He must turn the burden of himself over to God and let God be God. Then he will find release—and only then.

2. *Boredom causes exhaustion.* When one is interested in his work, there is no exhaustion. Harvard University investigations over ten years have come to the conclusion: "The phenomenon formerly called fatigue is better described as boredom. It is boredom that causes a reduced rate of working." Professor Edward L. Thorndike says that it is not actually an incapacity to work but a lack of desire to work which produces fatigue. When you are interested in your work, you are not tired by it. He concludes that boredom is the cause of 95 per cent of the decrease in mental work during the closing sessions in school, and that it is a major cause of fatigue in adult life. Interest in your work turns on the supply of hormones in the blood; a lack of interest turns them off. You can make your glands secrete or not secrete by your interest or lack of it.

A schoolteacher was preoccupied with herself and her own problems. She said that she looked over the heads of her children and wearily watched the clock. The days dragged on. Then she surrendered herself and her problems to God, was released, lowered her eyes from the clock to the faces of the children, and began to be interested in them. Her job became a joy, fatigue replaced by abounding energy.

O God, Thy boundless energy is mine, and I know it. I've been exhausting myself with impossible ways of life. And now I surrender them all to Thee, for I want to live and live abundantly. Amen.

AFFIRMATION FOR THE DAY: *I am healthy in Thy Health, strong in Thy Strength, and free in Thy Freedom.*

WORRY MAKES YOU TIRED

We ended yesterday on the fact that boredom is a major cause of fatigue.

3. *Worry is also a major cause.* A pilot of a plane on a trip to Latin America asked me if I enjoyed my lunch, and when I assured him I did and then asked him whether he did, replied, "No, I have an upset digestion." I inquired, "What are you worrying about?" He looked surprised and then said, "Yes, I am worrying. I am afraid they are going to put me on a run I don't want to go on, so I am worrying." I added, "That's what is the matter with you—worry is upsetting your digestive system." He asked, "Are you a Christian Scientist?" I replied, "No, just a Christian." And then he told me of another pilot so afraid of the examiner who was putting him through his final examination for a captain's status that, though he was "tops," he got mixed up and failed, had a nervous breakdown, and had to go on sick leave.

A woman, really upright, worried herself into invalidism about a sex-sin which was really nonexistent. When she surrendered it to God as we prayed, she exclaimed: "It's wonderful. I'm released."

There is an ulcer known as the "Dunkirk Ulcer," developed on a large scale by men waiting anxiously to be evacuated from the beach. An examining doctor told me that in a group of army inductees who came in one truck twenty-two out of thirty men had backaches. One had said that he had it, and the rest developed it. They were not imaginary—the aches were there, but emotionally induced. There is a "Soldiers' Rheumatism" which is not a rheumatism at all, but a functional disturbance as a result of anxiety and fear. Heart palpitation can come as a result of worry, and then worry over the heart palpitation increases the palpitation. It is a vicious circle. The trouble is entirely functional; the heart may be perfectly sound.

A schoolteacher waited on her sick mother and taught school. She began to feel sorry for herself, worried about herself, and developed a pain in her back. The doctors could find no reason, talked to her about the real source of it. She surrendered her self-pity and worry to God and the pain left her. She then served with reserves.

O God, I come to Thee with anything that hinders the flow of Thy resources through me. For I know that Thou hast them and I need them and that I can have them for life—now. So I surrender all the hindrances and take Thy health. In Jesus' name. Amen.

AFFIRMATION FOR THE DAY: *I am not a reservoir. I am a channel, a channel attached to Infinite Resources.*

FEAR PRODUCES FATIGUE

We come to the next cause of fatigue:

4. *Fear produces fatigue.* Fear is worry become acute. Worry is general; fear is specific. A Russian psychiatrist sat at the table in a railway diner with two men and a woman who wore a gold cross at her throat. She was an exuberant person and breathed poise and health. Suddenly the psychiatrist said: "If more people believed in and lived what that cross stands for, I'd have nothing to do. I see from seventy-five to a hundred patients a day, and the three things they suffer most from are fear, loneliness, and selfishness."

An able piano teacher wrote with great difficulty in a very shaky hand. She explained that she and her sister had written in longhand six hundred acknowledgments to those who had sent flowers and messages when the father died, and she had strained a muscle in her thumb. But in her playing the thumb was normal. Obviously the trouble was not physical but mental; the thumb was associated with writing letters on a painful occasion, the death of a loved one. The thumb nerves began to be upset because the emotions were upset, and the paralysis took place. Another woman put the matter to me this way: "I began to have asthma, and I saw it was rooted in the jitters. I gave up my fears to God, and the asthma has disappeared."

5. *Inferiorities produce fatigue.* When we are inwardly running away from things, the very thought of those things makes us tired.

6. *Resentments produce fatigue.* When one is chewing on inner resentments, there fatigue sets in. A girl in an elevator said to me with a shake of her head: "That porter is driving everyone around here nuts." "And especially himself?" I asked. "Yes," she agreed, "he is driving himself nuts." The resentments in everybody were throwing sand in the machinery of life.

A patient with a gastric ulcer got it as the result of the fact that, when he was a boy, the sound of the dinner bell was the gong that began the next round of a never-ending family fight. His stomach would go into spasms—stomach ulcer the result.

O God, I come to Thee to take out all resentments and fears that cause upset. I cannot take them out, but I can consent, and I do consent—wholeheartedly, now. I am free, for I give my free consent. Amen.

AFFIRMATION FOR THE DAY: *"Fear knocked at the door, faith answered, nobody was there."*

THREE MORE THINGS WHICH PRODUCE FATIGUE

The next cause of fatigue is:

7. *Indecision.* The person who takes a long time to decide things, and then after they are decided undecides them for fear of making a mistake, is always tired. The fear of making a mistake makes him make a continuous mistake, the mistake of keeping himself emotionally upset with indecision. Far better make a few wrong decisions than be indecisive. For the indecisive person is in greater danger of making wrong decisions by being emotionally upset over making any decision. Decide things, and if the decision is wrong do better next time. Don't wear yourself out by weighing endlessly the pros and cons.

8. *Oversensitivity produces fatigue.* There must be a toughening of the fiber of life, for if you're hurt by every passing event, you'll be continuously hurt and tried. Very often people have an oversensitive conscience and produce false guilts within themselves. They get into bondage over marginal things. They make God picayunish, looking for motes. Their consciences have blind spots; they are blind to the disruption they cause to themselves and others by being upset over little things. The conscience should be a healthy conscience, not a conscience that goes into a spasm at the sight of a mouse of defect of character.

9. *Inner guilt produces tiredness.* A doctor who has a great many patients a day has a number of copies of *Abundant Living* on the tables in his waiting rooms. The patients read them while waiting and ask where they can get them. He tells them to take one along. He has given away six hundred copies in this way. His reason: "I give the book to serve as a cathartic!" He knows that the patients are filled with fears and guilts, and no amount of medicine or physical manipulation can cure them until they get rid of these fears and guilts. Guilt produces conflict, and conflict wears out the physical organism. "There is no health in my limbs, thanks to my sins." (Ps. 38:3, Moffatt.) "He pardons all your sins, and all your sicknesses he heals." (Ps. 103:3, Moffatt.)

O God, I know that when I get rid of every vestige of guilt I shall be free—wholly free of conflict and fatigue. So here I am at Thy feet; take me, remake me. I rise up in Thee strong and well and unafraid. Here I live, and live with fear and fatigue. I thank Thee. Amen.

AFFIRMATION FOR THE DAY: *"A mind at ease is life and health, but passion makes man rot away."* (Prov. 14:30, Moffatt.)

STEPS TO ABOUNDING ENERGY

Steps to get rid of fatigue and to live a life of abounding energy:

1. *Get a physical checkup to see if there is any structural disease.* If there is nothing serious enough to cause fatigue, then look for the causes elsewhere. They are probably in the mind and attitudes.

2. *See if you have your minimum requirement of vitamins.* I get mine from "grass" tablets which have the whole range of known vitamins, and apparently some not yet discovered. They have a plus not known in synthetic vitamins. You may be vitamin-starved. There is an intimate connection between vitamins and nerves. If you are vitamin-starved, you will be tired and nervous.

3. *If you are bored with your work, change your job or change your attitude.* If it is not possible to change your job, then change your attitude toward your job. Do everything "for the love of God."

4. *Surrender to God everything which produces inner conflict.* Surrender self-centeredness, worry, fear, resentment, oversensitivity, inferiority feelings, and guilt. These make you tired, for they are not-the-way.

5. *Get interests outside yourself and give yourself to them.* Don't retire. The retired are the tired. Turn to new interests and new tasks. Someone has said that "life is counted not by the breaths taken but by the breaths not taken." You will be breathless with new interests and tasks. You will be gasping with surprise at a world popping with novelty and needs, and at yourself meeting those needs!

6. *Don't say, "I am tired." Rather say, "I am fresh in God."* The Africans have a saying, "Don't be tired tomorrow." Don't anticipate tiredness. Affirm health and adequacy. Autosuggestion? Yes, and good autosuggestion. Far better to suggest health than suggest sickness.

7. *"Turn on health" day by day by relaxed receptivity.* Let the healing grace of God into every brain cell and nerve and tissue by periods of quiet relaxation in His presence. In India there are stone slabs on pillars called *sumatungas* so the people carrying burdens on their heads can rest them. An Indian woman said, "Christ is my *Sumatunga*." He is.

O Christ, Thou are my *Sumatunga;* Thou art giving me rest. In Thee I am strong and well and rested. In Thee I am able for anything. Let life come on—I am ready. For I can be beaten by nothing, burdened by nothing. I am safe, and ready. I thank Thee. Amen.

AFFIRMATION FOR THE DAY: *"Come to me, all ye labouring and burdened, and I will refresh you."* (Matt. 11:28, Moffatt.)

HOW DOES GOD HEAL?

Disease can make one tired and unfit. What is the teaching of the Way about physical healing?

First, disease is not the will of God. Jesus never told people to bear disease as the will of God; it was an enemy to be banished. He healed men as a part of the coming of the Kingdom. Disease is not-the-way.

God is still healing today, in various ways through various methods. But in every case it is God healing. "We clear the way; God does the healing." God heals:

1. *Through surgeons.* A woman thanked me for telling her that my guidance was that she should go to a surgeon. She was cured by an operation.

2. *Through physicians.* God has laid up in nature various remedies which we are in the process of discovering. Use them. But a word of caution: To get the drug habit and begin dosing yourself for every little ailment is bad. A druggist was probably exaggerating when he said, "Eighty-five per cent of the stuff I sell is bunk," but he uttered a truth nevertheless. In spite of all this, there is a residue of real benefit from medicine.

3. *Through mental suggestion.* You can suggest sickness to yourself and you will be sick. "As he thinketh in his heart, so is he." On the other hand, you can talk health to yourself and it tends to heal. A man on a plane became ill: his heart was fluttering, he could not get his breath, the altitude was too high for him. A doctor on the plane asked him where he lived and received the answer, "Mexico City." The doctor informed him that he was only 2,000 feet high in the plane, whereas in Mexico City he was 7,500 feet high. The man got well immediately. There is such a thing as "blind men with perfect optic nerves, paralyzed men as sound in wind and limb as the doctors themselves, lame men who have never received a wound, deaf men who have never been near the front." Why? Because their mentality became twisted, their wires crossed because either the conscious or the subconscious mind played tricks on them and suggested disease as a way out of a tangle—an escape.

O Christ of the healthy mind and healthy soul and healthy body, make me healthy and harmonious and whole. For with Thee I too will health. Let the healing streams of health flow through me. Amen.

AFFIRMATION FOR THE DAY: *My mental processes surrendered to God are now surrendered to no false fear or false imagination. I am free.*

MORE WAYS GOD HEALS

We continue to look at the ways God heals.

4. *Through climate*. Although this is overstressed—for the real climate of health or ill health is within—nevertheless, some climates are conducive to health and some to disease. But don't take the climate business too seriously, for often—not always—when the doctor does not know what to do with you, he sends you off "for a change" to get you off his hands. I have lived in health in an "unhealthy climate" for years—emerged stronger, more fit.

5. *Through deliverance from underlying fears, loneliness, self-centeredness, purposelessness, resentments, guilts which produce disease*. "Ammon was so upset by his passion . . . that it made him ill." (II Sam. 13:2, Moffatt.) A newspaper item says: "It was reported today in Norway that the Nobel prize winner, the novelist Knut Hamsun, became seriously ill when he learned of the German defeat. Hamsun had openly supported Quisling and the Germans." "Banish all worries from your mind, and keep your body free from pain." (Eccles. 11:10, Moffatt.) Note the connection: "worries" . . . "pain." "So long as I refused to own my guilt, . . . life ebbed away. . . . My body dried up, as in summer heat." (Ps. 32:3-4, Moffatt.) "Some, weakened by their sinful ways, were sick and suffering through evil-doing; they had a loathing for all food, were on the verge of death." (Ps. 107:17-18, Moffatt.) "There is no health in my limbs, thanks to my sins. . . . My wounds are foul and festering, thanks to my sinful folly. . . . There is no soundness in my body. . . . My heart is throbbing, the pith of life has left me, light has gone from mine eyes." (Ps. 38:3, 5, 7, 10, Moffatt.) "My health is wasting under my woe, my life eaten away with sorrow. . . . My body falls to pieces." (Ps. 31:9-10, Moffatt.) "Trouble wears away my strength, I age under outrages." (Ps. 6:7, Moffatt.) "My health pines away under my trouble." (Ps. 88:9, Moffatt.) "A mind at ease is life and health, but passion makes man rot away." (Prov. 14:30, Moffatt.) "Revere the Eternal and draw back from sin: that will mean health for your body and fresh life to your frame." (Prov. 3:7-8, Moffatt.) "A glad heart helps and heals: a broken spirit saps vitality." (Prov. 17:22, Moffatt.)

O Christ, Thou art seeking to deliver me from all that produces upset in the body. I yield to Thee all things that keep me from being at my best. I put them into Thy hands for cleansing and release. Amen.

AFFIRMATION FOR THE DAY: *All that produces disease within me is surrendered to Thee. Therefore in Thee I am well and sound.*

HEALING THROUGH THE SPIRIT'S TOUCH

We conclude our observations on the method of healing through deliverance from wrong mental and spiritual states.

"None in the land shall say then: 'I am sick,' for all who live there have their sins forgiven." (Isa. 33:24, Moffatt.) A missionary had a pain in her shoulder, but the doctors could find nothing. She picked up *Is the Kingdom of God Realism?* and her eyes fell on the story of the woman with a pain in her shoulder who said she thought "she would be well if she could tell her husband to go to hell just once." The missionary discovered that her own pain was caused by a resentment she had toward a man who was deceiving a girl living in her home. She surrendered the resentment to God, and the pain left.

A man frozen to his job by government regulation became sullen, bumped his engine against trucks, endangering lives. He had a stroke and is now an invalid. The anger sent up his blood pressure and brought on the stroke. Dr. William Sadler, the eminent specialist in nervous diseases, says that "if people lived in a truly Christian way, half the diseases would drop off tomorrow morning, and we would rise up a new superior race of human beings." A carriage ran over a Pekingese dog that had leaped from a woman's lap. She vomited. After that, whenever she heard the yelp of a dog, she lost her meal. The connection was discovered, the whole thing brought out, and she was released. God heals through forgiveness, insight, and deliverance from all internal states that produce disease.

6. *He heals through the direct operation of the Spirit of God upon our bodies.* Those who know say that there is no nerve or tissue which is beyond the reach of the effects of mental and spiritual states. Then is it difficult to believe that there is no portion of our bodies beyond the healing touch of the Spirit of God? To me this has passed beyond belief—it is a fact. Starr Daily says, "I do not believe in prayer—I know it." Well, I too can say: "I do not believe in healing by the direct touch of the Spirit of God—I know it." For I was suddenly touched in a dark moment, and from that time I've known health and life.

O Christ of the Healing Hands, lay Thy Hands on me and make me well in every portion of my being. I take life from Thee, and in Thee I am well, I am strong, I am free. All my springs of health are in Thee. I am grateful. Amen.

AFFIRMATION FOR THE DAY: *"He . . . will also make your mortal bodies live by His indwelling Spirit in your lives"* (Rom. 8:11, Moffatt.).

THE FINAL CURE

We come to the final method of God's healing:

7. *God heals through the final cure—the resurrection.* Some diseases must await the final cure in the resurrection. We live in a mortal world, a world where physical death is a fact. It is a beneficent fact, for if we didn't pass away and make room for the next generation, the earth would be so crowded that there wouldn't be any but "Standing Room Only." But we are on the way to a world of immortality where decay will not invade. Here it does invade, by the very nature of things. The body must break down sometime. Just as the soul must die to live, so the body must die to live.

Some of the saints of the earth have not been healed—they have lain on beds of unrelieved suffering. Then does God not will to heal? Yes, but He postpones it for some, to await the final cure in the resurrection. He will heal later on. In the meantime He gives the sufferer power, not merely to bear his suffering, but to use it until the final release. To *use* it? Yes. There are those who are called to "the ministry of suffering," to bear a daily cross and to live "in spite of."

I was taken to see "the most eminent citizen of Columbus," an invalid, blind and paralyzed, but radiant. When asked what was the greatest lesson he had learned, he replied: "To see the love of God in everything and in everybody. Anyone who has achieved perfect happiness as I have is not to be pitied." Pitied? He dictates books, radiates good cheer, and lives so victoriously that well people come to an invalid to learn how to live. An invalid spreads health.

A woman who had been on her bed for forty-two years "did more for the Kingdom of God than all the ministers of the town," said a businessman. She did. When she died, she didn't die—"she just walked into the sunset." No, "she walked into a sunrise." Her victorious spirit now has a body to suit the victory of the spirit. "I wish I could get my resurrection body now," said the saintly P. M. Buck, as he pegged away on his typewriter with two fingers, the rest crippled with rheumatism, trying to finish a certain mapped-out number of books before he died. Now he has his postponed body.

O God, Thou art healing, healing, healing. I am under Thy processes of healing. I give them full sway within me, for I am being redeemed, soul, mind, and body. I feel the coursing of Thy life within me. Amen.

AFFIRMATION FOR THE DAY: *"I am myself resurrection and life. . . . No one who lives and believes in me will ever die."* (John 11:25, Moffatt.)

A WORD TO YOUTH

We come now to consider the time process which is carrying us on through youth, middle age, and old age—and into the arms of God. First, youth. You have three great decisions of life to make: (1) The choice of a life work. (2) The choice of a life partner. (3) The choice of a life philosophy.

Perhaps the last should be first, the choice of a life philosophy. I have mentioned the two most important questions about a life: "What is your center?" and, "What is your circumference?" If you begin at the wrong center, your whole life will go wrong with it. I need not tell you that I think Christ should be your center and the world should be your circumference. Choose Christ. A high-school student said to me: "If we don't get a faith to live by in high school, we will probably never get it." Statistics show that after twenty-one, the chances are three to one against becoming a Christian. Make the Way your way.

Your second choice is your life work. When God made you, He made you different, unique. He broke the pattern after making you. He has a special place for you to fill, a contribution for you to make. Don't be worried about finding it at once. It will unfold to you as you go along, obedient to His will as you see it. See page 287 of this book for the steps you are to take in trying to discover your life work.

"What, going up to see without a star?
What, going on a journey without a map?
What, going out to battle without a song?
What, going into life without love?"

The third is the choice of a life partner. Follow these steps: (1) *Take a second look."* If the proposed partner can't stand a second look, break the attachment. It is better to remain single than marry the wrong person. (2) *Choose one in whose conversation you will be interested when the physical side of marriage becomes dimmed.* (3) *Take a course in successful marriage relations.* Few divorces take place where there has been such a course. (4) *Find your mate in church circles—preferably your own.* A canary that is put with sparrows will chirp; the sparrows won't sing.

O God, help me to make these three decisions under Thy guidance. For I know that if there is no Hand on my helm, there will be rocks beneath my bow. Thou hast my life and my life choices. Amen.

AFFIRMATION FOR THE DAY: *I start with Thee. Cleanse my past, consecrate my present, clarify my future. I follow.*

264

A WORD TO MIDDLE AND OLD AGE

We will pause for just a moment to look at middle age. In many ways it is the most dangerous age. In middle age we begin to play safe, lose adventure, and perish of dry rot. G. B. Shaw says that most men's epitaphs could be: "Died at thirty, buried at sixty." In middle age many let down their standards and break morally. Sometimes with strange justification: "But you are a schoolteacher and a Sunday-school teacher—what can you teach your young people about living straight?" I asked of a woman who was having an affair with a married man. "But," she replied, "I can still teach them to be clean in youth, for I didn't start this until forty." At forty everybody should undergo reconversion on general principles. That is the period of sag.

But we must look particularly at old age. There should be training courses in how to grow old gracefully and happily. We have training courses in how to grow up, but not in how to grow old. They say, "You are as old as your arteries." Better, "You are as old as your mind." And your mind need never grow old. "Unlike the flesh, the spirit does not decay with years. Many of the happiest men and women in the world are those in their sixties, seventies, and eighties"—happiest and most useful. An old Quaker, eighty-two, with a beautiful face said: "I'm going to live till I die, and then I'm going to live forever." "I'm going to live till I die"—can we keep on living abundantly and creatively till we die, no matter at what age? Yes.

Dr. Martin Gumpert in his book *You Are Younger Than You Think* says that "idleness is the greatest enemy of the aged and presents them with their ticket to death." Sophocles wrote his famous *Philoctetes* at eighty-seven. Michelangelo was writing poetry and designing buildings up to the time of his death at ninety. Gladstone, prime minister at eighty-three, fought the greatest battle of his life for the passage of a home-rule bill. Goethe completed *Faust*, his greatest work, at eighty-one. Titan finished "The Last Supper" at eighty. You are younger than you think!

O God, help me to grow old gracefully and beautifully and creatively. Give me the strength and will to bring forth fruit even to old age. May I know in Thee the deathless life, and be unafraid of getting old. May I greet it with a song. Amen.

AFFIRMATION FOR THE DAY: *"Even to your old age I will be the same."* (Isa. 46:4, Moffatt.)

HOW NEVER TO BE OLD

Some people do their finest work in old age. The elder Cato began to study Greek at eighty. The duchess of Bedford was sixty-two when she took up flying, and made solo flights at seventy-one. She flew to Cape Town and back. Clara Barton founded the American Red Cross at sixty-one and was president of the organization for twenty-two years. She founded the National First Aid Association at eighty-four and was its active leader until she died at ninety-one.

Some time ago I was speaking at a church service which was broadcast. A listener told me that the broadcast was broken into by a few lines of "The Old Gray Mare Ain't What She Used to Be." My hearers may have thought so! But it would have been fatal for me to have done anything but laugh at it, and laugh it out of court! If that song breaks into your consciousness at any time, laugh at it—long and loud. For it needn't be true. Provided:

1. *You never retire.* If you give up your business, take up new interests or revive old interests and go to work again at the things you are interested in. Dr. E. H. Lines, of the New York Life Insurance Company, said: "Men who retire don't live long. They're not prepared for leisure. It's too great a shock for them."

2. *You learn something new every day.* The people who live longest are those who have a zest for living. That zest keeps them going. Mrs. Edna Grace Koch, mother of ten children, took her B.A. degree thirty years after her marriage, after all her children were grown and through college. She was the only one who graduated with honors, including her husband who was a professor.

3. *You don't depend on financial security for a successful old age.* Dr. Martin Gumpert says: "Financial premiums on retirement, which become automatically effective on a certain date, confer none of the blessings of real security, . . . are detrimental to the health of the individual." Contribute to the welfare of the life around you. A widow said to me: "I thought I was done for, so I just let go. Now I must make something of my life after hearing you." Never "let go." Rather, "Let's go"—into the finest and most fruitful period of living, ripe and beautiful old age. Sixty-two is wonderful. I wouldn't be twenty-two for anything! This is too much fun.

O God, I thank Thee for the years that come and go. I thank Thee that they grow more beautiful and blessed as they come and go. Amen.

AFFIRMATION FOR THE DAY: *O God, Thou art my rejuvenation. I am young in Thee.*

THE WAY IS THE WAY OF POWER

We have been considering the fact that the Way is the way of power, the way to use the raw materials of human life, good, bad, or indifferent, that may come to us.

But, you say, that sounds good, too good to be true. Where are we to get the power to do that? We must now consider *the Way as the way of power*. Jesus said, "I am the way," the acting; "the truth," the thinking; and "the life," the resources to fulfill the thinking and the acting. Without the Way as the way of resources, then it is all a recommendation instead of a realization—something presented, but not possible.

"Am I using all my talents?" asked a servant of God, greatly used, and the reply came from God: "Yes, and very much more; you are using my resources." That was the secret. He was going beyond his resources and was living on God's resources. I wrote in my notebook: "Am I living on reserves or on resources? Am I careful of my human reserves, because I have nothing beyond them to live by? Or have I learned to tap divine resources and live by them?"

If the Way is the way of good precepts, but not the way of power, then it fails us at the point of need. For it is at the point of power that we break down. But the power is all here. "*All* who touched him recovered." (Mark 6:56, Moffatt.) It wasn't a question of the power inherent in Jesus. It was all there. It was a question of touching Him by an appropriating faith. *All* who touch Him now by an appropriating faith recover—recover from whatever ails them.

But many of us are like the Chinese gentleman in Penang who, sitting in his new Ford car, had coolies push him up and down the street. When asked if there wasn't any power in the machine, he replied, "Yes, but I'm afraid to turn it on." We are afraid to turn on the power—it's here unused. That power is nothing less than the power of the Holy Spirit. The Way is the way of the Holy Spirit. A Holy Spirit—less Christianity is different from Christianity. It is a devitalized Christianity; it is less than, and therefore other than, Christianity. It is sub-Christian. The Way is the way of power, power to live the things it teaches.

O Christ, I know that Thy distinctive baptism is the baptism with the Holy Spirit and power. I need inner reinforcement. Then give me this power that will change the whole level of life for me. In Thy name. Amen.

AFFIRMATION FOR THE DAY: *"The Spirit makes alive."* (II Cor. 3:6, Moffatt.)

CONCERNING THE HOLY SPIRIT

The Way is the way of power. There are three facts about God: (1) God *for* us, (2) God *with* us, (3) God *in* us. God *for* us, the divine Intention, the Father; God *with* us, the divine Invasion, the Son; God *in* us, the divine Indwelling, the Holy Spirit. The divine Intention becomes the divine Invasion, and the divine Invasion becomes the divine Indwelling. It is not enough to have redemptive Intention and redemptive Invasion. They are both outside of us, therefore inadequate, for our need is within us. There must be Indwelling.

What happened in history in the Incarnation must move straight on inside of us in experience in the Indwelling, must do it or fail. The historical must become the experimental. Otherwise the Christian faith is a counsel of perfection, making impossible demands on human nature. But if the divine Indwelling is a fact, then everything is possible. I have quoted a sign on the walls of a Bible class: "I can do little, *we* can do anything." It was intended to mean the human "we." But the same thing can be said of the divine-human "we." God apart from us can do little. We apart from God can do little. Together we can do anything.

The Holy Spirit means the human-divine togetherness. In the Incarnation God came part way, in the Indwelling He comes the full way, comes into the citadel of our spirits. And He comes, not as a transient visitor, but "to abide with you forever." A minister suggested that "the Holy Spirit comes and goes as we need Him." That cuts at the root of the Indwelling. And the Indwelling is the focal point of redemption. Without Indwelling, redemption doesn't get at us *where it counts*. With the Indwelling, redemption touches the vital spot.

So the distinctive baptism of Jesus was the baptism of the Holy Spirit. He never baptized with water; He saved Himself to give the "one baptism"—the baptism of the Spirit. In that "one baptism" His redemptive work is potentially complete. In the baptism with water we surrender our sins; in the baptism of the Spirit we surrender ourselves. One is negative, the other is positive; for in the surrender of ourselves we put ourselves at the disposal of the Spirit; our interests and our capacities merge. Togetherness sets in.

O Christ, I want to be baptized with Thy Spirit. I am not content with any gap between us. I want to be indwelt. I want the Spirit to move into the very citadel of my spirit. There I would be one, and only one. Amen.

AFFIRMATION FOR THE DAY: *"Wherever the Spirit of the Lord is, there is open freedom."* (II Cor. 3:17, Moffatt.)

THE HOLY SPIRIT BRINGS UNITY

The Way is the way of the Indwelling. God's laws are written within us: "The kingdom of God is within you." This is without our consent. But the Indwelling is with our consent. In the Indwelling our personality is preserved, purified, permeated, and perfected.

We find a sevenfold statement of the Christian faith in the opening verses of the Acts (Moffatt). The Christian faith is this: (1) Jesus' life: "Jesus began by doing." (1:1.) (2) His teaching: "Jesus began by . . . teaching." (1:1.) (3) His death: "After his sufferings." (1:3) (4) His resurrection: "He had shown them that he was alive." (1:3.) (5) His coming within them in the Holy Spirit: "Issuing his orders by the holy Spirit." (1:2.) (6) The Kingdom of God as the total program: "The affairs of God's Realm." (1:3.) (7) His ascension to the right hand of power: "He was taken up to heaven." (1:2.) Here, then, was a movement founded on His life, His teaching, His death, His resurrection, His coming by the Holy Spirit, His program of the Kingdom for individual and collective redemption, a movement whose Author is at the right hand of power, has "all authority."

This movement operated by bringing a sevenfold unity into life. With the coming of the Holy Spirit these unities were realized: (1) Unity with God: "They were all filled with the holy Spirit." (2:4.) (2) Unity within the self: "They were all filled with the holy Spirit —the Spirit enabled them to express themselves." (2:4.) (3) Unity within the immediate group: "Peter stood up along *with the eleven.*" (2:14.) (4) Unity with all believers: "The believers all kept together." (2:44.) (5) Unity with other races: "We hear these men talking of the triumphs of God in our own languages!" (2:11.) (6) Unity in material things: "They shared all they had with one another." (2:45.) (7) Unity with all men in an all-inclusive love, including enemies: "For the promise is meant . . . for anyone whom the Lord our God may call to himself." (2:39.) When surrendered to and responsive to the Holy Spirit, we are at one with God, with ourselves, with our immediate group, with all believers, with all races, with material things, and with all men, including enemies, in an all-inclusive love. This is "the unity of the Spirit."

O living Spirit, I come to Thee for this living unity. I'm tired of being out of harmony. I would be made whole, and I would be made *one.* For I would know unity with Thee and with all others. Amen.

AFFIRMATION FOR THE DAY: *"Lead the life of the Spirit; then you will never satisfy the passions of the flesh."* (Gal. 5:16, Moffatt.)

"IT IS ALL EMPTY INSIDE"

The Holy Spirit is the center of our virtues. Our virtues are rooted in self-interest or Spirit-interest. One makes them pagan; the other makes them Christian.

Paul says: "I prove myself at all points a true minister of God, . . . with [1] innocence, [2] insight, [3] patience, [4] kindness, [5] the holy Spirit, [6] unaffected [7] love, [8] true words, [9] the power of God." (II Cor. 6:4-7, Moffatt.) There are four virtues on each side of the Holy Spirit, the central spring of all virtues. He is the spring and center of our goodness. The last is the "power of God." The power of God is behind all virtues which spring from the Holy Spirit. For all virtues not rooted in the Holy Spirit end in self-righteousness. Rooted in the Holy Spirit, they end in self-effacing dedication.

In our faith, in our unity, and in our virtues the Holy Spirit is central. But the Holy Spirit is not central in our present-day Christianity. The emphasis upon the Holy Spirit has been pushed from the main stream of Christianity into the cults. There the teaching has been thrown out of balance, often identified with rampant emotionalism. That queers it. The queer have queered Pentecost for many. And yet the almost entire absence of emphasis on the Spirit has impoverished the main stream of Christianity. It often degenerates into a humanistic striving to be good.

A leading psychologist said: "That Church of today is like an autumn leaf, dry and dead, but retaining its form and structure." Too sweeping, of course, but with just enough truth in it to make it sting. If this is true of the Church, then it is even more true of psychology, especially when it is pagan. The pagan psychologist goes on the assumption that all that is needed is to have yourself analyzed; all else will follow. The outstanding psychology is psychoanalysis, not psychosynthesis. Some of the most disrupted people in the world are the analyzed. They are picked to pieces, but not put together again.

But the Christians can't complain if men turn to pagan cults and pagan science when they themselves have lost, or have failed to realize, the central fact of their faith—the Holy Spirit. A minister stood up, put his hand over his heart, and said, "It is all empty inside."

O Spirit Divine, how dare I be empty within when all around me cries out for a way—the Way. With Thee I am able for anything. Without Thee I am doomed to sterility. So I open my heart. Come in. Amen.

AFFIRMATION FOR THE DAY: *I am "filled by him who fills the universe entirely."* (Eph. 1:23, Moffatt.)

HE BEGAN—THEY BEGAN

What is the part of the human in all this? The Holy Spirit does not mean the end of self-effort. It is the beginning of self-effort.

The opening verse of Acts says that "Jesus began" (1:1), but the next chapter says that "they began" (2:4). "All that Jesus began" is-sued in all that "they began." The coming of the Holy Spirit was an awakening stimulus, an imparting of an astonishing energy. Francis of Assisi speaks of "the holy energy that floods in through surrender to God."

It is said that "the harvest of the Spirit" includes: "love, joy, peace, good temper, kindliness, generosity, fidelity, gentleness, self-control." (Gal. 5:22-23, Moffatt.) Now note that it begins with "love" and ends in "self-control." The genesis of Christian virtues is not duty but love. We practice these virtues, not because duty compels us, but be-cause love impels us. But that love issues in "self-control." Spirit-control ends in self-control. The self-control is not the control that sits on a lid but a control through surrender of the self to the Holy Spirit. Then the lesser desires are caught up into higher desires, and we do the highest because we love the highest.

John the Baptist's first recorded word is, "You brood of vipers" (Luke 3:7, Moffatt); and Jesus' first recorded word is, "The Spirit of the Lord is upon me . . . to preach the gospel to the poor" (Luke 4:18, Moffatt). One begins with a suppression, the other with an expression; one with a brood of vipers, the other with a brooding Spirit. One was the gospel of a demand, the other the gospel of an offer; one talked of "the coming Wrath" and the other of "the coming Kingdom." John's baptism was with water, to get rid of; Jesus' baptism was with the Spirit, to get possession of. One movement died; the other lives on—forever. John irritated; Jesus inspired.

A minister said a penetrating thing in one of our Ashrams: "When I preach something ahead of what I am, I only irritate people; but when I preach what I have experienced, I inspire people." Our Chris-tian faith can be an irritation or an inspiration.

O Holy Spirit, I want goodness to be within me, not as an irritation to myself and others, but as an overflowing inspiration. Help me to have the contagion of the Spirit, make my virtues vital. In Jesus' name. Amen.

AFFIRMATION FOR THE DAY: *"Do not vex God's holy Spirit, by whom you have been sealed for the day of redemption."* (Eph. 4:30, Moffatt.)

TRYING TO KEEP UP

I sat alongside of Lake Massaweepie, in the Adirondacks, writing this book. Each morning a wild duck came by foraging near the shore with her brood. One duck seemed to be weaker than the rest and spent most of his time just keeping up with the others. He had no time to feed. Many of us spend most of our time keeping up with our tasks. We have no time to feed our inner spirits. We lack a plus, a margin of power that lets us meet our tasks with something left over.

Someone asked a dog trainer how he managed to do it. "It's simple," he replied, "for all you have to do is to know just a little more than the dogs." It's true of any job. You must know a little more than your job, be a little ahead of the procession, experience a little more than the group to whom you minister. It is that margin that counts. It is the "more" that decides every issue. A great teacher said to a group of teachers: "Don't teach too close to the margin of your knowledge." When there are reserves, they can be thrown into any situation.

Pentecost gives us that "plus"—that "margin" of power which makes men "more than conquerors." They conquer with enough left over for an extra task. Paul speaks of those "having a form of godliness, but denying the power," and he exhorts, "From such turn away." (II Tim. 3:5.) But the exhortation was unnecessary. We do naturally and normally turn away from those who have the form without the power. Our churches are often empty because the preacher is empty. Where the preacher finds, the pew fills. Then deep speaks to deep. One preacher was floundering in his message and getting nowhere when someone came up and offered him a throat lozenge, but the man said rather pathetically: "That won't do any good, not for the thing that's troubling me." He was empty, and he knew it. Someone described some of us ministers as being "4-F above the shoulders." There is enough truth in that to make it sting, but the deeper sting is that many of us are 4-F below the shoulders—our hearts are empty. In that case we are unfit for Kingdom service. That which is to reach the heart must come from the heart. If the heart is empty, then deep does not speak to deep. Shallowness speaks to shallowness.

O Christ of the full heart, make me full, full to running over. Make my heart a spillway, sharing my surplus with others in need. For I walk amid need, and I cannot walk amid it empty. Help me. Amen.

AFFIRMATION FOR THE DAY: *In the light of the world's emptiness I have no right to be empty when God offers me the fullness of the Spirit.*

A HOLY SPIRIT–LESS CHRISTIANITY

A Holy Spirit–less Christianity lacks contagion. It hasn't that plus that carries over from a contained faith to a contagious faith. Our Christianity can be contained, contained within us as a comfort, a refuge, a belief, a hope, an inspiration. Good, but not good enough. Nothing is ours that isn't shared; nothing is ours that cannot be carried over into duplication in other lives. Nothing really lives that isn't life giving. For the end of life is the procreation of life.

Someone has asked, "Are you a refrigerator or an incubator?" Some freeze life; others fructify it. Some throw a warm sympathetic glow around persons and situations that brings forth new life, new hopes, new aspirations. These people are spiritually creative.

Two preachers were being analyzed by two laymen. They came to this conclusion: "When one stands up to preach, he preaches eloquently, but he is alone. When the other man stands up, there isn't the eloquence, but the effect is astonishingly different. The reason is, now there are two." His abilities had been taken hold of by Another and heightened. His words had within them the Word. Here was the grain of wheat which had fallen into the ground and had died, died to itself as self-sufficient. And now it brought forth "rich fruit." The other man had not died, and so he worked by himself—"alone." One was a person in the hands of God. The other was in his own hands, or rather *on* his own hands, a problem to himself.

> "But oars alone can ne'er prevail
>   To reach the distant coast;
> The breath of heaven must swell the sail
>   Or all the toil is lost."

A Quaker said: "A man truly touched of God can influence the countryside for ten miles around." The five loaves and two fishes were insufficient for the five thousand while in the hands of the owner, but turned over to Christ—in His hands they were sufficient, plus something left over. And that is all there is to it. Life in our hands is life on our hands—a problem. Life in the hands of Jesus is no longer a problem; it is a possibility.

O Spirit of God, descend upon my heart. Take away the coldness by breathing within me Thy warmth. Make me a spiritual incubator. May I warm the cold, inspire the wavering, and make fruitful the barren. Amen.

AFFIRMATION FOR THE DAY: *"I am alive as he is alive by the power of God."* (II Cor. 13:4, Moffatt.)

ON POSSESSING THE SPIRIT

This matter of the Holy Spirit in Christianity is so important that we must spend another week upon it. The Church has in large measure tried to by-pass Pentecost and go out to its problem without the "tarrying." As a consequence it is exhausting itself against the problems of the day. Had the disciples tried to by-pass Pentecost, we would never have heard of them again. They would have exhausted themselves against the problems of that day. A river in California starts toward the sea but never gets there—it is lost in the sands. The spiritual life of many is like that. It starts, but it is lost in the sands of surrounding life; it doesn't get to its destination, its destination of contagion. It doesn't "get across." It doesn't "get across" because it doesn't "get" us.

Gypsy Smith once said of the difference between the singing of Negroes and whites: "The whites have the music, but the music has the Negroes." The whites sang music, but the music sang the Negroes —sang them with all the stops out, played them all over.

Halford Luccock said that "when a respectable middle-class Christian goes Christian—that's news." When the semibarren disciples surrendered to the Holy Spirit at Pentecost, it became news—good news to the world. That can happen now.

But the question is asked: Doesn't every Christian possess the Holy Spirit? And the answer is Yes. But the difference is probably this: In the new birth you have the Holy Spirit; in the fullness the Holy Spirit has you. Before Pentecost the disciples had the Holy Spirit, but after Pentecost the Holy Spirit had them. In Gal. 5:16-18 (Moffatt) we see three stages: first, "The life of the Spirit"; second, "the passion of the Spirit"; third, "the sway of the Spirit." These are the three stages: "The life of the Spirit," when new life is introduced within us by the Spirit; "the passion of the Spirit," when the new life bursts periodically into passionate operation; and "the sway of the Spirit," when the Holy Spirit exercises a perpetual control over surrendered powers and capacities.

O Spirit of the living God, I have found life through Thee, and some times it bursts into a passion for souls and for sacrifice; but I want most of all to have Thee as perpetual sway over me, a continuous possession and power. In Jesus' name. Amen.

AFFIRMATION FOR THE DAY: *Today I shall be: Spirit-saved, Spirit-stayed, Spirit-swayed, because Spirit-obeyed.*

THE SUBCONSCIOUS CLEANSED

We saw yesterday that the three stages as found in Gal. 5:17-18 were: the life of the Spirit, the passion of the Spirit, and the sway of the Spirit. We must return to our meditation upon these stages.

In conversion there is introduced into the soul a new life, the life of the Spirit; you are born of the Spirit. The birth of the Spirit may be very, very quiet like "an effortless sunrise." There are no fixed patterns: "The Spirit bloweth where it listeth"—differently in different persons. And yet the effects are substantially the same: "Thou hearest the sound thereof"—the sound of new life and victory. Life is on an essentially higher level.

And in this new life there are moments of "the passion of the Spirit." There are moments when "the passion of the Spirit" is upon you—you feel deeply, sacrifice really, are passionately Christian. But this is periodic; it comes and goes. "The passion of the Spirit" is succeeded by "the passion of the flesh." And these two are antagonistic: "The two are at issue, so that you are not free to do as you please." (Gal. 5:17, Moffatt.) "The passion of the Spirit" and "the passion of the flesh" cancel each other out, and you are divided, ineffective.

The reason for this clash? Probably this: "The passion of the flesh" is the unconverted subconscious mind. The three driving urges reside in the subconscious: self, sex, and the herd. These urges, through innate propensities and racial habit, drive for completion—fulfillment apart from, and sometimes contrary to, the new "life of the Spirit." "The life of the Spirit" is in the conscious mind. So conscious and subconscious mind are at cross-purposes.

This produces an up-and-down type of living. Sometimes "the life of the Spirit" is on top, and sometimes "the passion of the flesh." The spiritual life is unstable. We alternate between cold and hot; we do not "maintain the spiritual glow." A little boy, deeply impressed by Niagara Falls, tried to take some of it, roar and all, back to his home in a bottle. As he poured it out before the family, he sighed, "Oh pshaw, it's died." When we try to hand on the wonder and power of the new life, it often dies in the pouring out. It doesn't get across.

O Spirit of God, I want to know the continuing fullness of the Spirit. I want Thee, not as a periodic action, but as a continuing atmosphere. I want Thee as a Presence, always there and always available. Amen.

AFFIRMATION FOR THE DAY: *"He who has begun the good work in you will go on completing it until the day of Jesus Christ."* (Phil. 1:6, Moffatt.)

CONSCIOUS AND SUBCONSCIOUS UNIFIED

We saw yesterday that "the passion of the flesh" and "the passion of the Spirit" war within and leave us a house of Mansoul divided against itself. Is this the normal Christian state, the best that Christianity can do—to leave you a divided soul until the final release in death?

Some would reply in the affirmative and point to the seventh chapter of Romans as the normal Christian state: "I find another law in my members which conflicts with the law of my mind and makes me a prisoner to sin's law that resides in my members." (Rom. 7:23, Moffatt.) But that is not Christianity at all. It is entirely sub-Christian, for it is a description of Paul under the Law fighting it out with sin. Christianity begins with the closing verses of the seventh chapter and the opening verses of the eighth: "Who will rescue me from this body of death? God will! Thanks be to him through Jesus Christ our Lord! . . . The law of the Spirit brings the life which is in Christ Jesus, and that law has set me free from the law of sin and death." (Rom. 7:24-25; 8:2, Moffatt.) This life of victory is normal Christianity.

What has happened? The Holy Spirit has taken possession of the subconscious mind, has cleansed, redirected, and dedicated the three driving urges of self, sex, and the herd. Those urges are still there, for the person is not depersonalized. The self is there, but no longer at the center, no longer controlling life. The self is a Spirit-controlled self. Sex is still there, but no longer at the center, controlling the rest of life. The life is not sex-controlled, but Spirit-controlled. The herd urge is still there, but no longer fastened on such entities as class or race or nation as supreme loyalties. Now it is fastened on the Kingdom of God as the supreme loyalty, and all other loyalties are subsidiary to that absolute loyalty. The urges are under "the sway of the Spirit." So now conscious mind and subconscious mind are under one sway and control. The wrong attitudes which have fastened themselves around the legitimate urges are cleansed away, and the urges are now redeemed, harmonized, and dedicated. Therefore the person is a unit and therefore a power. He is no longer pulling himself to pieces. He is pulling his load toward one end under one Power.

O living Spirit, I want my whole being to be redeemed. Thy work is in the area of the subconscious, an area I can't control. So I turn it over to Thee, for Thee to cleanse and control and redirect. I thank Thee. Amen.

AFFIRMATION FOR THE DAY: *"Out of the wealth of his glory to grant you a mighty increase of strength by his Spirit in the inner man."* (Eph. 3:16, Moffatt.)

TO BE SPIRIT-POSSESSED IS TO BE SELF-POSSESSED

We saw yesterday that when surrendered to the Spirit we become inwardly harmonized and hence outwardly effective. One of the reasons why the disciples couldn't get the evil spirit out of the lad was because they were probably upset and jealous because they were not in the inner circle of the three who were on the mount of transfiguration with Jesus. They were jealous within and powerless without.

When you are Spirit-possessed, then you are self-possessed. For there is an affinity between the Spirit and the self. When we most belong to the Spirit, we most belong to ourselves. It is said of the disciples on the day of Pentecost: "The Spirit enabled them to express themselves." (Acts 2:4, Moffatt.) This is true self-expression. It is life reduced to the natural because it is life raised to the Supernatural. All extraneous inhibitions, fears, self-consciousness, complexes are cleansed away, and the life is now normal and natural and unaffected.

This surprised the disciples and their enemies. They couldn't understand men who did not cow before insolent might or despise the weak and broken. Their speech, cleansed from the devious, took on a new directness and power. Could speech be more reduced to simplicity and directness than these words from a formerly devious Peter: "Then Peter, filled with the holy Spirit, said to them: 'Rulers of the people and elders of Israel, if we are being cross-examined today upon a benefit rendered to a cripple, upon how this man got better, you and the people of Israel must all know this, that he stands before you strong and well, thanks to the name of Jesus Christ the Nazarene whom you crucified and whom God raised from the dead.'" (Acts 4:8-10, Moffatt.) No wonder "they were astonished to notice how outspoken Peter and John were." They were outspoken, for they were inspoken —the Spirit had spoken harmony and co-ordination to every part of their inmost beings.

When something happens *to* us, then something happens *through* us. A bishop asked a man of rather mediocre ability why it was that he was always being sought for by large churches. He replied, "I am a small man, but I have a great God." And the great God had him.

O Spirit divine, I come to Thee for an empowering. I want not a momentary uplift but a permanent lifting up of my entire being on a higher level of life. Fill me with Thyself so that I may shed all self-consciousness and fears and stand up unafraid and effective. In Jesus' name. Amen.

AFFIRMATION FOR THE DAY: *I am among those who know "the enraptured indistinction between themselves and the Divine Being."*

STEPS TO RECEIVE THE HOLY SPIRIT

We now come to the place where you not only see but seek. You want to know the truth of the Holy Spirit as a fact in your own life. You are not content to see others used of the Spirit and yourself by-passed. You put yourself into line for the fulfillment of God's promise. "Ye shall receive the gift of the Holy Spirit. For the promise is unto you, and to your children, and to all that are afar off." (Acts. 2:38-39.)

1. *Say to yourself: God has come a long way in His approach to me. He has come through an incarnation, an atoning death, a resurrection, down to the door of my heart. Having come so far, I know He will come the full way—He will come within me.* The Holy Spirit is God coming within me. Here He changes the "with" to the "in." I am grateful for the "with," but I cannot be satisfied this side of the "in."

2. Again, say to yourself: *I know I would not be called to the Way without being provided with power to walk in the Way.* If this were not true, then the Christian faith would be an irritation, an exasperation. We see something we would follow but cannot. The Christian faith would then be a mockery instead of a mastery. But every syllable of the Christian faith is sincerity. Would it reverse itself at the place where it counts, at the place of power to put it into operation?

3. *As I search the Scriptures, I note that the Holy Spirit is given on four conditions:* (1) I must ask: "How much more shall your heavenly Father give the Holy Spirit to them that ask Him?" (Luke 11:13.) (2) I must accept the Holy Spirit by an act of appropriating faith: "By faith we might receive the promised Spirit." (Gal. 3:14, Moffatt.) (3) But I cannot accept the gift of the Holy Spirit without paying the price of that gift—the gift of myself. If He gives Himself, then I must give myself. (4) I must obey Him: "The holy Spirit which God has given to those who obey him." (Acts 5:32, Moffatt.) I must therefore ask, accept, give, and obey. I am now committing myself with all my being to do those four things.

O God, I am now committed. I set my face to seek with all my being for Thy highest gift, the gift of the Holy Spirit. I am not entering this quest lightly; I enter it with no reservations, no halfway attitudes. I set my face and my life to seek and to find. Amen.

AFFIRMATION FOR THE DAY: *"By all your participation in the Spirit."* (Phil. 2:1, Moffatt.) *I do participate in the Spirit, for I am possessed by the Spirit.*

THE STEPS OF APPROPRIATING FAITH

Four steps in receiving and retaining the Holy Spirit: I must ask, I must receive by faith, I must give myself, and I must obey.

These four steps I am now taking. First, I am asking. But Jesus gave three stages of intensity: ask, seek, knock. The asking is intensified into seeking, and the seeking into knocking. The knocking means that I am on the threshold—right on the verge of entering. There is nothing but a door between me and entering. And that door turns out to be Christ: "I am the door." The Door in that case is not a barrier, but a means of entrance—it is an open Door.

Second, I am entering by faith. As a child of God I am heir to the best the Father has—Himself. I take the gift of the Holy Spirit, and I take Him now. I do not ask for evidence—His character is enough. I rest on His character and not on my feelings. My feelings come and go, but His character remains forever. "Faithful is he that calleth you, who also will do it." (I Thess. 5:24.) I rest on His faithfulness and not on my faith—not on what I do, but on what He is. I take this ladder of faith: "Now the confidence we have in him is this, that he listens to us whenever we ask anything in accordance with his will; and if we know that he listens to whatever we ask, we know that we obtain the requests we have made to him." (I John 5:14-15, Moffatt.) Here are the steps: (1) *Confidence:* "the confidence we have in him"—confidence in character of God as seen in Christ. (2) *Conversing:* "we ask anything." (3) *Condition:* "in accordance with his will." (4) *Conviction:* "we know that he listens to whatever we ask." (5) *Consequence:* "we know that we obtain." And now I am taking those steps: I have confidence in the character of God. I converse with Him and tell Him my need. I believe the condition is met—that this is according to His will. I have the conviction that He hears and that, as a consequence, I am now possessed and filled by the Spirit. I know that faith will turn to fact and the fact to feeling. I take the step of faith; the fact takes place, and the feeling will be a by-product. I am talking faith to Him.

O Father, I am talking faith to Thee. I "have access by faith into this grace" wherein I now stand. I am receiving into every fiber of my being Thy Spirit as the permanent cleanser and controller of my life. Amen.

AFFIRMATION FOR THE DAY: *"The God who gave you his holy Spirit."* (I Thess. 4:8, Moffatt.) *He has given me the Holy Spirit —now.*

THE LAST STEP—SELF-GIVING AND OBEDIENCE

We come now to the two remaining steps in the receiving of the Holy Spirit: self-giving and obedience.

Perhaps we should have put the step of self-giving before the act of receiving faith. It belongs before. You cannot accept the gift of the Holy Spirit without involving the prior gift of yourself. And yet it belongs after the acceptance too. For it is a once-for-all giving and yet it is a continuous giving. It is like being married—there is a completed act when each gives the self to the other in marriage, and yet marriage is a continuous process of mutual self-giving. It is crisis and continuity.

But, you ask, how shall I know I have given myself? Silence the heart before Him and see if anything arises to the surface unsurrendered. If nothing arises, then you must take it for granted that there is nothing left behind. To be sure that everything is covered, tell God you surrender all you know and all you don't know. If anything unsurrendered is shown to you in the future, then that belongs to Him too.

And now the continuous obedience. He is in control. He uses you as the instrument of His purposes, provided you co-operate. We retain the Holy Spirit as long as He retains control. When we take over, He quietly steps out—not completely out, but He shuts off the sense of His presence and power till we decide to give Him the reins again. "To these facts we bear witness, with the Holy Spirit which God has given to those who *obey* him." (Acts 5:32, Moffatt.) The "obey" is present, continuous.

The difference between the pagan outlook and the Christian is this: Know thyself, accept thyself, develop thyself—that is pagan. Surrender thyself, discipline thyself, obey Another Self—the Spirit of God—that is Christian. You lose your life and find it again. An African patient was puzzled because Dr. Albert Schweitzer was there: "Why did you come?" The doctor replied, "Jesus sent me." Where Jesus sends, the Spirit sways.

O Spirit of the living God, I consent—gladly consent—to Thy sway, for Thy sway is my way, my deepest way. For I am made for Thy sway. In that sway I find my life and my fulfillment. Thy will and my will are not alien but affinities. I thank Thee. In Jesus' name. Amen.

AFFIRMATION FOR THE DAY: *"As we live by the Spirit, let us be guided by the Spirit."* (Gal. 5:25, Moffatt.)

THE WAY IS THE WAY OF GUIDANCE

We come now to the question of guidance. The Way is the way of the God-guided life.

Usually men are guided by one or more of these things: (1) By what others do. (2) By chance happenings. (3) By superstitious beliefs. (4) By impulses. (5) Sometimes by conscience. (6) Occasionally by God.

But the one who is on the Way is on the way of God—God has direction of his life. How does God guide? Obviously God must guide us in a way that will develop spontaneity in us. The development of character, rather than direction in this, that, and the other matter, must be the primary purpose of the Father. He will guide us, but He won't override us. That fact should make us use with caution the method of sitting down with a pencil and a blank sheet of paper to write down the instructions dictated by God for the day. Suppose a parent would dictate to the child minutely everything he is to do during the day. The child would be stunted under that regime. The parent must guide in such a manner, and to the degree, that autonomous character, capable of making right decisions for itself, is produced. God does the same. When our daughter was married, I wrote her: "I hope I shall never be in the way and never out of the way." I would be there when needed.

And yet, having said that, I hasten to add that the guidance of God is more intimate than God standing by in case of need. It is willing co-operation. God gives us autonomy, and then we deliberately choose to co-operate with Him on the basis that He is the managing Director. He has the first, middle, and last word, and we are glad to have it so. For His will is our highest interest. "Thy hands made and moulded me, to understand thine orders." (Ps. 119: 73, Moffatt.) We are inwardly made to "understand" and to do the "orders" of God. And when we do them, we are free—free because fulfilled. Guidance then is guidance into our highest development and achievement. It is also guidance into liberty, for when we do the will of God, we are free. The will of God is always our will at its best.

O God, I come to Thee to be guided, for I know in Thy guidance is my only goodness and my only greatness and my only gladness. So I come to submit my way to Thy way, to align my will to Thy will. Guide me. Amen.

AFFIRMATION FOR THE DAY: *I no longer belong to those who "take bypaths of their own, badly made"* (Jer. 18:15, Moffatt); *I am under God's guidance.*

GOD GUIDES IN SEVEN WAYS

The will of God is our freedom and our fulfillment. How do we find that will?

We believe that God will reveal His will, and hence will guide us, through at least these ways: (1) Through the life and teaching of Jesus as recorded in the Scriptures. (2) Through the collective experience of the ages through the Church and society. (3) Through the counsel of good and intelligent people. (4) Through opening opportunities and needs. (5) Through the heightened moral intelligence. (6) Through conscience. (7) Through the Inner Voice.

Sometimes He will guide us in one of these ways, more often by a conjunction of these ways. The latter is safer. But a caution is necessary. Do not expect guidance to be as explicit and plain as two and two make four. There will always be a degree of probability in any of this guidance, for that degree of probability puts adventure and daring into life, and it is at the point of adventure and daring that we grow. Guidance must be sufficiently clear to act upon, but never so clear that an act of adventurous faith is not required. The act of adventurous faith is the growing point.

1. *God guides us through the life and teaching of Jesus as recorded in the Scriptures.* This is God's general guidance. For in Jesus we see the nature of God and Reality revealed. There isn't a thing in Jesus that isn't in Reality, and there isn't a thing in Reality that isn't in Jesus. Here the Mind of God came into embodiment. In any situation look at Jesus and do the most Christlike thing you know, and you will never go wrong. God will never, and can never, guide you in a way that cuts across the Spirit of Christ. He can never because He cannot act against His own nature. Suspect any "fancy" guidance that isn't Christlike. For instance, a girl had a dream that linked her life with the life of a man who was eligible for marriage. She was prepared to give up her job and follow the suggestions coming out of that dream. But that dream was obviously from her subconscious mind and, if followed, might have let her down hard.

O God, I see that I cannot do other than the Christlike thing and remain in Thy will. I want Thy will, so I ask Thee to guide me according to Him. Then I will be safe and assured. I do not ask Thee to do something Thou canst not do. Amen.

AFFIRMATION FOR THE DAY: *"I will instruct you and teach you what is the road to take; I will give you counsel, O humble soul."* (Ps. 32:8, Moffatt.)

GUIDANCE THROUGH COLLECTIVE EXPERIENCE

We pursue our study of guidance. We said yesterday that God cannot guide you in any way that is not Christlike. Jesus was supreme sanity. There was nothing psychopathic about Him. He went off into no visions, no dreams. He got His guidance through prayer as you and I do. That is, He got His guidance when in control of His faculties, and not when out of control as in dreams. I do not say that God may not guide through a vision or dream; but if He does, it will be very seldom, and it will be because He couldn't get hold of our normal mental processes to guide them. For God is found most clearly and beneficially in the normal rather than in the abnormal. And Jesus is the Normal, for He is the Norm.

2. *God guides us through the collective experience of the ages through the Church and society.* There is a deposit of experience being laid up in the Church and society, experience as to how life works and how it will not work.

It is possible that both the Church and society can become tyranny to the soul when they assume to control the destiny of the individual. We cannot turn over our conscience to the Church or to society. The state recognizes that and gives the right of "conscientious objection." It thereby acknowledges that God is supreme and not the state. If the state is not supreme, neither is the Church. And for the Church to say that unless you obey its decrees you are damned is an insufferable arrogance that has become blasphemy.

But while we reject an overlordship of Church and society, nevertheless God may guide us through them—guide us, but not override us. God's guidance frees us from the tyranny of Church and society, and yet makes us free to use any guidance we can get through them. Someone has said that "every man is a prisoner of his date," but a God-guided man is no longer a prisoner of his date, and yet he is free to take from his date anything relevant and contributive. God guides through the Church and society to the degree that the Church and society are guided of God. "Copy me, as I copy Christ," said Paul (I Cor. 11:1, Moffatt), and it is sound advice—and Christian.

O God, I want to know Thy will and to follow it. If Thou hast any word to speak to me this day through the Church and through society, let me take that word and follow it. But give me discernment to hear Thy word amid the words. Amen.

AFFIRMATION FOR THE DAY: *"Whoever reverences the Eternal, learns what is the right course to take."* (Ps. 25:12, Moffatt.)

GOD GUIDES THROUGH OPENING OPPORTUNITIES

We continue to look at the methods of God's guidance:

3. *Through good and intelligent people.* Note that I link "good and intelligent." I would not trust the guidance of a person whose intelligence is not linked with goodness. Intelligence not linked with goodness is no longer intelligence—it is learned ignorance. On the other hand, be sure the person who gives advice is intelligent as well as good. Unintelligent goodness is not a safe guide either.

4. *Through opening opportunities and needs.* You are now a Christian, and "a Christian is one who cares." As you get into closer touch with Christ, you will "care" more and more for everybody, everywhere. You will now see needs not hitherto seen. Your sympathetic imagination will be quickened. You will project yourself into other people's situations, and you will see and feel from their standpoint. Dick Sheppard said: "Christianity does not consist in abstaining from doing things no gentleman would think of doing, but in doing things that are unlikely to occur to anyone who is not in touch with the Spirit of Christ." You will be guided to see needs to which the unguided are blind or obtuse. The Spirit will create "a concern" where others are unconcerned.

Perhaps you can apply the fourfold method of science in getting guidance through an opening need or providence: first, study of the problem; second, unconscious incubation; third, emergence of the solution; fourth, verification by experiment. Study of the problem means to gather all the information possible. Unconscious incubation means that you may get guidance through the subconscious mind. "He giveth his beloved sleep," is more correctly translated, we are told, "He giveth unto his beloved in sleep." God speaks through the subconscious in sleep. You awaken in the morning, and all is clear. The emergence of the solution may come through conscious or subconscious processes. When it does come, try it out—verification by experiment. If life approves of it, go on with it. You will find that life will approve only what Life approves.

O God, open my eyes to see, to see the needs around me. I promise that I will give myself to meet these needs with all I have and am. For I want to be guided into something that takes me and my energies and my love. I will follow—lead Thou me on. In Jesus' name. Amen.

AFFIRMATION FOR THE DAY: *"The hidden issues of the future are with the Eternal our God, but the unfolded issues of the day are with us."* (Deut. 29:29, Moffatt.)

GOD GUIDES THROUGH MENTAL PROCESSES

We continue our consideration of the methods of guidance:

5. *Through heightened moral intelligence.* Perhaps this is the most general way of guidance—and perhaps the safest and most beneficial to character. For the end God has in view must be the production of the kind of character which will autonomously see the right and do it. Jesus said, "Why even of yourselves judge ye not what is right?" (Luke 12:57.) The highest kind of character is that which spontaneously takes the right attitudes. Someone has said: "No man is safe in a crisis unless he has carry-over forces of accumulated habit." He spontaneously does the right.

Take the case of Peter being led out of prison. An angel awakened Peter, led him past the first and second guards, through the iron gate; "and after they had gone through one street, the angel immediately left him. Then Peter came to his senses. . . . When he grasped the situation, he went to the house of Mary." (Acts 12:10-12, Moffatt.) Note that the angel led him past difficulties which Peter unaided could not surmount, but the moment they arrived at the place where Peter's intelligence could take over the angel left him. He got guidance —so far! To have guided Peter beyond that point would have weakened him.

A good deal of thought regarding "guidance" would have insisted that the guidance be continued clear up to Mary's door, where a pause would have been made to see if there was guidance as to whether the latch should be lifted or not. That kind of guidance weakens character. And more, it often produces crossed wires. For if "guidance" isn't forthcoming in the minutiae, then it is often manufactured, unconsciously of course, out of the subconscious.

God will guide us, but only so far! He guides us up to the point where we grasp the situation as Peter did, and then heightened moral intelligence can take over. Just as God uses guidance enough to show us He is there, but not too much to weaken initiative, so God works miracles, but sparingly. His revelation of Himself is not a magical but a moral revelation. Just enough miracle to fortify the moral.

O God, my Father, I thank Thee that Thou art making out of me the kind of person who will react to the right by habit. Make me that kind of a person more and more. In Jesus' name. Amen.

AFFIRMATION FOR THE DAY: *"The meek will he guide in judgment."* (Ps. 25:9.)

GUIDANCE THROUGH CONSCIENCE AND THE INNER VOICE

We come to another method of guidance:

6. *Through conscience.* Conscience is a capacity to distinguish between right and wrong, but what it distinguishes as right and wrong is determined largely according to training. Conscience can be trained to approve diametrically opposite things. I asked a Hindu once what would happen if he should break caste and no one should know it. He replied that his conscience would trouble him. My conscience would trouble me if I kept caste! Our consciences have been trained to approve diametrically opposite things.

Conscience, therefore, is not a safe guide unless it is trained at the feet of Christ and there taught to approve the Christlike thing. Paul says, "My conscience bears me out in the holy Spirit." (Rom. 9:1, Moffatt.) A conscience corroborated by the Holy Spirit is safe. "Conscience," says Huckleberry Finn, "takes up more room than all the rest of a fellow's insides." And a small boy said: "I have something inside of me that I can't do what I want to with." Conscience is authoritative, but you must put Christian authority within it. Teach it the highest and it will lead you into the highest.

7. *The Inner Voice.* God guides through the Inner Voice. God still speaks after the Scriptures were closed. "God kept on talking when His book had gone to press." One has to learn to distinguish between the Inner Voice and the voice of the subconscious, our deep desires projected into consciousness. We can learn to distinguish by two outstanding criteria: (1) The Inner Voice always tells you to do the Christlike thing; the voice of the subconscious tells you to do the thing you want. (2) The Inner Voice is authoritative, quietly so. It does not argue. It commands, and its commands are self-authenticating. The voice of the subconscious argues; it tries to convince you, and its voice lacks moral weight. You will learn to distinguish. An aviator and his wife driving a car got a flat tire and stopped at a garage. The garageman heard the Inner Voice, "Ask that man if he is a Christian." He shrank from it, but obeyed. The aviator was interested, responded, and found a change within. Half an hour later his plane crashed in a take-off and he was killed. The Voice was right.

O Voice Divine, make me acute to listen to Thee, for when I listen to Thee I listen to Wisdom and Good Will and Redemption. Give me strength to obey when Thou dost speak. I want to be God-guided. Amen.

AFFIRMATION FOR THE DAY: *Today I shall listen to "the internal testimony of the Holy Spirit."*

GUIDANCE IN THE CRISIS AND IN THE CONTINUOUS

We add additional thoughts on guidance:

1. In order to get guidance in a crisis, remain in the will of God in the continuous. "I being in the way, the Lord led me." (Gen. 24:27.) If we take our own way in the ordinary, we can't expect God to give us His way in the hour of need.

2. Sometimes you will have to act on probability without specific guidance. Douglas Steere says: "If the way is 95 per cent dark and 5 per cent light, make your decision on the basis of the 5 per cent light." And when there isn't 5 per cent light, listen to this word: "Whoever is walking in the dark, without a ray of light, let him have confidence in the Eternal, and lean upon his God." (Isa. 50:10, Moffatt.) Trust the character of God. There may be guidance in the absence of guidance; the guidance is to trust where you cannot see.

3. In order to find out your life work, take these steps: (a) Make an unconditional surrender to God. (b) Ask where is the greatest need. (c) Ask through what vocation you can express your life to meet that need? (d) As you study, confer with people and pray what is the inner urge for you to do? (e) What you ought to do, you will do.

4. Learn what Emerson calls "the secret of lowly listening." Relax in His presence; practice lowly listening. "Your Teacher never leaves you now; you see your Teacher for yourselves, and when you swerve to the right or left, you hear a Voice behind you whispering, 'This is the way, walk here.'" (Isa. 30:20-21, Moffatt.)

5. Change the saying from, "Where there is a will, there is a way," to "Where there is God's will, there is a way." "For if God guides you, He provides you"—provides you with power.

6. Remember we are made for His will, and only in His will can we succeed. "Man thinks out many a plan, but 'tis the Eternal's purpose that prevails." (Prov. 19:21, Moffatt.)

7. Don't ask for the whole way; ask for the next step. "The steps of a good man are ordered of the Lord," every two and a half feet. "Thy word is a lamp unto my feet," showing the next step.

O God, I would say in the words of Mary, "I am here to serve the Lord." I have one purpose and one aim—to serve Thee. So take my life, my powers, my all, and make them the very best they can be. Amen.

AFFIRMATION FOR THE DAY: *"Let me listen to God speaking, speaking surely words of prosperity."* (Ps. 85:8, Moffatt.)

THE WAY IS THE WAY OF SIMPLICITY

We turn now to consider *the Way as the way of simplicity*. The Christian way is the way of complete simplicity.

Evil is always complex, roundabout, tangled. Goodness is always a reduction of life to simplicity. Lies are roundabout, complicated. Truth is straightforward and uncomplicated. If you lie, you have to have a good memory; you have to remember each time what you have said. But if you speak the truth, then you don't have to remember what you have said; you simply tell the truth each time. All great discoveries are a reduction from complexity to simplicity. There is a motto on the walls of the office of the research department of General Motors, at Dayton: "This problem, when solved, will be simple."

Life for the Pharisee was very complicated. For Jesus it was very simple. The Pharisee lived by innumerable taboos and regulations and laws. Jesus reduced these hundreds of laws to two: love to God and love to man. That is genius. If beauty is "an absence of superfluities," then Jesus was beautiful in character and life and must have been in appearance, for there was an absence of superfluity and pretense. His words were stripped of all useless verbiage, and were so near to fact that they were fact. It was said of Cromwell that "his words were half battles." But Jesus' words were whole facts. The religious man of the East tries to make his language impressive by swearing by everything in heaven and on earth. Jesus said, "Swear not at all. . . . Let your communication be, Yea, yea; Nay, nay: for whatsoever is more than these cometh of evil." (Matt. 5:34, 37.) You don't have to strengthen truth by an oath, trying to get this, that, and the other thing behind the truth, for the universe *is* behind the truth. It is self-verifying. Nothing is behind a lie; it is on its own; hence men try to bolster it with loud affirmation and oaths. A man who swears is unsure of himself, so he tries to make his statements emphatic by profane assertion. Swearing isn't the sign of a he-man; it is the sign of a weak man; and the more he swears, the weaker he is. If "the adjective is the enemy of the noun," then swear words are the enemy of emphasis. The more you swear, the weaker your statements.

O Christ, make me simple and straightforward as Thou art. I would be cleansed of all complications and roundaboutness. I would be direct and self-verifying, simplehearted, of simple speech and simple love. Amen.

AFFIRMATION FOR THE DAY: *"All who swerve from thy will, thou spurnest; their notions end in nothing."* (Ps. 119:118, Moffatt.) *My notions end in nothings.*

SPEECH REDUCED TO SIMPLICITY

We continue the Way as the way of simplicity.

The Quakers introduced "the one-price system" into Europe in obedience to the suggestion of Jesus that "your communication be, Yea, yea; Nay, nay." This abandonment of the bargaining system which was prevalent in Europe, as it is now prevalent in Asia, has saved civilization millions of years in time and untold bad temper.

The account says, "He was speaking the word to them." (Mark 2:3, Moffatt.) What was "the word"? Not some written scripture. It was "the word" amid the multiplicity of words. When men heard it, they said, "This is the word." When the greatest orator of the day spoke at Gettysburg, men heard a torrent of words, words which have been forgotten. But afterward when Lincoln spoke out of the depths of sincerity words reduced to simplicity, men heard the word, the word of democracy. His speech is deathless.

When Jesus stood before two groups, they asked Him innumerable questions to which He answered nothing. But when each group came to the crucial question, His answer was as clear as crystal. The Jews wanted to know the answer to this: "Tell us if you are the Christ, the Son of God!" "Even so!" answered Jesus. The Roman governor wanted to know, "Are you the king of the Jews?" "Certainly," replied Jesus. (Matt. 26:64; 27:11, Moffatt.) The rest is silence. When a relevant issue arose, He was simple, direct. In regard to the irrelevant He maintained a majestic silence. His enemies paid tribute on another occasion to this quality of simple directness: "We know you are straight in what you say and teach." (Luke 20:21, Moffatt.) He was straight in His unstudied moments, "in what you say," and in His studied moments, "in what you teach." In both He was straight and simple. Paul caught this simplicity from his Master: "I state the truth openly and so commend myself to every man's conscience before God." (II Cor. 4:2, Moffatt.) The truth he preached—Christ (vs. 5) —and the conscience are made for each other. Said an old Quaker to me: "I wondered how you would use words to get beyond them, but I believe you did it." I brought them to the Word—Christ.

O Christ, Thou art the Word, the Word made flesh. Help me to be the word made flesh, in a very insignificant way, and yet nevertheless in a real way. I give up all affectation, all unreality. Amen.

AFFIRMATION FOR THE DAY: *"Let what you say be simply 'yes' or 'no'; whatever goes beyond that springs from evil."* (Matt. 5:37, Moffatt.)

LIFE REDUCED TO SIMPLICITY

Jesus not only was simple Himself but demanded simplicity. And demanded it as a condition of entrance into the Kingdom of God: "Unless you turn and become like children, you will never get into the Realm of heaven at all." (Matt. 18:3, Moffatt.) Unless you reduce life to simplicity of spirit, you cannot get in.

Within that Kingdom nothing is revealed except to the simple-hearted: "Revealing it to the simpleminded; . . . such was thy chosen purpose." (Matt. 11:26, Moffatt.) Is this the chosen purpose of God, in nature and in grace? Do the simplehearted, the simple-minded know, and do the rest go blind? Apparently.

Jesus said, "Do not trouble yourselves about how to defend yourselves" (Luke 12:11, Moffatt); for if you are in a state of self-defense you are complicated, you will get tied up within. Let your life and conduct be your defense; don't nervously go around trying to explain things. Be the kind of person who can afford to "wait till the years and the centuries speak against the hours." Moreover, you can afford to confess mistakes because you are essentially right. You are not afraid to be thought wrong because you are so conscious of being right. Small men are always defending themselves; big men can afford to wait till time will defend them.

You can be rich in two ways: in the abundance of your possessions or in the fewness of your wants. When your wants are reduced to simplicity, then you are rich. Someone asked a radiant person who had suffered much how he did it, and the reply was: "I think little about what I haven't and much about what I have."

Our definition of Christianity then becomes simple. Complicated creeds and systems give way to the simple. A visiting and very pompous bishop asked some village people in India who were candidates for baptism, "What is it to be a Christian?" and expected a theological reply, but got the answer instead, "To live like Mr. Murray." Mr. Murray was the missionary who had taught them. The word of Christianity had become flesh in him. It was so in Jesus.

O, living Christ, make me simple and unaffected and unafraid. Give me the mind that was in Thee; then I too shall be simple and straightforward and loving. I would have the heart that loves the simple and the true. Give me that heart. Amen.

AFFIRMATION FOR THE DAY: *When I am on the defensive I am living by fear, not by faith.*

STEPS TO SIMPLICITY

We come now to the steps to gain simplicity of life and character:

1. *Go over your life and see if there are complicated motives that produce outer complications in attitude and act.* If there are mixed motives owing to mixed loyalties and loves, then that produces complication. Perhaps these mixed motives are in the subconscious mind. The lid may have been put on them so that they are suppressed. You are at war with yourself. Conscious and subconscious minds are at cross-purposes. That makes complications and compromises.

2. *Still the mind and let all motives and loyalties and loves come to the surface.* In that relaxed mood look at them and see them for what they are. Do not fight them; look at them calmly and straight-forwardly.

3. *Make up your mind which motives are worthy, which shall stay, and which shall go.* You are in the hour of pruning, the pruning of the extraneous, the unnecessary, the wrong. Ask God to give you clear sight and courageous decisiveness. You have come to the cross-roads, one road leading to complication on complication, the other leading to simplicity and sureness.

4. *Surrender all that complicates into the hands of God.* Don't become tense and begin to fight these complicating things. That makes the roots cling all the tighter. Give inner consent for God to take them out. He can, and does, take them out, with your consent, your *full* consent. He has your motives under His control and direction.

5. *Let these simplified motives, now purged of complications, work out into simplified living.* The outer manifestations must be simplified in order to keep the inner simplified. For if you *act* complicated, then you will *be* complicated.

6. *Start from a simple premise:* "I have no responsibility except to live in union with God." That reduces life to the simple and the vital. You do not have to think about many things. Think of one thing, and all else follows. That one thing: "Abide in me." "If ye abide in me, . . . ye shall ask what ye will." (John 15:7.) One responsibility: Live in union.

O Christ, I see. I have been nervous and anxious and complicated. And now at long last I am coming to the simple. I am in union with Thee. That is my primary and only responsibility. I accept it with joy. I am a child again, simple, happy, unafraid. Amen.

AFFIRMATION FOR THE DAY: *"Leave it all quietly to God, my soul."* (Ps. 62:1, Moffatt.)

MORE STEPS TO SIMPLICITY

We continue our steps to simplicity:

7. *Since you have one simple responsibility, and that is to live in union with God, now you have one simple attitude toward people: Give out love and only love.* As a friend says, "If you give out heaven part of the time and hell part of the time, you will be in heaven part of the time and hell part of the time." You will be in that which you give out. If you give out love all the time, you will be in love all the time.

Moreover, you are born of that which you give out. If you give out criticism habitually, you will become a critical person in the very essence and make-up of your being. The output becomes the instay. The person who manifests love always becomes lovable—always.

8. *You now look no longer at the end results, but you do the right thing and let results take care of themselves.* If you are always looking at the end results, you are always nervous and complicated. Act from a simple premise: Do the right thing, then the results can take care of themselves. Those results will always be right *in the long run*. It is impossible that the right thing should have a wrong result in the long run. And it is impossible that the wrong thing should have a right result in the long run. The man, referred to previously, who paid three thousand dollars to be told that he needed a new philosophy of life, went out to give to industry a simple idea—to him revolutionary: "Do the morally right thing in every situation, and don't even think about end results. The universe will take care of them."

9. *You can now afford to confess mistakes of speech and act, for you no longer feel it necessary to defend yourself. You are fundamentally simple and therefore sound.* Go over your life and cut out all affectation in speech and act. Make everything ring true—especially your speech. Cut out all useless adjectives, all talking for effect, all weasel words. The Chinese say, "Words are the sounds of the heart." Your heart and your words now have the same sound, the sound of simple love.

Now you can say: "I have soothed and stilled my soul. . . . My soul is like a weanèd child." (Ps. 131:2, Moffatt.)

O Christ, make me like a weaned child, weaned from all that complicates and all that is out of harmony with love. For I must have within me nothing but simple love, and I must act on nothing but simple love. Amen.

AFFIRMATION FOR THE DAY: *"Let all that you do be done in love."* (I Cor. 16:14, Moffatt.)

WEANED FROM MANY THINGS

We must follow up these steps to simplicity by some general thoughts that gather up the implications of simplicity.

You are now weaned from the necessity of always being entertained. You don't need to be entertained at all. You *are* your entertainment. Your world of entertainment has become simple. When there is nothing to entertain you from without, you can do what the ancient scripture says, "draw waters out of your own well." The reason for the passionate demand for entertainment and diversions is that the well within is dry. So life has to be primed from without. But now you can live on simple pleasures, simple loves, simple things. You do not despise entertainment, but you do not depend on it. You can have it or do without it.

You are also weaned from the necessity of success. A great many are nervously feeling the necessity of always succeeding. They are in bondage to success. But now you do not have to succeed. All you have to do is to be true to the highest that you know, and success and failure are in the hands of God. That emancipates you from the bondage to succeed. The most successful Man that ever lived failed, by all the standards of success. He left no money, no book, no property. All He left when He went away were some seeds sown in the hearts of some doubtful followers. But those simple seeds have transformed the world. You don't have to succeed. Sow the seeds of love and truth, eat and sleep, and the earth will bring forth fruit of itself. The universe will take care of success. You can even "loaf dynamically."

Again, you are emancipated from insult. Said someone of another: "Insult doesn't get him; it goes over his head. He doesn't know when he is insulted." When you are lowly and humble, then insult goes over your head. You know you are simple and sound, so what other people say doesn't affect you. You can smile at insult, for you have an insulation—the insulation of simplicity. An officer of the Confederacy, in Virginia, was challenged to a duel. He put an advertisement in a paper: "I have a greater responsibility than to defend my honor. I am a Christian. And to duel is unchristian." This wiped out dueling in Virginia overnight. Simple courage changed the attitude of a state.

O Christ, I have come to the place of the great Immunity. Now I do not go up and down with my circumstances, for my life is within. I am therefore released from dependence on outwardism. I thank Thee. Amen.

AFFIRMATION FOR THE DAY: *"Love is my only obligation."*

FREEDOM THROUGH SIMPLICITY

One more day we must spend on the implications of simplicity. At a railway station in India I turned to an Indian gentleman and asked if he was going on my train. "No," he replied, "there are nothing but third-class carriages on this train." (In India there are four classes on trains: first, second, intermediate, and third. Third class means wooden benches and crowds.) "I'm going on it," I replied. "Yes, you can go on it," he answered, "for you are a religious man. If you go first class, it doesn't exalt you; and if you go third class, it doesn't degrade you. You are lifted above these distinctions, but I have to keep them up." I could have danced on the station platform! I was free from the vast complication of keeping up a position. I could go first class, or I could go third class—my values were elsewhere. I had to keep up nothing, for I wanted nothing. I had emancipation by elimination.

A British ambassador's wife sent a request to reserve a front seat at one of my meetings; it was explained that "an ambassador's wife should never sit with anyone in front of her." What a complication to live by! I could sit anywhere; I was free! Bondage to prestige is bondage.

The successes of life are often through the simplicities of life. Alexander McLaren preached a whole series of sermons to win one skeptic of powerful intellect to Christ. At last the man presented himself to join the church. McLaren was delighted and asked which sermon had helped him to the decision. He replied: "None of them. I helped an old woman down the steps, and she turned to me and said, 'Oh, thank you,' and added, 'Do you love Jesus Christ, my blessed Saviour? He means everything to me.' I did not love Him then, but her face and her words arrested me, and I found I was on the wrong road. So I've turned." Simplicity won where learning failed.

A rich Mexican suffering from stomach ulcers traveled at great expense to Battle Creek, was expecting a complicated remedy, but got this prescription: "Stop worrying and drink seven glasses of water a day." He did—and got well. Simplicity heals as well as saves.

O Christ, Thou art asking me to give Thee one thing—myself, my all. It is all so simple, and yet when we do it, we see how profound it is. Everything falls into its place, and everything works with everything else. I thank Thee. Amen.

AFFIRMATION FOR THE DAY: *"Thou hast given me room to move, and a foothold sure!"* (Ps. 18:36, Moffatt.)

THE WAY AND IMMORTALITY

When men die, do they live again? Open the question of religion in club or school or forum, and one of the first questions which will arise will be this question: "Is there immortality?" So we ask: Is the Way the way everlasting, or does it end in a dead end—at death?

First of all, our answer must be this: If the Way does not reach out beyond death, but ends abruptly at death, then it would make no essential difference in my allegiance to the Way. For up to death it is a better way to live. If the Way has no future, nevertheless it has a present—it works out better now. A group of Latin American intellectuals, very skeptical, asked: "Isn't Christianity a reward morality, a promise of future life in heaven if you obey it now?" I replied: "Wipe out the idea of a future life, and I would take the Christian way as the way life approves now. It works better, so I cling to it." They replied, "Now we are satisfied."

Someone asked an old saint what would happen to her if, when she got to the gates of Paradise, they should refuse her admission. She replied: "I'd shout all around the walls and rejoice over the wonderful time I've had coming up this far." She uttered a profound truth. Someone put it this way: "Now that I am a Christian, I feel much better when I feel bad than I did before when I felt good." So immortality or no immortality, the Christian way is the sensible way to live now. There is more joy to the square inch in Christ than there is to the square mile outside. Inside of Christ there is life—now. Outside of Him there is death—now. So the Christian is not particularly worried about life after death, since he has life before death.

Someone came to Emerson quite upset: "Oh, Mr. Emerson, they tell us the world is coming to an end. What shall we do?" "Oh, that's all right," said Emerson, "we can get along quite well without it." He had a world of his own—within. The Christian way has a way now, and it is the way where life is adequate, victorious, effective, and happy now—apart from immortality.

O Christ, I thank Thee that in this betting of my life on Thee I can't lose. For if there is no future, I win now. I win, for I've found in Thee Life. What can lesser life do to Life? I am immortal even if there is no immortality. I thank Thee. Amen.

AFFIRMATION FOR THE DAY: *I am immortal till my work is done, but as I have eternal work to do, I am eternally immortal.*

WHY WE CAN BELIEVE IN IMMORTALITY

We saw yesterday that the Way is a better way now even if there is no immortality. The Christian way is not dependent for its validity on an event at the end of life, but upon the reality of the facts of life now. But I hasten to say that I do believe in immortality.

1. *If there is no life after death, then what is the alternative?* The alternative is unthinkable: Life comes to an abrupt end, even when life is often at its best and finest. What kind of universe would this be if it could approve of that? The universe seems to have meaning, value, purpose, but does it reverse all that process of meaning, value, purpose at its highest point—in the life and character of man? Does it all suddenly turn meaningless, valueless, and purposeless at that highest point of existence, by snuffing it all out at death? If so, the processes of the universe end in an anticlimax, and worse—they end in immorality. By what moral outlook could it be justified to let a man attain a character through struggle and discipline and then at the end wipe out the results by death? The universe would not only be a disappointment; it would be positively immoral. The essence of the universe would not be morality but mockery.

2. *If there is no immortality, then present morality lacks eternal support and is thereby weakened.* Truth by its nature is universal. There is no such thing as a local truth. Truth by its nature is also eternal, for if it isn't valid everywhere, for all time, it isn't valid anywhere at any time. To make morality valid for a brief period, but to give it no eternal support, is to weaken morality now. And that is exactly what happens. When a future life is not believed in, present life becomes cheapened and its moralities undermined. Life becomes, "Eat, drink, and be merry—if you can—for tomorrow we die." At one of our Round Table Conferences in Singapore a Chinese said: "I am trying to live by Confucian ethics, but when it comes to death, it is all black—I can't see anything." While the ship on which he was traveling neared Australia, he jumped overboard. There was nothing else to do! No eternal meaning—no meaning now.

O Christ, I know that there is something so immortal in Thee—and hence in me, for I am in Thee—that these things are impossible not to believe. I know that. Thou art my Eternal Verity and my Eternal Validity. I thank Thee, thank Thee. Amen.

AFFIRMATION FOR THE DAY: *The life I live in Thee has the feel of an Eternal Validity upon it.*

FURTHER REASONS FOR IMMORTALITY

3. *In the universe there is a conservation of energy. Is there no conservation of values?* They tell us that no energy is lost; it is only transmuted into other forms. If the universe is careful about conserving energy, is it careless about the conservation of value? Especially where value is the most valuable thing in the universe—moral character? Then the universe is not only bad; it is stupid. If, at the end, I should find that there is no future life, I would look the universe straight in the face and say: "I thought better of you. I thought you made sense. Now I see you make nonsense. I'm sorry. You've let me down. In this hour of dissolution I'm better than you are. I thought morality had eternal significance. It doesn't. But I thought thoughts higher than you sustain, so I'm superior to you. You are insignificant —not I."

A lad in Vancouver said to his father: "Stanley Jones is happy, and he has something to be happy about." True. But suppose at the heart of that happiness the worm of a question about immortality were eating? Wouldn't the happiness become a happiness with a doubt at its center? For ultimately you can rejoice only in that which has ultimate significance. Emily Dickinson sings:

> "The only news I know
> Is bulletins all day
> From Immortality."

4. *Those who believe in and realize immortality now live better than those who do not.* I say "believe in and realize immortality" because it is not enough to believe in; you must partake of eternal life now to make it a reality. Otherwise it is a superstition with no effect on life. "I want to belong to the church so if I should die drunk I would have a chance through purgatory of getting to heaven," said a young woman, and said it seriously. She didn't believe in immortality; she believed in immorality and practiced it. But those who really believe in and experience immortal life have life heightened, cleansed, dignified, and value-imbued.

O living Christ, I know that Thou art the center of all my values, the center of my life. Can this life within me die? It seems immortal; it seems that death is impossible to it. So I rest in glad assurance—forever. Amen.

AFFIRMATION FOR THE DAY: *"The crown of a good life awaits me."* (II Tim. 4:8, Moffatt.) *Can the crown of a good life be eternal nothingness?*

THE BEST MAN THAT EVER LIVED BELIEVED

We come now to our crowning reason for believing in immortality:

5. *The best Man who ever lived on this planet believed in it, practiced it, demonstrated it, and proclaimed it.* Jesus was so right in everything. There isn't a thing He uttered that is not valid for today. There isn't an attitude He took that isn't the highest attitude now. There isn't an act of His that is not now a universal norm. He touched life in all its phases, and everywhere He touched it He rang true—more, He rang Truth. Then when He touched this matter of immortality, was He wrong here? Right every other place, the ages being witness, was He wrong *here*—here where it really counts? If so, then it casts a shadow on all He said and did, a very dark shadow too: *None of it is eternally real.* That would be a fatal shadow.

Instead, He throws a light, an eternal light, upon everything He said and did, and the light is this: *Goodness has eternal meaning and cannot die.* That makes every virtue, all goodness, all morality stand up straight, the Light of Eternal Meaning upon their brows. It does more: it makes goodness sing and dance and shout—it is deathless. Morality becomes gay. It has a song in its heart and a deathless message on its lips.

For it is founded, not on a belief, but upon a demonstration—the *resurrection of Jesus from the dead.* Jesus not only proclaimed life after death; He demonstrated life after death. Without that demonstration belief in immortality might be strong; this makes it sure. Did He rise from the dead? The answer is that if He didn't, then He ought to have done so—the whole account would come out wrong. Two things take us all—sin and death. Jesus rose above sin; would He rise above death? The account says so. It fits His life. He conquered everything in life; would He conquer man's last enemy, death? With that enemy unconquered, there is the shadow of final defeat upon everything. With that enemy met and conquered, then the boards are swept. Everything has been mastered. The Way is the way, everywhere for everything.

O Christ, hadst Thou stalled at the last ditch, hadst Thou been beaten at the barrier of death, then we would be stalled—eternally stalled with Thee. But now we go over the barrier with Thee, all barriers with Thee. Nothing can stop us now. I thank Thee. Amen.

AFFIRMATION FOR THE DAY: *I live in a resurrected Christ. Since He cannot die, neither can I.*

298

WHY WE BELIEVE IN JESUS' RESURRECTION

Four things make me believe in the resurrection of Jesus:

1. *The life of Jesus.* This claim is not made concerning an ordinary man. This Man has been the most influential person in all history—influential for good, yea, for redemption. Wherever life gets into touch with Him, really into touch with Him, it is lifted, changed, saved. There is an extraordinary life here. That extraordinary life makes it possible for me to believe in His extraordinary rising. We do not discuss "resurrection" by itself, we discuss the resurrection of Jesus. Would such a Man as this rise in such a manner as this? Everything within me says Yes. He carries the Resurrection; the Resurrection doesn't carry Him. I believe in it because of Him.

2. *The fact of the empty tomb.* Within a few days after His death the disciples were charging the leaders of Jerusalem with His death and doing it publicly. Why couldn't these leaders walk straight to the tomb and point out the body of Jesus? It would have settled everything, for them. They didn't. Why? If the weak answer is reiterated that the disciples stole the body while the soldiers slept, then the answer is simple. How could they have done it without somebody seeing them, or without somebody giving them away? There were those who proved faithless; wouldn't they divulge the awful secret of the theft and justify their relapse? No whisper has ever come down through the ages of such divulging. Besides, do these disciples look like men who hold a guilty secret, who proclaim a vast hoax, who live on a lie? Do they look like body snatchers? Their hangdog faces would have shown it; the guilty secret would have eaten out their message. That message would have fallen dead upon the ears of the world, as all lies do. But these men, on the contrary, are radiant and irresistible. They laugh their way through persecution, sing their way through prisons, and smile their way through death. For what? A hoax? Well, hoaxes don't produce hallelujahs, nor does body snatching produce transformed lives. Like produces like.

O living Christ, Thou who art true in every word, every deed, dost Thou foist upon us a lie? If so, nothing is true—nothing. But Thou art Truth; everything within cries out that it is so. And Thou art risen; everything good says so. I thank Thee. Amen.

AFFIRMATION FOR THE DAY: *I cannot be alive in someone who is dead. I am alive in Someone who is alive!*

WHAT PRODUCED THE NEW TESTAMENT CHURCH?

The next fact that makes me believe in the resurrection of Jesus: 3. *The fact of the New Testament Church.* It arose immediately after the death and resurrection of Jesus. It didn't emerge after long years, giving time for myths to grow up upon which the movement could live precariously. It arose at once. At one moment the disciples were timid believers "behind closed doors for fear," clinging pathetically to a blasted hope, a hope that had been blasted by His death. The next moment they were irresistible apostles, out from behind closed doors facing Sanhedrins and crowds from all over that ancient world, and proclaiming with joy, an amazing, irrepressible joy, that Jesus had arisen and that He was Lord and Saviour. They did it with such power and assurance that the multitudes who had witnessed His death saw in these men His resurrection.

What could have produced that Church? A dead Christ? It would have been an effect all out of harmony with the cause. After the battle of Waterloo the news was signaled: "Wellington defeated . . ." A mist came over at that point. England plunged into sadness. Then the mists arose, and the full message came: "Wellington defeated Napoleon." Sadness turned to joy. The news was signaled from a hill called Calvary, "Jesus defeated . . . ," and the mists came over for three days—the saddest days of human history. Then on Easter morning the mists cleared, and the world got the full message, "Jesus defeated death." And the world has never been the same since. Nor has death been the same since. "O death, where is thy sting? O grave, where is thy victory?" Earth's blackest day and earth's brightest day are only three days apart. But those three days divide the ages. On one side, doubt and despair; on the other, hope and happiness.

We rose in an airplane outside Balboa, Canal Zone, in the darkness, and blinds were over the windows lest we see military secrets. We were shut in, blind to what was going on outside. And then the blinds were taken down, and lo, a marvelous sunrise, white clouds tinted pink and red. The world started in the dark after the Crucifixion, shut in to the fact of death's triumph; and then the third day took down the blinds, and lo—the Sunrise! He is Risen!

O Christ, I thank Thee for the Victory—the Victory Thou didst bring when from the dead Thou didst arise. That Victory is mine. Help me to live by it and for it. I am grateful to my depths—grateful forever. Amen.

AFFIRMATION FOR THE DAY: *Resurrection is inherent—in the seed, in Jesus, in me.*

IS JESUS ALIVE NOW?

We come to our last reason for believing in the Resurrection:

4. *Jesus is alive now.* Two irreligious young men were discussing the Resurrection, telling each other why it was impossible to accept the doctrine. An old man whom they knew to be a Christian went by, so they asked him: "Tell us why you believe that Jesus rose again." "Well," said the old man, "one reason is that I was talking with Him this morning."

Those who expose themselves to Christ by surrender and obedience know Him to be alive—He lives within them. The historical has become the experimental. This fact of the living Christ is the best corroborated fact in history; for in every clime, in every age, among all peoples the experience is the same: Christ—alive, redeeming, joy-producing, love-creating—moves straight into the hearts of people everywhere as a present Fact. We not merely remember Jesus; we realize Him.

Heaven for us is thus no longer future; it is here and now. Therefore it will be hereafter, for we take heaven with us, in us, as we go. There is no feverish setting the house in order as we go. We await heaven, because we have heaven. A daughter asked if she should read the Bible to her dying Scotch father. The old saint replied, "Na, na, lassie, I thatched my house before the storm began."

When you have Christ, you have immortality. "I am the resurrection, and the life." He is the initial life, the "resurrection," and the sustained life, the "life."

Will we know each other in the immortal world? The answer is: Will we be less intelligent then than we are now? Know each other? We shall know each other perfectly, love each other deeply, and enjoy each other wholly. Now the barriers of a decaying flesh separate us; then we can love without those barriers. While there will be no flesh, there will be form—an immortal body. Your love for your loved one is immortal, and will be immortally embodied in everlasting fellowship.

O Christ, I thank Thee that Thou hast "brought life and immortality to light through the gospel." We know this is true, for in Thee we know that there cannot be death. It is all so deathless. And so sure—as sure as Thou art. I thank Thee. Amen.

AFFIRMATION FOR THE DAY: *"Because I live, ye shall live also."* (John 14:19.)

THE MARKS OF THOSE ON THE WAY

We turn now in our study of the Way to the marks of those on the Way. If the Way is the way—the way to do everything—what are some of the characteristics of those who follow the Way?

I am picking out the most Christianized person in the New Testament to study in him the marks of a Christian—Stephen. In Stephen, Christianity was simple, unaffected, unprofessionalized. It is significant that the most Christianized person in the New Testament was a layman. The "leaders" were too conscious of being "leaders," and in that consciousness lost some of the Christian spirit.

Stephen belonged, not to the "Twelve," but to the "seven." And yet before long that word "seven," spelled thus in Acts 6:3 (Moffatt) became "the Seven" in Acts 21:8. Evidently those men, by their life and character and contribution, turned a common noun into a proper noun. Any word or person getting into touch with Jesus is heightened, for Jesus turns all our common nouns into proper nouns. The word "love" gets into contact with Him, and you have to spell it "Love"— it's different now. Jesus turns the nobodies into the somebodies and the insignificant into the significant. Stephen too heightened everything he touched. He dignified the commonplace, took a job the apostles turned down as beneath them and made it more significant than anything the apostles themselves were doing.

1. The first mark, then, of the Christian is this: *He was a man who made the insignificant the significant by the spirit he put into it.* It is not *what* you do that counts, but *how* you do it—the spirit you put into it. You can do great things in a little way and little things in a great way. Stephen was great, not only in what he did, but in how he did it. The spirit in which you do a thing is the aroma surrounding the deed and makes the deed smell good or bad. Stephen "served tables," but he did it in such a way that table serving became sacramental—those tables became a veritable table of the Lord, "The Lord's Table," and around them people of all races ate the bread which became the Bread. Stephen was a deacon who became a beacon —a light to all the ages, especially on the commonplaces of life.

O Christ, if I have the little things to do today, help me to do them in a great way with a great spirit. Save me from pettiness lest my great deeds become petty in the process. For how I do a thing makes me in the doing. Help me to be Christian—always. Amen.

AFFIRMATION FOR THE DAY: *"I bear branded on my body the owner's stamp of the Lord Jesus."* (Gal. 6:17, Moffatt.)

BASIC HONESTY AND GRACE AND POWER

We saw yesterday that the thing that matters is *how* you do the things you do. A sign along the railroad going through Chester, Pennsylvania, says: "What Chester makes, makes Chester." Whatever the Christian makes, makes the Christian—especially the spirit in which he makes it. In whatever spirit you work, that spirit works into you. You are born of the spirit in which you work.

2. *He was basically honest.* Stephen was basically honest, a man "of honest report." (Acts 6:3.) This is fundamental, for nothing can atone for a lack of basic honesty. No amount of "fancy virtues" or "fancy spirituality" can take the place of simple honesty of character. The ultimate question about any man's character is: Are there any circumstances under which that man will lie? If so, he has a worm eating at his heart. Jesus said: "If . . . ye have not been faithful in the unrighteous mammon, who will commit to your trust the true riches?" (Luke 16:11.)

3. *He was "full of grace and power."* (Acts 6:8, Moffatt.) Note the combination: "grace and power." But note that "grace" was first, and "power" the by-product of the "grace." If you seek power first, you will not get it. For that means that you are the center—you want power. The probabilities are that you will want power to use to enhance yourself. You will probably put the word "spiritual" to the power, but down underneath there is the desire to be at the center of the picture, the man greatly used of God. But if "grace" is first, then you are centered in God, not yourself. You long for and seek the unmerited favor of God. You are at His feet; you want only Him. Then as a by-product of that fact God can and does give you "power." Those who seek power do not get it, but those who seek God first, last, and always get God—and power. Then the power can be given; it will be used for Kingdom ends and not for personal ends. God can give power only to surrendered souls who have come to an end of themselves. Any other kind of spiritual power is spiritual powwow, verbal instead of vital. Jesus said: "Ye shall receive power," only when you become "witnesses unto me"—not of yourself.

O Christ, I know that power is for the simple, surrendered will. I would make my will just that. For I know Thou canst not entrust power to unsurrendered wills. Take mine—fully. Amen.

AFFIRMATION FOR THE DAY: *"I am alive as he is alive by the power of God."* (II Cor. 13:4, Moffatt.)

FULL OF THE SPIRIT AND OF WISDOM

We continue the study of the marks of a Christian:

4. *He was "full of the Spirit and of wisdom."* The Christian has "the Spirit," and "the Spirit" has the Christian. The prayer I find myself praying most is, "Lord, you've got me." It runs like a refrain through my prayers. If so, that settles all. If we are on our own hands, we are like the five loaves and two fishes in the hands of the little boy —inadequate. But if we are in His hands, we are like those same loaves and fishes in the hands of Jesus—adequate for a multitude.

It isn't enough to be full of the Spirit. We must be full of wisdom as well. Spirituality directed by wisdom is beneficial, but spirituality directed by ignorance is blighting. Some have the Spirit and no wisdom, and some have wisdom and no Spirit. Both alone are weak. Together they make the Christian.

The account says that in the discussions "they could not meet the wisdom and the Spirit with which he spoke." (Acts 6:10, Moffatt.) Note that the translator felt he must put the word "spirit" as "Spirit." You could not tell where Stephen's spirit ended and the Holy Spirit began. They were blended. That is the Christian's privilege—he can have all his powers heightened by the Spirit. A plus is added to life. There is "something more" added to all he says and does.

5. *He was made by a task too difficult for him.* The race question arose for the first time, and the Church had to face it and solve it. They solved it by generosity: "If you think the Grecian widows are neglected, we turn it over to the Greeks to manage." Every one of the Seven had a Greek name except Stephen. When it came to him, the reaction was: Well, he belongs to everybody; he has transcended race. So they chose him with the Greeks, for he was universalized. The choosing of a nearly all-Greek group threw the responsibility into the hands of those supposedly wronged, and that put it up to the Greeks to do better and make no distinction. They settled it by generosity. The difficulty of his task made Stephen. Always get a task you can't do, one that is beyond your powers. That throws you back on divine grace.

O Christ, do not give me tasks equal to my powers, but give me powers equal to my tasks. For I want to be stretched by things too great for me. I want to grow through the greatness of my tasks, but I shall need grace for the growing. Amen.

AFFIRMATION FOR THE DAY: *"My qualifications come from God."* (II Cor. 3:6, Moffatt.)

STEPHEN BRIDGED GAPS

We pursue our study of the marks of a Christian.

6. *Stephen bridged the gap between the secular and the sacred.* The apostles felt they should not "drop preaching the word of God and attend to meals. . . . We will continue to devote ourselves to prayer and the ministry of the word." (Acts 6:2, 4, Moffatt.) It sounded spiritual. That tradition has continued until today. But it introduced into Christianity a dualism between the secular and the sacred—a disastrous dualism. It did several things: It made spirituality function in terms spiritual, instead of in the total life, material as well as spiritual. It made ministers the ministers of a vague spirituality instead of a vital, whole-life impact. It also made for unreality. If the minister wasn't "spiritual," he had to act like it, so he put on spiritual tones and spiritual dress. And the laymen? They dealt with secondary things—the material—and therefore lived a secondary life. It took the sense of mission out of the laity, and life sagged. They were not in a first-rate calling, so they didn't have to lead a first-rate life. This has driven a disastrous wedge into Western civilization. It must be withdrawn. All life must take on the sense of the sacred, and all callings be divine callings. Holiness must get back its original thought, wholeness. Holiness is wholeness.

This dualism was not in Jesus. He preached and taught and healed and fed, all as part of one impact of the Kingdom. But Jesus was a layman and had the lay mind—life was all of one piece. The apostles missed their step at this place and moved out of the line of succession of Jesus. The "apostolic succession" therefore is not the Christian succession; it is the apostolic succession, and they missed their step. Paul got back into the line of Jesus, so he could say: "These hands of mine provided everything for my own needs and for my companions." (Acts 20:34, Moffatt.) His work as a tentmaker was a part of his Christian calling. He mended the seamless robe of Jesus which the apostles had torn asunder. Stephen was in the line of succession of Jesus. He made his spirituality function in terms material. His interpretation of the Christian gospel was in life terms instead of lip terms. His Christianity walked—and what a walk!

O Christ, I too would make my Christianity walk. I would make it function in terms material, for I cannot live except in terms material, for I am embodied. Help me, then, to live a life in terms of life—of all life. Amen.

AFFIRMATION FOR THE DAY: *Today all my tasks shall be sacramental; the sordid shall become the sacred by being done "unto God."*

MAKING THE SECULAR INTO THE SACRED

We saw that Stephen did everything in a sacred way. But while he gave himself to serving tables, he wasn't swamped by the job. He did not become so immersed in it that he had no time or heart for evangelism. The fact is that he became more evangelistic than the apostles, who were supposed to do nothing but evangelize. The longest recorded sermon in the New Testament was given, not by any of the apostles, but by a layman—Stephen. (Acts 7.) And the only man in the New Testament called an evangelist was a member of "the Seven"—"Philip the evangelist." (Acts 21:8, Moffatt.) Stephen too would have earned that title had he not precipitated such a crisis by his preaching, a crisis that brought on his early death. Philip had such a mighty revival in Samaria that two apostles were sent down to regularize it! Laymen produced the revivals which the ministers could not produce, but could regularize!

7. So the next mark of the Christian is: *Stephen did serve tables, but served them so well and efficiently that he had time and disposition for evangelism.* Stephen combined the qualities of both Martha and Mary. In the house of the Christian soul Mary and Martha should be one. All Martha is weak, and all Mary is weak, but a combination is very strong and very effective. Our greatest need is laymen on fire with evangelism.

8. *He was so positive that he aroused opposition.* Stephen stood for something, and so some stood against him. The business of many Christians is the inglorious business of keeping their heads stuck in. Result? There isn't an idea in those stuck-in heads worth getting excited about. They become the dull and then the null.

9. *As they lied about him before the Sanhedrin, "his face shone like the face of an angel."* (Acts 6:15.) Stephen had the power to turn lies into light. Even their lies became useful; they broke into light as they fell upon him. That is mastery, a power to make lies serve. The man who stands for something will have a shining face—in spite of all. The man who stands for nothing has nothing on his face—becomes nothing.

O Christ, help me to stand for something, no matter the cost. Help me to get used to the sight of my own blood. For only as I bleed can I bless. Take out of me all dodging of issues, all the cowardliness that makes no issues. Help me to have the mark of courage. Amen.

AFFIRMATION FOR THE DAY: *Today I shall stand for something. My opinions shall become convictions.*

THE CHRISTIAN IN THE CRISIS

We saw yesterday that Stephen had a shining face in the midst of calumny. Nietzsche said, "The Christians will have to look more redeemed for me to believe in it." Stephen looked redeemed at the place where redemption counted—at the place of persecution.

10. *To resist Stephen was to resist the Holy Spirit.* "You are always resisting the holy Spirit." (Acts 7:51, Moffatt.) Stephen was the kind of man whom when you resisted, you resisted the Holy Spirit. Very often to resist us is not to resist the Holy Spirit, but the spirit of egotism, the spirit of stubborn pride, the spirit of petty opinionation. But Stephen was so merged with the Spirit that their interests were one, and hence their oppositions were one.

11. *He was a man who looked above trouble and saw the glory of God.* "They were furious and gnashed their teeth at him. But he, full of the holy Spirit, gazed up at heaven and saw the glory of God." (Acts 7:54-55, Moffatt.) Had we been there, we perhaps would have seen trouble and not the glory of God. He saw the glory of God as the big thing, the all-important thing, and the trouble as the little thing, the incidental. His eyes were in focus—the Throne was at the center and the trouble on the margin. The Way is the way of perspective; the Big is big, and the little is little.

12. *They couldn't rush him off his feet into their attitudes.* The account says: "With a loud shriek they shut their ears and rushed at him like one man." (Acts 6:57, Moffatt.) They rushed at him like one man, but they couldn't rush him off his feet into their attitudes. He kept his own. He kept his own spirit because he let Jesus keep it for him: "Lord Jesus, receive my spirit!" And He did—He kept it intact, unspoiled, uncorrupted by what they did. He didn't allow the other man's conduct to determine his. He worked from his own principles, not from their pressures. The tragedy of opposition is that we often take our opponent's weapons and fight with his instead of our own. If we use hate, we become hateful. We are born of that which we give out. Stephen gave out love and was born of love.

O Christ, I come to Thee to ask Thee to keep my spirit intact. Help me not to be rushed off my feet into unchristian attitudes and acts. For when I do, then my opponents have won—have won me to their method and spirit. Lord Jesus, receive my spirit and keep it intact. Amen.

AFFIRMATION FOR THE DAY: *"Leave me not speechless for the truth."* (Ps. 119:43, Moffatt.)

THE SUPREME MARK—FORGIVENESS OF INJURIES

We come now to the last mark of the Christian as seen in Stephen:
13. *He forgave his enemies at the very moment of the injury.*
"Then he knelt down and cried aloud, 'Lord, let not this sin stand
against them!'" (Acts 7:60, Moffatt.) His last word was "them."
Instead of a thought of himself in self-pity his last and dominant
word was "them." In his hour of pain thinking of "them" was his
deepest concern. That is Christianity in action. Here the high-water
mark of morality came to its highest. Outside of the Master upon the
cross, crying, "Father, forgive them; for they know not what they do,"
here is the most magnificent Christian spirit ever recorded. To forgive
your enemies is the authentic Christian spirit at its best. The crushed
violet perfumes the heel that crushes it.

A father held his only little boy in his arms and watched him die.
The doctor had made a mistake in giving the boy an inoculation
when the boy was allergic to it. The father put the dead child down,
put his arm on the doctor's shoulder, and said, "Doc, I feel terribly
sorry for you." And he prayed a prayer for him—forgave him then
and there! Then the father dedicated himself to helping young people
through college.

But the reply is made, "What good does it do? The last word is
with force, for at the end was not Stephen under the stones? Didn't
the stones win?" Apparently, but only apparently, for look at the
sequel. The young man Saul standing there "quite approved of his
murder." For a time—and then something rose within him that didn't
approve of the murder, nor of Saul. That face, that prayer of Stephen
—he could not forget them! They haunted him! He kicked against
the goads. Then on the Damascus Road Jesus met him; he fell
blinded, was radically changed, became the greatest Christian of the
centuries. Stephen, in his fall, raised Saul up. Which won, stones or
spirit? The stones are now scattered stones on a Palestinian roadside.
The spirit of Stephen marches deathless through the ages. The spirit
wins. The Christian spirit always wins. Bury it, and the third day
it will rise again. Stone it, and you scatter it through the earth.

O Christ, I follow Thee, the deathless. This Way is the way around,
over, through everything, including death. I am so grateful, for I have hold
of something that nothing can hold. It conquers everything. Amen.

AFFIRMATION FOR THE DAY: *"Never think, 'I will treat him as he
treated me. I will pay back the man for what he did.'"* (Prov.
24:29, Moffatt.)

THE MARKS OF A CHRISTIAN CHURCH

We studied last week the marks of a Christian. We must now go a step further and look at the marks of a Christian church. For the Way is not the solitary way; it is the social way. "To be is to be in relations." And church relations are the best of our planet. If you wipe out the Church today, you will have to put something in its place tomorrow, for it is rooted in the necessities of human living. With all its faults, the Church is the best serving institution on earth. It has many critics but no rivals in the work of human redemption. It has filled the earth with schools, hospitals, orphanages, blind and leper asylums, churches—everything to lift the soul of the race to higher levels. While divorces are now one out of four as a general average, there is only one out of fifty among church people.

So the Way is a way of association, of corporate living under the spirit of Jesus. When the spirit of Jesus is brought to bear upon corporate living, what kind of a society emerges? To see a society that has been Christianized let us turn to Antioch. In Antioch the Christian spirit first came to its own in corporate living. It was no mere chance that "it was at Antioch . . . that the disciples were first called 'Christians.'" (Acts 11:26, Moffatt.) The name was not just a label stuck on them, for names were given in those days according to characteristics, and if the characteristics changed, the name changed. Barnabas was called Joseph, literally "One More." He probably belonged to a large family, and when they came down to him, they ran out of names and called him Joseph—"One More." But when he fully surrendered to God, he was not merely "one more"; he was a whole multiplication table; he was a plus; so they called him Barnabas—"Son of Encouragement." It was his dominant characteristic. James and John, before being changed, were called Boanerges—"Sons of Thunder." They were tempestuous—their characteristic. So when the people saw the disciples at Antioch, they could think of but one characteristic—they were Christ-ians. The characteristics of Christ were dominant and determinative. In Antioch the Christian way came into its own. It did not come into its own in Jerusalem.

O Christ, I thank Thee that Thy characteristics live in men. Let them live in me, in us as a society. For Thy way is the Way for the corporate life as well as the individual. Let Thy Spirit possess and rule us. Amen.

AFFIRMATION FOR THE DAY: *"In him you are yourselves built into this to form a habitation for God in the Spirit."* (Eph. 2:22, Moffatt.)

THE MAKING OF A CHRISTIAN CHURCH

We saw yesterday that the Christian way did not come to its own in Jerusalem. Why? Well, Jerusalem never quite got over being Jewish. Everything in Jerusalem was limited by that fact. Peter was a product of Jerusalem, and when he went to Gentiles, he went with reservations. He ate with them, but drew back if anyone from Jerusalem was looking. Paul was a product not of Jerusalem but of Antioch, so when he went to Gentiles, he went with no inhibitions. The Gentiles accepted him as "the apostle to the Gentiles." Peter never became a world evangelist; he was caught in a racialism and never quite got free. The roots of our Western Christianity are in Antioch, not Jerusalem, for it was out of Antioch that Paul went to spread the gospel to Europe, and hence to us.

Three things went into the making of this church:

1. *Men who suffered for their faith founded it.* "Those who had been scattered by the trouble which arose over Stephen, made their way as far as . . . Antioch." (Acts 11:19, Moffatt.) The marks of the cross were upon the founding of the church. The cross was in it; hence the lift of the Resurrection was in and through it. If our faith costs nothing, it contributes nothing.

2. *An international mind went into the making of the church.* The Jews preached the gospel only to Jews; but the Cypriotes and Cyrenians, bringing to the gospel a wider outlook, an international mind, preached to the Greeks as well. "The strong hand of the Lord was with them" (Acts 11:21, Moffatt), as it is always with those who think and love in large terms. This bringing of an international mind to the situation was important, for God guides within the framework of our thinking, and it was from the framework of that thinking that Paul was sent to Europe and to us.

3. *The third element going into the making of the church was Barnabas, the most Christianized of the group at Jerusalem.* He was the kind of man who could rejoice in the work of another—when he "saw the grace of God he rejoiced." (Acts 11:23, Moffatt.) The test and sign of a real Christian is to rejoice in someone else's work. He was interested in the Kingdom, not in his part in that Kingdom.

O Christ, give me largeness of heart and the disposition to rejoice in what others do for the Kingdom. For it is the Kingdom that matters. Then take from my spirit all pettiness. In Thy name. Amen.

AFFIRMATION FOR THE DAY: *Today I shall not be, as the Africans say, "A small-date man." I shall be large in spirit and outlook.*

A STRONG CORPORATE SENSE

We noted yesterday that Barnabas brought his own great spirit to this church at Antioch. He also brought to it Paul. When he saw this kind of a Christian church, he said to himself, "This is the place to bring up that young man Saul." So he "went off to Tarsus to look for Saul" (Acts 11:26, Moffatt.) To bring Saul to Antioch was a great stroke of Christian genius, for it determined the nature of the Christianity which spread from it in the person of Paul. Paul's nature was changed by Antioch, so after Antioch his name was changed to Paul. The stamp of Antioch was upon Paul.

We must now look at the marks of a Christian church.

1. *There was a strong corporate sense.* Paul and Barnabas were "guests of the church" for a whole year—guests of the church, not of individuals. As the people "were worshipping the Lord and fasting, the holy Spirit said, 'Come! set me apart Barnabas and Saul for the work.'" (Acts 13:2, Moffatt.) They were so one that the Holy Spirit could speak to the whole church and guide it. They were not a group of worshiping individuals but a corporate body—"an organism of the Holy Spirit." The thing that won that ancient world to Christ was not only the message but this new society, an undecaying society in the midst of a decaying society, a society that loved and loved widely and without barriers in the midst of a society that knew only how to hate or love in grooves. It was a society that had faith, hope, and courage in the midst of a society that had lost its nerve and its hope.

Sydney Cave says: "The early preachers of Christianity could not get used to the wonder of the gospel, nor to the wonder of the church." Men and women crowded into this undecaying society for the sake of salvation. Yes, and also for the sake of security—mental and spiritual and social security. Men want to feel they "belong." Without that belonging there is a sense of orphanage, of spiritual loneliness. The Church of today must regain that sense of corporateness, of being a society that has meaning for all life, that when men belong to it they belong to something that has present and ultimate meanings.

O Holy Spirit, indwell us by Thy power and life, so that we may have a sense of togetherness—a sense that when one is hurt, all are hurt, and that when one rejoices, all rejoice. Give us the sense of a Body. Amen.

AFFIRMATION FOR THE DAY: *Help us this day as a group not merely to talk about the Kingdom of God but to be the Kingdom of God—in miniature.*

THE WORTH OF A PERSON AS A PERSON

We come to the next mark of a Christian church:

2. *There was the sense of the worth of a person as a person—class was abolished.* In the naming of those who constituted the prophets and teachers of Antioch, Barnabas was named first and Saul last; they were not headlined at the top. In the midst of the list is "Manaen, a foster brother of Herod." To catch the brother of a king was a big catch. We would have displayed it. They tucked Manaen in the center with a man from North Africa and a Negro above him. (Acts 13:1, Moffatt.) Evidently all class distinction was wiped out, and a person was a person—"a man for whom Christ died." It was a vast leveling process. A new worth and dignity came into every human being as a child of God and therefore equal to everyone else. A classless society emerged. Had this spirit been maintained, it would have captured the earth. But the Church later could sing:

> "The rich man in his castle,
> The poor man at his gate,
> God made them, high or lowly,
> And order'd their estate."

The early Church would have choked on that. The later Church swallowed it, and became class-filled and *Christ-empty*. Something universal died, and the ugly spirit of class was born. The Christian faith began to be a class faith. Unless we regain the original spirit of a classless society, the Communists will beat us to it. Communism's astonishing spread leads Harold Laski, the brains of the Labour Party in Britain, to say that it is going to replace Christianity, for it has a passion for people, the common people. This is no idle threat. If the Church does not stand for people, the people will not stand for the Church. The Church must have a passion for souls, but it must also have a passion for people—soul, mind, and body. For it is possible to love people's souls and be unconcerned about what happens to their bodies, their minds, their dwellings, their environment. Is there class in a real home? How can there be? for love is equal and equalizing. The early Church was a home; hence there was no class. Where Christ is, class is not.

O Christ of the all-embracing love, give us again the love that loves all and loves equally. Thy love is so utterly class-blind. Give us Thy love. Amen.

AFFIRMATION FOR THE DAY: *Since I have "a faith of equal privilege"* (II Pet. 1:1, Moffatt), *I shall give equal privilege to all.*

ALL RACE AND CLASS BARRIERS REMOVED

We come to the next mark of a Christian church:

3. *The church had wiped out race and color lines.* In the account of the prophets and teachers at Antioch there is mention of "Symeon (called Niger)" (Acts 13:1, Moffatt)—literally "Symeon (called the Black)." That was the place of the black man in the early Church. He was not just tolerated, on the edge, patronized. He was at the center, having an honored place among "prophets and teachers," and his hands were laid on Paul and Barnabas as they went forth to preach the gospel to white Europeans. Ordained by a black man! When we depart from that, we depart from the original gospel. No amount of orthodoxy can atone for a lack of this orthopraxy. To treat a man on the basis of color is to introduce into the Christian Body a foreign substance, a foreign substance which will fester and poison the whole Body. This foreign substance is now festering, and no amount of plasters of rationalization can cure this festering sore. It can be cured by an attitude of equality of opportunity for all, apart from race and birth and color.

4. *The church had a sense of economic solidarity.* The account says that when a famine befell the church at Jerusalem, the disciples of Antioch "put aside money, as each of them was able to afford it, for a contribution to be sent to the brothers in Judaea." (Acts 11:29, Moffatt.) The Christians drew no line between the spiritual and the economic. Life was one. They didn't do what the Africans depict:

> "The full-bellied child
> Says to the empty-bellied child,
> 'Be of good cheer.'"

They shared the total life, including the economic. They did it out of Christian impulse. We must now harness these impulses into constructive planning, a planning that will make a co-operative order, a society of each for all and all for each. The outer wars are the outer expression of an inner war constantly taking place in society, at the basis of life, the economic. That basis must be Christianized. If not, then we will be marginally Christianized and centrally paganized. "A civilization saves or damns its soul by the way it wins its bread."

O Christ, who didst turn the hearts of Thy early followers to this way of organized love, turn our hearts too that we may put love at the center of our living. Then we shall be truly Christian. In Thy name. Amen.

AFFIRMATION FOR THE DAY: *Let the Church be organized love—to all.*

HOLDING TOGETHER CONSERVATIVE AND RADICAL

The next mark of a Christian church is:

5. *The church held together in a living fellowship the conservative and the radical.* "In the local church at Antioch there were prophets and teachers." (Acts 13:1, Moffatt.) The teacher is usually the conservative, conserving the values of the past. The conservative has a real function in human society. The good of the past must be wrought into the structure of the present; we live by yesterday as well as by today and tomorrow. A present cut off from yesterday becomes a cut-flower civilization, without roots. The conservative conserves.

On the other hand, the prophet is the one who believes that the values of the past should be applied to the present and the future in ever-widening areas of application. He is the radical. Strangely enough, the word "radical" comes from a word meaning "the root." A real radical has the root of the past in him, but demands that that root bear fruit now in the total life. He demands that implications become applications.

The church held radical and conservative together in unbroken fellowship, each cross-fertilizing the other. They were both held together in a living tension. That tension produced a growing point. The church that does not hold both conservative and radical in a living tension will have no growing point; it will become sterile. "An arid liberalism and an acrid conservatism" are both alike sterile. Together they could be fruitful.

The Church must not allow these two groups to split and sink a cleavage down through the life of the Church. We need a radical conservatism and a conservative radicalism. Jesus was both: "I am not come to destroy, but to fulfil."—that is conservatism. "Ye have heard that it was said by them of old time . . . but I say unto you."—that is radicalism. The past married to the future brings forth the living present. But conservatism married to nothing but itself, or radicalism married to nothing but itself, brings forth nothing—nothing but controversy or conjecture. Married, they bring forth progress. The conservative has something, the fundamentals of the gospel; the radical has something, the demand that those fundamentals be applied now.

O Thou who art gathering up the ages, gather us up and make us one, one in spite of difference, perhaps because of difference. For in Thee all things cohere. Hold us together in a coherent whole. Amen.

AFFIRMATION FOR THE DAY: *I shall be a conservative in my faith and a radical in its application.*

HOLDING TOGETHER STRONG MEN

We come to the next mark of a Christian church:

6. *The church held together in an unbroken fellowship strong men who differed.* Paul and Barnabas parted "in irritation" (Acts 15:39, Moffatt) over the question of taking John Mark because he had deserted them at Pamphylia. Here was a good chance for two denominations: one the Barnabasites, those who believed the Church should be redemptive—Mark should be redeemed and given another chance; the other the Paulites, those who believed the Church should be kept clean—Mark should be cleansed away. Both very good ideas for a new denomination! Better than some that now produce a new one! But the church at Anitoch held them in an unbroken fellowship. As they parted, they were "commended by the brothers to the grace of the Lord." (Acts 15:40, Moffatt.) I am sure they commended them to the grace of the Lord with a twinkle in their eyes: "Brothers, you both need it!" They parted, but they both came back to Antioch, their spiritual home, held together in spite of difference.

7. *The church was redemptive.* As the church received Mark and Barnabas into their fellowship in spite of Mark's lapse, they made him over again by the loyalty of Barnabas and the healing fellowship of the Church. Paul sat down in later years and dictated to his amanuensis: "Pick up Mark and bring him along with you, for he is useful in helping me." (II Tim. 4:11, Moffatt.) I can see the amanuensis glance up with a quizzical smile, and Paul thinks for a moment and says: "Yes, I mean just that. Barnabas was right. He was a better Christian than I was. He was always taking people no one else would take; he took me when nobody believed in me. Grand Christian, Barnabas"—and a tear trickles down his cheek. The church was redemptive.

8. *The church was creative.* As they fasted and prayed, the Holy Spirit said, "Separate me Barnabas and Saul for the work whereunto I have called them." (Acts 13:2.) The whole history of Western civilization was in that hour, for out of that hour went two men who gave the gospel to Europe—and us. When the Church listens to the Holy Spirit, it becomes creative. New movements are born.

O God, we surrender to Thee and listen to Thee. Make us creative. Help us to bring new souls and new movements into being. Amen.

AFFIRMATION FOR THE DAY: *Today there is a power working in me —"A power which operates with the strength of the might which he exerted in raising Christ."* (Eph. 1:19, Moffatt.)

THE WAY IS THE WAY OF CREATIVE CONTAGION

We ended yesterday by saying that the church at Antioch was creative. Dynamic impulses went out from that little group which remade the individual and collective life of many a land. *The Way is the way of creative contagion.* The Way is a way of cultivation, but it is also a way of contagion. Everyone who adopts it feels the impulse and the obligation to share it. If there is no impulse to share it, then the life within is dead or moribund. For the creative impulse is within this new life by its very nature. Evangelism, therefore, is not something imposed. It is inherent.

Evangelism is not something specially connected with an occupation—certain people set aside for it by vocation and occupation. It is not an occupation but an outcome. It is the outcome of the nature of the life itself. Inherent in all life is the impulse to create—life produces life. If it doesn't create, it dies.

This impulse to create and share is seen in Philip. He was given a job which was not supposed to be evangelistic. In fact, the apostles gave up this work of serving tables so they could be evangelistic. But, strangely enough, the only man who had the title of "evangelist" was the man who had a layman's job imposed upon him and was not supposed to do evangelistic work. But the impulse was greater than the imposition. The reach of his soul went beyond the reach of his hand; he shared a gospel as well as goods. "Philip the evangelist" (Acts 21:8) was an example of a man who embodied the evangelistic impulse in and through and beyond his occupation. A lay evangelist kept the apostles trotting to keep up with him. He went beyond the apostles in several ways.

First, in his message. When he went down to Samaria, he "preached Christ" to them, and "the crowds attended like one man to what was said by Philip." (Acts 8:5-6, Moffatt.) Why? The verses below interpret what the gospel which he preached was: "the gospel of the Reign of God and the name of Jesus" (vs. 12)—a new Order, the Kingdom of God, and the Person, Jesus. He combined in his message the necessity of an Order and a Person, a gospel for the whole of life.

O Christ, I too would have this creative impulse within me, for this and only this matters. I know this, for it matters everything to me. Help me to share this with everybody, everywhere. For it was shared with me and became everything to me. Amen.

AFFIRMATION FOR THE DAY: *I will not remain evangelical unless I become evangelistic.*

THE WAY IS THE WAY OF RECONCILIATION

We saw yesterday that Philip grasped the essential Christian message—Christ, the Person, embodying the Order, the Kingdom of God. These two must be together, for the Order without the Person is too impersonal, and the Person without the Order is too personal, lacks corporate meanings. But together they comprehend the whole of life. The conservatives emphasize the Person; the liberals emphasize the Order. But Philip put them together. So did Paul: "He preached the Reign of God and taught about the Lord Jesus Christ" (Acts 28:31, Moffatt.) The two men who most clearly caught the essential elements of the Christian gospel were both laymen, outside the stream of "apostolic succession." They were both the most evangelistic and, as a consequence, the most evangelical. Running streams are usually clearer than stagnant pools. Their theology was out of Life to life.

Second, Philip went beyond the apostles in his reconciling impact. His evangelism was what all evangelism should be—reconciliation. Through everything he did reconciliation runs. And that is the heart of evangelism. The one verse which sums up the Christian gospel better than any other, I believe, is this: "God was in Christ, reconciling the world unto himself, . . . and hath committed unto us the word of reconciliation." (II Cor. 5:19.) God was reconciling men when they didn't want to be reconciled, and the price He paid to get to men in spite of their sins was the cross. And what God does we must do; we must reconcile men even though it costs a cross. For the chief business of the Christian is to reconcile others. We must reconcile in four directions: between man and God, between man and man, between man and himself, and between man and nature. This fourfold reconciliation is the one business of the Christian; all else is subsidiary. If we are not reconciling, we are not Christian. The Way is the way of reconciliation.

The center of that reconciliation is the reconciliation between man and God. As long as the central estrangement is there between man and God, then all relations have the shadow of estrangement upon them. Life lacks central harmony. Unreconciled with God you are unreconciled with yourself, with your brother, with nature.

O God, Thou art reconciling us when we fear reconciliation, for we have become naturalized in the unnatural—we have tried to be at home away from Home. Help us to be reconciled and to reconcile. Amen.

AFFIRMATION FOR THE DAY: *Today I shall touch everything with a healing touch.*

BRIDGING GAPS

We saw yesterday that the essence of the Christian impact is reconciliation. And the world needs it. For there are broken bodies, broken hearts, broken homes, a broken Church, a broken world, and broken hopes. Philip reconciled in these directions:

1. *He bridged the gap between the material and the spiritual.* He spiritualized the material, and he materialized the spiritual—made it walk in flesh and blood. Someone spoke of a certain great Christian as a man who was "a mystic who had a strong sense of double-entry bookkeeping." We need practical mysticism and mystic practicality. Philip was at home in two worlds at once. He served tables as a deacon, but he won people to Christ as an evangelist, and the two were not two, but one.

2. *He bridged the gap between Greek and Jew.* He was a Greek wholly trusted by the Jews. When the race question arose, he was the one to settle it in his own person. He belonged to everybody because he belonged to Christ. The Christian is pro-everybody, he is only anti-evil. "Is So-and-so a pacifist?" was asked of a certain Christian. The reply: "Like his Master, he is not an 'ist' of anything. He is not a pacifist, but peace itself—he heals everything he touches." We need people not to bring races together so much as to rise above race and see in every person a person and treat him as such. In many interracial meetings race sticks out everywhere. We need people who are unconscious of race but deeply conscious of people. Philip, without mentioning race, solved the question in his own person, by his transcendence of race. A Greek served Jews and did it racelessly.

3. *He bridged the gap between Jew and Samaritan.* The tension between Jew and Samaritan was great. The Samaritans would not receive Jesus and the disciples because their faces were set in the direction of Jerusalem, and to call a Jew a Samaritan was to abuse him. But here was a Greek reconciling Jew and Samaritan. (Acts 8:5-6.) He did such a great work among the Samaritans that the apostles had to come down and lay their hands on them that they might receive the Holy Spirit. Hitherto they had wanted to call down fire on them to destroy them; now it was the fire of the Spirit.

O God, in a world torn and fragmented help me to heal everything I touch, and help me to touch everything. Give me the healing hands and the healing heart. For Thou art sending me to reconcile everywhere. Amen.

AFFIRMATION FOR THE DAY: *Today I shall reconcile, reconstruct, and release.*

RECONCILING BETWEEN RACES

We pursue the reconciling spirit of Philip:

4. *He reconciled between black and white.* The Spirit told Philip to join himself to the chariot of an Ethiopian. He obeyed implicitly. (Acts 8:27.) Philip didn't see the man's skin; he saw his soul. And it was a great soul.

Skin is precarious. The African thinks the white man is one who is wearing his skin inside out. A little Chinese girl put her arm alongside the white arm of the missionary and said, "You must have been very sick." A little girl who had never seen a black child before went up to her and passed her fingers over her face to see if the color would rub off; when she found it didn't, she kissed her. The child bridged the gap through simplicity. Philip did it through his Christian faith. But some people's Christian faith does not function at this point. Someone said to a deacon who was expressing pronounced racial prejudices, "But what does God say about it?" The deacon replied, "I don't care what God thinks about it; this is what I believe." And he still thought he was a Christian. His racial self was dominant and vocal; his Christian self was inoperative. In a Christian center there is a building called "The World Brotherhood Building" in which a Negro is not allowed to stay. Another Christian center talks brotherhood by the square yard and practices it by the square inch, for Negroes are not allowed to take part in the proceedings. When I called attention to this, a woman naïvely said, "But there are a lot of them working around on these grounds." As if to have them there as servants fulfilled the Christian conscience! A colored soldier was asked to get out of a car into a Jim Crow car, and as he hobbled away on crutches, he said, "I was crippled for this." On the other hand, look at this picture: At a mass meeting for women, a colored woman's baby began to cry, and she got up to take it out. A white woman took the baby from the mother, took it outside and attended to it during the rest of the service so the mother could stay. Early Christianity bridged the gap in the person of Philip; he reconciled between black and white.

O God, who hast made of one blood all men everywhere and hast bound us at Thy feet in brotherhood, help us to get rid of everything that makes for separation between man and man of whatever race or color. For all are equal in Thy sight. Amen.

AFFIRMATION FOR THE DAY: *Today I shall see in every man of every race not a problem but a possibility.*

APPRECIATING PEOPLE WITH DISABILITIES

Yesterday we saw how Philip reconciled between white and colored.

5. *He reconciled between the physically defective and the physically whole.* He talked to the eunuch with the same respect that he would accord a physically whole person. To be able to see the man behind the physical defect is a Christian attitude and accomplishment. Men have despised the cripple and the blind and the leper. When the blind man called to Jesus to have mercy on him, the people told him to keep still, and then Jesus stopped and asked him to be called. Then they ran to him and said, "Courage! Get up, he is calling you." (Mark 10:49, Moffatt.) They were not interested in him until Jesus was interested; their interest followed His. It is still true. He makes the uninteresting interesting. Even a eunuch becomes creative, on other levels, under His touch.

Tyranny had laid hold of the eunuch, had mutilated him to make him useful and safe in a royal court among women. He was cut off from all procreation. Society does the same today, but in other forms. It lays hold on people, compels them to live in crowded slums where soul and body and mind are mutilated and rendered noncreative. This is all so subtle and hidden and camouflaged that only experienced eyes, and Christian, can see it. Again, when it kills off our youth in war and makes marriage impossible for a great many young women, denies them a home and children, it is still in the process of mutilation. When it drops bombs out of God's skies on whole populations and makes little children start life under the Great Terror with stunted minds and bodies, this again is mutilation. When we keep food from getting to the hungry because, while God's earth is bountiful, we refuse to get past the key jam of distribution, then this too is mutilation. Today our Christianity must function in terms of the underprivileged and the mutilated. When news of the end of World War I came to the bishops of the Methodist Episcopal Church, then in session, they called on the great orator Bishop William A. Quayle to speak. He said one sentence: "We must now be decent to the Negro." It was his most eloquent speech.

O God, we come to Thee to be awakened to the worth-whileness of men everywhere. Stab us broad awake and make us sensitive to any human need, anywhere. In Jesus' name. Amen.

AFFIRMATION FOR THE DAY: *"Democracy is that madness that believes about men what isn't so, and yet without that faith they will never become what we believe them to be."*

SPINSTERHOOD A CHRISTIAN INSTITUTION?

We now look at the final reconciliation which Philip affected:
6. *He reconciled between the married and the unmarried state.*
The account says that Philip had "four unmarried daughters who
prophesied." (Acts 21:8, Moffatt.) To have a grown unmarried daughter was almost unheard of; to have four was news. Marriages in those
days, as in the East today, were arranged by the parents. To have four
daughters unmarried showed parents who were very remiss, or daughters who were very remarkable. The latter is probable, for "who
prophesied" gives us the clue. To prophesy meant not so much to
foretell as to forth-tell. These young women were so creative in passing
on the message that they were not frustrated at all. They sublimated
their sex life in creative work, in new-born souls, creating hope and
new movements. They were not suppressing sex, but expressing it on
another level.

So spinsterhood is a Christian institution. It grew out of the fact
that the Christian impact made creation possible outside of marriage,
and thus opened up harmonious living whether within or without the
marriage relation. Spinsters, then, are in a line of creative succession.
And they have kept it up. Their contribution to American life
through teaching school and in other ways is perhaps the greatest
contribution of any group. Here's to the spinsters who have uniquely
helped to make America what it is! They deserve our gratitude, God
bless them! And they perhaps have been as happy and adjusted as the
married. Maybe more so, if the divorce courts are any indication. .

Philip is the patron saint of the unmarried, for he showed four unmarried daughters so useful that it had to be recorded for all ages. He
reconciled the married and the unmarried state as equally fruitful if
lived under the will of God. So "Philip the evangelist" drew everything together. He healed everything he touched, and he touched
everything. As Ted Adams was ordained by his father, the sermon
outline was: (1) Keep close to God. (2) Keep close to man. (3) Bring
man and God together. Philip did that—the reconciler.

O living Christ, make my heart the place where everything is brought
and everything is healed. Make me a reconciler everywhere, to everybody, in
everything. For it is a broken world, and in Thee we have the healing—
the only healing. Amen.

AFFIRMATION FOR THE DAY: *Today I shall see every man in God and
what he can become in God.*

EVANGELISM THE LIFE BLOOD OF THE CHURCH

We come now to sum up the study on the evangelistic impulse.

It is said in the last book of Scripture: "Blessed is he who reads aloud" (Rev. 1:3, Moffatt)—who passes on to others what he reads, the outgoing, sharing type. No benediction is pronounced on those who read to themselves only. Nor does it say: "Let the redeemed of the Lord keep their mouths shut." Psychology is saying the same thing in psychological terms—you must be the sharing, communicative type to be healthy-minded. It is said: "They overcame him by the blood of the Lamb, and by the word of their testimony." (Rev. 12:11.) They conquered by what He did for them—"the blood of the Lamb"—and by what they did for Him—by "their testimony." Here was taking and telling, the alternate beats of the Christian heart. For when something happens to us, then something happens through us.

Two things characterize the real Christian: he listens to God, and he talks to people. Many reverse that: they listen to people, and they talk to God. It was said of John the Baptist: "He came for the purpose of witnessing." (John 1:7, Moffatt.) That is psychologically sound. The center was outside himself; he was not talking about himself. That made a healthy-minded person—and effective.

As soon as one finds Christ, there is an impulse to find another and bring him to Christ. In the first chapter of John there are three "finds"—Andrew "finds" Peter, Jesus "finds" Philip, and Philip "finds" Nathaniel. The gospel is a gospel of finding. Of the forty healings in the Gospels, all but seven were brought in by someone else.

As Jesse M. Bader says: "You can be a clerk or a salesman—the clerk waits for a customer, and the salesman goes out for him. We should be ringing door bells, instead of church bells; we have been doing by proxy what we should do by proximity; by purse instead of by person." George Lansbury, a leader in the British government, said to me: "I have not been unsuccessful in politics, but if I had to do it over again, I would invest my life in people, in personally changing people, rather than investing in programs."

O Christ, Thou hast given me the greatest work in the world, the work of bringing others to Thee. Help me here and now to dedicate myself to that simple task, and help me to be faithful to that dedication. For nothing counts so much as this. In Thy name. Amen.

AFFIRMATION FOR THE DAY: *Nothing is really mine till I share it.*

WHAT CAN WE BELIEVE ABOUT WAR?

We come now to face a question we were bound to face sooner or later: the question of the Way and war. We cannot by-pass this question and keep our moral integrity. For war does not by-pass any of us, anywhere. All of us are affected by war. But all are not affected in the same way.

There are those who say that when we are involved in war, we are all involved in the same way. Those who approve of war and those who do not are all equally involved; therefore there is no moral distinction. This is shallow. We are all involved, but those who approve of war and those who do not approve of it are involved in morally distinct ways. One gives inner moral assent and the other withholds moral assent. The moral results are very different. Can approval and disapproval produce the same moral results? Then what kind of a moral universe is this?

While giving freedom of conscience to others and refusing to de-Christianize those who differ from me, I must give the reasons why I have had to withhold inner moral consent to war. I believe that the Way and war are incompatibles. If the Way is right, then war is wrong. If war is right, then the Way is wrong.

It is largely your beginning place that determines your conclusion. If you begin with the Way and then look at war, you will probably come out to one conclusion. If you begin with war and then look at the Way, you will probably come out to an entirely different conclusion. Your starting point will determine your ending point. Some theological students asked a prominent Christian why he abandoned his former position against war for one of moral approval. In reply he unfolded a map of Europe, pointed to it and said, "That map is my reason." He got his morals from his map, instead of from his Master. He looked at the Nazis instead of the Nazarene. And that is essentially the wrong starting point. The Christian begins at Christ and works from Him out to problems.

O Christ, I know where I should begin. I should begin at Thee. Like Peter, when I take my eyes off Thee, I sink into the moral morass of the hour. Help me to see Thee; then I shall see clearly the moral issues of the passing hour. Help me to see war clearly. Amen.

AFFIRMATION FOR THE DAY: *Today I shall not begin with a problem. I shall begin with the Person and work from Him down to my problems.*

RAISES MORE PROBLEMS THAN IT SETTLES?

Yesterday we saw that we must work from Christ to the problem of war. The objector replies: "It's all very well to talk about getting your eyes on the Nazarene instead of the Nazis, but what are you going to do with Hitler?" The answer is a simple one: "He and his brood were not my babies; they were yours. You produced them out of your method, then lay them on my doorstep and say, 'What are you going to do with them?' I wouldn't have produced them. If you had taken my method and program, Hitler and his kind would not have arisen. You produced them out of your method, and then say we must get rid of them by the same method. It won't work; it's a vicious circle."

General Dwight D. Eisenhower, just back from the war in Europe, said a significant thing: "You cannot produce peace by hate and a club." But hate and a club are the stock in trade of war, the very essence of it. According to Eisenhower, you will have to abandon the mentality and the method of war if you are to have peace. I would suspect a mentality and a method I have to abandon at its moment of greatest triumph. The mentality and the method must be wrong.

At the close of the war I have not had to abandon either my mentality or my method to have peace. My moral universe was the same before the war, during the war, and at the close of the war. And I'm certain that if men will apply the mentality and the method of the Christian, there will be no more war. "But if men will not respond to the Christian way?" Then the answer is: "Increase the dose." Because the patient doesn't get well when we give him small doses of the Christian spirit and big doses of the war spirit, we should not abandon the giving of the healing Christian spirit and give nothing but the poison of the war spirit. It doesn't make sense. Increase the Christian dose.

A soldier fresh back from devastated Europe said to me: "We've raised more problems in Europe than we've settled." What a verdict! After pouring out the blood of millions of men and expending billions in money we come out to that result—more problems raised than settled!

O Christ, forgive us that we've missed the Way. For we know that this is not the Way. The sense of futility that settles upon us as we begin to see the results makes us sure that this way leads away from Thee. Then put our feet again upon the Way. For we perish. Amen.

AFFIRMATION FOR THE DAY: *Nobody wins in war. Everybody loses. It is only a question of the degree of the losses.*

WORSHIPING GODS CONQUERED IN WAR

Yesterday we saw that the method of war is incapable of producing the results expected of it. The means are out of harmony with the ends sought. For getting rid of evil by evil means you infect yourself with the very evil you try to get rid of. It is written: "It was after his return from the massacre of the Edomites, that Amaziah brought the gods of the men of Seir and set them up to be his gods, bowing in homage before them." (II Chron. 25:14, Moffatt.) We worship the gods of those whom we conquer in war. We adopt their ways. In getting rid of militarism by military methods we are militarized. One of the evil results of this war will probably be peacetime conscription. In getting rid of military nations, built on universal conscription, we end up in adopting the thing that led to their militarization and to their downfall. We do the thing that was their undoing. We end up in worshiping the gods of the nations we conquer. We thus take the slippery road down which every military nation has slid to its doom.

We build a structure for peace, and at the center of that structure we put force, lodged, not in collective security, but in five nations as the final authority of the world. We adopt Hitler's principle as the center of a world structure for peace. His principle wins. We become infected by the thing we try to overthrow. No wonder the prophet cries: "The toil of the nations ends in smoke, and peoples wear themselves out for naught." (Hab. 2:13, Moffatt.) Take another picture: "Then Abner said to Joab, 'Let the young men get up and have a fight before us.' 'Very well,' said Joab. So the young men got up. . . . Each caught his opponent by the head and stabbed him in the side, so that they all dropped together. . . . That day the fight . . . was most fierce. . . . Abner called to Joab, 'Is the sword to devour forever? Do you not know the outcome will be bitter?'" (II Sam. 2:14-17, 26, Moffatt). This is war. Leaders start it; young men fight it; even the leaders get sick of it and cry: "Do you not know the outcome will be bitter?" Outcome bitter? Yes, and the process too is bitter. And nothing good comes out of it, except that which could have been accomplished by other and better means.

O God, forgive our stupidity and our perverseness. We try to make life work in unworkable ways. And we get hurt. We have been hurt, terribly hurt. And now help us to begin again. In Thy name. Amen.

AFFIRMATION FOR THE DAY: *It is a new world for everybody, or a new world war for everybody.*

THE STEPS DOWN

A vivid illustration of how militarism, after initial successes, defeats itself and becomes worm-eaten is seen in the case of Herod. In Acts 12 it says that "king Herod laid hands of violence on some members of the church." Now note the steps down: (1) "James . . . he slew with the sword." (Vs. 2.) (2) Seeing this succeeded, he goes a step further: "He went on to seize Peter." (Vs. 3.) (3) Peter was imprisoned. (Vs. 4.) (4) He began to be disconcerted at deliverance of Peter. (Vs. 19.) (5) Asserts his peeved authority again, orders the guards to death. (Vs. 19.) (6) He retreats to Caesarea, baffled. (Vs. 19.) (7) Arrayed royally, he talks big, "It is a god's voice, not a man's!" (Vss. 21-22.) (8) Eaten of worms, he dies, a worm-eaten god. (Vs. 23.)

These are the exact steps down for militarism. It succeeds, goes further, overreaches itself, can't understand the imponderables, retreats baffled, talks big, rattles the sword, becomes worm-eaten—dies! War is a worm-eaten god. The magazine *Time* says: "It is a law of history that power, even the power of evil, eventually produces the power that supersedes it."

Science, in the service of war, discovered the ultimate power at the base of the universe—the power wrapped up in an atom. We were triumphant, and frightened. A commentator said that for three days following its first use he didn't see a smile on a single face on the streets of Washington, and that a wisecrack would have been as much out of place as at a funeral. We discovered the ultimate power, grew frightened, saw that war dare not handle it, for it would ruin the used-upon and the user. We knew that it would have to be surrendered into the hands of good will to use constructively—or else! In other words war, which depends on power, got power, grew frightened of the thing it was after, turned to goodness, and said, "Save us, we perish." Did a method ever reveal its inner bankruptcy so absolutely? It got what it was after and then begged someone else to take it over. I am against a method which, when pushed to its ultimate conclusion, means universal ruin. Something is fundamentally, basically wrong with it.

O Christ, help me to see clearly this evil that has gripped the world in its tentacles. It uses so many good things—patriotism, courage, self-sacrifice—and yet it itself is evil. Amen.

AFFIRMATION FOR THE DAY: *If war is right, Christ is inherently wrong. If Christ is right, war is inherently wrong.*

WHICH JESUS BAR-ABBAS?

A year before the end of the war, as I passed by on the train the New Mexico desert with its wired-off area and knew they were searching for superpower, I knew not what, I wrote in my notebook: "Paul went into the desert of Arabia to learn the secret of power, emerged to transform the world; the United States military forces along with science have gone into the desert of New Mexico to learn the secret of power—will they emerge to destroy the world?" Little did I know that I framed a question which is haunting many minds.

These powers must be handled according to the Way—or else! The words of Lew Ayres are true, "It is Christ or rubble." But the Christian Way must cease alliances that weaken and absorb its strength. It must be itself. Clemenceau said: "When a Christian decides to live his Christianity, then a real revolution starts."

But the Christian must discover the real Way and cease to take a camouflaged thing. When the moment of the world's great choice came, two figures came before the Jewish leaders to choose from— Jesus and Jesus. (Matt. 27:17.) They both had the same name, according to Moffatt, and the same title: Jesus Barabbas (literally, Jesus, son of the father) and Jesus Bar-Abbas (literally, Jesus, Son of the Father). Jesus means "savior" in both cases, and in both cases they were sons of the father (Father). The difference was the capital F and the small f. They both came as the savior of the nation—one taking the method of force for deliverance from the Roman yoke; the Other, the method of dying for men to reconcile them to God and to each other. They were so alike—the nomenclature the same, the purpose the same. But the content was utterly different. The nation chose Jesus Barabbas, the man of force, and in choosing perished. Roman power destroyed their city. They took the sword and perished by the sword.

Today two different religions stand before the world, both with the same name: Jesus Barabbas and Jesus Bar-Abbas. One relies on the method of war for the deliverance of the nations; the other relies on basic good will and justice for all. Which Jesus are we choosing?

O Jesus, to give Thee Thy names of "Saviour" and "Son of the Father" and then to put another content into them—that for Thee must be the ultimate crucifixion. Save me from that. Amen.

AFFIRMATION FOR THE DAY: *Today I shall have a Christianity that is Christian.*

LET THE CHURCH KEEP ITS MESSAGE

We saw yesterday that there are two religions both using the same names, declaring the same ends, but with utterly different contents. A devotee of the one faith said over the radio: "We must breathe a prayer of thanks to the Ordnance Department for the weapons provided." A prayer to the Ordnance Department—to his god! If we look to the Ordnance Department as our "god," and pray to it, then we turn pagan, no matter what Christian names we may still use. It is another Jesus, with another content.

Let the Church keep its own message and pray to its own God. In front of the First Baptist Church, Richmond, Virginia, there stands a great church bell which was taken down to be melted into shot and shell for the Confederate Army. A man bought it at a good sum to redeem it from the intended purpose and to save it so it could continue to toll out, "On earth peace, good will toward men." If we allow our organization and influence to be melted down into shot and shell, then who is there left to proclaim the only thing that can heal: "On earth peace, good will toward men"? Nobody. In that case we take our place among the high priests of whom it was said: "Swords and cudgels . . . from the high priests." (Matt. 26:47, Moffatt.) What an output from religion—swords and cudgels! Love and sacrifice from Jesus, swords and cudgels from the high priests. These died; the Other lives on. If the Church becomes the religious impulse for swords and cudgels and baptizes them with its blessing, then the Church too will die as the high priests died. They belonged to the not-the-way.

If the Church will not stand for this message, then secularism will be bound to, for life demands it. On the base of a monument to a celebrated Brazilian, Marshal Manuel Luiz Osario, are these words: "The happiest day of my life will be that day when they bring me the news that the civilized peoples are celebrating the festival of their brotherhood by burning down their arsenals." A cartoon in a daily newspaper depicts a bloody sword, and under it these words: "This might have been a scalpel." We must make it one.

O Christ, I know that Thou hast a better way—Thy will. If this way of hate and war is right, Thou art wrong. If Thou art right, then this is wrong. I choose Thee. For Thou shalt be standing on the horizon as the smoke clears away—our one hope. I thank Thee. Amen.

AFFIRMATION FOR THE DAY: *"Atomic energy knows neither friend nor foe. It is a primeval force. It is a new beginning, or it is the end."*

A PERSONAL WORD

In closing this week upon the Christian attitude toward war I want to add my personal word. Better men than I have approved of war. I respect their consciences while disagreeing with their attitudes. I do not judge them. But I must register my own convictions.

During the First World War I got as far as this in my thinking: I preached a sermon during that war on two texts: "Herod with his men of war set him at naught"—militarism sets Jesus at naught. "When they saw . . . the soldiers, they left beating of Paul"—militarism protects the innocent and the weak. Therefore I can support this war. I got that far. Then the period of disillusionment set in. I saw that the basis on which I could support war was flimsy and based on a fallacy: militarism protects the innocent and the weak. I saw that innocent and guilty alike were unprotected in war—it made no moral distinctions. Further, I saw that war did not protect the weak; it involved them and hit them especially. Whatever power militarism has had in the past to protect the innocent and the weak, it has lost all such power. More civilian casualties took place in this war from wounds, famine, and disease than military casualties. War protects no one—anywhere. It does the opposite.

I saw that the whole thing was a vast waste of men and goods. Joseph M. Dodge, head of the War Department Adjustment Board, said: "Since war goods are being purchased with the taxpayer's money and represent economic waste in their use, there is every reason for holding their price as low as possible and restricting profit." Economic waste! I saw that war was a vast illusion, a vast waste. It built nothing. It blasted everything. It built nothing beneficial that we could not have built without war.

Then I saw that not only did life not approve of it, but Life also. When I worked from Christ down to this business of war, it seemed so utterly incompatible with everything I knew about Him that it just didn't fit. So I repudiated it and determined I would give the balance of my days to finding a better way for myself and mankind.

O Christ, I thank Thee that the conflict within is over. No doubts remain. I am committed and committed forever to getting rid of this awful monstrosity. Give me courage to face misunderstanding and to love those who disagree. In Thy name. Amen.

AFFIRMATION FOR THE DAY: *"Victory may be achieved through armaments, but not world peace."*

WHY WE GO TO WAR

We studied last week the incompatibility of war and the Way. Many—shall I say most?—people will agree with me that the Way and war are incompatibles, but they ask, "What's the alternative to war?" Are we to sit down and let evil overrun us? Is that the answer of those who repudiate war? No, a thousand times, no. We don't want evil to overrun anybody, least of all ourselves. We are against evil in all its forms, against it so much that we do not believe in creating one evil—war—to get rid of another evil. Two evils never make a good. A war poster says: "Whoever wins the war, the kids lose." Yes, but everybody loses—victor and vanquished. No one can win a war. It's only a matter of which side loses most, but everybody loses.

For two or three years during the war I said to audiences something like this: "There is a difference between this war and other wars, and the difference is profound. It is this: Nobody believes in this war. Even those who support it don't believe in it. Their mood is: 'Yes, we are caught by the war; we're in a jam; we've got to go through with it; it's a nasty mess to clean up; but this isn't the way—this isn't the way to settle international disputes. Why should we burn down the house of civilization periodically to get rid of a few rats? Can't we build a house of civilization that is ratproof?'" That is the mood. When I first began saying that, I thought that I would get a comeback. I bowed my head for the recoil. Not one person has ever come up to me and said, "You're wrong. I believe in it." Not one. Why? Well, we don't believe in it. This is sheer gain. Humanity has come to the place where it doesn't believe in its chief occupation—making war.

Then if we don't believe in war, why do we go to war? The answer is simple: *We have no alternative.* There is no other method to settle international disputes. There is no world government over us to which we can refer international disputes for settlement. With all the good will in the world, we will continue to go to war until we get a government over us. International anarchy is the cause of international war.

O God, Thou art teaching us, slowly teaching us in spite of our costly stupidities. Open our minds that we may see, and seeing, help us to act and to act with decisiveness and fearlessly. For mistakes and prejudices cost blood. Help us. Amen.

AFFIRMATION FOR THE DAY: *"It is love, as the outward expression of one spirit within, which is the means of making oneness of mankind a genuine reality."*

EVERYTHING THAT MAKES FOR WAR

We left off yesterday at the place where we said that we go to war because we have no world government over us to which we can refer our disputes. In these United States we have everything that produces war between nations: sectional differences, religious tensions, racial clashes, class differences, vested interests, selfish men wanting power. Besides, we have a heterogeneous people out of many racial backgrounds with a history of hate and war in Europe. And yet with all that we do not go to war. Why? Because we have a government over us to which we can refer our disputes for settlement. That government has three things: moral authority, courts of justice, and police power sufficient to bring the culprit before the bar of justice to be tried by a tribunal of right.

Before government was established in the sparsely settled West of the United States, men went armed; and when any dispute arose, they shot it out. Were they more warlike than others? No, but they had no alternate method of settling disputes. When government was established, those pistols dropped away, and men argued it out before tribunals instead of shooting it out. The thing that stopped the shooting was not mere good will but organized good will in government. That is lacking in international affairs; we have no government over us. And we will continue to go to war until we do.

That world government will take one of these two forms: a world state or federal union. I do not believe that an undifferentiated world state is possible or desirable. Had we tried that in this country, had we wiped out all state boundaries and functions and amalgamated them in one state governed from Washington, we would have failed. And rightly. For the one undifferentiated state doesn't provide for state rights, for local differences and responsibilities and freedom. Federal union does. It provides for union with local self-expression. It fulfills two instincts—the desire for union with the whole, and the desire for local self-expression through local self-government. It harmonizes two apparently opposite instincts—union and difference. Federal union is therefore founded on human nature.

O God, we thank Thee that Thou art leading Thy children everywhere to a union that will not wipe out our differences but will provide that they exist in a deep and fundamental union. Thou art teaching us. Help us to learn. In Jesus' name. Amen.

AFFIRMATION FOR THE DAY: *Love must be organized into corporate relations.*

THE MEANING OF FEDERAL UNION

We saw yesterday that federal union holds the only promise of a world union. Note that we say "federal union" and not "federation." Federation is a league of sovereign entities—they have delegated no sovereignty. Federal union is not a league of sovereign entities, but a union of those who have delegated sovereignty to that union. Under that union they have freedom, but the union is supreme and sovereign.

The United States is not a federation; it is a federal union. We came near forming a "League of Friendship" among sovereign colonies. Had we done so, what would have happened? We would have had forty-eight sovereign states, each with its sovereign government, its foreign office, military establishment, border defenses, tariffs, customs, fears—and wars. We would have been the cockpit of this Western world—the Balkans of the Americas. We refused that and asked the colonies to delegate that sovereignty to the union—to lose their lives to find them again in a brotherhood. How they were led to do it I cannot see, except by divine providence.

For these colonies were often very strained in their relationships with each other. An English visitor, after journeying a thousand miles among the colonies in 1760, reported: "Oil and water cannot mix any sooner than can these colonies." A delegate stood up in the assembly of North Carolina and pleaded that a Chinese wall of exclusion be placed on the northern border of North Carolina to protect the culture, the religion, the civilization of North Carolina from—Virginia! Norfolk debased her currency to get the trade away from Baltimore, which in turn debased hers to get the trade away from Philadelphia, which in turn debased hers to get the trade away from New York. New York state declared war on Connecticut over a boundary dispute, and Massachusetts declared her neutrality. Sounds modern! And yet these sovereign colonies lost themselves, made the union supreme. And found themselves! They fulfilled the law of the Kingdom of God deeply embedded in the nature of reality: "Whosoever will save his life shall lose it: and whosoever will lose his life . . . shall find it." We found ourselves in a stable and glorious union—a federal union. Unconsciously we became the archetype of world union.

O God, Thou whose Almighty hand hath led us thus far on the way, guide us to the consummation of our destiny—a world federal union. For Thou art guiding us, we feel it in our bones. In Jesus' name. Amen.

AFFIRMATION FOR THE DAY: *"There's a divinity that shapes our ends, rough-hew them as we will."*

SURRENDER OF SOVEREIGNTY

We saw yesterday how we, as colonies, were guided—divinely guided, I believe—to fulfill a law of losing life to find it again. The League of Nations broke that law and broke itself in the process. Each nation in the League of Nations saved its life, refused to surrender any sovereignty to the union, and lost its life in universal chaos and war. The League of Nations didn't fail because the United States wasn't in it, though we should have been in it. Had we been in it, it would have come to the same end, for it was trying the impossible—trying to have a union without any surrender of sovereignty to that union.

Suppose two people intending to form a union in marriage should say: "We will have a union, but neither of us will surrender any sovereignty to the union." How long would the union last? About as long as many marriages now last, and for the same reason!

Two patterns for peace are emerging: (1) Leagues, pacts, treaties, charters among sovereign nations. (2) A federal union of the world.

The first pattern for peace will not keep us out of wars. Leagues, pacts, treaties, charters among sovereign nations are only truces between wars. There is no government over these sovereign nations to decide matters of dispute between them. Hence every nation has to be ready to decide the matter itself on the basis of armed might. We had 4,800 treaties in operation when the last war came, and we broke them like Samson broke the green withes binding him when Delilah said: "The Philistines be upon thee." Leagues, pacts, treaties, charters between sovereign nations cannot by the very nature of things keep us out of war. To rely on them to keep us out of war is to lean on a broken stick which, when it breaks, pierces our hands—and our hearts.

The crux of the world problem is now bare before us: Will the nations delegate sovereignty to a world federal union, or will they refuse to delegate sovereignty and trust in leagues, pacts, treaties, and charters? All other questions are marginal; this is central. If they will not willingly delegate sovereignty for peace, they will unwillingly delegate it for war.

O God, we have come to the crux of the world problem. Both in the individual and in the collective we must lose our lives to find them again. Thou art bringing us to the Valley of Decision. Help us. Amen.

AFFIRMATION FOR THE DAY: *Every unit—individual, group, nation —must surrender itself to save itself.*

WE HAVE ALREADY DELEGATED SOVEREIGNTY

We ended yesterday by saying that it is not a question of surrendering sovereignty but a question of doing it willingly or unwillingly. For the moment war comes sovereignty is surrendered—to war.

The fact is that we in the United States have already delegated sovereignty. There is a commission called "The International Boundary Commission," made up of three Canadians and three Americans, into whose hands have been placed for decision all questions concerning the boundary, water rights, water pollution, fishing rights—all questions that arise concerning the boundary between Canada and the United States. For thirty years it has functioned and has settled some knotty questions. For instance, it found on resurveying the boundary between Maine and Canada that Fort Montgomery, a United States fort on which we had expended some millions, was on Canadian territory. A fort to protect the United States from Canada on Canadian soil! But the commission, used to dealing with large questions in a large way, simply drew a line around the fort, took it in, and then dipped down on the other side and gave Canada a corresponding amount of territory. Then the United States became ashamed of that fort. Wasn't it the only fort on three thousand miles of boundary line? And wasn't it the safest international boundary in the world? So we tore it down and used the materials to make roads between these two countries. On the West Coast the fumes from the Trail Smelting Works on the Canadian side came over and damaged the orchards of the American farmers, who put in a bill for $2,500,000. Expert testimony assessed the loss at $250,000, which was paid. Then the fumes had to be dealt with. The fumes were used to make fertilizer for the orchards!

For thirty years this commission has functioned, and never once has it failed to come to a unanimous conclusion. And the point of the story is this: The commission settles every question without reference back to the Canadian Parliament or to the Congress of the United States. In other words, we have delegated sovereignty to this commission. Nationally humiliated thereby? Ennobled.

O God, Thou art teaching us that the only way to find life is to lose it—to lose it in something beyond ourselves. Teach us the supreme lesson of losing our individual and our national selves in Thy Kingdom. Then we shall find ourselves—fulfilled. Amen.

AFFIRMATION FOR THE DAY: *I shall surrender myself to ever-widening loyalties, but shall make the supreme surrender only to the Kingdom.*

THE THREE STAGES FOR NATIONS

In a previous study we saw that the three stages of life for the individual were: (1) Dependence, the childhood stage. (2) Independence, the stage of adolescence. (3) Interdependence, the stage of maturity.

Nations go through those same three stages: (1) Dependence, the stage of imperialism where one nation tells another nation what to do. (2) Independence, the stage where all nations demand freedom for themselves. (3) Interdependence, the stage where, finding that independence is not all that it is supposed to be, that we are interdependent, we deliberately relate ourselves to something beyond ourselves and find ourselves in the process—come to the stage of maturity.

Humanity is strung out in all three stages. But we are coming—and coming inevitably—to the third stage of interdependence, the stage of maturity. As the individual very often never grows up, but continues to assert his independence, in other words his adolescence, so nations continuously assert their independence, saying they will delegate no sovereignty to anything, thereby showing they are not superpatriotic but merely adolescent. We will come to interdependence, and the pattern for that interdependence is federal union, for in federal union there is union with local independence and freedom. We thereby do not despise independence; we fulfill it under a higher interdependence.

In the words of President Truman: "We must come to a world republic. It will not be more difficult than the achievement of our Republic." The thing that led to the formation of our federal union, we are told, was the oysters of the Chesapeake Bay. No one could decide to whom they belonged, Virginia or Maryland. Of all the dumb things leading to a wise conclusion this takes the prize—dumb oysters leading to a federal union! It makes us hope that God will be able to use our stupidities to lead to a world union! World government must have three things: moral authority, courts of justice, and police power sufficient to bring the criminal before the bar of justice to be tried.

We in America have been God's proving ground to prove out a principle—the principle of federal union. The British Commonwealth of Nations has also been a proving ground. The principle works.

O God, our Father, slowly but surely we have seen the hand of destiny pointing us to federal union. Give us courage and largeness of heart that we may follow and follow unafraid. For Thou art leading us. Amen.

AFFIRMATION FOR THE DAY: *Only the immature and the unsure refuse to surrender to a higher loyalty.*

A UNION OF PEOPLES

In world federal union there would be a common citizenship, common currency, common postage, common defense, and a common loyalty to the union. That union must have in its original nucleus the representatives of all races and all colors. We must not try to form a union of the Anglo-Saxons and then invite others into it; that would be psychologically impossible. It must be a *world* union, and it must not be dominated by any nation or group of nations.

But an objection arises: If this federal union has moral authority, courts of justice, and police power, will this not mean that in the exercise of that police power coercion will be used; and if states are coerced, will this not mean war? We got over that difficulty in these United States by a simple expedient. We formed a union, not of the states, but of the people of the states. "We the people of the United States . . . do ordain and establish . . ." This had great consequences. When a person in a state committed a crime, we did not send a federal army to smash up the whole state. Instead we extradited the criminal and brought him before the bar of justice. We used just enough force to get him before the bar of justice to be tried.

We could do the same in regard to world union. It would be a union not of the states but of the people of the states. Therefore if a person or a group of persons went wrong in a member state, we would not send an army to smash up the whole state; we would extradite the criminals and bring them before a bar of justice. That would be a legitimate use of force, for the end is a tribunal of right. In war the end is not a tribunal of right but a tribunal of might. Police force and force used in war are different.

When the Constitution was being signed, the delegate from Frederick, Maryland, before he signed, said: "I am a citizen of the town of Frederick, of the county of Frederick, of the state of Maryland, and now I choose to be a citizen of the United States." Some day I hope I can say: "I am a citizen of Baltimore, of the state of Maryland, of the United States of America, and now I choose to be a citizen of the world."

O God, help us not to be like the children of Israel as they viewed the Promised Land but drew back and died in the wilderness. Help us to go in and possess the land, for Thou art leading us. In Jesus' name. Amen.

AFFIRMATION FOR THE DAY: *"I saw thrones with* people *sitting on them."* (Rev. 20:4, Moffatt.) *The people shall finally reign.*

THE KINGDOM OVER ALL

Last week we studied federal union as the form of world structure to which we believe we are destined to come. But we must now hasten to say that, while we believe in federal union, it is not our gospel. The Way is not the way of federal union but of the Kingdom of God. The Way may include federal union as one of the ways of expressing itself, but the ultimate order is the Kingdom of God.

If we should achieve the highest form of world federal union, it would not be the Kingdom of God. That Kingdom is the absolute. All our lesser orders are relativisms—related to something beyond themselves from which they draw meaning, value, significance. So the Kingdom judges and redeems the most nearly perfect human order. We give ourselves tentatively to human orders; we give ourselves totally to the Divine Order. The loon, a water bird, sometimes alights on a small body of water surrounded by a forest or hills; and since it needs a long water surface runway to get off, it finds itself landlocked and perishes in that confinement. We, as Christians, must not become landlocked in lesser schemes. We will give ourselves to them, provided there is always room to take off for the ultimate resting place—the Kingdom.

But even that comparison must be corrected, for we do not take off for the Kingdom; we take off from the Kingdom and give ourselves to the lesser. The Kingdom is our starting point.

For the Kingdom is the Way. Acts 19:8, 9 (Moffatt) says: "Paul entered the synagogue . . . , persuading people about the Reign [Kingdom] of God. But as some . . . , decrying the Way . . ." Here the Kingdom and the Way are used synonymously. The Kingdom, then, is the archpattern for nations and individuals. Everything that fits it lives, and everything that fights it perishes. The Kingdom is our collective destiny. After the end of the war two nations stand out, each embodying an idea—Russia embodying collectivism, America embodying individualism. They must both change and come to a third position, gathering up the truth in individualism and the truth in collectivism, making a society where you love your neighbor (collectivism) as yourself (individualism). That will approximate the Kingdom of God—our destiny.

O God, Thou hast a plan, and that plan is the Kingdom, and that Kingdom plan covers all life, individual and collective. Help us, then, to give ourselves to that Kingdom plan with all our hearts and minds. Amen.

AFFIRMATION FOR THE DAY: *The Kingdom as the over-all and the in-all is our central loyalty.*

THE KINGDOM HAS THE FINAL WORD

We saw yesterday that the starting point for the Christian is the Kingdom of God. From this he works down to all life. But this has to be clarified. The starting point is the Kingdom of God embodied in Christ—the Order embodied in a Person. Christ + the Kingdom = the Way.

Everything not conforming to the Kingdom is destined to perish. During the war I wrote an article, "The Score So Far," in which I traced the movements of events spelling out one thing: the moral universe will have the last word; we lose as we go against it. Now that the war is over, we can see who has won. The moral universe won! Japan, wanting to dominate China, succeeded only in kicking China into being a world power and kicking herself into the dust. America, thinking largely in money terms, comes out of the war with plenty of it—as debt. Britain, exploiting India, comes out in debt to India. Russia lost her moral prestige through imperialistic attitudes toward border countries. And thus it goes endlessly. The Kingdom always has the last word—always. When you go against the Kingdom, you go against yourself.

A woman writes: "Upon reading your book *Is the Kingdom of God Realism?* I whispered to myself, 'It is too hard.' Shortly after this I misplaced my affections and found I had taken the hardest road of all." A passage expresses the fact that everything against the Kingdom is "doomed to perish." (I Cor. 1:18, Moffatt.) On the contrary, for those in the Kingdom "there is no doom." (Rom. 8:1, Moffatt.) As the Apocrypha says, "For the world fighteth for the righteous," or, as Goodspeed puts it, "For the universe is the champion of the upright." (Wisd. of Sol. 16:17.) Everything that is un-Kingdom is undone. Christ is not only goodness; He is wisdom: "Whom God hath made our 'Wisdom.'" (I Cor. 1:30, Moffatt.) An army officer said: "I have come to the conclusion that I cannot be what I want to be without God." Whoever has the first or the intermediate word, God's Kingdom has the last.

O God, my Father, I see that Thy Kingdom is my good, and my kingdom is my bad. Help me, then, to give myself to Thy Kingdom with all my heart and with all my influence. For if this is true, then nothing else matters. But it is true. I know it. Amen.

AFFIRMATION FOR THE DAY: *"Thy kingdom is an everlasting kingdom."* (Ps. 145:13, Moffatt.) *All else has the doom of decay on it.*

HOW THE KINGDOM COMES

Yesterday we saw that the Kingdom of God is to be sought first, last, and always. If you seek something else first, an inner restlessness will possess you—you will have a dull sense that you are not on the Way. Jesus said: "So do not seek food and drink and be worried." (Luke 12:29, Moffatt.) Note that if you seek anything else first you do become "worried"—you know inherently that you've missed the Way. The Kingdom, then, is a total way for the total life, a complete totalitarianism. But when you obey it completely, you find complete freedom.

A good many earnest and sincere Christians feel that the Kingdom of God cannot be an issue now, since it will not come till Jesus comes. "No Kingdom without the King," is the slogan. "He will come to set up His Kingdom on earth, but till then we can do little or nothing to bring in a better order on earth. The best we can do is to rescue individuals, for the earth is going to smash, getting worse till He comes."

But as we look closely at the teaching of Jesus, we find the Kingdom comes in three ways. First, by gradualism. "First the blade, then the ear, after that the full corn in the ear." The Kingdom of God "is like a grain of mustard seed . . . ; and it grew, and waxed a great tree." The Kingdom of God "is like leaven . . . till the whole was leavened." These and other passages teach that the Kingdom will come by permeation, by gradualism. There are other passages which teach that the Kingdom of God will come suddenly, by apocalypticism, with the return of Christ. Some people extract the gradualistic passages, others the apocalyptic. That disrupts the account, for both are there, and we need both. The gradualistic gives me my task, and the apocalyptic gives me my hope. So I shall trust as if the whole thing depends on God and work as if the whole thing depends on me. As this passage puts it, "The hidden issues of the future are with the Eternal our God, but the unfolded issues of the day are with us." (Deut. 29:29, Moffatt.) I shall therefore deal with the unfolded issues and leave the hidden issues to God. "It is not for you to know the times or the seasons." (Acts 1:7.) Our task is clear: We can be the agents of the coming of that Kingdom now.

O God, I see that there have been many surprises in history—the greatest surprise the first coming of Thy Son. There may be another—His second coming. And yet He is always coming to me—now. Amen.

AFFIRMATION FOR THE DAY: *All of my influence, all of my power, all of my self are at the disposal of the Kingdom—today.*

THE ONLY KINGDOM THAT CAN STAND EVERLASTING INCREASE

We saw yesterday that the Kingdom comes both by gradualism and by apocalypticism. But there is another set of passages which teaches that the Kingdom *is*—not will come, but *is*. Jude speaks of God's "dominion and authority, before all time and now and for all time." (Vs. 25, Moffatt.) The dominion is "now." "He must reign, till he hath put all enemies under his feet." Not "when" but "till." He is reigning now even while those enemies are not under His feet. He reigns, and men get hurt when they do not obey that reign. "For thine is the Kingdom"—not shall be, but "is." Paul speaks of the "dethroned powers which rule this world." They rule, but they are "dethroned." They have the doom of decay upon them.

There is an important passage in Isaiah: "Of the increase of his government . . . there shall be no end." (Isa. 9:7.) Every government of every kind in every realm must not increase beyond a certain point. When it does, it becomes tyranny and causes disruption and confusion. Every government must have an end—beyond which it must not go. All except one—"Of the increase of his government . . . there shall be no end." His government can go on to the absolute and yet remain beneficial and freedom-giving.

Take sex. Within certain bounds and under certain restraints sex can rule your conduct. But throw the reins over the neck of sex and tell it to ride where it will—there is no limit. Result? Hell—here and now. The people who enjoy sex least are those who restrain it least. Of the increase of the government of sex there must be an end, or it is the end of the personality—it disintegrates.

Of the increase of the government of the self there must be an end. It is right to love yourself—"Thou shalt love thy neighbor *as thyself.*" If you didn't love yourself, you wouldn't improve yourself. But self-love can easily pass into selfishness. Of the increase of the government of self there must be an end—if not, disintegration.

Of the increase of human government there must be an end. Governments must govern only so long as they produce spontaneity within the individual. After that they produce only suppression and tyranny.

O God, everything that rules us must have a limit except Thy rule. There we come to life's fulfillment and completion. In that rule is our complete freedom. We have found that which fits life. Amen.

AFFIRMATION FOR THE DAY: *God's rule is the only rule that can be total and at the same time totally beneficial.*

AS IT GREW IT WITHERED

Yesterday we saw that every government has to have a limit—an end. All except the government of the Kingdom—"Of the increase of his government . . . there shall be no end." Nothing can stand infinite increase. "As it grew, it withered"—it couldn't stand increase.

There is this penetrating word about Egypt: "Their strength is to sit still." (Isa. 30:7.) They were so loosely hung together that movement would cause them to fall apart. So the prophet said: "Don't ally yourself to something that can't stand movement and growth." All institutions founded on maintaining the *status quo* belong to the category of those whose "strength is to sit still." But such institutions are doomed. If you cannot change, you cannot live, for life is change. "Don't rock the boat," means, "Don't leave the shore," for a boat that doesn't rock doesn't rove. As Halford Luccock says, changing the figure, "He has his feet on the ground," means, "He has his feet in the grave." Life is dynamic change. Therefore the Christian faith will never be outgrown, for we are not following a fixed unalterable code. We are following a living Mind. The more you see in Him, the more you see there is to be seen. He renders the good of today not good enough for tomorrow. The Christian way is therefore the Way for a growing world. For it grows with our growth, but it is always ahead of us. Heb. 2:10 (Moffatt) says: "It was befitting that He . . . should perfect the Pioneer"—One "perfected" and yet a "Pioneer"! The Perfect grows on us, therefore cannot be outgrown. With us and yet forever ahead of us! We have Him, and yet there is so much we haven't! "Of the increase of his government . . . there shall be no end." The more He governs, the more we grow. It is a Government for which we are made; its commands are our demands.

We are fighting the increase of government in our country. We are afraid of its powers. Even the Communists say that the state will eventually fade out. They thus witness to the fear of governments—beyond certain limits. But we have hold of a Government which we want to increase infinitely and infinitesimally. We are not afraid for its rule to be extended infinitely. Its rule is our release; its sway is our way—"the faultless law of freedom." (Jas. 1:25, Moffatt.)

O God, I thank Thee that in Thy Kingdom I find my home and my perfect release. I walk in it, bound in every fiber of my being, and yet I walk without restraint. I thank Thee for this perfect liberty. Amen.

AFFIRMATION FOR THE DAY: *Perfect law and perfect liberty, perfect restraint and perfect release—this is my paradox and my perfection.*

341

"THERE IS A GRANDEUR"

The Kingdom is the one Government of which there will be no end. The Chinese have a saying, "He has gone up into the horns of a cow"—gone up into something which ends in a dead end. There are no dead ends in the Kingdom.

A writer says: "Let us render thanks that we receive a realm [Kingdom] unshaken." (Heb. 12:28, Moffatt.) From my depths I do give thanks for a Kingdom unshaken amid a world shaken to its depths. A little boy looked at the oil on a puddle of water in a street and said, "There's a rainbow gone to smash." A lot of our rainbows have gone to smash. This Kingdom is unsmashed. Unsmashed? It is not even shaken. In the Panama Canal Zone the government is testing different kinds of rocks to see what they will stand. The ages have tested the rocks upon which men build, and only one fulfills all the tests—the Rock of Ages, the Kingdom of God.

And yet we cling to the little things in religion and miss this great thing—the central thing—the Kingdom. It is said: "Asher sat still by the seaboard, clinging to his creeks." (Judges 5:17, Moffatt.) Here was Asher by the side of the great sea, and yet he clung to his creeks; by the side of the big, he clung to the little. He was creek-minded instead of sea-minded. Many give themselves to the marginal in religion and miss this center. A father told me he took his little son to see the President, and the boy's eye got caught by a policeman's hat, and he would look at nothing else—and missed the President. We get caught with the policeman's cap in religion and miss the One embodying the Kingdom of God—the government of the universe.

Darwin said: "There is a grandeur in this view of life with its several powers, having been originally breathed by the Creator into a few forms or into one." Darwin was in search of origins; we are more interested in destinations. He wrote of the "Origin of Species," and we point to the "Destination of Species." And there is a grandeur, an unspeakable grandeur, in one Government bringing everything under its control and giving everything fulfillment.

O God, there is grandeur in Thy Will as the one unifying center for all life, bringing everything under its control and redemption. Here all compartmentalisms, all dualisms, are gone, and life is centrally unified. I thank Thee, thank Thee, thank Thee. Amen.

AFFIRMATION FOR THE DAY: *I shall work with, and not against, the Great Design.*

WE NEED A CENTRAL UNITY

We saw yesterday that we need something to bring all life into a central unity. Our world unity has been broken; life has become compartmentalized. Science is abstracted knowledge; it picks things to pieces in analysis, but doesn't know how to put them together again in a synthesis. As a consequence we live in an incoherent world.

A Chinese scholar recognizes three reasons why Christ attracts the Chinese mind: (1) Because He is the great Synthesizer—brings life into unity. (2) Because of His scholarhood, instead of scholarship —the latter is analysis, the other is synthesis. (3) Because of the Kingdom of God. Here is a great scholar seeing the great things in the Christian faith. But often the Church announces the big but deals with the little. A sign by the roadside said, "GREAT STRAWBERRY FESTIVAL SERVED BY CHURCH," in large letters, but in small letters, "*Owing to scarcity of strawberries, prunes will be served.*" Strawberries proclaimed, prunes provided! We must talk and provide the big, the ultimate; and the only ultimate is the Kingdom.

You take on the significance of the thing to which you are attached. If you are attached to money, you have the significance that money can bring; if to yourself, the significance that the self can bring; if to the Kingdom, then you have Kingdom significance.

A French diplomat refused to let me ride with him in the same car from Pahlevi to Teheran, saying, "I am a diplomat." I suppose I should have felt squelched, but I didn't. Inwardly I said to myself, "But I'm an ambassador." I was an ambassador of the Kingdom of God and had its significance. He had the significance of France, I of a universal Kingdom. France fell; the Kingdom abides forever. "Thy kingdom is an everlasting kingdom." Of no other can that be said.

The significance of the Way is that it is the way for everything in heaven and on earth, for God and man, now and forever. Our significance, then, comes from the fact that we are attached to the Way that is Relevance. Everything else is irrelevant. Everything else is "off the beam"; this is "on the beam." Said a businessman: "You have the only answer to our industrial situation." Yes, and for every situation.

O God, our Father, how can we thank Thee enough that Thou hast put us on the Beam. This is Life. We know it. We rejoice in it. Help us to shout our answer to the world, for it is not our answer, but Thy Answer. Thy Answer is the Kingdom. Help us to give "the glad news." Amen.

AFFIRMATION FOR THE DAY: *I am on the Beam. I shall arrive at Home —the Kingdom.*

IS THE CHRISTIAN WAY THE ONLY WAY?

We come now in our pilgrimage to the place where we can face this question: "Is the Christian way the only way? Cannot people find God through other ways? What about people who sincerely follow other faiths—are they lost? And what about those who lived before the coming of Christ—are they lost? Do we have to be exclusive?"

The Christian way is not a way set alongside of others; it is the Way which fulfills all others. Jesus said, "I am not come to destroy, but to fulfil." (Matt. 5:17.) This was locally applied to the Law and the Prophets, but it is a generic statement, capable of being applied to all truth anywhere. His very attitude was fulfillment, gathering up the fragments of truth found anywhere and completing and perfecting them in Himself. He is no enemy of truth found anywhere. How could He be, when He is *the* Truth? All the lesser truths are finger posts pointing to Him who is the Truth. In the others they are all ideas; in Him they become Fact. In Him the divine ideas which have wandered through the world did at last clothe themselves in flesh and blood; the idea and the fact became wedded forevermore.

As for those who lived before Christ, the answer is that nobody has ever lived before Christ. "Before Abraham was, I am." (John 8:58.) Of course men lived before the Christ became the incarnate Jesus. This eternal Christ is "the true Light, which lighteth every man that cometh into the world." (John 1:9.) The light that was in conscience, in insight, in illumination, in ideals, was the light of the excarnate Christ. If men lived according to that "light," they will be saved and be saved by Christ, however unconscious they may have been of Him as Christ. Men are judged according to the light they have. To whom little has been given, of him little will be required; and to whom much has been given, of him much will be required. A varying standard of judgment according to light will give men equality before God.

But why didn't Jesus come in the beginning of history instead of at the middle? He came at the very first moment He could, for preparation for His coming had to take place. Even then people misunderstood Him and crucified Him.

O Christ, I thank Thee that Thou hast not left any man anywhere at any time. Always Thou art pursuing Love. And always Thou art redeeming. I let Thy burning love into my heart, and I am evermore held by it. Amen.

AFFIRMATION FOR THE DAY: *"It is in Christ that the entire Fulness of deity has settled bodily, it is in him that you reach your full life."* (Col. 2:9, Moffatt.)

THE JUDGMENTS OF CHRIST AND THE JUDGMENTS OF LIFE

As we discuss this matter of Jesus as *the* Way and not a way among ways, we must get hold of the fact that He did not come to bring a religion but to be Religion. He didn't come to bring a set of truths but to be the Truth. He didn't come to tell us about life but to be the Life. He didn't come to show us the way but to be the Way.

And all life is corroborating that. The judgments of life and the judgments of Christ are the same. That will be the area of the great discoveries in religion in the future. Said a minister: "This saying that Christianity is written in the universe is long overdue." As long as we thought the Way was written only in books, we fought about authenticity of books. Now we go beyond that and say that if you should wipe out the books you would find the same facts written into reality. Of course the books bring into focus the scattered rays, and therefore we can never dispense with the books, but the corroboration is universal. Scratch life anywhere, and you find a witness to the Way.

For instance, take Epicurus, who taught that pleasure is the only good and the end of all morality. He placed "great importance on friendship," and asserted that "justice is necessary to a true life of pleasure." Why? The way of unfriendliness or injustice will not bring pleasure—the nature of the universe determines *that*. You can't have pleasure without relationship to the Way. If you don't fit into the Way, then the way of pleasure turns out to be not-the-way. At the bottom of a liquor price list in a dining car was the item, "Aspirin—25 cents." It was expected that the quest for pleasure through liquor would end in a headache, so provision was made for it. At the end of the Beatitudes there is no item which provides the equivalent of aspirin, for there are no headaches, no kickbacks, and no hangovers. Rather: "Rejoice, and be exceeding glad." You have hold of a growing joy as well as a growing answer in Christ.

Epicurus saw that pleasure could not be had when in violation of the moral law. When you go against that moral law, you go against your own self and hence your own pleasure. "He who spits against the wind spits in his own face."

O God, I know that this Way is inescapable, for how can I escape Thee? I cannot run away from myself and the laws written within me. Nor do I want to, for I would be escaping from salvation. Help me to obey and live and live abundantly. Amen.

AFFIRMATION FOR THE DAY: *"That in all things he might have the pre-eminence."* (Col. 1:18.)

"SHIP THE UNIVERSAL WAY"

We continue our emphasis on the Christian way as the Way—the Way universally.

I saw a sign which read: "Ship the Universal Way." Inwardly I said, "I am!" The Way is the universal Way. There isn't a realm in heaven or on earth or under the earth where it isn't valid now. And there isn't a realm anywhere where the unchristian thing isn't the foolish and impossible thing. In an address in Canada I said I was no statesman, but the Chinese ambassador came up and said: "You are not a statesman? If the statesmen had your point of view, our problems would be settled overnight." But my point of view was not *my* point of view; it was the Way! When Gladstone said, "Nothing that is morally wrong can be politically right," he was simply saying that when you run against the Way, it is bad politics.

A representative from Tennessee said in one of our meetings in Washington: "I used to plant corn, and I knew I was not doing the growing; the laws of nature were doing it. I knew I couldn't do anything except work with God. But I come up here, and I find the only people in the world who think they can do things alone, without reference to God and with their eyes on the exigencies of the next election." That is what is wrong with our politics—men are substituting their ways for the Way. And we pay for their stupidities.

The account says that Jesus was crucified at "the place of a skull" —at the place of brainlessness. To take something else and crucify Jesus is not only bad; it is brainless. For instance, they thought they could crucify Jesus "by subtility"—quietly without anybody knowing it—and they succeeded only in spreading his gospel over the world. When you crucify Jesus, you are brainless as well as bad.

Jesus said: "The word I have spoken will judge him on the last day." (John 12:48, Moffatt.) Yes, and it judges him now. Anyone who goes against the Way is judged by that very act. There is no need of pronouncing sentence on the last day, for life pronounces sentence now. When anyone lives according to the Way, "he will incur no sentence of judgment" (John 5:24, Moffatt). Life approves of him.

O God, how can I thank Thee enough for showing me the Way and for putting my feet upon it. I am atingle in every fiber of my being at the glory and wonder of it. Gratitude spreads its benediction over my soul. I thank Thee. Amen.

AFFIRMATION FOR THE DAY: *"I am Alpha and Omega"—the Christ of the Beginning Word and the Christ of the Final Word.*

ALL AUTHORITY IN HEAVEN AND IN EARTH

We are studying the Way as the Way. It must be burned into us. Jesus said, "All authority hath been given unto me in heaven and on earth." (Matt. 28:18, A.S.V.) Many people wonder if it is on earth. Daniel Webster answers with this profound word: "Everything that makes a man a good Christian makes him a good citizen." The Christian, when Christian, has authority on earth by his very fitness for living. And note, the authority is "on earth"—in its very structure. It is not imposed; it is inherent. The laws of everything are the laws of the Way. And this is for the nation as well as for the individual, for we are commanded to "make disciples of all nations." The nation was to become a disciple of the Kingdom. Instead of that, the nation acts as if it were God. Result? These periodic hells called wars—the nations' pay-off days for acting as if they were God. Again Jesus said, "I have come as light into the world." (John 12:46, Moffatt.) He is light in heaven? Yes, but He is also light now—in the world. In every situation He is light, and everything else is darkness. If you don't believe that, then you will have to find it out through experience. As an English professor put it, "Through an experience of good and evil we find that the good is best." Or as G. B. Shaw said in reference to forgiveness, "Forgiveness is the great way; it may turn out to be the only way." By trial we see that Jesus is the great way; by further trial we see that He is *the* Way. "Heaven and earth will pass away, but my words never!" (Luke 21:33, Moffatt.) Why? Because Reality cannot pass away, and His words are distilled Reality. "Everyone who falls on that stone will be shattered." (Luke 20:18, Moffatt.) You go against Him, and you will be shattered—life will go to pieces. And there are no exceptions—"everyone." Even if God should go against the Way, He would be hurt—He would cease to be God. Nothing can go against this Way. As Goethe says: "The devil wills the evil, but has to further the good." The Way will triumph:

> "That cause can neither be lost nor stayed
> Which takes the course of what God has made."

O God, my soul exults. The Invincible has hold of me. We together cannot be defeated. For the sum total of Reality is behind us. We are working with the grain of the universe and not against it. We are therefore treading the way of the unconquerable. Amen.

AFFIRMATION FOR THE DAY: *"Cling to the Rock, or break on the rocks."*

THE INVINCIBILITY OF THE WAY

We continue our study of the invincibility of the Way:

Two men, sons of the South, one white and the other black, but both children of the same Father, stood and earnestly talked: "We win —we win," said George Carver, the Negro saint and scientist. To which Rufus Moseley, also a saint and a scientist in spiritual things, replied: "Who win? Those who live by the will of God?" "Yes, that's it, that's it," Carver replied with glowing face. They were both invincible, for they both lived by "the good Spirit," by the Way.

A judge said to a minister: "You ministers try to prove your message. You should proclaim it and it will approve itself to people." He was right, for the Way is self-verifying.

John Foster Dulles, adviser to international conferences, went to these conferences for many years and found they were getting nowhere because the spirit and outlook were wrong. Discouraged, he drew up a list of the qualities of character that would make for a successful international conference, and to his amazement he found that every single quality of character was a Christian quality. He saw that you couldn't make an international conference work without the Christian spirit. So he who was skeptical became a convinced and committed Christian, pushed into it by the very pressures of life.

Dale Carnegie, in speaking and writing on how to win and hold friends, says in essence that you must think of the other man. If you are self-centered, you won't win others. In other words, you must love your neighbor as you love yourself. Carnegie gets paid for expounding a Christian principle and applying it to relationships. Take any way of life, and if it leads to real living, it merges into the Way. Someone asked Lord Grey, prime minister of Great Britain, if he had any difficulty reconciling his private morality and his public acts, and he replied, "No, for the right thing is always the right thing to do."

Paul sums it all up thus: "That all things in heaven and earth alike should be gathered up in Christ." (Eph. 1:10, Moffatt.) Both in heaven and earth "alike" all things find their fulfillment in Him. In Him they are "gathered up"; out of Him they fall apart.

O Christ, my eyes are open to Thy universal significance. There is no place Thou art not relevant. For there is nothing that isn't made by Thee and for Thee. In Thee I reach my full life; out of Thee I am stunted forevermore. I am grateful I am in Thee. Amen.

AFFIRMATION FOR THE DAY: *"May Christ dwell in your hearts as you have faith!"* (Eph. 3:17, Moffatt.)

WAS JESUS RELATIVE OR ABSOLUTE?

"But," says the critic, "when you speak of the absolute relevancy of Jesus, you forget the relativisms in the life of Jesus. Are there not a lot of relativisms there?" Yes, there are. He was a babe, growing in wisdom and stature, getting His guidance through prayer. And yet amid all these relativisms was an Absolute. Whenever you discover His mind, and not the mind of His disciples, you discover an Absolute. He is always right on every question and always final. In Him is the meeting place of the absolute and the relative—the God-man.

You can't put your finger on a thing that is good that isn't Christian, and on anything Christian that isn't good. But some ask, "Aren't people getting along pretty well without Jesus Christ?" The answer is that nobody anywhere is getting along pretty well without Christ. "Christ Jesus is within you. Otherwise you must be failures." (II Cor. 13:5, Moffatt.) Christ or failure. For "it is in him that you reach your full life." (Col. 2:9, Moffatt.) Everything remains arrested in development, stunted, unless somewhere along the line life touches Christ in some way or another.

Take this picture: Here is a man, hands drawn up over chest, his feet drawn up—couldn't walk. This outer tying up in knots was symbolic of the inner knots of the spirit—he was all tied up with sex. He had gone all over the country to doctors, and they couldn't do anything for him. But a simple Christian got him to surrender his sex life to Christ and to confess it. He did, and his hands straightened out, and he is now walking. He is completely released.

Here is another picture: I was being introduced to a high-school audience of four thousand by a girl obviously chosen because of her poise, her quiet ability, and her radiance. A pastor whispered to me as she stood up: "Six months ago that girl was the most disorganized girl in the whole school. A surrender to Christ has made the difference."

Another picture: A Jewess studied at various universities in Europe, and ended with a box full of degrees, but she said, "I knew nothing. I found Christ, and I knew everything." Her glowing face told everybody she had the Key.

O Christ, Thy law is our life, and when we take Thy law, we find our own liberty. In Thee we are free—free to be what Thou hast designed for us. I thank Thee, thank Thee. Amen.

AFFIRMATION FOR THE DAY: *In Christ I am alive. Cut off from Christ I am a withered branch.*

"UPON THE PATIENT'S BODY"

We saw yesterday that the Way works universally. An army general said to me: "If we don't do something like you suggested, we will be back at this business of war every twenty-five years." You can't get away from Christ, for when you do, you're up against it.

A doctor said: "In the first lecture on anatomy we got in medical college the professor said, 'Young men, from today you've got to be materialists. There is no such thing as soul.'" It was all material tissue. And now? The spiritual put out at the door came back by the window —and came back with a bang! Materialistic doctors had a generation on their hands filled with conflicts, neuroses, complexes. And these things could not be dealt with by physical instruments of science. As a member of the Mayo clinic put it: "We can deal with 25 per cent of the people who come to us by the physical instruments of science; 75 per cent we don't know what to do with, for they are passing on the sicknesses of their minds and their souls to their bodies." The mental and spiritual was back, and back in charge of the situation for good or ill. Dr. John Finney, of Johns Hopkins, said: "Upon a patient's body we read his present, his past, and his future. More than a priest, we should be worthy of a patient's confidence." And what was written in the body? The man's spiritual and mental attitudes in very large measure. Paul says, "That the life of Jesus may come out in my body." (II Cor. 4:10, Moffatt.) "The life of Jesus may come out." It is already there, written in nerve and blood and tissue. The laws of our physical life are the laws of Christ.

A brilliant woman made this observation: "The only objection I have against Christianity is that it makes everything digest and makes me fat!" Christianity not only makes everything digest; it makes all life work, everywhere. Life approves it and is against all that is unchristian. The universe backs the Way. The Way is easy. Only "the way of transgressors is hard." (Prov. 13:15.)

The Way is not a way. Paul says: "According to the Way, which they call a sect, I worship." (Acts 24:14. R.S.V.) The Way is not a "sect," dealing with a section of life—it is the whole of Life.

O Christ, I thank Thee that Thy yoke is easy and Thy burden light— I've found it so, I've found it so. In Thee I have the Key; everything unlocks with Thy Spirit. O Christ, give me sanity and sense, that I may follow Thy Way—to the full. In Thy name. Amen.

AFFIRMATION FOR THE DAY: *In Christ all Reality is behind me. Outside of Christ all Reality is against me.*

THE HAND OF GRACE AND THE HAND OF JUDGMENT

What are the prospects that men will choose the Way?

Well, if men will not choose the Way deliberately by intelligent choice, then they will be driven to it by disillusionment. God has two hands—the Hand of Grace and the Hand of Judgment. If you won't take life from the Hand of Grace, you will have to take it from the Hand of Judgment. A passage says, "When judgments come" (Ps. 1:5, Moffatt)—not "if" they come but "when." They are bound to come; judgments are taking place now. And slowly but surely men are bound to judge life as God judges it.

A Negro woman was asked to get up from a car and get into a Jim Crow coach. She slowly gathered up her things and said under her breath: "God is getting mighty tired of all this." That was the pronouncement of a prophet, the sentence of doom on a wrong—God's getting mighty tired of it.

Take this matter of racial superiorities. To bolster it up I have heard the passage of Scripture quoted where God is supposed to have cursed Ham (the black man) and made him the slave of Japheth (the white man). But if you look up the passage in Gen. 9:25-27, you'll find God had nothing to do with it. It was Noah who pronounced the curse—and on Ham's son Canaan, not Ham—and he did it when he was drunk. "And Noah awoke from his wine . . . : and he said." To take a drunken man's pronouncement as the code for the treatment of a race! Moreover, those who use this passage must acknowledge that Ham and Japheth had the same father and mother, so Ham and Japheth and their descendants are blood relations. And they are! God is getting mighty tired of religion that would lay hold on an obscure passage uttered by a drunken man to bolster up unchristian racial attitudes. If God had decreed that the black man should forever serve the white man because Ham told his brothers that their father was in an undignified state in his tent, I should lose interest in such a God. That God would be my devil.

The authentic voice of God sounds in these words: "What are you more than Ethiopians to me, ye Israelites? the Eternal asks." (Amos 9:7, Moffatt.) God is getting mighty tired of these injustices.

O God, I thank Thee that Thou art lifting the lid from our underlying paganism. Thou art showing us our unchristian depths. Help us to clean them out. Only thus can we be on the Way. Amen.

AFFIRMATION FOR THE DAY: *Today I shall be color-blind and class-blind—I shall see people.*

"GOD IS GETTING MIGHTY TIRED"

We saw yesterday that God is getting tired of a lot of things and that weariness of God with them is their doom. A marker put up by his colored comrades on a South Sea island reads: "Here lies a black man who died fighting the yellow man that the white man might be free." God and man are going to get progressively tired of that kind of freedom—freedom for some and not for others. A Negro minister said: "I've lived for thirty-six years as an American citizen in the American democracy, and for the first time I've lived these two weeks without fear and tension." That in a democracy! In a contest in Cleveland on what punishment should be meted out to Hitler, the prize answer was this one: "I suggest that Hitler be wrapped in a black skin and be made to live out the balance of his days in the American democracy." The girl who gave it was colored—she knew. God is getting tired of that kind of democracy.

And science is speaking more and more the Christian position in regard to race. The two chemicals that produce color in the skin are carotene and melanin. A preponderance of carotene makes the yellow skin, and of melanin the brown or black skin. But all races have both. It isn't that some have them and others haven't—all races have both. So superiority founded on color is precarious.

A United States senator started an investigation of a teacher who taught in a teachers' college "the equality of races." She was found to be "innocent" of that crime! Someday we will lay that alongside witch-hunting as a reminder of where we have come from.

Science and the Christian faith are converging on seeing humanity as humanity, and the differences between races as cultural, not inherent. Take the development of electricity: Marconi was Italian; Ampère was French; Faraday and Joule were English; Ohm was German; Edison was American; Volta was Italian. The first blood shed in the American Revolution was Negro blood. Washington said: "Some of the bloody tracks at Valley Forge were from Negro feet." The most decorated portion of the American Army in this last war was the Japanese-American unit.

O God, Thou art teaching us the hard way that men are brothers and humanity is one. We wouldn't have our race prejudice cleansed by the blood of Thy Son, and now we have to have it cleansed away in the blood of our sons. Forgive us. Amen.

AFFIRMATION FOR THE DAY: *One blood for us—the Blood of Christ. One blood in us—the blood of humanity.*

GOD IS GETTING TIRED OF RACIALISM

When God gets mighty tired of a wrong, He uses any instrument He can get hold of if His own people won't respond. The Christian Church in South Africa was filled with racialism. Gandhi, being brown, could not get into one of them. He was repelled, started a movement for the liberation of millions, discovered an essentially Christian power—the power of soul force, became the father of his country. Gandhi as a Hindu is used of God to do what He couldn't do through the Christians. God got tired.

I asked a porter in a train why he was reading a Bahaist book, and he replied: "It teaches me brotherhood." When I asked him if Christianity didn't teach him brotherhood, he replied: "Not this kind; this kind transcends race." God got tired waiting for the Christians to be Christian regarding race, so He uses the Bahaist movement with its roots in Mohammedanism to teach the Christian to be Christian.

I asked a Jewish woman in Russia why she preferred living in Russia, and she replied: "I was treated well in England, but I was always conscious of being a Jew. Here I am treated as a person and not as a Jew. Here I am not conscious of race." God got tired of an unchristian Christian society and used an atheistic people to teach the rest of us about the oneness of humanity.

And God is using atheistic Russia in another way. God is using Communism as a mustard plaster to make individualism change, as He is using individualism to make Communism change. The thesis is individualism; the antithesis is Communism, and out of the clash of opposites a synthesis, a third something, is being born. That third something is the Kingdom of God. God gets tired of our being so slow to change through the teaching of our faith, so He uses the dialectic of history to make us move to a higher level and a juster order—the Kingdom.

Jesus offered the Kingdom of God to His own people—they would be the agent of the coming of the new Order. They were bound by prejudice and ritual and wouldn't respond, so God grew tired and raised up the Church out of the nobodies. His own people were left standing behind a Wailing Wall.

O God, are we as a Church now going to be left behind standing behind a Wailing Wall? We know the Way is going to have the right of way, through either us or others. Help us to be the responsive channels. Amen.

AFFIRMATION FOR THE DAY: *Today's alternative: Disobedience and a Wailing Wall; obedience and an open vista.*

GOD IS GETTING TIRED OF UNEQUAL PRIVILEGE

Another thing both God and man are getting mighty tired of—the concentration of wealth in the hands of the few and the impoverishment of the many. The excuse cannot be given that one represents frugality and ability and the other represents prodigality and inability. Of course there is some truth in that in some cases. But where society is so organized that a great deal of this wealth can be passed on without regard to ability or frugality or character, the excuse goes lame.

There is no excuse for the spectacle of millions alongside misery. We must learn to distribute our wealth more widely to raise the level for all. If we do not, then we will have to put up with an unstable situation. For where there is lack of equality, there is lack of equilibrium. If you have an unjust society, you will have an unstable society. As long as society has wide differences in distribution of wealth, we are going to have strikes, lockouts, wars. When we come to a closer approximation to equality, then and then only will society become more stable.

This more equitable distribution can be carried on through: (1) profit sharing, or (2) co-operatives, or (3) revolution. We must make our choice. I vote for the first two. A leading industrialist in Canada said this to me at the close of an address: "You're right. My factory was a feud. I was giving as little as possible, and my employees were doing as little as possible. We were tied in knots. Then I saw that the basis was wrong, and I said to my employees, 'Hereafter you are going to have the right of hiring and firing. Moreover we are setting aside 23½ per cent of the profits for labor above wages. We are going to work this out together.' Immediately the spirit of the factory changed. The men weeded out slackers, for now they were slacking against labor as well as capital. It was to the interest of everybody to work harder and more intelligently. Everybody did more and got more. The spirit of the factory changed almost overnight. We are no longer a feud; we are a family." "Profit sharing works like magic," said an able management engineer who straightens out sick businesses.

O God, we know that Thou art teaching us to live as brothers, not only in Church but in the factory. Thou art teaching us the hard way. We should have learned it through our gospel; now we have to learn it through our tied-up economy. Save us from our stupidities. Amen.

AFFIRMATION FOR THE DAY: *Our alternative: Profit sharing for everybody or problem sharing for everybody.*

PLENTY FOR ALL—POVERTY FOR MANY

We saw yesterday that profit sharing would change employer and employee from competition to co-operation. Co-operation is a higher principle with a higher result. A management engineer puts it this way: "If a business insures the security of its employees by profit sharing, it automatically insures itself."

That same principle of co-operation must be applied to community relationships. Co-operatives may not be the final answer, but they are a step on the road to the final answer, for they distribute wealth widely through co-operative effort. They tell us that bees live through the winter by mutual aid. They form into a ball and keep up a dance. Then they change places; those that have been out move to the center, and those at the center move out. Thus they survive. Should those at the center insist on staying there and keeping the others at the edges, they would all perish.

An economy where the privileged insist on being kept warm by those on the edges of privilege is a doomed economy. Privilege must be distributed to all or be taken away from all. When Eisenhower was asked how he managed to keep the diverse elements together in the battle of Europe, he replied in the famous words: "Sir, it is one team or we lose." In a larger sense, "It is one world or no world."

> "The laws of changeless justice bind
> Oppressor and oppressed,
> And close as sin and suffering joined
> We march to fate abreast."

Someone reporting the saving of a woman and a child said: "It would be difficult to say it was the woman who saved the child or the child who saved the woman. For it is one of those unexpected miracles of living that when we protect another we often save ourselves." Miracle? No, a deeper-embedded law. You cannot hurt another without hurting yourself, and you cannot help another without helping yourself. An Oriental saying: "What has happened to you is poison to me." Any hurt to another is poison to me, and any help to another is food to me.

O God, Thou art teaching us through flood and dust and depression and war that we cannot live except in the Way. We see Thy awful hand at work in human affairs—its message: "The Way or the way of death." Amen.

AFFIRMATION FOR THE DAY: *I lose to live; I renounce to realize.*

"A FAITH OF EQUAL PRIVILEGE"

We saw yesterday that God is getting tired of man's exploiting man. Imperialism in economics, in politics, in international relations, anywhere, has the doom of God upon it. He is making it work out wrong; it adds up to tension, conflicts, war, impoverishment, hell. William Hard speaks of nations "all inspired by the suicidal idea that if we can only sufficiently impoverish foreigners we ourselves shall be rich." Suicidal? Yes, for the Way is against it. Hard further adds: "By such nonimperialistic actions the U. S. has won what no other power in all the world has won: the confidence of its small neighbors." But the moment she becomes imperialistic she will lose that confidence overnight. "The next century is the American century"—of decadence, if she embarks on imperialism of any kind. For God is mighty tired of imperialism. Every imperialistic country has decayed.

Peter speaks of "a faith of equal privilege." (II Pet. 1:1, Moffatt.) The corollary of a faith of equal privilege is a society of equal privilege; one is root, and the other is fruit. And this is founded in the nature of God as revealed in Christ: "By the equity of our God and saviour Jesus Christ." Any society that is founded on unequal privilege anywhere is against the nature of God—against the Way—and hence it is doomed. God has simply got mighty tired—that settles it—nothing can save it except repentence, complete and absolute.

And God has got mighty tired of selfishness in the individual. Man has thought he could make himself and his desires the center of the universe, thought he could become God and be happy. It has turned out badly. Someone has said that the history of the prodigal son can be summed up in three stages: sick of home, homesick, home. But the reason for the homesickness was self-sickness—he was sick of himself. "Give me" was his first step down. "Make me" was the first step back. To be self-centered is to be self-loathed. We wanted ourselves; now we have them, have them on our hands, as problems, problems which we frantically try to unload on doctors and psychiatrists. What's the matter? God's got tired, mighty tired of our acting as God.

O God, we see Thy Finger pointing again, "Weighed and wanting," and again we are afraid. Help us to cease our ways and take Thy Way. Thy Way is our way—we are made for it—and if we rebel against Thee, we rebel against ourselves. Forgive us, forgive us. Amen.

AFFIRMATION FOR THE DAY: *You cannot revolt against God without revolting against yourself.*

YOU CANNOT LIVE AGAINST THE GREAT DESIGN •

We ended yesterday in saying that man is not God and to act like it brings nought but self-noughting. This is true when we set up a portion of man and make that the center of life. For instance, sex. Sex is not something to be feared. It is God's gift by which we share with Him His creatorship. But make it a law unto itself, make it God, and it will be a worm-eaten god.

The pagan doctor or psychiatrist who recommends sex license as a remedy for sex problems is recommending to you to go straight to hell—hell now, on the inside of you. You will jump from the frying pan of sex difficulties into the fire of an inner conflict—"where their worm dieth not, and the fire is not quenched." If you won't listen to me, then listen to one who has tried it—a young woman who went through an extramarital experience: "Much is talked of the evils of frustration in the case of the woman who denies herself the physical experience of love. In my opinion that vague and periodic torment is as nothing compared to the frustration suffered by the woman who seeks happiness in love outside of marriage. With all the latent instincts of her sex released and intensified by the mating experience, awake for the first time to the full design of married love, she realizes with a sense of dumb defeat that for her the fulfillment of that design must remain, perhaps forever, an unaccomplished thing. It is a trapped, blind-alley feeling that only one who has experienced it can appreciate. The conflict set up as a result casts its dark shadow over an experience which one had expected to be all light and freedom." In other words, the judgments of Christ and the judgments of life are the same. The Way is written in the Bible, but also in the blood. It is written in the Incarnation and in the instincts—in our flesh and its relationships. It is written everywhere and operative everywhere, and every way that is anti-Way is anti-life.

God is mighty tired of our trying to live anti-Way, and the results are registered in a disrupted humanity. This disrupted humanity is also getting mighty tired of living against itself. It may choose the Way through disillusionment.

O God, Thy two hands are outstretched. Help us to take the Hand of Grace offered to us in Christ, instead of the Hand of Judgment offered to us by life. For outside of Thee is nought but sickness. Help me. Amen.

AFFIRMATION FOR THE DAY: *To have myself on my own hands is hell; to have myself in God's hands is heaven.*

A LADDER FOR YOUTH

In this last week of traveling as comrades of the Way, we give a series of ladders or steps that those who have not yet joined us may take to become committed also as comrades of the Way. Perhaps some are on the Way but hobbling along on only one foot. We want you to be as one man put it: "I'm on the Way with both feet."

These ladders will be miscellaneous, but we hope that in them the last straggling seeker may find one that meets his need.

We will begin with youth. As you start out in life, you will need five things: (1) *A faith to live by.* (2) *A cause to serve.* (3) *A fellowship in which that faith can be nourished and through which that cause can be served.* (4) *A decision to accept that faith, serve that cause, and enter that fellowship.* (5) *A life dedication to that faith, to that cause, to that fellowship—now.* Therefore, here and now accept that faith—Christ. Give yourself to that cause—the Kingdom of God. Enter that fellowship—the Church, with a life dedication now. That means you have a life pattern. A boy hit a baseball, ran to first, on to second, then hesitated and yelled: "Fellows, where's third base?" He had no pattern of the diamond in his mind, and so he broke down in confusion halfway. You have a pattern; you know what you want, and where you want to go. Then go!

Maybe there are blocks. Jesus spoke (Mark 10:21) to a young man who wanted to find eternal life: (1) *"Go"*—face the blocks, face your life. (2) *"Sell"*—get rid of the thing that stands in the way. (3) *"Give"*—change your center from yourself to others. These are the three steps away from the old ways. Now there are three more steps, and you are on the Way: (4) *"Come"*—you renounce to reconstruct; you give up to take up. (5) *"Take up your cross"*—it will cost you something, in the beginning. Afterward it becomes easy. (6) *"Follow me"*—your center is in Christ, not in this, that, or the other person. People may let you down; He never will. You now have an utterly dependable center of life—Christ. The first three steps which are away from the old life are steps into the void. The next three steps are into the victory. You are on the Way!

O Christ, I thank Thee for Thy gracious invitation to come to Thee. For I sense the fact that in Thee I have everything I need in earth and in heaven. Thou art my Satisfaction, and I know it. So here goes! I fling away every paltry thing that keeps me from Thee. I come. Amen.

AFFIRMATION FOR THE DAY: *I am on the Way with both feet and with my whole heart.*

358

VARIOUS LADDERS FOR VARIOUS PEOPLE

We continue our suggestions of steps "out of" and "into."

All steps down begin with a wrong idea. Here are the steps down: (1) Mixed up. (2) Messed up. (3) Screwed up. (4) Tied up. (5) Fed up. Remedy? Give up! Result? Fixed up!

Perhaps life is not so much mixed up and messed up as empty. You are not bad, but you are not overflowing. Then here is a simple ladder for finding: (1) "Ask." (2) "Seek." (3) "Knock." (Luke 11:10.) There are three stages of intensity here: "Ask," the stage of inquiry about what you want. Then the stage of seeking, setting the life in the direction of finding what you want. Jesus said: "On that day you will not ask me any questions. . . . Ask and you will receive, that your joy may be full." (John 16:23-24, Moffatt.) You will turn from questions to quest. You get beyond the question period to the questing period. Then you come to the third stage where you "knock." At the door you press for immediate entrance—now.

Take another statement of Jesus: "Everyone who comes to me and listens to my words and acts upon them, I will show you whom he is like. . . . A man [who] laid his foundation on the rock." (Luke 6:47-48, Moffatt.) Here are the steps: (1) "Comes to me"—not to this, that, or the other doctrine, rite, or church. You may get mixed up in these and never get to Jesus. Jesus said, "comes to *me*." (2) "Listens to my words." Some are always talking to God instead of listening to God. As someone has said: "Suppose you have an appointment with the President, and for fifty-five minutes you talk on and on, and then as you are about to go, you say, 'Perhaps, Mr. President, you'd like to get in a word.' " The art of listening is the art of living. For we "live . . . by every word that proceedeth out of the mouth of God"—not by the words that proceed out of our mouths. (3) "Acts upon them." If we do not act upon what we hear, we will hear nothing. The speaking begins again when we act.

When we come to Him, listen to His words, and act upon them, then we are on a rock; life sustains us.

O God, I thank Thee that in coming to Jesus I am coming to Thee, in listening to Him I am listening to Thee, and when I do so, Thou art sustaining me, backing me to the utmost. I am on the Rock. Come wind, come flood, I'm on the Rock. I thank Thee, thank Thee. Amen.

AFFIRMATION FOR THE DAY: *"Yet I am always beside thee; thou holdest my right hand, guiding me with thy counsel."* (Ps. 73:23-24, Moffatt.)

A LADDER OF FOUR "T'S"

We continue our ladders for triumphant living.

Perhaps you have been going in the wrong direction: (1) *Turn around.* No use going on if it gets you nowhere fast. Rufus Jones tells of a foot traveler who asked a youth he saw by the wayside how far it was to a certain destination and received this answer: "If you go on the way you are headed, it will be about twenty-five thousand miles, but if you turn rightabout-face, it will be about three." (2) *Turn down.* It is of no use to turn around if you don't turn down the old habits and ways. You have to say No to some things to say Yes to others, the real things. (3) *Tune in.* You are now set to hear. God will speak if you get His wave length and tune in. (4) *Tone up.* Your life needs constant toning up to standard tones. We get flat and out of tune. The Quiet Time is the time for toning up every chord, for one chord off will make a discord. (5) *Turn out.* The end of life is to get you beyond yourself, turned out, toward others. Psychologically all this is sound, for the self-centered are the self-disrupted, and the other-centered are the healthy-minded. A student had the letters "G.O.S." on his wall and wouldn't tell what they meant—said they were given to him by his mother and he was trying them out. At the end of the semester he would give the result. At the end he said: "It works. 'G.O.S.'—God first, others second, self last."

Perhaps the whole could be summed up in a simple ladder of three steps: (1) Repent. (2) Receive. (3) Release. The end is released—from yourself.

The same end can be seen in the statement about Jesus and the loaf. (Luke 24:30, Moffatt.) (1) "He took the loaf." Your life is no longer in your hands—it is in His; He takes it. (2) "Blessed it." He blesses your life with forgiveness, with power and usefulness. In His hands life is blessed; out of His hands it is cursed. (3) "Broke it." He often has to break us before He can give us. He breaks us by sorrow and disappointment. (4) "Handed it." He passes on our lives to others. We are outgoing.

O Christ, take my life and bless it and break it and hand it on to others, for I would be free of an inner tied-up condition. I would be free—to give. Thou hast given me all; help me to give all. Amen.

AFFIRMATION FOR THE DAY: *"Let me live unhampered, for I study thy behests."* (Ps. 119:45, Moffatt.)

STUDY, OBEY, TEACH

There are three steps for the Christian worker or minister: "Ezra had set his heart upon studying the law of God, upon obeying it, and upon teaching its rules and regulations in Israel." (Ezra 7:10, Moffatt.) Note the steps: (1) *"Studying."* When we cease to learn, we cease to live. No Christian can influence others who hasn't a growing mind and a growing experience of God. I saw a "dead glacier" in Alaska—a glacier that had ceased to push on and was receding. We are receding if we are not studying. (2) *"Obeying."* We must obey what we learn, or we will cease to learn. "If any man willeth to do [God's] will, he shall know of the teaching." (John 7:17, A.S.V.) If you are not willing to do, then the knowledge ceases. God shuts off the lessons if we shut off the living. (3) *"Teaching."* If we study and obey, then we can teach, and only then. The content of the teaching is determined by the studying and the living. In the teaching is our own illustration. "Character is caught, not taught."

For the Christian worker or minister we find three steps to getting a hearing: "Then Jerusalem and the whole of Judaea . . . went out to him." (Matt. 3:5, Moffatt.) (1) *A message of divine authority:* "Repent, the Reign of heaven is near." (Vs. 2.) John's message was the Kingdom, and in that framework he called for repentance. The authority of a totalitarian Order spoke in him. (2) *A message of human equality:* "Level the paths for him." (Vs. 3.) Equality of opportunity—"level the paths." We cannot speak for God unless we are speaking for man—and for all men of every race, color, creed. (3) *An identification with the people in his own life.* John ate locusts and wild honey, was clothed with camel's hair, and lived in simplicity. As he pleaded: "Let everyone who possesses two shirts share with him who has none, and let him who has food do likewise" (Luke 3:11, Moffatt), there was conviction in his words, for he was living his message. "Then"—note the "then"—"Jerusalem and the whole of Judaea . . . went out to him." (Vs. 5.) You get a hearing if you have a divine message, a human sympathy, and a life that illustrates the message.

O Christ, we thank Thee that we are drawn to Thee, for Thou art the message Thou dost proclaim. We see Thee as the Word made flesh, and we are drawn. Help me to be this Word made flesh too. For I must be the answer, as I proclaim the Answer. Help me. In Thy name. Amen.

AFFIRMATION FOR THE DAY: *If I ask people to obey, I must embody.*

A LADDER FOR THE COMMISSIONED

Paul has had a world hearing. Why? In Acts 26:17-18 (Moffatt) he tells us the points in the commission: (1) Rescued *"from the People and also from the Gentiles"* to whom he was sent. The first deliverance was a deliverance from a domination of the herd. Surrender to the herd instinct is the most dangerous thing in life. Jesus was crucified by it: "Their shouts carried the day. Pilate gave sentence that their demand was to be carried out." (Luke 23:23-24, Moffatt.) Surrender to the herd murdered James: "James . . . he slew with the sword, and when he saw this pleased the Jews, he went on to seize Peter." (Acts 12:2-3, Moffatt.) It kept Paul in prison: "As Felix wanted to ingratiate himself with the Jews he left Paul still in custody." (Acts 24:27, Moffatt.) The dominance of the herd over the individual is responsible for more collapsed moral standards, lowered tones of the spiritual life, than any other single thing. "Everybody does it" is sufficient to wipe out all the Christian standards and spirit from the individual. No minister can help his people if he isn't delivered from the people to whom he is sent. His herd instinct must be fastened on the Kingdom of God as the supreme loyalty. All lesser loyalties must fit into that.

(2) *"That their eyes may be opened."* You cannot open peoples' eyes if you see with their eyes. Only as you see and act differently can you make them different. (3) *"Turn from darkness to light."* It is not enough to let people see they are in darkness. They must turn. Conversion must be produced. (4) *"From the power of Satan to God."* Our message must bring light and life—it must bring power to break all tyrannies. (5) *"Get remission of their sins."* The estranged souls of men need forgiveness, reconciliation. (6) *"Consecrated by faith."* The end is a consecrated personality, delivered from and dedicated to the consecration of all ransomed powers. The end of evangelism is to produce an evangelist.

Another ladder leads to the same ends. (1) *Receptivity*—the first law of life. (2) *Resources*—keeping them intact by contact. (3) *Reserves*—always enough, and to spare, a plus. (4) *Release*—the end of the process is for your ransomed powers to be released for others.

O Christ, give me a deliverance from the people to whom I am sent. Save me from their standards and spirit and help me to help them by being different and better. Amen.

AFFIRMATION FOR THE DAY: *I have surrendered to God; therefore I surrender to nothing else.*

"FOR AS THESE QUALITIES EXIST AND INCREASE"

How do we "participate in the divine nature," become "active and fruitful"? II Pet. 1:3-8 (Moffatt) tells eight steps: (1) *"Faith"*— belief, surrender, obedience. (2) *"Resolution."* Resolution is second, after surrender. The Way is not primarily the whipping up of the will but its surrender, and then resolution. (3) *"Intelligence."* What does not hold the mind will soon not hold the emotion and the will. (4) *"Self-control."* Now self-control, following self-surrender, is God-control. (5) *"Steadfastness"*—no tentative attitudes. (6) *"Godliness."* This is Godward—the God-contact through prayer. (7) *"Brotherliness."* This is manward—the human contact through brotherly attitudes. (8) *"Christian love."* This is the atmosphere and attitude of the whole. "For as these qualities exist and increase with you, they render you active and fruitful." Here is a daily exercise:

"Begin the day with God:
    Kneel down to Him in prayer;
    Lift up thy heart to His abode
    And seek his love to share.

"Open the Book of God,
    And read a portion there;
    That it may hallow all thy thoughts
    And sweeten all thy care.

"Go through the day with God,
    Whate'er thy work may be;
    Where'er thou art—at home, abroad,
    He still is near to thee.

"Converse in mind with God,
    Thy spirit heavenward raise;
    Acknowledge every good bestowed,
    And offer grateful praise.

"Lie down at night with God,
    Who gives His servants sleep,
    When thou tread'st the vale of death
    He will thee guard and keep."

O Christ, help me to draw on the power of habit to reinforce these resolves. Help me to become natural in good, at home in the Kingdom. Amen.

AFFIRMATION FOR THE DAY: *My habits, being dedicated, work with me. Soon they shall make me automatic in my Christian responses.*

"THEY GET STRONGER AS THEY GO"

For our last day together on the Way we will meditate on parts of the eighty-fourth psalm (Moffatt). It sums up our experience together.

"Now soul and body thrill with joy over the living God." (Vs. 2.) In another song a psalmist said: "Body and soul, I thirst, I long for thee." (Ps. 63:1, Moffatt.) In one "body and soul thirst"; in the other "soul and body thrill." The "thirst" had turned to "thrill." Perhaps one reason is that in the first case "body" was first and "soul" was second and in the second "soul" was first and "body" second. When the body is first, it all ends in thirsts; when the soul is first, it all ends in thrills. But note that now "soul and body thrill"—the whole person in accord. No longer soul and body fight each other. Both have the same Lord, obey the same laws, and thrill with the same thrills.

"Happy are they who live within thy house. . . . Happy are they who, nerved by thee, set out on pilgrimage!" (Vss. 4-5.) Life has found its rhythm of living "within thy house," the passive, receptive; and setting "out on pilgrimage," the active, outgoing. Here again are the alternate beats of the Christian heart: receptivity, response; receptivity, response. Mary and Martha in the same home and at harmony.

"When they pass through Weary-glen, fountains flow for their refreshing." (Vs. 6.) We have found the secret of "how never to be tired." A woman doing the washing for twelve people, asked if she didn't get tired, replied: "I am convinced that to say one is tired is to say one is discouraged. I am not discouraged, by the grace of God, so I am not tired." "Fountains flow [from within], . . . blessings rain [from above]." Heaven and earth become one.

"They are the stronger as they go." (Vs. 7.) For they are not living on their reserves, but on Resources—His infinite Resources. Every step and every triumph makes more possible the next step and the next triumph, until we can say: "Wherever I go, thank God, he makes my life a constant pageant of triumph." (II Cor. 2:14, Moffatt.)

O Christ, Thou who art the Way. From my depths I thank Thee that I am on an Endless Way, with endless Resources, with endless Happiness, with endless Gratitude, under the process of an endless Growth. I thank Thee, thank Thee. Amen.

AFFIRMATION FOR THE DAY: *"The path of the just is as the shining light, that shineth more and more unto the perfect day."* (Prov. 4:18.) *The Perfect Way becomes the Perfect Day.*